D1277296

No Laurels for de Gaulle

No Laurels for de Gaulle

by ROBERT MENGIN

Translated from the French by Jay Allen

NEW YORK
FARRAR, STRAUS AND GIROUX

Foreword

At a time when the last war had run three quarters of its course, and when my country was three quarters liberated, I found myself in Washington with nothing, or almost nothing, to do. I had been posted there, during a period of convalescence, as Secretary to the French Naval Mission, after active service in Tunisia and at sea with the French Navy.

As I look back, it seems odd that at such a time I should have been given so little to do. But that is how it was, and I see no point now in going into the reasons why. In any case, with leisure on my hands, I thought to turn it to some account, and I did so by writing a long and detailed letter to my father, whom I had not seen since the spring of 1940, just before France fell to the Germans. He and my mother had been all that time in the village of Rogny on the banks of the Loing, south of Paris and not far from Fontainebleau, making out as best they could under the Occupation, with some fourteen German soldiers at a time living under their roof, uninvited and unwanted guests.

At that darkest of moments in our history when the French armies fell apart before the overwhelming might of the Nazi offensive, I was in England attached to the French Embassy in London. When I heard that Marshal Pétain had been appointed to negotiate an armistice, I immediately resigned my job as press attaché of the Embassy. For weeks thereafter I worked at the headquarters of General de Gaulle. I had listened to his famous radio appeal of

June 18 and was deeply moved by it. But I was not allowed to continue there. Why? Because I could not sign the Act of Engagement then required of any French citizen in England who wanted to go on fighting. As I read it, this remarkable oath committed a man to personal allegiance to General de Gaulle. I could not bring myself to put my name to anything of the sort. I then tried to join the British or the Canadian Navy but found my way blocked because of the agreement wrung from the English by General de Gaulle which gave him the exclusive right to any Frenchmen on British soil. It was General de Gaulle's "Free French" or nothing.

I then went to work editing the small newspaper called *Le Courrier de l'Air* which was dropped over Occupied France by the Royal Air Force and later on by the Americans. Although this was not what I wanted most to do when my country was prostrate before the invader, it seemed useful enough.

So it happened that I stayed on in England until the beginning of 1943. By then the Allies had landed in Morocco and Algeria and I was at last free to go back into the service of France as an officer in the Naval Reserve, where my oath to serve my country, and only my country, was quite sufficient. I went into action alongside American forces against the Germans in Tunisia and took part in the capture of Bizerte at the moment when the Americans, the British, and the French finally sprung the trap on the Axis armies in Africa, crowded into that northeastern corner of Tunisia.

After a brief period in charge of Radio-Algiers, I went back to sea, where I had wanted to be all along, seeing service on French warships in the Atlantic and the Mediterranean. I had the good luck to take part in the landings on Sicily, at Salerno, on Corsica, and on Elba.

When I was in Washington in 1944, then, I had for a brief time nothing much else to do, and there were four years of my life to account for to my mother and father in their village on the Loing, free now of their German guests. This explains why my letter attained the size of a book.

After my father's death, some ten years ago, the manuscript

came back into my hands. Then one day, mysteriously, it disappeared. I was the more disturbed by this because of an earlier and equally mysterious disappearance of a sheaf of documents I had deposited at the French Embassy in London, which, after England's break with the Vichy government, was left in the care of the chancellor. He was a thoroughly honorable man and not a Pétainist and therefore had English permission to remain and guard the archives. At the end of the war he was dismissed by the representatives of the new French government. At that time a number of things, far more precious than my papers, disappeared from the archives.

Of my lengthy letter home, all I had left were some rough drafts and a very bad copy. But I still had in my possession the big envelopes, carefully dated, in which all during the war I had kept such papers and documents as interested me. I had these with me in a valise that became heavier and heavier; one of the advantages of a sailor's life is that he does not have to pay for excess baggage on board ship.

In this book I am in a sense redoing my letter, but now it is not for my parents and other relatives older than I. It is addressed rather to my children and the new generation everywhere who did not know the last war at first hand. As for those who did go through it, I can only ask their indulgence to the extent that they are familiar with what I have to say. I am inclined to think that many among them are not.

Certain Gaullists will reproach me. They will say, I should imagine, that I have not shown the General in a light favorable to his glory or, as they will also surely say, to the glory of France. (I should here say that words such as *gloire* and *grandeur* appear frequently in Gaullist prose, and also that when this work was begun, the General was *not* President of the Republic.)

I cannot deny that it would have been agreeable for me, delicious even, to have been a good Gaullist in London in 1940. It would be more so in Paris in 1966. However, I would not want to give the impression that I was ever General de Gaulle's victim. Or that I am now. The truth is that in England during the first two and a half years of the war I was highly privileged, as were all the French there, in comparison with our compatriots in Occupied France and the nearly two million French prisoners of war and the forced laborers held in Germany. I have no complaints about anybody or anything.

Most of my relatives are Gaullists, or once were. Most of my friends, too. They have long deplored my not being with them, or, as they say, one of theirs. On this score there have been many arguments, sometimes lively, always with everyone free to speak his mind. The most amusing of these discussions are the ones in which lessons in Gaullism are offered by persons who at first condoned the armistice of June 1940 and then went along with it for periods of time that varied with their intelligence and perspicacity. Today they have become Gaullists retroactively. They write apologias in the General's defense. And they are much given to tracking down anyone who might offend him.

Gaullists have a perfect right to create for themselves a certain ideal of France and to love that France. And we have the right, we who are in the minority, anti-Pétainists and yet not Gaullists, to hold to another ideal of France, to love it and to defend it. By our numbers we constitute no very great threat; in London in 1940 there were hardly a dozen of us who rejected Vichy and the Marshal and General de Gaulle too.

For nearly a millennium the French have felt themselves to be a nation. Our unity as a people now cannot be very seriously endangered if some among us cherish ideals and ambitious for our country that differ from those held by the majority. My ideals, my ambitions cover rather a lot of ground. I would, for instance, like to make some contribution to the rehabilitation of patriots who have been vilified. My ideal is a France without double talk, without casuistry, without false front, without smoke screen. And (why not go all the way?) a France lucid in language as in mind, which exalts free will above conformism, which will behave fraternally to other peoples and not with suspicion and mistrust, which will strive for moderation rather than grandeur, for courtesy in place of haughtiness and arrogance.

So that once again the world may say of France what five hundred years ago Charles d'Orléans wrote when an exile in Dover:

> [1] *Qui se pourrait d'elle lasser!*
> *Toujours sa beauté renouvelle.*
> *Dieu! qu'il la fait bon regarder,*
> *La gracieuse, bonne et belle!*

Charles Duke of Orléans (1391–1465) was taken prisoner at the battle of Agincourt in 1415 by Henry V of England in his bid for the crown of France. He was held in English prisons a quarter of a century and is sometimes referred to as the "caged songster." (Translator)

[1] Who could ever weary of her!
Her charms forever new.
Oh Lord! how good to behold,
How gracious, how good and beautiful.

Contents

1939

September 1939

There can hardly have been a day more beautiful than Sunday, September 3, in London. After a heavy rain in the night, the morning was very bright, clear, and cool. Up at an early hour, I went out in uniform, for those were the instructions that all of us mobilized in London had received. As a reserve officer in the Navy, I was under the orders of our Naval Attaché. He had his offices in the Embassy, Albert Gate House, a large establishment that on one side looked out over Hyde Park and on the other on Knightsbridge. We lived, my wife Anne and I, only a few steps away. Instead of going straight to the office, I took a turn through Hyde Park to have a look at the antiaircraft batteries that even then were being set in place. The lawns, still wet from the showers of the night before, glistened in the sun. I circled back by Kensington Gardens, Queen's Gate, and South Kensington Station, where I took the Underground. A hundred or so schoolboys and girls were taking it too. They were evidently some of the poorer children of that well-to-do neighborhood, and they must have been almost the last of the children of London to be evacuated. It was high time: the war was to begin at eleven o'clock sharp. They stood in line on the platform all very quiet and well behaved, each one carrying a small suitcase and, slung over the shoulder, a gas mask. Some anxious mothers had made up sheaves of cloth to protect the cardboard box containing the mask. Fixed to the lapels of their jackets, the boys had cards giving their name and the name of the village to which they were being sent. The girls wore the cards around the neck. Very few of the youngsters seemed sad, yet, looking at them, I could not help but imagine the children of Poland already dead, wounded, terrified on this the third day of the German onslaught.

There was a rumor that France did not want to declare war, not in any case until the next day. We the French had most certainly given our promise to the Poles to go to their help immediately in the event of a German attack. We had already let two days slip by, and the English had finally said that they would wait for us no longer. Their ultimatum was about to expire, at eleven o'clock on that beautiful morning.

Georges Bonnet was our Minister of Foreign Affairs. While talking with him over the phone to Paris, our Ambassador had been very angry, or so we heard from General Lelong, the Military Attaché, who shared the office with the Air and Navy Attachés. Our Ambassador was Charles Corbin, an imperturbable, cold man, and so elegantly turned out that he always seemed to have just come from his tailor's. It was not easy to imagine him in a temper. But he was exasperated by the Foreign Minister. M. Bonnet had a way of sending telegrams of instructions which he would then cancel over the phone, a practice that upset M. Corbin because, as M. Bonnet well knew, there would not be any trace of the counterorders in the files.

At ten o'clock, General Lelong had an announcement to make: "We will be at war at seventeen hours today. Six hours after the British! Really, it is too disagreeable to have had to drag our feet like this! During this time the Poles are in their death agony!"

I caught myself glancing frequently at the clock on our office wall. The minute hand moved into the first minute after eleven, and the war was officially on. General Lelong, without the slightest change of expression, kept on with his exercises in penmanship on the sheet of paper before him. He was seated in front of me, a little to the left. Directly across from me, Colonel Fournier, our Air Attaché, did not look up from the book he was reading. To one side of me, on my left, and thus facing General Lelong, was the Naval Attaché, my chief. He was a captain and he was droning along about money with his chief petty officer, who handled supplies. The minute hand seemed to be moving very slowly. But time nevertheless was passing, and nothing was happening. Exactly the way war is most of the time.

Our two tall windows opened on Knightsbridge, which runs parallel to Hyde Park. We could see, without moving from our chairs, that there was not the usual Sunday crowd. No nannies in sharp competition over the elegance of the baby carriages they were wheeling. No horses whose riders reined them in to show them off before admiring eyes. Only couples dressed for church, the men with their umbrellas tightly rolled, their wives in printed frocks.

At 11:30 a siren wailed, then another, then all the sirens, one after the other, uncoordinated—a wailing, wavering, panting sound. In later raids, the eerie sirens usually went off in unison. In our office, none of the warriors moved a muscle. I tried to imitate them. But why deny that this imperturbability of the career officers got on my nerves? I got up as if to stretch and walked to the window. The passers-by had lost their grave Sunday demeanor. They were running now toward the bomb shelters, gas masks bouncing on their rumps. The buses pulled up to the curbs. Drivers put on their brakes nervously and ended up half on the sidewalk. They jumped out, lifted the hood, and removed the distributor as they had been instructed (so that their cars could not be used by German parachutists). We did not, of course, know it then, but just up the way, by Queen's Gate, Winston Churchill, the new First Lord of the Admiralty, was at that moment being hustled along with Mrs. Churchill to a shelter a hundred feet or so from his front door.

This flurry of excitement, with just a hint of panic, I remember so well because I was never again to see its like in London, even during the worst of the bombings later. It was hardly surprising. Everybody knew from the newspapers that the Germans were bombing towns and villages in Poland. And for years, since well before Munich, we had been hearing that great capitals would be demolished by bombs within minutes after the declaration of war. (That was, in fact, one of the reasons why in England and

France people accepted the shame of Munich.) From American experts, one a great aviator, we heard that the German fighters and bombers were ready in overwhelming numbers. They were ready all right, but the bombings in the West had yet to come. And, as for their numbers, it turned out that these could be matched, surpassed even. We also knew, if I remember rightly, that some two hundred thousand beds were ready for the expected casualties.

Knightsbridge was empty save for the buses and cars left hastily at, or over, the curbs. The only human beings in sight were two policemen walking their beat. Against the sky line, I could see the balloons of the famous balloon barrage—cylindrical they were, and painted silver—rising to the end of their tethers, thick steel cables. These were supposed to create a jungle into which no bomber would care to dive to bomb at a low altitude or machine-gun people in the streets.

I left the window, and, back at the table again among my silent associates, I perused intently a chart with the inter-Allied signal code for use at sea.

Happily, Colonel Fournier, in front of me, decided to break silence. He actually moved, got up, took his cap off the hook, and said with extreme unconcern, "I am going up on the roof and have a look round. They don't seem to have wasted any time, *les Boches*, in getting their crates into the air!" At that period in history, military men of a certain age, who had gone through the preceding war, still said *les Boches* to designate the Germans, who shortly came to be known by other names.

Soon the Colonel came back down from the rooftop terrace and, hanging up his cap, said, "*On ne voit la-haut que le soleil qui poudroie et l'herbe qui verdoie.*" [1] The thought crossed my mind that Sister Anne, on reporting this to her hapless sister from the top of Bluebeard's tower, might have had an accent of distress which was altogether lacking in the Colonel's voice. For a second I think he even seemed relieved. And then he really was so, for at

[1] From Charles Perrault's *Bluebeard:* "I see nothing but the sun which makes a dust, and the grass, which is green."

that very moment the sirens began to wail, now no longer panting in their urgency, but in the long sustained single note that would later, for months on end, be the sweetest possible music to the ears of Londoners.

At about twelve-thirty, our office door opened and in walked a slender fellow dressed as if for travel, a blue-jay feather in the ribbon of his *chapeau de chasse*. He looked very unhappy. It was Commandant de Brantes, our assistant military attaché, returning from leave in France to rejoin his post.

"I don't know where to hide my head," he said. "I've had all of London running like mad! You can see how it was: these Air Force gentlemen [making a little bow toward Colonel Fournier] neglected to report our take-off and flight plan. I am in fact the cause of the sirens!"

He had the look of a guest who has just spilled a cup of coffee on his hostess's dress.

It was thus that the twelve million inhabitants of the London area got their first cold chills, all because of the oversight of a pilot. An enormous practical joke, but a poor one. As far as I remember, the truth never came out in the press. But a legend did develop, the way legends do, and suddenly you heard it all over London: the unidentified plane that caused the alert was bringing home some reveler who had gone over to Le Touquet to try his luck for the last time at the roulette tables. It became a kind of game; whenever Commandant de Brantes made his appearance anywhere, somebody would always call out, "Here comes the reveler!"

He was to be killed in the Resistance later on.

I could not very well relate everything I saw and heard in London during the months that were known in France as *la drôle de guerre* and in England as "the phony war." This term was thought to have been first used by the Ambassador of the United States, Joseph Kennedy, whose handsome second son, John Fitzgerald Kennedy, was then serving unofficially as his aide. Ambassador Kennedy used to go about saying that if England and France thought what they were engaged in was war, they would lose it. He turned out to be not far from wrong. Actually, the expression "phony war" seems first to have been used by Senator Borah of Idaho, thought of as an isolationist. He had been indignant at the British and French policies of surrender that led to Munich and was apparently now implying that the failure of the Allies to do anything effective to honor their commitment to Poland, such as an all-out attack from the Maginot line, or bombing raids on the Ruhr, could only mean that they were still hoping for some sort of negotiated peace.

The "phony war" may well have been phony, but in France the *drôle de guerre* was far from *drôle*. It was terribly wearying, boring, and not a little nerve-racking because of the dangers ahead that one could only vaguely sense. First there was the startling contrast between London and Paris. In France, where I went twice during that long winter, everything and everybody was lugubrious. I am not saying that the French had gone off to the war without courage. But it seemed almost as if they were making a deliberate effort to be despondent, as if they were in advance mourning for afflictions still to come. Lamentations preceded the tragedy and they helped bring it on.

In February I went way out in Brittany to see Anne and hold our first baby in my arms. While I was there I met only one person who was actually gay. And that was Armand, Anne's brother. But he was bitterly critical of the smugness of the naval officers under whom he was serving, at first on the *Dunkerque*, our new battle cruiser, which with her sister the *Strasbourg* was more than a match for the German *Scharnhorst* and *Gneisenau*. In Paris, on my way back to London, I saw my elder brother. He had distressing reports to give me about the airfield to which he was assigned as liaison officer with an English unit. Among our fellow Frenchmen he saw incredible negligence, equipment badly kept up, officers frequently drunk. He found them one day dancing a jig in delight at the news that an English battleship had been torpedoed. (This may have been the *Royal Oak*, sunk inside Scapa Flow on October 14, 1939, by a German submarine.)

In Paris I also ran into Jean Berard, a classmate of mine who had become an archaeologist. He was up from Rome, where his brother, Armand, who was to become French Ambassador to the United Nations after the war, was then Secretary of Embassy under François-Poncet. Jean and his brother were both partisans of a policy of firmness in our relations with Mussolini, still technically a neutral at that time but all too obviously restive in that role, hardly able to wait until it seemed safe to emulate his Axis partner in the role of great conqueror. At the Quai d'Orsay, however, Georges Bonnet harbored intentions that were quite different from what they had in mind, the exact opposite in fact.

Before leaving, I saw my father. He was brimming over with optimism of sorts. He went with me to the airfield at Le Bourget, where I was to take my plane for London. It was a dark morning, with a lowering sky that promised snow. And the highway from Paris to Le Bourget takes you through areas that are as squalid as any the industrial suburbs of Paris can offer. But when my father was along, all nature smiled. A cup of chicory in a dirty bar at the airfield was pronounced by my father to be marvelous coffee. He talked enthusiastically of an article he was about to send to the *Revue de la Societé d'Acclimatation.* He then turned his attention to the war.

"What are we waiting for to attack? More arms? But do we really think the Germans aren't making use of the time we give them to produce as much as we, or even more?"

I told him that in London the French propaganda line—the line intended for English officials—was that we dare not launch an attack on the Germans until we had transferred our arms factories from their vulnerable locations in the north and east to the south of France.

"Bah!" he said, shaking his head in dismay. Then he added, "Well, let us be patient: victory should not be more than six or seven years off!"

When he voiced his peculiar optimism at home, he gave my mother a terrible fright. She could not imagine any of us surviving that long. This brings to mind one of my earliest childhood memories. My father married at rather an advanced age. He was over fifty when war came in 1914, and so was not mobilized, although he did volunteer for auxiliary services. He took my elder brother and me—we were eight and six years of age—to witness the departure of a regiment of dragoons bound for the front. They were already mounted on their horses in the great inner court of their barracks at Melun, south of Paris. Their polished helmets caught and reflected the first rays of the sun. They seemed so splendid, invincible, to the eyes of a child. Through the ornamental iron grille that closed off one end of the courtyard, a proud and excited crowd watched them, and some of the people shouted, "Bring us back Alsace and Lorraine!" One of the more exuberant dragoons called in reply, "Give us just six weeks!"

On the way home, my father said, for the benefit of my mother and my maternal grandmother, "Those poor people! They don't realize that if it lasts only six weeks we will be beaten!" My grandmother objected indignantly. But my father was right: he remembered 1870, when the Germans won a lightning war but surely would have been defeated in a long war.

Now at Le Bourget I reminded him of this childhood recollection of mine just when my plane, a tiny military machine pretty as a toy, taxied up to the ramp, ready to take off. As soon as the passengers were on board and the door closed, the plane taxied down the field, turned around, and took off, soaring past the ramp. I looked the other way so as not to take with me a last image of my father diminished by distance. As things turned out, I was not to see him again until the liberation, four years hence.

I did go back to Paris once more in March, but my parents were by then in the country south of Paris, in the little house at Rogny which after June they were to have to share for the rest of the war with fourteen Germans. They had taken under their protection a Mme Willard, the mother of a Communist lawyer. She was not herself a Communist, but she was Jewish. They introduced her as an old cousin. Half the village knew that this was untrue, and the other half suspected as much. But nobody gave her away.

I went by sea in March because for several days fog had grounded the liaison planes between London and Paris. At least a dozen sacks of official mail had accumulated, and I was ordered to take them to Paris. The Germans had thoughtfully moored magnetic mines to block Newhaven Harbor. Wooden trawlers had to go ahead of us and fish them out, so by the time my ship reached Dieppe, the Paris train connection had long since gone. I caught a local for Rouen and there got aboard another train bound for Paris, where I piled up my mail sacks in the corridor, contrary to all the rules. A Norman family who had been standing used them as seats.

That evening in Paris at the Air Ministry, rue des Belles-Feuilles, I was made to feel about as welcome as a dog in a game of bowls. The colonel who was to take over my consignment of official mail was in a hurry to go home for dinner. He was just closing his desk.

"A fine hour to show up!" he said angrily. "Leave your sacks in the checkroom and come back tomorrow and I will sign the receipts!"

To that I replied that I would take all of them over to the Ministry of Foreign Affairs, to which some of the sacks were destined anyway. "They must still be open for business over there," I said. The colonel seemed to smell trouble, so he recovered his manners, had me sit down, opened his drawer and signed the receipts, and then asked if I couldn't use a voucher to go and dine at I forget what military club.

I have cited this incident because it struck me then as characteristic of the state of mind of the military in Paris. I refused his voucher with thanks and went off to find Anne. She gave me an even more unpleasant welcome than the colonel at the Air Ministry. She had just come from Brittany, where she had left the baby. After the birth, she had been ill. I can only describe her illness as a wasting away, and she believed that because of it she was losing her beauty. She was depressed and in a frightful state of nerves. I saw her and her mother off the next night at the Gare de Lyon for Genoa, where they were to board an Italian liner; they had both been invited to spend some time in Florida, and the doctors assured her that a sojourn there, away from the war and its privations, would restore her health in a matter of months.

I went back to England by sea. The fog had lifted. For the first time in my life, although not the last, I actually saw mines. They had either been torn away from their moorings by the storm or had been dropped expressly to drift into the path of ships. I don't know which. They were floating on the surface, ugly-looking objects. We could have exploded them with cannon or machine-gun fire, as was done often later on in the war when it was no longer phony, much less *drôle*. But our ship prudently veered away and signaled to the trawlers, wooden craft, which fished them up with extreme delicacy. The British Admiralty wanted them intact so they could be defused and taken apart. Volunteers did this hair-raising job. If one hears the click of the timer, one has seventeen seconds to find cover. Now and then the explosion would occur without any warning click.

Back in London, I found a sort of gaiety. Faces were not mournful as in Paris. For this, my comrades at the French Naval Mission gave me an explanation: the English did not have six million men mobilized; and anyway they are insensitive, a stolid lot, as everybody knows. Insensitive or not, the English had losses far greater than ours, because of the war at sea, the only phase of the war in the West that was active at the time. Rationing in England was much more severe than in France. The celebrated blackout of London was far more strict than any blackout in Paris, where at night there was usually a kind of macabre twilight.

After the summer of 1940, the French were reduced almost to famine. The English, throughout the war, were never so reduced. The French experienced the horrors of the invasion and the occupation. The British did not, except for Jersey and Guernsey. But before the defeat, suffering in France was principally the result of apprehension. Apprehension, let me also say it, was the fashion, the mode. Everything in France, said Stendhal, is a matter of mode. Even to do battle, on the frontiers or on the barricades. Even the idea of *la patrie*, of fatherland; in my father's generation *la patrie* was the mode among the students of the Left and the extreme Left. In the next generation or two, patriotism was quite unfashionable.

The matter of fighting, of standing up to be shot at, is now even more unfashionable. In 1958 in France we experienced a revolution from the Right, with not a single person on the Left risking even a scratch to oppose it. In the generation that came after the victory of 1918, at the moment when France found herself, for a very short time, the greatest military power on earth and possibly the greatest power politically as well, one would hear, "A *bas l'Armée!*"

When I was a student at the Lycée Henri IV, nobody ever cried "*Vive la France!*" except in derision. During my military service at sea, when the bugle sounded to colors it was thought in good taste for the younger officers standing at attention on the quarter-deck to murmur under their breath a jingle that was then very much in vogue:

> [2] *Et si jamais la France*
> *A besoin de défense,*
> *Je n'serai pas le dernier*
> *A me tirer des pieds.*

If a man went on to advanced military studies, he risked being taken for one of the boys of the extreme Right, such as the Action Française and other breeds. In my generation, the most brilliant students who entered the École Polytechnique or the École Normale Supérieure did not stay on in the Army or even in teaching: the idea of serving the state, the nation, was no longer the fashion among the intellectuals.

Nearly all my comrades, and my elders too, who were gifted students, considered themselves anti-militarists. And they were. But when war threatened, they split into two groups. One group,

[2] And if ever France
Needs defending,
I won't be the last
To drag my feet.

not very numerous, did not betray the spirit or the intellect. Quite naturally, Jean-Paul Sartre, anti-militarist, was among those who really fought. Like Alain, the philosopher and pacifist who volunteered in World War I when he was past forty-five years of age. Like Socrates, a pacifist too, who fought heroically at Potidaea and at Delium. But to the majority of the intellectuals of the middle class, or those who aspired to belong to the middle class, anti-militarism served handily as a pretext for not fighting. When the war came, they discovered, many of them, that they had gifts not as military combatants but as military propagandists.

Winter, 1939–40

In Simone de Beauvoir's *Memoirs of a Dutiful Daughter,* there is a character called Herbaud who is the prototype of the ambitious but fearful French intellectual. The Herbaud she depicts is the son of a poor schoolteacher, but his ideals are those of the more prosperous French *bourgeoisie.* He is constantly seeking to pull himself up by his own bootstraps, to improve his situation in life. He is completely, almost deliberately unaware of the spiritual anguish of his times. His manner is offhand, and he is far from dependable. Where women are concerned, he has no discernible conscience. He seeks out men when he thinks them *interesting,* for which read "useful." Sartre is *interesting.* So he cultivates Sartre. Clairaut is not *interesting*; in other words, not useful, so to Clairaut he never bothers to speak. To the Dutiful Daughter he says, "You are wasting your time with people who aren't worth the trouble, who won't repay your efforts." He also informs her that she should *profit,* a word that is very much his, by his presence in Paris, even though he has a wife and, at Coutances, he is *interested* in a third person.

The Herbauds of my generation bear a heavy responsibility for the astonishing spiritual decadence of France between 1918 and the present. In 1939, after the outbreak of the war, they discovered that they were all patriots at heart. But not combatants, please! They swarmed into all the rear-guard operations, became what my American friends were later to call the chair-borne troops. They found themselves particularly fitted for the special jobs involving the confection of wartime propaganda and the peddling of it.

The more important among them became heads of departments; the least lucky had to get along behind a typewriter. Some of them actually put on uniforms and thereby ran some minor risk of being sent to the front. I remember one of this breed, a true Herbaud, in Algiers in 1943. He was propagandizing so furiously in behalf of General de Gaulle and against the Americans that he got himself in somebody's bad book and it was suggested this true-blue patriot should be sent to the front in Tunisia, to the scene of hostilities. He was called up, put through a medical examination, given typhus shots, and stuffed into the uniform of an infantryman. I have never seen such indignation. To send him into action, he, a Herbaud? What did they take him for? Suppose he was wounded? Suppose he came down with some illness? Suppose he got killed? Did they not know that he was soon to be called to the role of Minister in the service of General de Gaulle?

This final argument, that he had a great role ahead of him, won the day. He was thereupon discharged, and he eventually became a Minister.

1940

Spring, 1940

In London, during the weird spring of 1940, the French Ministry of Information followed a peculiar line. This ministry was staffed by a talented troupe with no small number of Herbauds among such genuine first-class intelligences as Jean Giraudoux—first-class but ineffectual. The ministry persisted in telling the British and the world at large that the French Army was the best in the world. I did not understand this. It seemed to me that we would do better to proclaim our relative weakness, proclaim it from the housetops. After all, the Germans knew all about it, but not the English. The way to get the English to raise a huge army, equip it, and send it to France was to frighten them, and the truth was frightening enough. A great many people in France knew it. Either they did not work for the Ministry of Information, however, or they did and did not or could not speak out.

I discovered the reasoning behind this strange propaganda of ours. It is almost unbelievable. First, it was thought that if the English ever discovered how weak we were they would leave us in the lurch. This was the opinion of our ministers, and it gives the measure of their capacities. The reason why in June 1940 the Pétain–Weygand–Baudouin government of the Republic of Bordeaux, soon to become the Vichy regime, was in such a hurry to sign the fateful armistice was that they believed the British would sue for peace the moment the French armies ceased to be their shield against the Germans.

Then there was the French General Staff's worry that the English would send us too many soldiers. This would mean, according to the beliefs current at the Château de Vincennes, where Generalissimo Gamelin held court, that we would no longer dominate the High Command.

Our Generalissimo made appearances in London several times during the early months of the war. At the Embassy I once watched him when he was on his way up to the first floor, where our Ambassador, Charles Corbin, was giving a dinner in his honor. The diplomat "Torcy" was at the dinner, and when I saw him next day I asked what kind of an impression our Generalissimo had made on him. He said that all during the repast General Gamelin had talked of nothing but philosophy and Italian painting.

"If anybody had launched upon such subjects in the presence of Papa Joffre," he went on, "the old man would have opened his eyes as wide as—no, not saucers, plates. Listening to the Generalissimo discourse on philosophy and art, I felt a cold draft at my back."

(Under the pseudonym "Torcy" I refer to a man who resembled Jean-Baptiste Colbert, Marquis de Torcy, who was Secretary of State for Foreign Affairs at the end of Louis XIV's reign. He had that statesman's modesty, self-abnegation, courage, and remarkable sureness of judgment.)

For several weeks I was transferred from my job at the Embassy to the French Naval Mission, which was known as the FNLO —that is, the French Naval Liaison Officer. The French Naval Liaison Officer in the flesh was Admiral Odend'hal, the most courteous man in the world, with all the prejudices then treasured by the French Right. There were quite a few people on his staff, and there was little to do. When I was on day duty, my work consisted mainly of watching others work. When I was on duty nights, I spent the hours before dark having dinner in the office or reading some novel, and then I would settle down to sleep on a camp bed. Now and then the man on duty at the teleprinter would come and shake me awake. That would mean a message from Maintenon, the village near Paris where Admiral Darlan had seen fit to transfer our Admiralty. When it was in cipher, I would decode it, and, if it was urgent and addressed to the English, I myself took it to their Operations Room.

The British Admiralty, however, had not budged from Whitehall, in the heart of London. (True, they had built a vast underground shelter near Admiralty Arch that served them in good stead later when the bombs began to fall.) They assigned the French Naval Mission three sizeable rooms on the top floor of the "Old Building," a structure that came by its name honestly. The stairs had a pronounced list out toward the stairwell. The parquet floors were not consistently level; in spots they dipped, and you could imagine, if you shut your eyes, that you were walking on a ship's deck in a choppy sea. Off the landing at the head of the stairs there was an immense room, or hall, lined with Victorian washbasins of flowered china. There, in the mornings, we made small talk, a towel over one arm, a cake of soap in the hand. An English officer, trying out his French on me, once said, correctly enough but with a strong accent, "What do you think of the Admiralty as a hotel? Believe me, the servants here wear more gold braid than in any hotel in the world!"

One evening when I took a message as far as the door of the Operations Room, I noticed a dinner jacket among the uniforms. The man wearing it was small and round-shouldered, or, rather, with shoulders hunched forward. His head was that of an English baby. He had almost no neck, and his feet and hands were tiny. It was Winston Churchill. He was then neither Sir Winston nor Prime Minister, but First Lord of the Admiralty. The First Sea Lord was showing him something.

Churchill was said to be unpopular with his admirals. They reproached him for having meddled in strategy during the First World War and for having thought up the unlucky expedition to the Dardanelles. They now seemed to fear that he would try to make up for that setback by imposing his own tactics on the fleet, a prospect that did not make them happy. He was better liked by the younger officers. As for the sailors in that room, they could not keep their eyes off him. He was not smoking his celebrated cigar, and I found myself thinking that perhaps he sported it mostly in public.

I was exasperated at having so little to do. Any signalman could have handled everything. Or better still, some older officer from the Reserve. I went periodically to see the Admiral and ask for sea duty. I had a nostalgia for ships, for the life at sea. I saw myself on a bridge sparkling in the Mediterranean sun, or swept by ocean spray; or in pursuit of raiders. This is how one sees things from afar.

Admiral Odend'hal would listen patiently to my request and, with a smile, send me on my way. "You can go to sea if Italy declares war. Meanwhile, try not to step on our feet, and see if you can't learn to obey orders."

That spring I was assigned to another post, at the Embassy once more, and still further from the sea; I was Press Attaché. Here it should be said that the civilians under our roof were, with rare exceptions, more valiant than the military. The Ambassador was imperturbable in any crisis. Roger Cambon, who held the rank of Minister, never during the whole war missed a single bombing of London. The First Secretary, Roland de Margerie, had volunteered for the *chasseurs* at the very beginning. He had been at first with the troops on the Maginot line, and later, much against his wishes, had been called to the General Staff at Vincennes. Quite recently Paul Reynaud, Daladier's successor as Prime Minister, had appointed him chief of his diplomatic cabinet. In his place as First Secretary in London we now had Boni de Castellane, whose father was the celebrated Boni of the Palais-Rose on the avenue du Bois and whose mother was the former Anna Gould. His health was not good; otherwise he would have been in the war, as he had strong military inclinations. Another of the Embassy staff, François de Rose, had been discharged for reasons of health, but this did not keep him, after the armistice, from working with General Weygand in North Africa and on the Tunisian front. Our two junior members, François de Watteville and Jean de Montoussé, had gone, the first to the Army, the second to the Navy. Watteville was killed after the armistice in 1940. Montoussé enlisted in the Free French

Naval Forces and on the corvette *Roselys* served on the terrible Murmansk run.

Toward the end of spring, in my new job as Press Attaché, I had one of the worst shocks of my life. An older friend of mine and a distinguished newspaper correspondent, Frederick Voigt came to me with a most unusual proposal. He said he wanted to discover what my reaction might be to certain information that he would show me. Voigt was a specialist on German matters, and all the better equipped because he was of Prussian origin. Since 1934 he had been saying over and over again in the *Manchester Guardian* that Hitler could only be stopped by force, and that the quicker it was done, the better. He had been asked by the Foreign Office to organize their intelligence service for Germany. In this department they also turned out pamphlets intended to inform the German people and to counter the false reports put out by Hitler's Propaganda Ministry. Planes of the Royal Air Force dropped these pamphlets over Germany instead of bombs. This was done, not because the British were particularly short of bombs, but because the French government had objected to bombing the Reich for fear of retaliation.

Voigt believed in the value of the information gleaned by his department but not in the efficacy of the pamphlets that were supposed to enlighten the people under Hitler. He believed that the most dangerous aspect of the German character was its lack of any critical sense. It was this, he felt, which at times made the Germans so dangerous to the world and to themselves. "The French have too much of it, and the Germans not enough. The Germans will go on believing Hitler and his lies, and they will believe him right up to the moment of defeat!"

This view of the German character seems harsh. I cannot say whether it is justified or not. But I find myself wondering if the war was cut short by a day, even an hour, because of the pamphlets rained on Germany by the British and later by the Americans. Who can say? But this I do know, that of all the commodities circulating among mankind the most difficult to convey is the truth, the easiest is the lie. For the lie has something contagious about it, and on an epidemic scale.

An hour or so after leaving London, we reached the village of Bletchley and there took a right turn. Then Voigt laughingly proposed that he should blindfold me; the location of his special Foreign Office section was a secret. When I saw just ahead the high walls of rose-colored brick, I had no trouble recognizing the admirable park of Woburn Abbey, the largest of its kind in England. The walls extend for nearly twelve miles and there are at least three thousand acres in the park, not to mention the many adjacent properties belonging to Woburn. At the time there were perhaps three thousand deer, many of them of an unusual breed called Père David. There was a herd of European bison. Highland cattle roamed about. There were wild ponies from the Gobi Desert, and a thousand other animals. There were perhaps a hundred thousand birds, some of them magnificently exotic. The oddest of all the creatures there was the old Duke of Bedford, the eleventh duke, I believe. A relic of Queen Victoria's reign, he lived alone in the Abbey surrounded by some fifty domestics of various kinds, maids, footmen, and the like, and served out of doors by an army of gamekeepers, foresters, and gardeners. He had been president for years of the Zoological Society. A true friend of animals, he was less fond of human beings. With his more than £200,000 a year, he was a very generous man, except where members of his family were concerned.

He was morose and formidable, for his lengthy silences were broken only by an occasional monosyllable. People avoided him when they could. His servants tried to melt into the walls when he passed. Workmen actually had to be hidden from sight, and footmen were posted in the halls where work was underway to see that they disappeared before he came by. At this time, the Duke was seeing nobody except his doctors and the three teams of nurses who looked after him around the clock. Lord Halifax, then Secretary for Foreign Affairs, had been a friend, and the Duke, now nearing the limit of his years, had loaned him the use of several buildings within the domain, notably the indoor riding school and the indoor tennis court, both of them beautiful eighteenth-century structures very like the Jeu de Paume and the Orangerie in Paris, only gayer in effect. These were to house the Secret Services.

He had also given the Foreign Office temporary use of a number of buildings around the edges of the park and in the neighboring countryside. It was at one of these, called Crowholt, that we first went to lunch with some of Voigt's associates. Naturally, what we talked about was the war, which had suddenly taken a disastrous turn. Then Voigt, without warning, fired a question at me: was the French government going to ask for a separate armistice?

I was thunderstruck. I don't know what I answered, nor does it matter. What I do remember all too clearly are the documents Voigt showed me that afternoon. They had come to him from Berlin, I believe, and their gist was that the French government consisted, to a dangerous extent, of defeatists. The Prime Minister himself, although considered fairly resolute, was under the spell of Mme Helène de Portes, who was set on peace at any price. The Vice-Presidency of the Council of Ministers had been entrusted to Marshal Pétain, known to stand for a compromise peace, and the Secretariat of the War Committee to Paul Baudouin, a long-time appeaser who was thought to be pro-German.

I confess that I was stunned by all this, and I suspect that Voigt was disappointed. He had clearly thought that I would be able to reassure him with a ringing denial of some sort. But I was in total ignorance of such dangerous trends within my government.

Back in London, another unpleasant surprise awaited me. I went at once to see Torcy to ask if there was any truth in the alarming reports shown me at Woburn. Torcy was in his office, which had just been done over in a soft shade of green. He was unhappy that such effort had been put into interior decoration in the middle of a war; he said the color made him think of a tearoom and he felt like a petit-four. (This image was all the funnier because Torcy is tall, very serious of demeanor, and not at all socially inclined.) Any hope that I may have had that the German reports shown me by Voigt were groundless was dashed when Torcy told me that it was indeed against the danger of France's backing out

that Neville Chamberlain had signed the March 28 agreement
with Paul Reynaud by which both France and Britain agreed not
to enter into separate negotiations with the enemy, either for
armistice or for peace. Reynaud had dug up this treaty from Quai
d'Orsay files after his cabinet had been confirmed in power on
March 22 by a one-vote majority. In London he had explained to
the British that he had to rack up a diplomatic success, which the
signing of the treaty might be thought to be.

Right after this conversation, all of us in London were dismayed
by the news that during the night of May 18 to 19 Paul Reynaud
had relieved Alexis Léger of his functions as Secretary-General of
the Ministry of Foreign Affairs. This was a blow at the Franco-
English alliance that M. Léger, better known today as the poet
Saint-John Perse, had fought to defend. It was a victory for the
defeatist camp of M. Baudouin, Mme de Portes, Marshal Pétain,
and the others.

I was in a position to think of myself as reasonably well informed, but I had never dreamed that the French Army could
prove so vulnerable. When the Germans launched their massive
assaults on Holland, Belgium, and France, I could hardly compre-
hend what was happening. But it should have been easy for anyone to see the extent to which the first battles had dislocated the
entire military and administrative machinery of France. At the very
moment when maximum efficiency was needed, nothing worked
any longer. Try to imagine some tremendous fire, and at the outbreak three quarters of the firemen are dead and wounded and the
rest have fire hoses without water or water without fire hoses.

The English knew of course that their neighbor's house was on
fire, but they did not grasp what it meant. They were not fully
aware, they were dazed, they were really stupefied, if one can use
the word. Inability to grasp reality at such a time can serve as in-
sulation against fear. As the English proverb goes, ignorance is
bliss, or can be.

May 1940

The French government had tried very hard to get people to believe that the French Army was the best in the world. Well, it can be said that of all the government efforts during the war this was the only one that met with any success. The awakening was disagreeable. But the English people are not overly endowed with curiosity. Very few of them were in a mood to ask: But what on earth happened? Why were we told such lies? Nevertheless, the minority in England who did want an explanation got one. And this explanation little by little got around. It consisted of just two words: stupidity and betrayal. The French Army, the story went, was not really bad, but it was poorly led; French tanks were not in such short supply as had been believed, but they were badly distributed, not properly concentrated; and there were traitors in high places.

As to tanks, General de Gaulle affirms that toward the end of May we still had great numbers of them. In his memoirs he states that we had 1,200—a considerable figure. After the war, General Weygand denied it vehemently.[1]

The English were not upset by these explanations. On the contrary, they seemed to find comfort in them. Bad generals and trea-

---

[1] ". . . On June 1, I went to see General Weygand, who had summoned me. . . . Then he asked my opinion on what it would be best to do with the modern tanks—1,200 or so—which we still had at our disposal." *The War Memoirs of Charles de Gaulle*, Vol. I (New York: Simon and Schuster; 1955), p. 50. Hereafter known as *Memoirs*, I.

"By counting generously . . . we reach at most a total of 250. We are far from 1,200 tanks. . . . How could he have given such a figure?" Maxime Weygand: *En lisant les Mémoires du guerre du général de Gaulle* (Paris: Flammarion; 1963), p. 28.

son: it really was all quite simple. We have no traitors in our midst, they said to themselves. And our soldiers, who invented tanks, know how to use them. Thus we run no risk of a disaster such as struck the French.

It was only later, at the time of the German drive into Russia, that the English began to understand the fundamental cause of the French defeat: namely that, numerically and in point of matériel, the German Army was infinitely more powerful than the French Army; that it was a formidable instrument of war which could face the most desperate resistance, which could lose many hundreds of thousands of men and still continue, as if inexorably, its advance. The day—it was near the end of 1942, if I remember rightly—when Churchill made his public statement that the German Army had lost on the Russian front alone more men than on all fronts during the entire First World War, he aroused in England not so much a feeling of optimism as a great retrospective wave of fear. For the first time the English understood why the French Army had so easily been smashed. For the first time they understood the magnitude of the danger from which Great Britain had escaped.

The mistake my generation, and the one decimated in the First World War, which preceded mine, made was to let this mighty machine come into being and to leave the profession of arms in the hands of men of such limited understanding. Even the most intelligent, like General de Gaulle, never understood the importance of a combat force of planes to accompany tanks as they forged ahead, bombing and machine-gunning anything and anyone that tried to hold them up. The mediocrity of our officer corps was all the more disastrous since at the same moment in Germany a military career was so highly honored. Luckily, in the Soviet Union it was also held in high esteem.

While our armies were coming apart, the Franco-English entente was going awry. Mutual confidence was draining away. It began to go at Dunkirk. To my generation, this episode of the war is still all too vivid. But a new generation has come along. To them let me explain Dunkirk briefly. The Allied armies had been cut in two by the German offensive on May 20 when General Guderian's armor swept through to the Channel at the mouth of the Somme with such speed that at Abbeville they caught French troops drilling on the parade grounds and captured a British battery, with all its guns, in the market square at Albert. In some places the population mistook them for English troops. Nearly a million Allied troops were thus cut off not only from Paris but from the British supply ports in Normandy and Brittany.

The First French Army, to which the British Expeditionary Corps was attached, proceeded to dig in around Dunkirk. The question was whether it could stay there and hold off the Germans, receiving supplies by sea, or whether it would have to be evacuated. And that also would have to be by sea.

Since May 19, the Supreme Allied Command had been in the hands of General Maxime Weygand. The new Generalissimo decided that these units should hold on; that, far from being evacuated, they should strengthen their entrenched camp, or, as it was called, the Dunkirk perimeter. The English command, on the other hand, was for evacuation, particularly now that the capitulation of the Belgian armies had uncovered their left flank and the Germans were already in Nieuport. (The English would leave all their arms behind, except for some of the Guards, who held on to their rifles.) They contended that if the Franco-English armies tried to make a stand where they were, their perimeter would inevitably grow smaller and smaller and they would be overwhelmed, beaten down by Nazi planes and by artillery, which was well within range. In the end, the British maintained, the men would all be killed or taken prisoner.

This difference in view between the English and the French command was due, up to a point, to reasons of sentiment. You may remember the opening pages of Stendhal's *The Charterhouse of Parma*. After the defeat at Waterloo, the "beautifully groomed colonel" is cut down by a cavalryman's saber. A white-haired colonel takes over his command, and young Fabrizio del Dongo hears him roar at the soldiers scrambling away in retreat, "F—! In the time of the Republic we waited to give ground until the enemy forced us back! . . . Defend every inch of terrain and get your·

selves killed. . . . It is now the soil of *la patrie* that these Prussians want to invade. . . ."

For us, the French, the perimeter of Dunkirk was the soil of *la patrie*. For the English it was a battlefield like any other; and in this particular case, it was a mouse trap. They insisted on pulling out. We answered that there was no question of pulling out, and anyway an evacuation *would meet with certain disaster*. Those were our very words. The English from then on said nothing more; they proceeded to make their arrangements in secrecy.

I remember all too well the evening late in May—it was the twenty-seventh—when Admiral Odend'hal, of the FNLO, came back to London from Dover. He had gone to Dover to meet Admiral Abrial, who was making a round trip across the Channel. Abrial, who was called Admiral North, was in command of the entrenched camp at Dunkirk. While Admiral Odend'hal was waiting for him on the Dover docks, he saw a number of British Navy officers clad in khaki who seemed to be engaged in some rather odd preparations. He asked them what they were doing, and they replied that they were setting out for Dunkirk to commence the evacuation.

One can understand that Admiral Odend'hal was not at all pleased. Only by chance had he discovered at Dover what the British Admiralty should have told him in London but had instead sedulously kept secret from him. As for Admiral Darlan, Commander-in-Chief of the French fleet, his reaction was to blaze with fury at the English. As the Chinese say, here we saw the first crack in the porcelain.

This crack would grow larger and larger. Why? Because the English would be the first to be evacuated from Dunkirk. And why first? Quite simply because they were, at the outset, the closest to the shore of the Channel. This disposition of troops had been ordered by the High Command, which was French. It was doubtless logical since the British Expeditionary Corps had to be supplied by sea, while the French were supplied by land—until they were cut off from the main body of their army. But the old Duke of Bedford, whom I mentioned above, used to say, "We must always emplace our troops as far as possible from the shore, without any hope of retreat or withdrawal. People are always asking why the French Foreign Legion, besieged by Arabs in their desert forts, always fight like lions. Good Lord, it's because they haven't any other choice!"

The Duke also quoted some words of Clemenceau, the authenticity of which I cannot guarantee. He said: "Ah, that old Monsieur Clemenceau! He knew how to talk to us the English. One day he said to Lloyd George: 'If I don't have eighty British divisions on the front in France, I will make peace!' That's the kind of language our donkeys in Whitehall understand."

Things really went to pot on the day the English announced they were calling a halt to the evacuation, after having brought back from the Dunkirk inferno some 288,000 men, both French and English. Henceforth, they said, the operation would prove too costly: German cannon fire was reaching the beaches and the sea where the boats were loading, and the Stukas never let up, roaring down on the hundreds of thousand of soldiers huddling on the dunes, and on the fantastic fleet of ships, some four hundred in all—craft of every kind, from cruisers, destroyers, and minelayers to merchant ships, tugboats, fishing smack, and pleasure craft. At that moment, those taken off the beach numbered more than 200,000 English and less than 50,000 French. A great howl of indignation went up from French sailors: "Now that you have saved your own, you abandon ours, the men who covered your retreat! Very well then, we will carry on with the evacuation alone." (In fairness it must be said here that for three days the French had had no orders to pull out, even though Churchill had insisted that they were to go along with the British "arm in arm." Moreover, no French ships were allocated for them until the very end.)

The French Navy had to face up to the facts, however; in its desperate last efforts at evacuation it lost more sailors than it saved soldiers. They could only reduce their losses. But an old undercurrent of jealousy and Anglophobia came to the surface.

June 1940

Hearing the gunfire, Anne had returned from America. An officer's daughter, she claimed to adore the idea of combat, and I believed her, hard though it was for me to imagine that anybody could have a liking for the sounds and alarms of war. She had managed to get on the Italian liner *Rex*, which was making what was to be its last crossing, and she threw me into a state of confusion and apprehension. I was afraid that Italy might declare war while she was at sea and when she reached Naples she would be interned.

But Ambassador Corbin calmed me. I had to go to him to get his permission to cable the French consul in Gibraltar asking him to get Anne off the *Rex* when it called there. The Ambassador assured me that Mussolini would never dream of undertaking hostilities against the Allies until he was absolutely sure that the fate of France had been sealed by his German partners. That had not quite happened yet, so I let Anne sail into the Mediterranean. She was able to embark without hindrance in the country where the orange trees flower, and was able quietly to take a berth on one of the last trains for Paris from Naples and Rome. Once in Paris, she hesitated between going to see the baby in Brittany and going to join me. She decided that she could do with a brief sojourn in London first and reached England by one of the last commercial planes to leave France. With her she brought clothes to last her for three days. She was to stay for three years.

I found her lovely and, to all appearances, much restored. But she still seemed a little fragile. This did not, however, prevent her from accepting an invitation to aid in setting up facilities for the French wounded evacuated from Dunkirk, to be located in what was called the "Narvik Communication Line." This meant that it was comprised of the medical personnel of the French division evacuated from Norway. With this outfit was a doctor, a colonel by rank, who was constantly in tears over his separation from his family in France. One sometimes wondered in those days whether we French had not become a little too timid for war. On the divisional medical staff there was also a brilliant interne, the colonel's exact opposite; he took everything with an air of cool detachment so impenetrable that one had to assume that he had consciously put it on like armor. He was competent and intelligent and got on with the job while his colonel wept.

Anne was in his confidence. Too much so, she thought, for he left her monstrous responsibilities. She might ask him what to tell the English surgeon who wanted to know whether to amputate.

"I leave that up to you," he would say. "Answer him as you think best."

She was indignant at first. Soon she became so absorbed in her work that the world outside the hospital all but ceased to exist for her. In the evening she would bring home perfect strangers, some of them startling characters. There was, for instance, a nurse by the name of Mme Casimir Périer who had saved two hundred of her wounded at Malo-les-Bains by swimming out, under German fire, to a British ship; once aboard, she pointed out where her patients were hidden along the shore and supervised their removal under cover of darkness. She introduced us to Nescafé, then fairly new, and while showing us how easy it was to prepare over an alcohol burner, she set fire to a carpet and a table. She was so bighearted, and had such a gift for breaking dishes and mending limbs, she reminded me of an aunt of mine who was a nun. Like all nurses, she had harsh things to say about doctors. Shortly she was to leave us to go back to France.

Our poor country was going under. We were on the shore, spectators to its shipwreck and unable to lift a finger. Lucretius wrote:

> 'Tis pleasant, when the seas are rough, to stand,
> And see another's danger, safe at land.

I cannot share this feeling. Did Lucretius have no friends on board the sinking ship? Nor do I understand the moralist who maintains that the misfortune of others can always be borne.

As she sank beneath the waves, the ship answered more and more feebly to calls from shore. Then came the day when the tele-printers stopped working. The lines had been cut, at Rennes, I think. Reestablishing telephone connections between London and Paris involved immense detours in the circuits. One had to scream to be heard, and, as a result, little was understood. This was a foreshadowing of the final breakdown of understanding between the two countries. On June 7 I sent off my last telegram to my parents, urging them to leave Rogny and seek safety south of the Loire. It never reached them, and that was just as well.

Unable any longer to communicate by telephone, French and British leaders went to each other. Churchill flew to Paris, then to the Château du Muguet near Briare, and then to Tours. General de Gaulle came to London.

June 9, 1940

It was on June 9, a Sunday, that in the vestibule of the Embassy I saw a man in khaki uniform who was remarkably tall. I could easily guess that this was General de Gaulle. We knew he was in London.

He was just coming out of Ambassador Corbin's office, and I noticed that the kepi the footman handed him looked quite new and the oak leaves embroidered on it in gold gleamed in the sun-light of that June day. His promotion from colonel to brigadier was of very recent date. In fact, he had won it in May after having had reportedly stunning successes in the Battle of France at the head of the best tank division that could be thrown together. General

Weygand, by then Commander-in-Chief, had given him a magnificent citation, beginning with the words: "Admirable leader, audacious and energetic."

We were then aware only of these first words. I had myself given them to the English press when the General became Under-Secretary of State for National Defense in the Reynaud Ministry. The rest of the citation, which came to my attention later on, said that he had attacked a bridgehead, made an advance of five kilometers, and taken several hundred prisoners.

For a long time, rumor in London had General de Gaulle smashing ahead in several victorious attacks, just as the Germans were doing with their armored divisions.[1] So it was that the news of his appointment as Under-Secretary gave rise to two quite different reactions. One was that, as adviser and friend of Prime Minister Reynaud, who had called for his help, he would perhaps be able to save the situation by advising the strategic measures so sorely needed. The other reaction was one of regret that such a remarkably gifted tactician was being retired from the front. Making use of the unchallenged power he then still had, why did Paul Reynaud not hand over to this brilliant innovator, who had just demonstrated in battle the worth of his theories, the command of absolutely everything in the way of armored forces that could still be scraped together? Why could Reynaud not have appointed de Gaulle generalissimo? After all, Napoleon had been ten years younger when he became supreme commander.

I myself long believed in the legend wherein General de Gaulle had trounced the Germans two or three times on a scale compara-

[1] "I know of a certain armored division, improvised in the midst of combat, which inflicted on the Germans exactly the same treatment that their eleven *Panzer-divisionen* inflicted on us. . . ." From a speech by General de Gaulle, London, March 1, 1941.

"The final objective was Mont Caubert . . . 5 p.m. was our zero hour. The slopes of the hill were reached, but the crest remained to the enemy. . . . On May 30, the 51st Scottish Division . . . came, all fresh and spruce, to relieve the 4th Armoured Division. This regrouped near Beauvais. . . . Our losses were heavy; less, however, than those of the other side. We were bringing five hundred prisoners to be added to those of Montcornet (130), and a large quantity of arms and matériel." De Gaulle: *Memoirs,* I, pp. 46, 47, 48.

ble to what they had done to us. The truth, however, is different.
General de Gaulle relates in his memoirs what he did. There were
two engagements. In the first, in the neighborhood of Laon, the
General advanced to the river Serre and then had to withdraw. The
second was against the German bridgehead across the Somme at
Abbeville. He took two German defense lines but had to stop short
of his objective, which was Mont Caubert, a height dominating the
bridgehead. As he himself says, he took a total of less than 650
prisoners in the two actions. After the failure of his Fourth Armoured Division to reach the top of Mont Caubert, it was relieved
by the Scottish Fifty-first (Highland) Division. General de Gaulle
handed over his command and went to Paris to take his place in
Paul Reynaud's Ministry on June 6.

It is nevertheless true that General de Gaulle obtained two partial successes which were all the more admirable in a succession of
battles in which the French forces were constantly falling back.

He had been in his office at the Ministry exactly three days when
he was ordered to London on a special liaison mission. He saw first
the French Ambassador and his closest assistants: needless to say,
as Press Attaché I was not present at the conversations. I was not
even hiding under the table. But I was a member of the staff and
I can report on what I learned.

Ambassador Corbin, before accompanying the new Under-
Secretary to see the English, asked what could be said to them.
What was the French plan? What could still be done in this tragic
hour? Three defense bastions must be constituted, General de
Gaulle answered; one on the Maginot line, which was still holding; another in the Massif Central; the third in Brittany, in what
was called "the Breton Redoubt."

The Ambassador was not a strategist, but he wanted to know
what all this meant. So he put a question of his own to General
de Gaulle: What would happen if the enemy hurled the major part
of its forces against the first bastion, then against the second, and
finally against the third? The General had no answer. None at least
that the Ambassador was able to understand.

Another question: What did we expect from the English?

The General replied that primarily he had come to ask them to transfer to France, south of the Loire, the major part of their co-operation fighter planes, which had been based in England since just before Dunkirk.

Ambassador Corbin did not think that Churchill, Prime Minister since Chamberlain's resignation on May 10, would consent to anything of the sort.

The General was also to ask for reinforcements—for troops.[2]

English reinforcements? But, whether the three bastions held or not, had it not been decided immediately to begin the evacuation to North Africa of all troops that were not indispensable to slow down the advance of the enemy and thereby enable the others to be evacuated? Was it not strange, if this was indeed our decision, to embark French troops to Africa and to disembark British troops in France? Once again, the Ambassador was unable to understand the General's reply to his question.

Thereupon, they went to see Churchill at Downing Street. And, surprise! what interested the Prime Minister primarily was not the

[2] In presenting his request for British fighter squadrons to be sent south of the Loire, General de Gaulle should have been aware that his Premier's frantic demand for these, transmitted to President Roosevelt by Ambassador William C. Bullitt, and relayed on June 4 by the President to Churchill and the War Cabinet, had been flatly rejected. Sir Ronald Campbell, the British Ambassador in Paris, had explained to the French government and to Bullitt that the rate of destruction was so great that if Britain sent her remaining planes there would be none left in two weeks. Britain was now facing an invasion, and its fleet could not hold the narrow Channel without supremacy in the air. Bullitt, outraged, informed Washington that the British might be conserving their fleet and their planes to use as bargaining counters in separate peace negotiations with Hitler. The President and Cordell Hull most definitely did not share his view, as they were quickly to demonstrate. According to the British, all but three of their fighting squadrons had been thrown into the battle over northern France and Dunkirk, and during May and June they had lost several hundred pilots. At the beginning of July, Metropolitan Fighter Command were able to put into the air only forty-two of the sixty first-line squadrons the Air Ministry considered essential to the country's safety. If General de Gaulle knew of this overture by President Roosevelt, and of its rejection days before by the British War Cabinet, he nowhere says so.

military situation at all but the question of morale—to put it more precisely, the morale of his opposite number in France, Paul Reynaud.

It is not difficult to suppose that Churchill must have had some alarming reports from the English Ambassador in Paris. As I said, the English—and not only the English—were all too well informed of the campaign being waged in Paris by Mme de Portes and her friends to blunt the edge, such as it was, of Reynaud's supposed determination to fight on. Her efforts were strident, public, and ceaseless. (And she shared the Prime Minister's apartment in the Place du Palais Bourbon.) She was openly anti-English and anti-American. Her friends were the friends of Mussolini, and some of them, of Hitler. Most of this was known in London, though it was talked about only in whispers.

What Churchill now wanted was General de Gaulle's frank opinion of just how firmly resolved Reynaud might still be in the face of all this. Would Paul Reynaud stand firm? After all, he was the chief. Not all of his colleagues would follow him to Africa? So much the better; he could then rid himself of the defeatists.

General de Gaulle was reassuring. He affirmed that Reynaud's resolution was unshakable, that his spirit was firm, to an exemplary degree.[3] Churchill gave a sigh of relief upon hearing de Gaulle's assurances. He experienced an immediate sense of confidence in the General and in what he had to say. As Simone Weil was to write later, one immediately believes what General de Gaulle says, *"because he has the accent of sincerity."*

The General now detailed the requests he had been ordered to present to the British government. With regard to the planes, Churchill's answer was no. In the matter of troops, it was yes. He would immediately send a British division to Normandy. But the few fighter planes he still disposed of would be kept in England. To do otherwise would be to risk losing the war, for, *if* Hitler succeeded

---

[3] *Of Reynaud as French Prime Minister in 1940, General de Gaulle writes:* "He faced the storm with a steadfastness which did not waver. Never, during those days of drama did M. Paul Reynaud cease to be master of himself. . . ." De Gaulle: *Memoirs*, I, p. 78.

in knocking out France, he would launch an assault by air on England in the hope of clearing the skies for the invasion.

Many Frenchmen have in my hearing expressed the opinion that the British should not have refused to send over their fighter planes. Ambassador Bullitt was livid on the subject and attributed the darkest motives to Britain. However, Cordell Hull, the American Secretary of State, said in his memoirs that neither he nor President Roosevelt shared the Ambassador's belief in a British double cross. I am no expert in these matters, but I have long since been convinced that the Battle of France would have been lost even if the English fighter planes had been committed. My feeling is that we in France should burn a beautiful candle to Churchill's memory because he so resolutely refused to send the planes. Suppose he had yielded to General de Gaulle's request that the planes be sent: the very thought makes one tremble.

General de Gaulle went back to France with one refusal. But he had two successes to his credit: he had restored English confidence in the morale of his chief, Paul Reynaud, and he had prevailed upon the English to send another British division to France. For, contrary to popular belief, there were still British troops fighting in France after Dunkirk. On the very day that the British government was agreeing, at the General's behest, to send more troops to France, the Fifty-first Highland Division, ordered to retreat to Le Havre, found itself cut off. (Efforts by the British fleet to evacuate it from near Saint-Valéry on the eleventh and twelfth failed because of a heavy fog. The division was all but annihilated.)

General de Gaulle had not come to London alone. With him was a captain of the *chasseurs alpins*, a slim man of finely chiseled, expressive features, his look quick and intelligent. When he spoke, his meaning was perfectly clear and unmistakable. He was Roland de Margerie. I have mentioned how, for his sins, he was taken from the front by Reynaud to serve as chief of his diplomatic secretariat. He did all he could to stiffen the Premier's courage. But I very much doubt that he would have felt up to affirming, as had General de Gaulle, that Reynaud's courage would never give way. Indeed, he was extremely apprehensive of the combination of forces that now faced France: the might of the German armies, *and* in addition the influences that were at that moment being brought so heavily to bear on the French Prime Minister.

June 10, 1940

On the morning of June 10 we learned that, the last battle for France on the Somme having been lost, Mussolini, as had been foreseen, at long last had got up his courage to declare war on us. I went at once to knock on Admiral Odend'hal's door at the Admiralty. I demanded sea duty; that is what he had promised me in the event of war with Italy. He raised his arms to the heavens, saying: "Do you really think I have the time to attend to individual cases? You're so eager to fight, can't you wait until war comes to you! That will be soon enough, believe me!"

I returned to the Embassy and, in the performance of my prescribed duties, went from office to office. Castellane was reading the telegram that Prince Umberto of Piedmont, Commander-in-Chief of the Italian army that was supposed to be invading France, had dispatched to Mussolini: "Straining toward certain victory, the troops of the Army Group of the West wish to renew to the tireless Builder of the Fatherland their promise to dare all, so as to follow worthily in the footsteps of the Legions of Rome." I might here say that the Duce's new Roman legions numbered thirty-two divisions, and their exertions against France with approximately six divisions got them as far as the suburbs of Menton at the armistice. By then the Germans had been crashing down the Rhone Valley in the French rear.

Despite his ancestry, or perhaps because of it, Castellane was not a Royalist. And he particularly loathed the House of Savoy. Putting down the telegram, he said, "If ever that idiot of a son of a perjured father sets foot in France after the war, he'll get a kick in the rear from every passer-by." He could not know, of course, that the Count of Paris, Orléanist pretender to the French "throne," would prove less vindictive and invite the former Prince of Piedmont, then ex-King of Italy, to his children's weddings. True, King Umberto had in the meantime become a faithful ally.

"As for Musso," Castellane went on, "I am turning over in my mind a personal project, which is to spit in his face. But not before I have liberally partaken of a fine onion soup!" [1]

I went up to the second floor, where I had my office. The Embassy had just been enlarged; an apartment in the adjoining building had been acquired and the wall had been broken through to make a passageway. But our various departments were already short of space. After the war, it was to be even worse. The structure that had housed the Ambassador and all the offices used by his small staff in the days of the entente cordiale were found to be no longer adequate to the new French policy of *grandeur*. The Ambassador was thereafter lodged in a separate residence bought for the purpose. (The truth is, now that the diplomatic representatives of France abroad no longer possess anything near their former power and responsibility, our embassies have sunk to the level of provincial prefectures, where everybody is hard at work at a hundred thousand little things. Great affairs are handled between planes by Cabinet Ministers dropping in from Paris, and quite often by the Prime Minister himself, who knows very little about the country he is visiting, and continues anyway to make domestic policy while abroad. This kind of thing is not, I must say, peculiar to France and her diplomacy.)

To return to 1940: Torcy observed these efforts to embellish and enlarge the Embassy with a skeptical eye. "Just wait and see," he told me. "Once it is all finished, we will go away, leaving the key under the mat."

I asked him if he thought our government would really move to North Africa.

[1] These words were all the more striking because the Marquis de Castellane always spoke in the most proper manner. He was the kindest of men.

"If we had Clemenceau at the helm, I would not be worried. Our people would know how to die in France, rifle in hand, and continue in Africa. But instead of that—wait and see—they will cover the walls of all the villages of France with posters inviting the population to receive the invaders calmly and with dignity! It's disgusting, disgusting!"

June 15, 1940

From June 11 on, after the meeting with the French at the Château du Muguet at Briare near Orléans, the English government was for the most part doubtful that Paul Reynaud would leave for North Africa. The British had unhappy impressions from Briare. Generalissimo Weygand had asked for *all* of Britain's fighter squadrons. "Here is the decisive point," he said. "Now is the decisive moment. It is . . . wrong to keep *any* squadron back in England." Churchill had previously reached agreement on this matter with his Air Marshal and the Cabinet. We learned that he replied to Weygand in these words: "This is not the decisive point and this is not the decisive moment. That moment will come when Hitler hurls his *Luftwaffe* against Great Britain. If we can keep command of the air . . . we will win it all back for you." Twenty-five squadrons must be maintained for the defense of Britain and the Channel. And here let it again be said that they were to prove none too many.

At Briare the English had learned that their heavy bombers massed near Marseilles for a combined naval and air attack on Genoa had been stopped on orders from Air Chief General Vuillemin and Admiral Darlan. (Several days later, this attack did take place, on a lesser scale.) To be certain that the bombers could not take off, peasants and workmen near the airfield had driven trucks and dragged peasant carts onto the runways. The French command feared reprisals against their petroleum reserves, which they did not have the fighter planes to protect; the people feared the effects of a retaliatory bombing. One can only speculate now, so many years later, on what the effect of an all-out naval and air attack might have been on the Italian public: it might well have forced a change in high places that would have spared Italy the years of misery and destruction that lay ahead.

At Tours on June 13 Churchill, summoned back to France by Premier Reynaud—his last visit for four years—was asked tentatively whether he would consent to relieve France of her pledge of March 28. Reynaud said that he was making one last appeal to President Roosevelt and that if the answer was not "in conformity to our wishes" (which he, of course, knew it could not be), he would ask that France be released from its commitment not to seek a separate peace. In answer, Churchill expressed sympathy for France's plight but said that before she was released from the March 28 pact, there would have to be a "full discussion." Reynaud was asked to promise to do nothing before meeting with him again. Reynaud agreed.

The British ministers would have been even more fully enlightened had they been present on the twelfth at Cangey, the headquarters of President Lebrun. (They had already flown back to London.) Here the Generalissimo gave vent to his grievances against his predecessor and against the English, saying: "As a soldier it breaks my heart to say it, but we can no longer put off asking for an armistice."

Paul Reynaud and others objected, pointing to France's "pledged word" to the British. Weygand was then ordered to prepare to continue the war from North Africa. But Paul Reynaud did nothing at this cabinet meeting to put the Generalissimo in his place. Neither did he take any steps when General Weygand got himself tangled up in a transparent misstatement of the facts of the situation in Paris. A peculiar psychosis about the Communists was prevalent at this time.

It was, I believe, on June 15, although I would not swear to it, that the Embassy received its last telegram from General Weygand. He asked that the Royal Air Force be sent with supplies for the French armies cut off in the north. They still had munitions but were short of food.

It was not an easy request to present. Ambassador Corbin sent Torcy with it, as he was on close terms with Lord Lloyd. Torcy pleaded Weygand's case so well that he convinced the English Minister. But, said Lord Lloyd, before speaking to the Prime Minister "I would like now to hear not the opinion of the Commander-in-Chief, nor that of the diplomat who has come in his name, but I wish to know whether you, Torcy, in the interest of our common cause, are personally in favor of the operation."

Torcy replied, "You will lose ten percent of the fighters accompanying your bombers. The Army Group of the North will not fight. Keep your planes for the battle which is about to break over England." He told me later that this was the most terrible moment of his career. You will note that his advice was the exact opposite of that given by General de Gaulle some days earlier.

June 16, 1940

Later, Churchill was to see Reynaud much more clearly, as we all did. But at this moment he still trusted in General de Gaulle's assurances and believed in the French Prime Minister's determination to keep France in the war. The government would go to North Africa. There was one reason for apprehension, however: General Weygand was opposed to the move and claimed that it would only draw the Germans in the wake of the French. Then Morocco, Algeria, and Tunisia would be lost too. He was within his rights to think this, and to say it. But the French Prime Minister thought, or was reputed to think, otherwise. Why did he not dismiss General Weygand and appoint a new Commander-in-Chief to carry out his wishes?

The question was asked in many quarters at that time. We now know that Paul Reynaud was then no longer thinking in terms of continued resistance at all. He was really engaged in exerting pressure on the Generalissimo to get him to capitulate. He wanted General Weygand to shoulder the responsibility. But General Weygand would not hear of it. A dry little man, an ultra-conservative in politics, and steeped in the traditional military virtues, Weygand would *never* capitulate. And so he said. To do so would disgrace the flag.[1] Furthermore, capitulation by a commander on the field of battle was strictly forbidden by the code of military justice. Never would he consent to be a Marshal Bazaine; never would he be a General Dupont.[2]

To a French military man, the difference betwen capitulation and armistice is considerable.

Since capitulation had proved so unpalatable to General Weygand, the Prime Minister concluded that the only way out was through a political armistice. This was what General Weygand

[1] "From then on the Generalissimo, carried away by a current he was no longer trying to master, was bound to seek the solution within his reach: capitulation. But as he did not intend to assume the responsibility for this, his action would consist in steering the government towards it." De Gaulle: *Memoirs,* I, p. 52.

"That a man writing his memoirs should give his estimate of men and events could not be more natural, or even more desirable. But that he should pretend to plumb consciences, and that he should attribute degrading motives to the actions of those who do not share his way of looking at things, is neither worthy of one who has placed himself so high, nor comprehensible." Weygand: *En lisant de Gaulle,* p. 36.

"The question of the continuing action of the war is political and a matter for governmental decisions. . . . Capitulation is an act exclusively military by nature. . . . Capitulation is punishable by death or dismissal from the service. . . . M. Paul Reynaud suggested to me . . . the capitulation of our Army. I rejected this proposition with as much indignation as firmness. . . . I repeated it in a voice loud enough to be heard by everyone that I would not agree to put such a stain on our flags. . . ." Weygand: *En lisant de Gaulle,* pp. 66–9.

[2] Marshal Bazaine capitulated at Metz in 1870 after the defeat and capture of Napoleon III at Sedan, and General Dupont surrendered to the Spaniards at Bailen in 1808, an act for which Napoleon I never forgave him.

and Marshal Pétain had been trying to impose upon him. As Prime Minister, he, not his commanders, had the prerogative of decision in matters of such high import. Before he could request an armistice of the Germans, however, he first had to obtain a formal release from Britain; after all, it was at his own instigation that the March 28 pact had been signed by which each government pledged not to treat separately with the enemy.

When General de Gaulle reached London, on June 16, the British War Cabinet was still studying Reynaud's somewhat oblique and conditional requests for a release from the pact of March 28.

There seemed to be little reason for de Gaulle to say any more about his Prime Minister's unshakable resolution. Nobody, except perhaps Churchill, believed a word of it any longer. The British were now looking for some way to hearten Reynaud, to give him some backbone. He needed arguments to use against the defeatists in his Cabinet, Marshal Pétain at their head. It was in such circumstances that the British government came forth with its remarkable proposal for union between England and France.

This proposal, made in the best of faith, was a sensation at the time, but only briefly so, because events were moving so very fast. By its terms, France and Great Britain would become one country. Englishmen would become French and Frenchmen would become English. Obviously, the French would not be able to back out of the war, because they would have been English as well as French. Nationality would be double; France and Great Britain would no longer be two separate nations but a single Anglo-French one.

Churchill did not father this project. It was born while Chamberlain was still Prime Minister, and it was allowed to remain among the glass jars in the museum of freaks left behind by his Cabinet. In the emergency, Sir Robert Vansittart, permanent Under-Secretary of State at the Foreign Office, remembered it and brought it out. "Let's try this," he said. Working on the project along with Sir Robert was Jean Monnet, himself a living symbol of double nationality in his role as purchasing agent for both France and Great Britain. The problem was to find someone to sponsor it. Who could sell Churchill on the idea?

Their thoughts turned to General de Gaulle, who had just arrived. And the choice was good. The Prime Minister had been, one might say, smitten with General de Gaulle. He swore by General de Gaulle. (These sudden enthusiasms were in character with Churchill and were a gauge of his generosity of spirit.)

Ambassador Corbin and Jean Monnet went together to see the General early that morning at his hotel. What did he think? Did he approve of the project? Did he think that his chief, M. Reynaud, would approve of it? De Gaulle could not have been more positive. The project of union would indeed give Reynaud fresh courage and would prove helpful to him in convincing his Cabinet that France must continue to fight.[3]

Torcy's opinion was exactly the contrary. But it was decided to follow the General's advice. Nobody knew the French Premier better than he, and nobody was better informed on the state of mind of the Premier's colleagues in the Ministry. And so, during luncheon that day at the Carlton Club the General urged Churchill to sponsor the proposal.

"Do you really think," Churchill asked, in substance, "that this proposition will have a tonic effect on the French government?"

The General answered that he had not the slightest doubt of it. Had he thought otherwise, would he have urged this action upon the Prime Minister?

Churchill then made his decision. He called the British Cabinet together, and he in turn convinced his colleagues that the proposal would do wonders. General de Gaulle called his Premier on the telephone. From Downing Street the text was telephoned to Bordeaux, where the French Ministry was about to meet, Reynaud being unable to postpone it any longer.

---

[3] "Above all, I thought, like M. Corbin and M. Monnet, that the proposal was of a nature to provide M. Paul Reynaud, in the supreme crisis in which he was plunged, with an element of comfort and, vis-à-vis his Ministers, an argument for tenacity. I consented, therefore, to do what I could with Mr. Churchill to get him to adopt it. . . . After some discussion, the Prime Minister fell in with my view." De Gaulle: *Memoirs,* I, pp. 75–7.

The cure worked wonderfully and instantaneously: it killed the patient. The partisans of the cease-fire wanted no part of the British proposal. They derided it and cast ugly aspersions on Britain's motives. Even the wily ex-Premier Camille Chautemps, who was not one of the professional Anglophobes and was at that moment a man of peace, said that the British offer was designed to make France "just another dominion." Other self-proclaimed patriots said loudly that they would rather see France a mere *Gau* under Hitler than a dominion under perfidious Albion. As a direct result of this proposal of integral union, the defeatists and even the pro-Germans were able to pose as patriots determined to save France from British domination; the alternative was made to seem not so bad. In the face of this storm of anti-English feeling, Paul Reynaud chose to resign his high office, though he was not legally obliged to yield to a majority vote within his own Cabinet. After he had done so, he decided to let President Lebrun entrust Marshal Pétain with the task of setting up a new government, a task the old gentleman had been waiting impatiently to perform. Nobody, least of all Paul Reynaud, was unaware of Marshal Pétain's determination to ask for an armistice. Nor was anyone, including Paul Reynaud, unaware of the Marshal's intention in respect to the Third Republic.

General de Gaulle's admired and respected chief, Paul Reynaud, had yielded to the many pressures on him, both public and private.

As these events were taking place in Bordeaux, General de Gaulle landed there in an English plane from London. Churchill had told him that if things turned out badly he might return to England by the same plane. To arrange that, he had merely to speak to Brigadier-General Spears, the Prime Minister's personal representative in France. Churchill had already received on British shores the Queen of Holland, the Belgian government (at outs with its king), and the King of Norway; he would be happy also to welcome the French government, whether its intention was to remain there or to proceed via London to North Africa. This concept of Churchill's, which has not become very well known, might, to my way of thinking, explain the welcome he was soon to give to General de Gaulle, and likewise his willingness to recognize the General almost immediately as chief of all Frenchmen who would themselves recognize him in that role: for that was the initial formula.

Churchill's idea was that the plane that took General de Gaulle to Bordeaux could return, if developments warranted, with several of the high-ranking political personalities of France, perhaps with Paul Reynaud himself.

When General de Gaulle arrived in Bordeaux the evening of June 16, Reynaud had already resigned and Marshal Pétain was getting together a ministry.[4]

There was not much time. General de Gaulle arrived at nine-thirty and Marshal Pétain became Prime Minister at ten o'clock. But Paul Reynaud considered himself still in charge of interim affairs and was thus able to facilitate the General's departure by handing over to him 100,000 francs from the secret funds, which would, of course—amusingly enough—be charged to Marshal Pétain's Ministry. This money was to cover the General's needs after his arrival in London; whether Reynaud was aware of his former Under-Secretary's vast ambitions is not clear. But what about the General's wife and children? They were in Brittany, at Carentec. It was agreed that they should be sent to England ahead of the German armored columns then driving west. Passports were hurriedly issued for them by Roland de Margerie (who had also returned from England) and sent north by motorcycle couriers breasting the tide of refugees fleeing the German advance. They reached Mme de Gaulle in time for her to catch the last ship leaving Brest for England.

[4] "This meant certain capitulation," wrote de Gaulle later. "My decision was taken at once. I would leave as soon as morning came." He went to see his former chief, Reynaud. "And I found him with no illusions," he said, "about what the consequences would be of the Marshal's taking power, and, on the other hand, like one relieved of an intolerable burden." De Gaulle went on to say, however, that, in the face of hideous reverses, the Premier "had not wavered!" Or "ceased to be master of himself." But "the spectacle . . . was a tragic one." (De Gaulle: *Memoirs*, I, pp. 78–81.)

June 17, 1940

When the General left Bordeaux on the morning of the seventeenth, he did not wait for any of the political personalities Churchill thought might decide to join him in his British plane. Why the hurry? General Spears subsequently gave two reasons: first, that General de Gaulle had reason to fear that he might be arrested, and second, that he wanted to reach London as soon as possible so that he could launch his appeal.

There is really no need to ask why the General wanted to be the first to arrive in London. He makes it abundantly clear in his memoirs that as early as June 17, while he was flying to England in an English plane, he had already decided what he wanted to be: the repository of French sovereignty.

Anyone who doubts this interpretation should reread his words as they appear in his memoirs.[1] He had already, to use his expression, *assumed* France. He was already the government of France, the state and the nation all rolled into one person. He was already troubled by what he calls "parallel" enterprises, which were in fact rival enterprises, he says; enterprises, ambitions on the part of men who *could* take his place. His essential preoccupation was to perpetuate French power at this worst moment of the war, but on the side of the Allies, and to keep it until the Allied victory. Of the inevitability of an Allied victory nobody in London was in any serious doubt, as I can testify. Actually, their reasons for certainty were not as good as they thought then. But in London on the sixteenth, before flying off to Bordeaux, General de Gaulle had seen the temper of English opinion, their

[1] De Gaulle: *Memoirs*, I, pp. 81–3.

absolute conviction of victory, just as I had, though in the rest of the world, even in the United States, very few persons were at that somber hour betting any money on England. Very few indeed. (Anyone in America who doubts this should consult the newspaper files for June, August, September of that year, and even later.) But President Roosevelt, Secretary of State Hull, and Secretary of War Stimson did not believe that England was lost; otherwise, as Hull later said, they would not have immediately shipped off to Britain all those millions of rifles, rounds of ammunition, and the rest.

I myself confess that, in spite of the amazing temper of the English people, I thought the Germans might succeed in invading and occupying England. But I could not see how they would cope with the British fleet or how they could hope to vanquish the Commonwealth—in other words, how they would achieve that last victory without which no war is won.

When de Gaulle saw Churchill on the seventeenth, he was of course warmly received. The General asked to be allowed to speak right away over the BBC. Right away? The urgency was not so apparent to the Prime Minister. The Franco-German armistice was not yet signed and would not be for some days. Any precipitate action in London might risk creating in Bordeaux an effect quite contrary to what was desired.

On the seventeenth, after Marshal Pétain called on the French armies to stop fighting and asked for talks with the Germans with an armistice in view, I went to Admiral Odend'hal to say that, for myself, I would not obey the cease-fire order; for me the war was still on. He gave me an indulgent look but made no reply. I then went to make the same statement to Torcy, saying further that I was abandoning my functions as press attaché. He gave me his approval at once; in his eyes, I presume, my decision seemed natural. He was not in a particularly good humor that morning. An Embassy secretary who came in to report on a rumor that hostilities had begun between Germany and Russia was sent on his way without formality.

"Don't bother me with such nonsense!" Torcy said in his coldest tone. "We won't be talking about that for at least a year!"

As for the Ambassador, he was preparing to inform Bordeaux that he could not continue in his post. This model diplomat, normally so reserved, so imperturbable, so careful of his appearance, now let himself be seen with eyes red with tears.

I told no one else at the Embassy of my decision. In the corridor, near the office of the Military Attachés, a lively argument was in progress among a group of officers who had gathered, I suppose, to hear the news. "In wartime," one of them was saying, "a man can't just resign. Resignation equals desertion. One receives an order, one carries it out, and no nonsense!"

"I beg your pardon," said another. "Nobody is obliged to carry out an order that appears to him to run counter to the interests of the service!"

"The formula used in the Navy when an officer takes command of a ship is that you are to obey your superiors 'in any order they give for the good of the service and the success of the arms of France.' In other circumstances, one must disobey. . . ."

"But look, that's anarchy! . . ."

Just before noon, another group of officers came crowding into my office to listen to the radio, which was replaying Marshal Pétain's appeal. It is, or should be by now, all too well known.

> *Français!*
> *. . . Je fais à la France le don de ma personne pour atténuer son malheur. . . . C'est le coeur serré que je vous dis aujourd'hui qu'il faut cesser le combat. . . .*[2]

---

[2] "I bestow on France the gift of my person to alleviate its misfortune." The eighty-four-year-old Marshal of France made his broadcast at 12:30 in the afternoon of June 17, ordering French troops to lay down their arms, before any understanding had been reached with the Germans. The Germans continued their smashing advance, crossing the Loire, bombing heavily as far west as Rennes and Lorient. The Marshal's government (General Weygand as Defense Minister, notably) neglected to give its British and Polish allies advance notice of such a possible "cease-fire"—under the terms of which they would have to be interned. The British commander in France, General Alan

The recording over, the arguments started up again and became quarrels.

I went downstairs, but, before going out, I knocked on Castellane's door. He had a book in his hand and read aloud, for my edification, a passage from the Apocalypse in which he claimed to find a prophecy of the coming of Hitler, of his tanks and of his Stukas.

> And power was given to him over the four parts of the earth to kill with sword, with famine, and with death . . . and the sun and the air were darkened with the smoke of the pit. And from the smoke of the pit there came out locusts upon the earth. . . . And the shape of the locusts were like unto horses prepared unto battle. . . . And they had breastplates as breastplates of iron, and the noise of their wings was as the noise of chariots . . . and the heads of the horses were as the heads of lions: and from their mouths proceeded fire, and smoke, and brimstone.

He was at this point in the Scriptures when a liveried footman appeared with the Ambassador's little dog on its leash. He was taking the dog out, a ceremony that occurred a number of times every day, dogs being what they are. Castellane's office, once a waiting room, was the only one that opened level with the strip of lawn between the Embassy and Hyde Park.

At the appearance of the dog and its attendant, Castellane dropped the book, snatched his hat off the hook, popped it on his head, and, imitating some courtier of our grandiose past in the throes of an awful fright at having almost neglected a sacred

---

Brooke, did not learn of the Marshal's broadcast until a telephone call reached him from London at 1:15 in the afternoon. The French had not had the decency to inform him of developments. In midafternoon he was stunned to learn that one of his liaison officers, on his way to Cherbourg, had found himself *in the rear* of a German armored column in Rommel's command. That same day the Germans crossed the Loire at La Charité, and there found vast supplies of matériel, and all the documents of the French general staff. And by that night the French Second Army Group on the Maginot line had been encircled.

duty, scurried to the French door leading to the lawn. Throwing
it open, he swept off his hat in a deep bow *à la mousquetaire* and
as the tiny griffon padded by him, he called out portentously:
"Le chien de Son Excellence!"

Castellane then resumed his declamation of the Apocalypse.
I decided to get out of there. The kind of hysteria that was beginning to manifest itself on several faces can be contagious.
Robert, the Embassy porter, looked as though he had been hit
on the head. And old Dan, our *homme à tout faire*, was seated on
the steps, head in hands, bawling like a calf.

When I reached the house, which was quite near, it was past
one o'clock. But Anne was not home yet. Waiting for her, I found
myself standing by the window staring out at the trees in the
square, a rich green, and at the silver barrage balloons swaying
above them.

At last the automobile bringing Anne home drew up before
our entrance. She didn't quite get out, but, with her hand on the
door, talked animatedly for a few minutes with the ambulance
driver who had brought her. When she finished, I went down to
meet her. For the past two weeks she had been following developments as if from a great distance. She knew, of course, that the
war was going badly, but she seemed to feel that it had to be like
this before the eventual victory. She was remembering how it had
been in the last war. But this time there was to be no miracle
of the Marne.

"It is all over in France," I blurted out. Only later did I realize
how brutal this was. I did not mean it to be.

"What's all over?"

"Marshal Pétain has entered into negotiations with Hitler."

"Have all of you gone mad? Rumors, that's all! The rumor
I like best is the one that was going around this morning at the
hospital. Russia waited until Hitler was in it up to his neck in
France, and is now invading East Prussia!"

If I was to bring her down to earth, I must do it gently. But
at that moment the radio, which I had left on, tuned to a French

wave length, began to rebroadcast the rusty, creaking voice of the old man with its message of despair.

Je fais le don de ma personne . . .

"But it's Marshal Pétain!" she exclaimed.

She listened. She understood. And she slumped down on the sofa, buried her head in her arms, and sobbed . . .

That was when her illness began. It was to last for months. Since her return from Florida, she had been working past the point of exhaustion. Then, too, of all the Frenchwomen in London, she was perhaps the one least prepared to hear such words from a Marshal of France. For her it was the end of the world to which she had given her heart, the end of the world of her girlhood, when France was still victorious.

To return now to the events of June 17: at the darkest moment in French history, Churchill made a statement consisting of only six sentences which merit repetition. He said:

> The news from France is very bad, and I grieve for the gallant French people who have fallen into this terrible misfortune.
>
> Nothing will alter our feelings towards them, or our faith that the genius of France will rise again.
>
> What happened to France makes no difference to British faith and purpose.
>
> We have become the sole champions now in arms to defend the world cause. We shall do our best to be worthy of that high honour.
>
> We shall defend our island, and, with the British Empire around us, we shall fight on unconquerable until the curse of Hitler is lifted from the brows of men.
>
> We are sure that in the end all will be well.

June 18, 1940

As his confidential agent, General Spears, was no longer in Bordeaux, the Prime Minister decided to send on the morrow some other top-ranking government figures: Mr. Alexander, First Lord of the Admiralty, Sir Dudley Pound, First Sea Lord, and Lord Lloyd, by far the most dynamic personality in the War Cabinet.

Jean Monnet agreed with the Ambassador and with Torcy that he and Emmanuel Monick also should go to Bordeaux, along with two secretaries, René Pleven and Robert Marjolin. At this time, Jean Monnet was much better known for his determination to go on with the war than was General de Gaulle. (And evidently Monnet had no anxiety about being arrested in Bordeaux.) There seemed to have been some question of the General going with them; his reasons for staying behind in London were at that moment not very clear. They were to become clear before the day was out. For it was from London that very night that the General intended to broadcast his now celebrated appeal.[1]

The two missions, one English and the other French, were to

[1] Churchill and his associates were so shocked by Marshal Pétain's incredible appeal for a cease-fire and by his failure to acknowledge in any way the British offer of union made to Reynaud the night before that they did not see anything else they might usefully attempt along diplomatic lines. But on the evening of the seventeenth the Marshal's new Minister of Foreign Affairs, Paul Baudouin, had gone on the air in the hope of undoing some of the damage. He had said, "France will never accept shameful conditions which would mean the end of all liberty for the spirit of her people. . . ." His words were taken to mean more or less what they said. And Marshal Pétain had that same day assured Sir Ronald Campbell, His Majesty's Ambassador to France, that if the German terms proved unacceptable, the fleet would be scuttled and part of the French government would move to North Africa, out of the enemy's reach. So on the morning of the eighteenth, Churchill and his War Cabinet decided that all need not yet be considered lost in Bordeaux.

make an attempt in Bordeaux to reverse the strong defeatist current by setting forth just what the English could do to help with the conduct of the war from North Africa with the part of the Army that could be sent off ahead of the Germans, and with the fleet intact. The English were haunted by thoughts of the French fleet, and Sir Dudley Pound's objective in Bordeaux was at all costs to maintain an entente with Admiral Darlan. With these missions went Colonel Bonavita of the Inter-allied Committee on Military Plans, who was to transmit the British government's offer of shipping to carry French troops and equipment to North Africa. He was supplied with precise indications of the tonnage that could be allotted to this operation and was instructed to submit these to the French Ministry of War and the French General Staff.

Churchill determined also to order all British consuls and agents throughout the French Empire to place themselves at the disposal of the French authorities, military or civilian, with whom they normally dealt and to aid them in whatever they might attempt to keep the war going. The important thing was not to give the impression, now or in the immediate future, that the bridge between the two allies was down. Neither should anything be done to give anyone reason to think that French authority was being set up, with English help, on soil that was not French. Otherwise, what unpleasant conclusions might be drawn in Bordeaux, Algiers, Rabat? Admiral Darlan, to mention only one, would assuredly not place himself alongside, and much less under the orders of, some supposed French authority established in London and functioning with money advanced by the English. Anything of the sort would immediately, if not irremediably, compromise efforts to keep the fleet out of the armistice negotiations so that it might continue fighting or resume fighting later on. It was therefore essential to behave prudently in London and to make as few political manifestations as possible. It was in Bordeaux that quick action was indicated.

This conception, as you see, was diametrically opposed to the conclusions reached by General de Gaulle as early as the seventeenth, which he was to broadcast over the London radio, in the name of France, on the eighteenth.

Anne had a cousin who worked for the French Blockade Mission, one of a number of very pretty girls there. For some days these young ladies had nothing to do. Their chief was Paul Morand, diplomat-novelist (it was as a novelist that he made a name for himself between the First and Second World Wars), who was soon to resume his diplomatic career in the service of Marshal Pétain. One of the girls got a call from Geoffroy de Courcel, whom she knew, asking her to come and help the General. There was something that needed typing.

The text she was asked to type was that of General de Gaulle's famous appeal of June 18.

When we learned that the General was going to go on the air at six o'clock, some of us got together in my former office, where I still went despite my resignation. Pierre Maillaud was there. There was no secret about any of this. General Lelong, the Military Attaché, was giving anyone who asked for it the General's address, 8 Seymour Place. However, I cannot say for certain that Churchill had found the time to read the text, which had been submitted to him earlier in the day by General Spears. The Prime Minister had an enormous number of things to do that day and was himself to pronounce a historic speech before the House. Whatever the case, some hours before the General, standing tall in his uniform, was to read his celebrated appeal, Churchill, the little man in black jacket and striped trousers, his watch chain looped through a buttonhole of his waistcoat and his bow tie, had gone to the House of Commons. And there he spoke these words, which are worthy of being engraved in our memories.

> We do not yet know what will happen in France, or whether France's resistance will be prolonged, both in France and in the French Empire overseas. . . .
> The House will have read the historic declaration in which, at the desire of many Frenchmen and of our own hearts, we have proclaimed our willingness to conclude at the darkest hour in French history, a union of common citizenship (*Cheers*). How-

ever matters may go in France, or with the French government, or with another French government, we in this island and in the British Empire will never lose our sense of comradeship with the French people. . . . If final victory rewards our toils, they shall share the gains (*Hear, hear*), aye, and freedom shall be restored to all. . . .

Let us therefore address ourselves to our duty. . . .

One does not have to have been an admirer of the old British Empire, or even of the late Sir Winston, to recognize that Churchill's qualities of heart radiated from his words, as they shone out in his actions. He will surely have a statue in France some day. He was the incarnation of a double generosity, American through his mother, English through his father. And this is something that de Gaulle, otherwise so intelligent, seems never to have understood.

He never understood it, or perhaps he had no wish to admit its existence. If Churchill did indeed declare in advance that the French people would share fully in the benefits of an eventual victory, it hardly makes sense for the Gaullists to give the General the credit for having wrung these benefits out of the English. If Churchill's sincerity at the start is to be admitted by General de Gaulle, all the suspicions that de Gaulle entertained over the years and expressed over and over again add up to gratuitous insults to the good faith of Winston Churchill.

The General's appeal of June 18—its real text, I mean—is little known and is all too often quoted incorrectly, or with parts cut out or parts added. It bears rereading.[2] The General on that day

[2] *Appeal by General de Gaulle to the French people, June 18, 1940*

The leaders who, for many years past, have been at the head of the French Armed Forces, have set up a government.

Alleging the defeat of our armies, this government has entered into negotiations with the enemy with a view to bringing about a cessation of hostilities.

It is quite true that we were, and still are, overwhelmed by enemy mechanized forces, both on the ground and in the air.

It was the tanks, the planes, and the tactics of the Germans, far more than the fact that we were outnumbered, that forced our armies to retreat. It was the German tanks, planes, and tactics that provided the element of surprise which brought our leaders to their present plight.

expressed admirably what all of us in London were thinking: namely, that the defeat of France was principally due to our weakness in machines of war. And by a surge of strength in just such machines of war, the Allies would finally win over Germany. And such a victory would also be the victory of France, because our country was not alone.

Our country was not alone, nor was General de Gaulle alone, nor were any of us; we felt ourselves surrounded by friends, by our allies of that moment in history, and others who were to become our allies. And we were surrounded, too, by that comradeship of which Churchill spoke in the Commons just before de Gaulle launched his appeal.

As for myself, I was carried away by the General as we heard him that night. I already had his address and his telephone number. So, once home, I called Lieutenant de Courcel, his aide-decamp, and was given an appointment for the next morning, June

---

But has the last word been said? Must we abandon all hope? Is our defeat final and irremediable? To these questions I answer—No!

Speaking in full knowledge of the facts, I ask you to believe me when I say that the cause of France is not lost. The very factors that brought about our defeat may one day lead us to victory.

For, remember this, France does not stand alone. She is not isolated. Behind her is a vast Empire, and she can make common cause with the British Empire, which commands the seas and is continuing the struggle. Like England, she can draw unreservedly on the immense industrial resources of the United States.

This war is not limited to our unfortunate country. The outcome of the struggle has not been decided by the Battle of France. This is a world war. Mistakes have been made, there have been delays and untold suffering, but the fact remains that there still exists in the world everything we need to crush our enemies some day. Today we are crushed by the sheer weight of mechanized force hurled against us, but we can look to a future in which even greater mechanized force will bring us victory. The destiny of the world is at stake.

I, General de Gaulle, now in London, call on all French officers and men who are at present on British soil, or may be in the future, with or without their arms; I call on all engineers and skilled workmen from the armament factories who are at present on British soil, or may be in the future, to get in touch with me.

Whatever happens, the flames of French resistance must not and shall not die.

De Gaulle: *Memoirs*, I, pp. 83–4.

19. That same evening Pierre Maillaud (who was later to adopt the *nom de guerre* of Pierre Bourdan) dropped in at our house, and when I told him about it, he wanted to go with me. Again I telephoned Courcel. "Certainly. The General will receive you both."

June 19, 1940

A little before nine o'clock, Pierre Maillaud came by to pick me up. Off we went, the two of us, on foot, diagonally across Hyde Park from Albert Gate to Stanhope Gate. On the way, Maillaud talked to me about his projects. He was then the second man in the London bureau of the Havas Agency, the director being Paul L. Bret, a distinguished French correspondent somewhat older than we. Since the beginning of the war, Bret had been chief of the French Information Mission and so, to all intents, left Havas to Maillaud. Now that France had been invaded, Bret and Maillaud had decided to transform the London bureau of Havas into the headquarters of a free news agency.

Of all the people I knew in London, Pierre Maillaud was one of the best informed. On our way across Hyde Park he told me that Sir Dudley Pound, the First Sea Lord, had come back from Bordeaux the night before with reassuring news: Admiral Darlan, hitherto Chief of Staff of the French Navy and now Minister of Marine under Marshal Pétain, had sworn that our fleet would never fall into German hands. That Darlan was extremely anti-English, there was not the slightest doubt. But his oath that the Germans would never get their hands on the fleet was grounded in his own deep personal interest and in the interest of the government that he had just become part of. For the fleet was practically the only trump card Marshal Pétain would now hold if he was to avoid being totally crushed in the armistice negotiations with Hitler and later during the difficult period of collaboration in varying degrees. In the hands of Marshal Pétain and Admiral Darlan, the French fleet was essentially the means by which the prisoner could blackmail his jailer. And it was clear, or should have been, that it would never be given up.

Knowing our sailors, officers and men alike, as I did, I told Maillaud that Darlan's word had a much higher value than some might think: for it represented the deepest feelings of the officers and the crews. No navy in the world likes to see its ships taken from it. And a ship at sea does not have to let itself be caught like a regiment that has been surrounded. Ships can take flight; or they can scuttle.

As we neared Seymour Place, where General de Gaulle then lived, we fell into conversation about him again. Pierre Maillaud had sent out the June 18 appeal over the Havas network. He had also sent the text to Iverach McDonald, who, it turned out, had already received a copy. His paper, *The Times*, printed it in its entirety and in a good spot, the center page. The same issue of *The Times* carried an article giving instructions to the civilian population on how to behave during the invasion, which was then thought imminent: if the Germans come, "stay put!" In England, memories were still fresh of the confusion caused by the flood of refugees on the highways of France.

Seymour Place is an elegant sort of dead end just off Park Lane. At Number 8 there is a rather handsome building. (There is or there was. I have not been back to see whether it was destroyed during the bombings.) The apartment occupied by General de Gaulle was the London home of Jean Laurent, who had been his chief of secretariat in the Reynaud Ministry. It was in Bordeaux that Laurent had given him the keys.

In the anteroom we were met by Lieutenant de Courcel, the General's aide-de-camp, tall, blond, rosy-cheeked, and very polite. He told us that the General had people with him but would see us shortly.

It was not long before the General's callers emerged from the *salon.* We recognized them as prominent members of the French colony in England. They seemed already to have that preoccupied look, that kindly and protective smile of men who felt themselves weighted down by ministerial responsibilities to come.

"Be good enough to come in," Lieutenant de Courcel said.

The room was vast, and flooded with sunlight. At the far end, his back to a window, stood General de Gaulle, immobile and statuesque. After we had been introduced, Pierre Maillaud led off in a complimentary vein, saying that he had come to place himself at the General's disposition in response to his magnificent appeal of the night before. In what way could he be useful?

"What exactly is your profession?" the General asked.

Maillaud told him, but the General seemed to have heard only that Maillaud's job had to do with a news agency.

"Very well," the General said, "tell me the news!"

This reply was hardly expected, but Maillaud did as ordered. He gave the General the latest news, some of which, by the way, turned out later to be untrue. Then, doing his professional duty, Maillaud asked the General if he had any statement to make about his immediate plans. The General's answer was that he would speak again over the BBC that evening, addressing himself to all Frenchmen everywhere but especially to those in North Africa, to tell them where their duty lay. He felt in his heart, he said, that he was speaking *in the name of France.*

I looked. I listened. I had come with a great store of admiration. But I felt it beginning to ebb away, giving place to a sense of constraint, due in part, I think, to the General's appearance. He was seated in an armchair facing the two chairs to which he had motioned us, and as he talked to Pierre Maillaud, I could see only three quarters of his face. The one eye visible to me somehow suggested the eye of an elephant, quite round when the heavy eyelid was raised. (Later, Jean Oberlé told me that he, too, had the impression of an elephant's eye.) He had very little chin, so little that I found myself wondering whether it wasn't the result of a war wound. Yet it gave no impression of weakness, but rather of smugness, of self-sufficiency, as did also the mouth under the

little brush of a mustache, really a very small mustache. I saw in
him the characteristics of the officer-actor found in vast numbers
in the Navy. There was also something that suggested a very tall
Boy Scout, too tall, really, to be still a Scout.

Then suddenly he turned to me.

"And you, monsieur?"

Taken by surprise, I said only that I wanted to go to sea at the
earliest opportunity now that I was free, having resigned from the
French Embassy on June 17.

"On the seventeenth?" the General asked, with a quick glance
that seemed not quite friendly. He then got to his feet and we
took our leave most ceremoniously. In the street, Pierre Maillaud
asked what my impression had been. I answered that the General
seemed inflated.

"No, not that. That isn't quite the word."

"But *I* think it is the right word. You haven't had to do your
military service, so you have had no experience with that kind of
officer—inflated with the concept they have of themselves. If you
stuck a pin into them, you'd hear it—their idea of themselves—
come out whistling like the air from an inner tube."

We went on home, Pierre Maillaud and I, across the park the
same way we had come. We disagreed, so instead of arguing it
out we said nothing. I well remember that return home across the
park as the last silence I knew in London. People were coming and
going about their business with long springy steps. There were
very few cars and they seemed to be traveling slowly, noiselessly,
as if coasting along with engines off. The sky was of the purest
blue. The lawns were still green. That silence, that purity, that
freshness overwhelmed you with a sense of transience and fragil-
ity. But what was most extraordinarily comforting was the unanimity of the people's resolve. It is hard to convey an idea of how it
was. With us, in France, unanimity is accompanied by great bursts
of enthusiasm, as in 1914 in the first days of World War I. With
the British it is almost phlegmatic, if that is the right word to
describe quiet, almost shy determination. They rarely said what
they felt. They left that to Churchill, who said things so very

well. He said them sometimes with a passion that would have embarrassed most Englishmen, even though he did faithfully express what they were thinking deep inside themselves.

It would be too easy to think that this quiet determination to fight it out was due entirely to the eloquence of Winston Churchill, great though it was. Churchill had the merit, not negligible by any means, of using words that aroused in the English mind echoes from the days of the Armada and other times of great peril to this island land. As he said himself, he did not create the lion but he was privileged to give the roar. A not inconsiderable achievement! But the same Churchill had for years warned with marvelous clairvoyance of the Nazi peril, and had scarcely been heard. The English people do not close their ranks entirely, solidly, as in 1940, until they have their nose right in the facts, in the truth, so to speak. Whether it is Churchill who gives the roar, or Chamberlain who points the way with his umbrella, the lion charges.

Find some Englishman who argues that without General de Gaulle the French people would not have resisted as they did, and tell him that without Winston Churchill the British would have capitulated before Hitler. See how he takes that! The cult of personality, I understand—but not to the point where you equate a people with a man, any man. Not at any rate a people like the English, like the French, or the Americans. And then, too, a leader cannot be called great if he has only sheep to lead.

On this subject there is an anecdote of that day, June 19, which I did not hear until later. At about the time that Pierre Maillaud and I were so ceremoniously bowing out of the presence of General de Gaulle, a financier prominent in the City rang the doorbell of Lord Tyrell's home. Lord Tyrell had long been a diplomat, and he had a quality rare among diplomats—he knew and understood his own country. He had been Ambassador from the Court of St. James in Paris before the war and was now living in London in semi-retirement. His advice, however, was sought—and listened to. That was why the financier in question had come to see him.

"Lord Tyrell," he began, "you have read, as I have, the speech

that Churchill made in the House yesterday. He says that we are
to fight on the beaches, in the towns, and I don't know where else,
and that we will never give up! Good, very good! A fine speech!
Exactly what should be said! But, good Lord, it's not what should
be done!"

"What are you trying to say?"

"What I am trying to say is that we cannot fight, whether on
the beaches or anywhere else. It's absurd. Listen to me a moment:
we have a navy, of course. But, in the final analysis, the Italian
Navy must now be counted with the German. And tell me, what
will the French Navy do?

"Our Air Force? A handful of planes and pilots! Our Army?
None really! We are naked. All our equipment was left behind in
France. Even the rifles. The Guards were the only regiment to
bring back theirs. In brief, the adversary is ten or twenty times
stronger than we are. I grant that at the race track one can bet on
odds of ten to one, or twenty to one. But surely we cannot allow
the fate of the country to be gambled away like that. It defies
common sense!"

"But what would *you* do? There is no choice!"

"No choice? But there is, there is indeed a choice! We must
conclude a truce, as we did in 1803 with Napoleon. Hitler will accept it. Now the British people have at least understood. They
will work. They will produce shells, tanks, planes. America even
will come awake. Then, in two years, or three years, we will again
be able to make our voices heard loudly and firmly. We can then
even go to war if you want. We can even win it. But today we must
ask for an armistice! We must be sensible!"

As I heard the story, Lord Tyrell's answer went like this: "If you
want to talk sense, I could show you where you are wrong: we have
a *very good* chance of winning the war. England, the Commonwealth, that constitutes a huge, an enormous piece of the earth. I
could equally show you how, if we were to follow your counsel,
what we would lose would be precisely the Commonwealth! India
is already on the point of bursting like an overripe pomegranate, but
she will stand by us until the end of the war. South Africa, New

Zealand, Australia, and even Canada would part company with us. England would become a Spain shorn of empire. But I don't want to waste my time going into all that. I have a much stronger argument for you. . . ."

As he said this, Lord Tyrell took his caller by the arm, led him to the window, and pointed to one of the lampposts in Chesham Place.

"Do you see that gaslight? Good! Now let me tell you, sir, that you are lucky that you expressed yourself to me alone as you have done, in a room with the doors shut. But don't repeat what you have just said out in the street! For you and your kind would be hung on that lamppost by the people of Britain! Do I make myself clear?"

It was said of General de Gaulle that in 1940 he was a man alone. The truth is that the man alone in England in June 1940 is best symbolized by the financier who wanted to be "sensible."

Can it be said of General de Gaulle that he was alone in London, among so many French people? No. The ten to fifteen thousand French people living in London were unanimous in wanting to go on with the war at the side of the English. They made this clear, they proved it, in all sorts of ways. Only the nonresident French, the functionaries, military men attached to missions, hesitated, divided, and thought of going home to France. The French who were in London at that moment, whether as permanent residents or just passing through, never felt alone, for they were surrounded with warmth and comradeship. To that I can testify. There is an English saying, trite perhaps but very true and very touching when its truth is so demonstrated: "A friend in need is a friend indeed." In June of 1940 it went like this: Do you need money? Do you need work? Hospitality? There is our purse, there is our factory, there is our house. You are at home. And when English friends knew French, and most did, it was: *Vous êtes chez vous!*

So from nation to nation, from the British to the French. As early as June 19 Duff Cooper, Minister of Information, spoke over the BBC, and in his speech he said that France had lost a great

battle but that this was not the first time that a great nation had
been defeated and then had risen again, as France would rise again,
with the aid of her Allies.

All over London posters appeared with tricolored borders, topped
with the crossed flags of France:

A TOUS LES FRANÇAIS
La France a perdu une bataille!
Mais la France n'a pas perdu la guerre! [1]

Fabre-Luce, an author with whom I have little in common, says
that these were the words of General Spears, who himself got them
from Duff Cooper.[2] But Duff Cooper's words were not quite the
same. General Spears himself told me that he had assumed the responsibility of having the poster made up; it was designed by a
Richard Temple, who did not ask to be paid. Temple also drafted
a text, but General de Gaulle blue-penciled it and wrote down the
two celebrated lines in his own hand. They appear in none of his
published speeches, but they are very much his. They were also, in
a sense, the creation of the English people, for the sentiment they
expressed was heard in one form or another all over London. Every
Englishman you met would say that or something like it, some
giving you a pat on the back, others smiling broadly, and the ladies
with moist eyes.

"You are our allies! You will remain our allies! You will share
equally in the fruits of victory. Fear nothing! You have only lost
a battle. Not the war!"

Would we have behaved the same way if the roles had been reversed? I am sure we would have. I thought the response of the

[1] To ALL FRENCHMEN/ France has lost a battle!/ But France has not lost the
war!
[2] Subsequently, when these famous words came to be attributed to General de
Gaulle, there was a riposte from the gallant Antoine de Saint-Exupéry, never a
Gaullist. "Tell the truth, General," he said, "France did lose the war but her
allies will win it." Cited by Henri de Kérillis: *I Accuse De Gaulle* (New York:
Harcourt, Brace; 1946), p. 79.

English was beautiful, but it was exactly what one would expect from one's allies.

When it is said that General de Gaulle was a man alone,[3] is there a suggestion that he was alone in comparison to Frenchmen who stayed in France? No one could mean that. Nor could anyone mean that without General de Gaulle the French people would not have resisted. Resistance in France was a spontaneous phenomenon sparked by the presence of the invader and by the invader's characteristic behavior. It was a phenomenon that in France, as in the other occupied countries, would grow in volume with the increase of hope for an Allied victory. General de Gaulle was not the only Frenchman to wish for the country's liberation. Nor was he the only one to save the honor of France, as if the honor of a people could depend on one man, its one and only guardian.

Other occupied countries which had no de Gaulle to speak to them through a microphone in London were able to resist just as valiantly as ours, and some contributed armies of volunteers proportionately much more numerous. Up to the time of the invasion of French Africa by the Allies, something over two years, General de Gaulle had not yet drawn as many as twenty thousand fighting men to his standard. At that time the Polish government in exile

[3] "Go on with the war? Yes, certainly! But to what end and within what limits? Many, even among those who approved of the undertaking, wanted it to be more than aid given by a handful of Frenchmen to the British Empire, still standing and in the fight. Not for a moment did I look at the enterprise in that way. For me, what had to be served and saved was the nation and the state. . . . What I knew of men and things left me with no illusions about the obstacles to be surmounted. . . . There would be the so-called "parallel" but in fact rival and opposing enterprises. . . . In short, limited and alone though I was, and precisely because I was so, I had to climb to the heights and never then to come down. . . . Already in the afternoon of June 17 I outlined my intentions to Mr. Winston Churchill. . . . To begin with [he] put the BBC at my disposal. We agreed that I should use it after the Pétain government had asked for the armistice. That very evening the news came that it had done so. Next day, at 6 p.m., I read out at the microphone the well-known text. . . . At the age of forty-nine I was entering upon adventure, like a man thrown by fate outside all terms of reference." De Gaulle: *Memoirs*, I, pp. 81–4.

had an army of a quarter of a million men. And it was more difficult to come out of Poland than it was to come out of France.

As for the French Resistance, its role was perhaps unequaled.
The Allied commanders are all on record as to its value in gathering vital information, in sabotaging German installations, and, at
the great moment in 1944, in hampering German troop movements. It was just as spontaneous in France as in Holland and in
Poland. And, in my opinion, the many thousands who gave their
lives perhaps did not do so for the ideals now dominant in France.

On June 19 General de Gaulle gave the impression that he was
ready to put himself under the orders of any general senior to him
who was willing to go on with the fight. At the same time he indicated that he had already made his decision, confirmed in his
memoirs as dating from June 17, "to climb to the heights and
never then to come down."

In his second appeal he claimed to speak in the name of France.
On the same day he telegraphed General Noguès, then Commander-in-Chief of all French forces in North Africa, that he was
ready to do battle under his (General Noguès's) orders. On that
same day he telegraphed to French communities abroad, inviting
them to designate representatives to his person, implying that he
was to be considered as the center and as the leader. To the French
in North Africa he spoke over the head of General Noguès, the
Commander-in-Chief, who at that moment was still very much opposed to concluding an armistice. To other generals, commanders-
in-chief in their areas, he sent telegrams exhorting them to continue
the struggle.[4]

4 *Contradictions*

   On the same day, June 19, General de Gaulle:
   (1) Put himself at the disposition of General Noguès
*Telegram from General de Gaulle to General Noguès, Commander-in-Chief
of the North African theater of operations, Algiers:* [London, June 19, 1940]
"Am in London in unofficial and direct contact with British Government. Hold
myself at your disposition, either to fight under your orders, or for any *démarche*
which might seem useful to you."
   (2) Told General Noguès what Noguès's duty was
Appeal broadcast by General de Gaulle on the BBC: [London, June 19, 1940]

June 19–25, 1940

On June 19 in Bordeaux, on the morrow of General de Gaulle's appeal "in the name of France"—in fact, while Pierre Maillaud and I were making our bows to the General—the British and French emissaries, together with the British and American Ambassadors, were exerting every pressure imaginable.[1]

On that day Marshal Pétain told the two ambassadors that although he would remain in France ("Like the captain of a sinking ship," someone later said), the President of the Republic, M. Lebrun, ex-Premier Herriot, Speaker of the Chamber, and M. Jeanneney, President of the Senate, ex-Premier Daladier, and many others were to proceed to Algiers to establish an overseas government that would continue the war. Colonel Bonavita was much in evidence around the War Ministry, trying to implement

---

"In the Africa of Clauzel, of Bugeaud, of Lyautey, of Noguès, everyone with a sense of honor has the strict duty to refuse to carry out the enemy's conditions."

(3) Spoke in the name of France

". . . In the name of France I formally declare . . . every Frenchman who is bearing arms has a sacred duty to continue the resistance. . . . And now I speak above all for a French North Africa. . . . It is intolerable that the panic of Bordeaux shall spread beyond the seas."

[1] On receipt of word from Bordeaux on the seventeenth that Marshal Pétain had asked for an armistice, President Roosevelt by executive order froze all French assets in the United States, and Secretary Hull informed the German, Italian, and French governments that in reference to French and Dutch colonies the United States would recognize no transfer of territory in the New World from one non-American power to another non-American power. Cordell Hull further advised Marshal Pétain that the United States was prepared to set up an inter-American trusteeship over France's American possessions until France regained her independence. Ambassador Biddle was instructed to go with the French government to North Africa.

the British offer of ships for the vast migration of men and matériel that supposedly had been planned.

Herriot told Lord Lloyd and the others that he and Jeanneney
were agreed that France was bound to keep her pledges to Britain
and they saw no reason why resistance could not be continued
from North Africa. During these talks Herriot had a notably
acute observation to make: the defeated French generals and admirals were heaping blame for the debacle on "the politicians,"
the Communists, and the English (in that order) but were in
no way to assume any of the blame themselves. He knew that a
vicious anti-parliamentary movement was underway, though he
could not have foreseen how rabid it would become, with prison
in store for himself and a number of other "politicians" of the
Third Republic who did not share the ideas of Pierre Laval and
his associates.

In the two days since the appeal for an armistice, Pétain, his
Foreign Minister, and Admiral Darlan had been lavishing assurances on the British and American governments, in response to
the vigorous demands of both. In Washington, as we soon learned,
the French Ambassador had told Cordell Hull that France would
accept no terms that proved humiliating. Admiral Darlan on the
seventeenth had ordered the fleet to continue fighting and to pull
out of Atlantic ports that would soon be overrun by the Germans.
He at first promised that the fleet would take refuge in British
ports—a move the British demanded as the price for releasing
France from her pledge of March 28. He then said on the nineteenth that the fleet would be sent to ports of "a friendly power"
(he seems to have meant the United States). Then that it might
be scuttled. Then that it would never be allowed to fall into the
hands of the Germans. Admiral Pound and Mr. Alexander were
inclined to take his word but told him they did not believe the
Germans would allow him to keep it.

From the new "Minister of Defense"—General Weygand—
Lord Lloyd got no assurances at all. They were old friends. Indeed, Lord Lloyd had been one of Weygand's greatest admirers
in England. On this occasion unforgettable words passed between

them, and next day in London Lord Lloyd said that Weygand was now "nothing but a stunted, embittered little man."

While all this was taking place, a handful of men—really alone and without help—were making a desperate effort to keep North Africa in the war and to set up a French government there. I cite the names of these men because it is in London or from London that they operated: Jean Monnet, Torcy, and Emmanuel Monick, Financial Attaché at the French Embassy. These three were convinced that their efforts to set up a French government in Algiers would be jeopardized by the creation in London of a committee presided over by one man speaking in the name of France. They thought that this man, General de Gaulle, should cease to speak in the name of France, at least for several days. Anyway, that is what they asked of him. Jean Monnet was their spokesman.

Two of the three, Monnet and Monick, had returned from Bordeaux in a British seaplane. In Bordeaux the partisans of an immediate armistice were more numerous and more powerful than those who advocated continuing the war. However, nothing was yet lost; the armistice had not yet been signed. The possibility still existed of installing a government in North Africa. Indeed, Governor Le Beau, in Algiers, was making preparations to receive the government.

Aware of what General de Gaulle was doing, Jean Monnet tried to prevail upon him to call a halt to his actions and his words. "You will kill the project in the egg," he told de Gaulle. "You must immediately stop sending off telegrams right and left. Those to whom they are addressed cannot help but think that, with the help of the British Prime Minister—and they are bound to think you have his help, for how, otherwise, could you make use of the English radio and telegraph—you, a young French general, are arrogating to yourself the right to represent France. They, your seniors in age and service, are to take orders issued in London! From foreign soil!" To behave in this manner, Monnet thought, was deliberately to abort the efforts being made to keep North Africa in the war. Monnet considered North Africa the principal bastion around which the other overseas territories of France could rally, and, one day or other, the French fleet. No more telegrams, then! No more *démarches* to constitute a National Committee in London. . . .

Jean Monnet already had an international reputation at this time. He had served as First Deputy Secretary-General of the League of Nations. He never chose to appear center-stage, but, as chief of the Franco-British Purchasing Commission in the United States, he ranked among the top Allied personalities.[2] Thus he felt free to indulge in some straight talk with de Gaulle; he was possibly a little blunt.

The General brushed these warnings aside and continued his efforts to set himself up as France's representative: "to climb to the heights," according to the ideal that he had set for himself. On June 23, he obtained an official declaration from the British government—two, in fact: the first stating that the government of Marshal Pétain was not an independent government; the second taking note of the formation of the National Committee by General de Gaulle.

Quite suddenly, Jean Monnet understood: everything he had said to the General to halt him seemed rather to have encouraged him and encouraged him to go all the way. It was then that Monnet quit General de Gaulle's service, leaving behind a letter warning de Gaulle "for the last time" that he was committing "a grave error." What he *said* to the General personally is starchier still.

Torcy also understood equally well. The project he had tried to get underway among the French in Bordeaux, with the help of Monnet and Monick, and with the cooperation of Lord Lloyd and others among the English, was irremediably lost. That is not to say that General Noguès in North Africa did very much to help.

Jean Monnet left for the United States, where until 1943 he worked as a member of the British Supply Council by personal

---

[2] Writing of him later, Ambassador Robert Murphy said, "It can be plausibly argued that Monnet has been the most influential man in France of his generation, and he also has exerted a major influence upon the affairs of the United States, Great Britain, and other countries." Robert Murphy: *Diplomat among Warriors* (New York: Doubleday; 1964), p. 178.

appointment of Churchill. It was America in the immediate future that mattered to the world.

Emmanuel Monick went to Morocco, hoping the French would resume the war there. Torcy remained in London.

The truth of the dire predictions of Monnet, Monick, and the others began to be evident in Bordeaux on the twentieth. On that day Admiral Darlan issued his own "cease-fire" orders to all ships of the French fleet and sent out the first of a series of instructions to his commanders to put their British liaison officers ashore and to cease communicating with British ships or bases. General Weygand, as Minister of Defense, called a halt to all plans for shipping men and supplies to North Africa. Fully aware of British efforts through diplomatic and consular agents and of General de Gaulle's sudden (and seemingly contradictory) appeals to the French proconsuls, Weygand dispatched sulfurous messages to Algiers, Beirut, Saigon—all over the Empire—blaming Britain for France's defeat, and predicting that Britain herself would be forced to sue for peace or "have her neck wrung like a chicken's."

In the French overseas capitals confusion reigned, but only briefly. General Catroux telegraphed from Saigon to congratulate General Noguès, then in Algiers, on his reported decision to resist, and heard, in reply, that he had been misinformed. The proconsuls had not been impressed on the seventeenth, eighteenth, and nineteenth by what some called "the hysteria of Bordeaux." As I said, Governor Le Beau in Algeria was preparing to receive the government. But now the climate changed. From Tunis, on instructions from Weygand, Marcel Peyrouton went to Algiers to make sure that Noguès understood and that Le Beau would be neutralized. To Dakar, where there was strong pro-English feeling, Weygand and Darlan dispatched Admirals de Laborde and Platon to enforce discipline. As Monnet, Monick, and Torcy had predicted, General de Gaulle's appeal proved more than unavailing: there was a hardening of anti-British feeling and a heightened feeling of loyalty to Pétain, Weygand, and Darlan, to legal authority, in other words. The replies, such as they were, of the five-star generals of France, the proconsuls, and the governors of overseas France, were foolish and vain, but these men would not follow a two-star general speaking from London.

In London, then, it was General de Gaulle's concept which carried the day against that of Monnet, Torcy, and Monick. The General had all-powerful support, Winston Churchill's. By June 23, the British Prime Minister had already given him the most essential element of that support, the use of the BBC, from which the General had spoken *in the name of France*. And Churchill had taken note, favorably, of the creation of de Gaulle's National Committee.

What he had done, Churchill could presumably also undo. I will try to explain why, in my opinion, he did it in the first place, and why he was in fact never able thereafter to undo it; why, having helped the General to establish and consolidate his power, Churchill was involuntarily to increase de Gaulle's stature by allowing him to take on the appearance of an adversary.

Churchill's behavior with respect to General de Gaulle is to be explained by his very nature. Churchill was courageous, generous, impulsive. One of his most characteristic traits was the manner in which he made friends, and in which he kept his friends. He had a capacity for friendships that were spontaneous and immediate but indestructible. He never had all that many friends. Let me mention a few who are typical. First there would be the Prince of Wales, who became Edward VIII and, on his abdication, Duke of Windsor. Then there was Lord Beaverbrook, whose ability nobody disputes, but in his newspapers he played tricks on Churchill which only a hanging could have expiated. Then there was Sir Edward Spears, who, after having been de Gaulle's first patron, quarreled with him so furiously. One might also mention the Duke of Westminster, who made rather an unsuccessful career of marriage and, in the process, three Duchesses of Westminster. With all of these Churchill remained friends and would remain friends for the rest of his long life.

In May and June 1940 Churchill took to General de Gaulle. He saw in the General the very model of a French hero, a Bayard *sans peur et sans reproche*, upright, simple of soul, with all the frank, rough manners of a soldier. He also took him for a great Anglophile and, astonishingly enough, for a true democrat, qualities that one would generally have thought rare indeed among French soldiers. I feel sure that up to the very end of his life, in spite of the many wrathful moments, the many disappointments, Winston Churchill remained in his heart faithful to his friend General de Gaulle. He no longer thought him simple of soul or frank or Anglophile or a democrat. But I must here repeat that this great, proud heart never disowned friends.

At the start, the Prime Minister gave de Gaulle all he asked: broadcasting facilities, money, declarations of recognition; he promptly sent packing anyone in the British Cabinet or in the Armed Services who raised objections. The General was England's friend, give him what he asks. And don't waste my time with your carping.

The other reason for the General's initial success in London was that Churchill was swamped with duties, worries. For the first time in a hundred and fifty years a powerful enemy was crouching fifteen miles across the Channel from the White Cliffs. Churchill had only a minute or two a day to think about the General. Try and imagine the days and nights of the Prime Minister during the weeks that followed the end of the fighting in France. Not only did the invasion seem imminent, but there was almost nothing with which to oppose it. Almost no cannon, no tanks, almost no rifles, a small Air Force—but very, very good, as we learned. As for the fleet, its supremacy on the seas would be lost if the French ships fell into German hands.

The French Navy, built up by successive governments during the Third Republic at Admiral Darlan's insistence, boasted two of the world's most powerful battleships, the *Richelieu* and the *Jean Bart*, the first all but finished and the latter not too far from completion; two fast heavy cruisers, the *Strasbourg* and the *Dunkerque*; many fast modern cruisers with eight-inch guns; submarines; destroyers. . . . In tonnage the French fleet came to about one third of the British fleet but it boasted a high proportion of speedy, modern ships. In combination with the British Mediterranean fleet, it could have destroyed Italian sea power, the big new battleships and all, in

the first days after Il Duce plunged his country into war—long before German planes made their appearance over the Mediterranean.
(And there are many Italians and many friends of Italy today who
wish the French and British had done just this, and so spared the
Italians the agonies to come.)

The British and French navies together had been conducting a
fairly effective blockade, except along the Norwegian coast. Now,
with France out of the war, Britain the blockader became Britain
the blockaded, with German submarines taking up stations in
French Atlantic ports. And Britain's sea route to Egypt, to the oil
of Iraq and Persia, to India, Malaya, and Australia, was threatened.
Britain was outflanked along nearly 4,000 miles of its territory by
enemy shore: in the Bay of Biscay, the Mediterranean, and the Red
Sea. Between Gibraltar and Alexandria, British ships had only one
base left, Malta, sixty miles from Sicily and eight hundred miles
from the nearest friendly base; gone were Oran and Bizerte.

It was not until June 22 that the armistice[3] was finally signed by
Marshal Pétain's envoys and the generals of a jubilant Hitler in the
famous railway carriage at Rethondes in the Forest of Compiègne,
where the Germans had been humbled in 1918. The article dealing
with the fleet was by far the most disturbing part of it.

Article 8 of the armistice agreement did not say that the fleet
was to be handed over to the Germans, but there was an ominous
stipulation that the ships were to go back to the ports where they
were normally stationed in peacetime, and there disarmed—as for
instance, the port of Brest, now occupied by the enemy. If this
stipulation was fulfilled, how could the French fleet ever hope to
reenter the struggle against the Axis? And what guarantee was

[3] Hitler at Munich, June 18: ". . . With regard to the French fleet the
Führer said that the best thing that could happen would be to have the
French sink it. The worst thing would be to have the fleet unite with the
British, because, in view of the larger number of light French ships, the united
British–French fleets could organize extensive convoys. . . . Britain could sup-
ply herself without difficulty, and could transport (from the mother country,
from Canada, India, etc.) large forces to all sorts of places (from Egypt to
Portugal), thus maintaining or creating a series of theatres of operation. . . ."
Graziani Papers, cited in William L. Langer: *Our Vichy Gamble*, p. 48.

there that it would not fall into the hands of Hitler, who held all French ports on the North Sea, on the Channel, and on the Atlantic, and was within easy striking distance of Toulon on the Mediterranean, as events in 1942 were to demonstrate?

What then had happened to all the assurances given the British and American ambassadors and the French and British emissaries? The assurances that a French government would be set up in Algiers, empowered to carry on with the war—all that had been, said Marshal Pétain, "vain and idle words." And Baudouin's assurances that if the German terms proved "humiliating" they would be rejected? The Bordeaux government was given little opportunity to quibble over, much less resist, the Germans' terms. With the Wehrmacht relentlessly advancing northwest, southeast, and southwest, the Nazi government waited forty-eight hours before so much as acknowledging the Marshal's broadcast of the seventeenth, and did so, on the nineteenth, only to ask for the names of the French delegates to the signing. That same night—June 19 to 20—German and Italian bombers roared in low over Bordeaux, bombing indiscriminately. And they returned in the morning. Hundreds died in the city, whose normal population had been swollen by refugees to 700,000. When Pierre Laval was asked why this bombardment, he gave an informed reply: it was Hitler's answer to those who were trying to trick him by "subterfuges" such as a move to Algiers. Laval knew, as he was in close touch with the Nazis through the Spanish Ambassador.

On June 20 the British and American Ambassadors saw that whatever will there had been in Bordeaux to resist had been badly shaken by the bombing of the night before and by developments in Munich (of which more later). Indeed, it had largely drained away. Whatever the terms, Marshal Pétain's government would have to sign; the alternative was to refuse and make a quick dash for Algiers, Marshal and all. But this, the ambassadors realized, was not the intention of the officials at Bordeaux.

On the morning of June 20, Marshal Pétain was prepared to see President Lebrun and the others leave. But by that afternoon he had changed his mind. Pierre Laval had intervened, brutally and effectively. If Lebrun left with the seals of state of the Third Republic, Laval said, the Marshal's government would have no legal authority to negotiate with the Germans. Laval had his plans well laid for scrapping the Republic altogether. (The more determined deputies who did leave by ship on the twenty-first—Daladier, Mandel, and others—were placed under restraint on their arrival in Casablanca.)

The hapless French delegates reached Rethondes late on the twenty-first and were presented Hitler's terms by General Keitel. Around midnight they telephoned them to Bordeaux.

Early on the twenty-first, Sir Ronald Campbell had sent a note to Paul Baudouin reminding him that the British government had to be consulted before any armistice arrangement whatsoever was signed. "Naturally!" was Baudouin's reply. At nightfall that same day, Sir Ronald and Mr. Biddle learned that the terms would reach Bordeaux and be passed upon by the Marshal and his ministers, who would be meeting at 1 a.m. Quite obviously, Baudouin was not going to keep his word. Sir Ronald then sent a note to Marshal Pétain, Admiral Darlan, and M. Baudouin recalling the promises made him since the seventeenth—namely, that the fleet would go to English or American ports (as required by the British notes conditionally releasing France from her solemn pledge of March 28) and that at least part of the government would carry on from Algiers.

It was not until 3 a.m. (the night of June 21 to 22) that Sir Ronald was permitted to see Baudouin. The French Foreign Minister appeared in pajamas and read out to him draft pages of Article 8 (concerning the fleet). He then snapped, "That's all that concerns you!" and turned to leave the room. Sir Ronald followed, stopped him, and snatched the pages from his hands.

At daybreak next morning the Ambassador went to Marshal Pétain to protest. The sly old soldier expressed mild surprise at British apprehensions and assured Sir Ronald that, whatever happened, the Germans would not touch the fleet; it would be scuttled first.

Later that day Baudouin went to some pains to show Sir Ronald just how wrong he was to doubt French intentions. "Why, Article

8 will never be carried out! Do you expect the Germans to force our ships to return to the ports now occupied by their army? They would have to catch them first! So, go along and sleep in peace! The only party who has reason to be disturbed is Hitler: our ships will always be a threat to *him!* They will comprise the one arm by which we can hold him off if he tries to strangle us. With the Fleet our only means of blackmailing him, we certainly have no intention of surrendering it to him!" This argument might make sense. But who is now advancing it? It is Paul Baudouin, former governor of the Banque d'Indo-Chine, champion of Munich, the man who had had himself appointed Secretary of the War Committee, by Paul Reynaud, only to become a partisan of an armistice. And now he was detailing just how he and his associates intended to break their word to the Germans, having just defaulted on their promises to the British.

The British Ambassador was not impressed. With the German army about to enter Bordeaux, he took his leave and, boarding a British cruiser moored off Saint-Jean-de-Luz, headed for England. Churchill was not happy to see him back in London and greeted him less warmly even than he had greeted Brigadier Spears. The conversation went something like this:

"Why did you leave?"

"Why, sir, to avoid being taken prisoner by the Germans. They're on the point of arriving in Bordeaux."

"Well? A fine thing if you'd been caught. But you shouldn't have left! You shouldn't have let either the Marshal or the Admiral out of your sight for one minute! They should be threatened and cajoled all day, over and over, they should be told without ceasing that we'll be victorious, told unmistakably that if even a single French rowboat falls into German hands, we'll go to war against the Marshal! But now what would you have me do? Send a new ambassador? Impossible, our relations are half severed now."

The role so described by Churchill was in fact carried out by a remarkable man: the Canadian chargé d'affaires, Pierre Dupuy, who realized that he must not leave, and stayed close by the old Marshal at Bordeaux and later at Vichy.

As late as June 25, Churchill sent Lord Gort and Alfred Duff

Cooper to Casablanca to try to communicate with Daladier and other French statesmen who had left France on the liner *Massilia* in the belief that resistance was to be resumed from North Africa. But the British envoys were not allowed to see anybody at all. General Weygand had done his work well with General Noguès. And General Dillon, the British liaison officer in Rabat, was being held in his quarters under guard.

Did the Pétain regime have any right to sign a separate armistice with the Germans? Of course not! The British had formally authorized their defeated ally to negotiate an armistice *on condition that the fleet was excluded from it.* And the fleet was not excluded. But no one in the new government was in any mood to honor engagements to an ally they considered doomed as well, an ally whom in their bitterness, moreover, they blamed in part for their own plight. Weygand gave Britain three weeks. Admiral Darlan generously allowed a few more weeks; but inevitably she would be starved into surrender as the German noose was drawn tight around her.

June 30, 1940

By its failure to exclude the fleet from the armistice negotiations with Germany, the government of Marshal Pétain had violated the Franco-British alliance, which by then was three quarters disrupted anyway. Charles Corbin had been appointed French Ambassador to London expressly to conduct a certain policy within the alliance. He declined to follow any other kind of policy, and put in for his retirement, handing the succession over to Roger Cambon. That an ambassador should wish to keep within the sense, within the meaning of his mission, is a concept that sometimes eludes diplomats. They want to be ambassadors; don't ask them where, or for what purpose, for they would reply: "Just to be ambassadors."

Roger Cambon agreed to take charge of the Embassy for several days, only so that he could defend the alliance "to the last cartridge." He was encouraged by the English to do this. "Relations between our two countries must be preserved through the bars of the cage," Churchill said.

On June 30 a French vice-admiral, Émile Muselier, reached London. Answering his call, a number of French ships of war had rallied to him in Gibraltar and he had convinced their officers and men to carry on with the war. He had thereby brought into being the nucleus of the glorious Free French Naval Forces. Before reaching England, he had decided that his ships, to distinguish them from other French vessels, were to display the Cross of Lorraine, as he was himself from Lorraine.

The Admiral had more stars than General de Gaulle. But he reached London thirteen days later. To escape from France he had to go by sea from a port on the Mediterranean, passing through Gibraltar. He was General de Gaulle's superior in rank, and why would he not now try to set up a "parallel enterprise"—which was how the Gaullists later came to describe any rival efforts in behalf of France? He had already, independently of the General's authority, created a fighting force.

On reaching London, he went straight to the Admiralty, where he had many old friends and comrades-in-arms. His arrival there was the occasion for a celebration. He did not go until afterward to see de Gaulle. He told everyone that he was unaware, when he left France, that the General was in London. Nevertheless, the first contact between the two men could hardly have been more cordial. Having no political ambitions, the Admiral allowed the General to appoint him Chief of the Free French Naval Forces, which of course established a relationship of superior to inferior. It would be by the grace of a general with two stars that an admiral with three stars would henceforth hold his command—while the general held it. But Admiral Muselier asked nothing better. To him the only thing that mattered was to create a navy, to fight, to see a maximum of unity among Frenchmen determined to carry on the war.

July 1–3, 1940

Anne was feeling better. This was due to her youth and also to her determination to get back her strength at the earliest. She wanted to go to France to nurse the wounded. What an idea! I refrained from any opposition, not daring to risk a setback by contradicting her, and anyway, with Anne, arguments rarely accomplished anything. So I simply said that in wartime it was not of course unnatural for a husband and wife to be apart; as for me, I was not going back to France. I did not want to leave the English. The invasion, if there was to be one, would provide a spectacle without precedent in the last nine hundred years. A man would have to be sadly lacking in curiosity to chance missing that.

But I would go ahead dutifully and make all arrangements so that she herself could return to France. I would get visas and a cabin on the *Orduna,* the old royal mail liner on which toward the middle of July various services of our Embassy were to be repatriated via Lisbon. To make sure that these facilities would not be withheld, I had disclosed my decision to stay on in London to only three people at the Embassy, all trusted friends. I put in my request, then, for a cabin on the *Orduna* for Anne and myself and for visas for the two of us. I was not unhappy that I would thus be able at some future time to furnish proof that I had remained behind because I wanted to and not because I had no way of leaving. In fact, I have kept as a trophy of sorts our diplomatic passports, stamped with all manner of visas, including that of Canada. For it was not at all easy to leave England. One had to have exit visas, and landing visas. Furthermore, people were scrambling for passage on the *Orduna.* The ship was to sail with all her lights on, display-

ing on her stern an enormous sign reading DIPLOMAT, and two similar signs in huge letters along either side, and all three would be
floodlit during the night at sea. To travel on such a ship in wartime, a man would have to be not overly proud!

On July 1 Anne said, in a small voice meant to be timid, "If I
stay, I would very much like to have the baby with us here."

Stay? She had never once said that—always the exact opposite.
My silence had worked.

To go and pick up the baby in Brittany did not strike me as such
a difficult enterprise. Even today, with a fuller knowledge of the
conditions we would have to cope with in France, I believe that it
was a sensible idea. The Germans had hardly begun to patrol the
Channel. Our only problem was how to get started. We had to
have a boat, not a very big one, and gasoline. I counted on getting a
launch or some other small vessel through some of my old shipmates on the French warships that had reached Plymouth, the
Courbet, the *Léopard,* the *Savorgnan-de-Brazza,* the *Pollux.* However, Anne, who wanted to go with me, was thinking of an English
doctor friend. According to her, he knew all the fishermen around
Penzance, and through him we could buy a motorboat. (We could
hardly count on renting one for a cruise of that sort!) Through him
we could also get gasoline; doctors had access to as much gasoline
as they wanted. We would have to be very unlucky not to find a
compass. And wouldn't we be able to tempt some old fisherman
familiar with the currents of the Channel to go with us?

No sooner said than done. I withdrew all that was left of our
money at the bank in those beautiful white ten-pound notes. We
took the train, third class. We would set out that same evening to
make the Channel crossing in the darkness, and would spend the
next day in Brittany and return that night. It would be easy to hide
our boat in a little inlet of the Île de Callot, near Carantec, where
the baby was, from which at low tide one can walk to the main-
land.

We had a happy time in our compartment, lunching on
sandwiches, drinking up one of my last bottles of Beaujolais, and

poring over the tide tables and a Navy chart. But our luck failed us when we reached the home of the doctor on whom Anne had founded such high hopes. We found his household in a state of confusion, his young wife down with double pneumonia. When one of their own is ill, doctors are inclined to lose their heads. This one was nearly out of his mind. And it was we who had to hold his hand and comfort him all night long. Gone was any hope of getting him to find a fisherman for us. His wife fortunately made a quick recovery, but he himself died shortly afterward. We were no longer there, however, for on this morning of July 3 we left for Plymouth.

In Plymouth there was not a single French sailor in sight. They were all behind bars—prison bars! The English had that morning seized their ships while the crews were asleep. On the submarine *Surcouf*, shots had been exchanged, and three Englishmen and one Frenchman lay dead.

The fishermen, too, were confined to port. It was hardly the moment for us to ask the British authorities for a boat. A boat? For what? To go and pick up a baby in France? They would never have believed *that*. And what other pretext could we dream up? To this day I rejoice at having put on civilian clothes for our expedition. In uniform, I would have found myself rejoining my shipmates in the internment camps to which they had been escorted at bayonet point.

An English admiral—Jarvis, I believe his name was—gloried in that fine exploit, which turned countless French sailors into Anglophobes. But Jarvis was only an instrument. Churchill had given the orders. He certainly did not attempt to glory over it, but the events of that day showed how high suspicion of the French Navy had risen. Where lay the blame? The answer is not as simple as some might think.

We learned later that a fateful decision had been reached in London: the French fleet, not to be trusted in such a dangerous pass, was to be immobilized wherever possible, or crippled, rendered incapable of action.

Meanwhile, messages from Admiral Darlan to his commanders

had been intercepted: they were to avoid the English like the plague, to put ashore all English liaison officers, to cease using Allied codes, to leave English convoys for French ports.

Crestfallen, we took the train back to London. It was the evening of July 3. Our night was brightened for us by two incidents, each tied in with the other. We found that we had fleas or bedbugs, I don't know which, in the upholstery of our compartment; whatever they were, their attentions kept us awake. We had the compartment to ourselves, but in the middle of the night a soldier came in. There was only the dim blue night light, so thinking us asleep, he tried to snatch Anne's handbag, in which she had stowed our small fortune. Caught in the act, he froze for a moment and then leaped at the window, which shattered at the impact of his forehead. Was he trying to hurl himself upon the tracks? My guess is that he was off his head, for he wasn't drunk. He slumped back on the seat, bleeding badly. Anne at last had a wounded soldier to care for.

The conductor arrived. There was an involved discussion, and he decided that he liked neither our story nor that of the soldier, so he stopped the train at a wayside station, the name of which had been torn away, and had a colleague telephone ahead to London. The rest of the night he stood guard over us and the soldier, by then sunk in silence, until we reached Victoria Station. On the platform, in the wan light of early morning, two policemen were waiting for us. Did we wish to lodge a complaint? No, no, no! The hapless soldier went off, escorted by the two policemen and the conductor.

Humiliated, and dazed by sleeplessness, we took the Underground home. Our old Mary welcomed us, delighted to see us back, though we were speechless with frustration. For she had been sure that we would either come back like this, our expedition a failure, or never. A hot bath, clean linen, breakfast on a table polished as bright as a mirror, gave us a sense of luxury and tranquillity that could never end.

At precisely the moment that we were taking the evening train from Plymouth, astonished at finding not a single French sailor anywhere in view, "Force H" from Gibraltar, under the command of Vice-Admiral Somerville and speeding in line of battle at twenty knots before Mers-el-Kebir, was killing 1,147 French sailors in less than sixteen minutes, afterward disappearing behind a smoke-screen.

For those who are too young to have known this tragedy or who have forgotten it, I should explain. Mers-el-Kebir is a port running deep inland, a little to the west of the city of Oran in western Algeria, not far from the Moroccan border. At the time of the armistice, a sizable part of the French fleet was assembled there under the command of Admiral Gensoul: the two fast, modern battle cruisers, the *Dunkerque* and the *Strasbourg*; two battleships; and a number of light cruisers, destroyers, and submarines.

Admiral Somerville's Force H, under explicit orders from the Prime Minister and the Admiralty, sailed from Gibraltar at dawn on July 3. It consisted of the battle cruiser *Hood*, the battleships *Valiant* and *Resolution*, the carrier *Ark Royal*, two cruisers, and eleven destroyers. The destroyer *Foxhound* dropped anchor off Oran at 7:00 a.m., and the rest of the British force arrived at 9:30 a.m. and, at a safe distance offshore, proceeded to cruise back and forth during the long hours until 5:54 p.m.

The armistice clauses had finally been accepted by Marshal Pétain's government, but on the express condition that the fleet was to remain French. The Germans, understandably suspicious, sent an ultimatum on July 3; either your ships return to France or the entire armistice will be put in jeopardy. Return to France? If that meant their former home ports, then the greater part of our ships would enter the German trap. At Mers-el-Kebir, the crews knew, or thought they knew, that the fleet was about to sail. But for where? Though a former reserve officer in the Navy, I cannot say for sure, even today. Sailors on liberty in Oran, promenading up and down the streets, told persons I knew: "We are going back to Brest." Others interrupted: "But no! We are going to Toulon!"

Toulon or Brest—that makes all the difference. Brest was in the zone occupied by the Germans, which comprised the whole North Sea Channel and Atlantic coast of France. Toulon was in what people were beginning to call the "Free Zone," or unoccupied France.

Admiral Somerville sent Captain Holland of the destroyer HMS *Foxhound* as far as the boom blocking the harbor entrance, to deliver an ultimatum to Admiral Gensoul. Captain Holland was chosen because he had formerly been British Naval Attaché in Paris and spoke excellent French. Admiral Gensoul refused to receive him. The ultimatum, which he did receive, gave the French a choice of five courses of action. It began: "It is impossible for us, your comrades until now, to allow your fine ships to fall into the power of the German or Italian enemy. . . . We will fight to the end. . . . Should we conquer, we solemnly declare that we shall restore the greatness and territory of France. For this purpose, we must make sure that the best ships of the French Navy are not used against us by the common foe. . . ."

The choices were:

First: sail with us and continue the fight

Second: sail with us under reduced crews to British ports, to be interned. The crews would be repatriated

Third: sail beside us with reduced crews to some French port in the Antilles such as Martinique

Fourth: sail to the United States to be interned there

Fifth: if you refuse these offers, you will be required to scuttle your ships within six hours

If none of the five choices was accepted, the ultimatum read, "I have the orders of His Majesty's Government to use whatever force may be necessary to prevent your ships from falling into German or Italian hands." In other words, I will sink you.

The British Admiral had overwhelming superiority. He was in the open sea, free to maneuver as he wished, whereas the French warships were at anchor deep inside the harbor and had no visibility. Admiral Gensoul, unwilling to act on his own responsibility, had been in close touch with Vichy. He was forbidden to give way, of course. By this time he had agreed to see Captain Holland, a friend of happier times. In reply to the ultimatum, he handed Holland a written statement: the French would never allow their ships to fall into German hands—which had all been said before, and on higher authority.

At 5:54 p.m. Admiral Somerville, on orders from Churchill, had opened fire—and in sixteen minutes the harbor waters were covered with red pompons.

The *Bretagne* blew up. The *Dunkerque*, her control tower hit, ran aground. The *Provence* was beached. But the *Strasbourg* escaped, hugging the shore line, and was soon joined by cruisers from Algiers. With reinforcements from Toulon known to be heading in their direction, Force H retired to Gibraltar, and the *Strasbourg* and her accompanying cruisers finally reached Toulon.

One hundred and twenty-five years had passed since Englishmen and Frenchmen last fired on each other—at Waterloo. Churchill, always aware of historical precedent, later said he had been thinking of Copenhagen, which Nelson and Wellesley (later Wellington) between them had ravaged in 1807 in a surprise attack, destroying some fifteen Danish warships and thirty other vessels. Churchill also said that he had in mind that desperate moment in the French Revolution when Danton cried out: "The coalesced Kings threaten us, and we hurl at their feet as a gage of battle the head of a King!"

Was there really a sound analogy between the head of Louis XVI and the 1,147 red pompons floating on the waters of Mers-el-Kebir?

I should touch now on several points on which not enough light has been shed after all these years. At first nothing was published in France about two of the choices offered Admiral Gensoul; namely, internment in the United States or in a French port in the Antilles. Even Marshal Pétain was not told of these until six months later. Furthermore, nothing was said in France, of course, about Churchill's serious reasons for feeling no confidence whatsoever in the good faith of the new French government in Bordeaux. I have already described how the Bordeaux government behaved: as liars and perjurers. That partly explains why the British Prime Minister was afraid. For he was afraid—but afraid of what? Of losing the war no less, if the French warships fell into the hands of the Germans.

Was it likely that they would have, thereby giving the German and Italian fleets preponderance on the seas? No, it wasn't—unless the British were dealing with madmen. Churchill, however, did consider Admiral Darlan to be not only a "crook" but mad, for if he were not mad, he would have continued to fight at England's side with his fleet intact and the whole French Empire behind him. He would have been a de Gaulle ten times over, and after the victory he would have had France in his pocket.

Then, too, there was the opinion of General de Gaulle.[1] Earlier,

[1] *Successive declarations of General de Gaulle regarding the French fleet*

(1) June 16, 1940, speaking to Churchill: "Whatever happens, the French fleet will not be willingly surrendered. Pétain himself would not consent to that. Besides, the fleet is Darlan's fief. A feudal lord does not surrender his fief. But for it to be possible to be sure that the enemy will never lay hands on our ships, it would be necessary for us to remain at war . . ." De Gaulle: *Memoirs*, I, p. 76.

(2) June 24, 1940, to a correspondent of the Press Association: "I have reasons to believe that the French fleet will not give itself up. . . . I am convinced that all parts of the French Empire will continue to fight. I am in telegraphic relations with General Noguès . . . with General Mittelhauser [Commander, Middle East] . . . with General Catroux." London *Times*, June 25, 1940.

(3) June 26, 1940, on the BBC, publicly addressing Marshal Pétain: "Our entire army demobilized, our officers and our soldiers prisoners to be kept in captivity, our fleet, our planes, our tanks, our arms to be delivered intact so that the adversary may use them against our allies. You have gambled, lost, thrown away your cards, had our pockets emptied . . ."

(4) July 8, 1940, on the BBC: ". . . The frightful shelling at Oran. I shall speak quite frankly on this subject, for the present drama is one in which the future of each country is at stake, and it is therefore imperative that men of feeling should have the courage to face facts and speak their minds. Let me, then, say here and now that there is not a single Frenchman who did not learn with grief and anger that certain vessels of the French Fleet had been sunk by our Allies. This grief and anger come from the innermost depths of our being. We have no reason to dissemble our feelings and, personally, I am prepared to express them openly. I therefore ask the British to spare us, as well as themselves, any portrayal of this hateful tragedy as a direct naval success. To consider it as such would be both unjust and out of place. . . . By virtue of an agreement contrary to all honour, the Government then established in Bordeaux

before the armistice, General de Gaulle had put forth the idea that Admiral Darlan was comparable to a feudal lord. A feudal lord, de Gaulle said, does not give up his fief. Since the armistice, on June 24, the General had been telling the English press that he had reasons to believe the French fleet would not give up. On the very day of the armistice, he had been certain that the entire empire was going to continue to fight. Yet, two days later, on June 26, he affirmed that Marshal Pétain *had agreed to hand over the fleet, intact, as well as our planes and our tanks, for the Germans to make use of them in their forthcoming attack on England.* If de Gaulle himself, a Frenchman, a patriot, an officer, could believe that other Frenchmen, soldiers and sailors, were capable of surrendering their ships, how could Churchill not think the same?

July 4, 1940

It was while we were finishing our breakfast after our unhappy return from Plymouth that morning of July 4 that a BBC bulletin brought us news of the tragedy. I hurried off to the Embassy to learn whatever I could, and in the vestibule I caught sight of Ro-

---

agreed to place our ships at the mercy of the enemy. There cannot be the slightest doubt that, on principle and of necessity, the enemy would have used them either against Britain or against our own Empire. I therefore have no hesitation in saying that they are better destroyed." De Gaulle: *War Memoirs, Documents* (1940–1941) (New York: Viking; 1955), pp. 20–1.

Statement by General Menzies, Chief of the Intelligence Service, on Mers-el-Kebir

"We had false information that the French fleet was going to be ceded to the Germans. . . . Don't forget, moreover, that the French in London contributed to this state of mind by affirming that the fleet was going to fall into the hands of the Germans." Cited by J. H. Tournoux: *Pétain et de Gaulle* (Paris: Plon; 1964), p. 229.

land de Margerie, who had just arrived from France and was lean-
ing over the Reuter's teletype by the elevator, reading the latest
reports. He seemed to understand better than the rest of us the
causes behind the horror. "When a man has had to see what I was
witness to in Bordeaux!" [1] He said this with a gesture that con-
veyed much more. At that moment, Roger Cambon, his tall figure
seemingly more stooped than ever, crossed the hall on his way out.
He was going to the Foreign Office to make the last official call of
his diplomatic career. His purpose was to lodge a protest, in the
name of France, over what he called an unacceptable ultimatum.
He had had no instructions from Bordeaux to do this, but he
needed none.

His breed of diplomat is now—in 1965—all but extinct.

What made this ultimatum unacceptable (or, as we say rather
better in French I think, *irreceivable*), I repeat, was the threat at
its core. True, any ultimatum implies by its very nature, if it does
not explicity state, a threat—do this or else—and an ultimatum
such as was presented at Mers-el-Kebir would be considered unacceptable only because of a proud and arrogant sense of military
honor. Good enough! But it was to military men that the ultimatum was addressed; it would be sensible to expect them to react as
such. Consider this analogy: there are two friends, and one is suddenly struck down with a mortal wound. The one who is still intact says to his sorely injured friend: "You have on your person a

[1] And what had he seen in Bordeaux? From what I heard later, he had seen
plenty: the 300 *Luftwaffe* pilots shot down and captured by the RAF were to
have been sent to England by virtue of a pledge made by Paul Reynaud. The
Marshal's government released them instead to the Germans in time for them
to take part in the Battle of Britain. And the top-secret results of British
research on radar, which was on the verge of success, were delivered by Admiral
Darlan and his associates to the Germans. As for the Poles and the Czechs,
who were eager to go on with the war against the Reich, they were no longer
treated as the loyal allies they had been, but as enemies. And by virtue of one
of the most humiliating articles in the armistice agreement, France handed
over to the Gestapo the anti-Nazi and anti-Fascist allies who had trusted in the
historic right of asylum. Moreover, Admiral Darlan as Minister of Marine under Minister of National Defense Weygand saw to it that the Germans were
supplied with detailed information on the movements of British ships.

redoubtable weapon; entrust it to me, or bury it or toss it into the lake. These proposals of mine are fair and honorable. But I must warn you that if you decline to follow any of the three courses I have outlined, I will make use of my own weapons to take yours from you." In such a case, I say that the wounded friend will refuse; the threat should not have been uttered.

After handing his protest to the Foreign Office in the name of France, Roger Cambon returned to the Embassy and fired off a telegram to the government of Marshal Pétain informing them of what he had done. He then carefully drafted his letter of resignation to that same government, to Baudouin, the Minister of Foreign Affairs, who had worked so long and so hard to make "peace" with Hitler and to put together a Ministry in which foreign affairs would henceforth be truncated, a Ministry in which he was to find that his relationship with Germany would be that of the vanquished to the victor. Roger Cambon would not serve the chief of state who was about to sunder relations with the English, accept "collaboration" with the invader, and renege on the country's past.

This was a resignation pure and simple, yet unique, I believe, among the career diplomats of that chaotic time. For Cambon did not invoke any of his retirement rights, which would naturally have included a pension. On the other hand, he did not even for a moment consider joining de Gaulle. He admired the General's soldierly gesture but not his political designs. By his resignation, then, Cambon abandoned all his property in France. Until the peace he would live as a man of no means, from time to time helping others even worse off than he. The English insisted that, as the son of one ambassador and the nephew of another, whose names were woven into the very fabric of what was l'entente cordiale, he must at least retain his diplomatic privileges, but he declined. For the entire war, which had another five years to go, he would not leave London, save for one brief visit to Algeria.

On resigning his functions, he handed over the succession to the Marquis Boni de Castellane, who accepted, though not without a sense of sacrifice, for he was not happy at the prospect of being the French diplomat to break with England. And as chargé d'affaires, he would have the less than agreeable job of repatriating all the members of the Embassy and of various other French missions in London who wanted to go home. Once this task was accomplished, he would go to Tangier to work with the English, but would not join General de Gaulle.

The bloody business at Mers-el-Kebir brought a cry of indignation from the French volunteers in England. The sailors were outraged, and many tried to pick fights with Englishmen at every turn. Some even used knives, with which they were proficient. They could not understand that it was madness, panic that brought the English to this action which killed more than a thousand of their comrades, defenseless on ships anchored in the far end of a harbor known to them all, from which offensive action was not possible.

July 5, 1940

Cambon was the first and only Frenchman on July 4 to protest the action on Mers-el-Kebir. The next day, July 5, there was another protest, though on a level appropriate to the rank of the man making it, Admiral Muselier. Muselier went straight to the First Sea Lord, Sir Dudley Pound, and told him flatly that if any more blood was shed between English and French sailors he would ask to be interned. He demanded, and obtained, an agreement for indemnification for the wives, children, and families of the victims of Mers-el-Kebir.

In the afternoon, on the street, Anne and I quite by chance met an English officer, Commander Younghusband, of a celebrated naval family. In front of a fellow officer who was with him, he exclaimed, "I am ashamed of what we have done!"

The English love their country. But they have no hesitation about criticizing their government, even in the middle of a war, even when bearing arms. Any Englishman, no matter who, has the right to say what he likes about the Prime Minister without risking prosecution. If the King—and, naturally, his family—is shielded from criticism, it is because, as a sovereign, he is politically above the battle and not responsible for the acts of his government.

In the United States, where the Chief of State is also Commander-in-Chief, one can with impunity say anything one likes about him. In the middle of the war I myself heard President Roosevelt called almost every name in the calendar of abuse. It was magnificent! At that time Marshal Pétain, with the help of Hitler, had a gag firmly fixed on the mouth of France.

July 6–8, 1940

One man did not protest Mers-el-Kebir on July 4. Or on July 5, or 6, or 7, or even on the eighth. He merely let Vice-Admiral Émile Muselier—to whom he appeared to be "in a state of collapse"—do so himself. Actually, how could he have protested? Churchill could quite simply have countered: did you yourself not say that those ships would certainly end up in German hands?

So the General held his peace. Meanwhile, however, wrath was growing apace among the volunteers of the Free French Forces. He had to make a stand. Four days after the event, he made up his mind. In his speech over the BBC on the evening of July 8, he started off by saying that he was going to speak frankly, *without circumlocution,* because in the present drama of war, *men of heart* must speak out with *frankness.* In what he had to say, he was going to *express himself openly.*

He then stated that "there is not a Frenchman who did not learn with sorrow and anger" that the French fleet had been sunk by France's allies. But he did not say against whom this anger was directed: against Vichy only, against London only, or against both? In the latter part of the speech, some light was shed on this when he declared vigorously that if the English rejoiced in this fratricidal combat as a glorious victory, they would be taking an unjust and odious position. For the fleet at Mers-el-Kebir could not defend itself.

No doubt about it.

But who among Englishmen with any sense of responsibility even dreamed of making of the tragedy a "glorious victory"? I saw not a one. On the contrary, the English, particularly the sailors, were more inclined to blush than to give evidence of pride in their eyes. *The Times* wrote of the affair with embarrassment. The House of Commons, united in an implacable determination to win the war, showed their approval of Churchill when he spoke of Mers-el-Kebir as a "lamentable episode." In his memoirs he referred to "these sombre events," "this mournful episode." [1]

Then the General, in his broadcast, reached his main point. He repeated the declaration he had made before Mers-el-Kebir. The government of the Marshal, he stated, *had agreed to turn over our warships* to the enemy, who would have used them either against England, or against France itself.

Was Churchill pleased with this reaffirmation that justified his action? He let it be known that he was. And he said so later as well: in his memoirs he gave the General a "well done."

[1] From Madrid, where he was in very close touch with the French Ambassador and with those members of the Franco regime who were not blatantly pro-Axis, Sir Samuel Hoare (Lord Templewood) in a letter to Lord Halifax made perhaps the most apposite comment on the tragedy at Mers-el-Kebir. ". . . This blow against France . . . has upset the many people who were beginning to think upon this Latin bloc line. My conclusion would be that so far as Spain is concerned, we may get away with it, provided that our action is really justified by success. By this I mean that we have really captured, immobilised or destroyed the effective part of the French Fleet. *If we cannot point to successful results, Spain will regard it as a mad dog act against one of the Latin countries. . . .*" (Italics are the author's.) Sir Samuel Hoare, Viscount Templewood: *Complacent Dictator* (New York: Alfred A. Knopf; 1947), p. 69.

July 8, 1940

Around us the tragedy provoked the most passionate reactions. On one aspect of it only was there unanimity: by its very violence, the action showed the world the quality of Britain's determination. It was grim and ruthless in the face of a grim and ruthless enemy.

Otherwise, in the weeks and months that followed, the English we saw we found to be divided into two camps stirred by contradictory ideas. By far the most numerous were those who approved the ultimatum and praised the Prime Minister for having broken off with cannon fire all relations with an unworthy France from which nothing good could any longer be expected. All hopes in this camp were to be placed henceforth on the France incarnated by, and animated and directed by, General de Gaulle. He alone was faithful to the alliance, he and his followers. Now, with Admiral Gensoul's rejection of the ultimatum, and after the cannonade, people knew where they were! They would henceforth have no trouble distinguishing between white and black. On one side, the white, was General de Gaulle, England's friend. On the other side were the friends of Germany, and at their head were Marshal Pétain, Pierre Laval, and Admiral Darlan.

Was there any reason to think that, if they had temporized, Admiral Darlan would one day have turned his coat? That he would have come over with the entire French fleet, bringing in his wake the overseas territories of France? And that, commanding such considerable forces, he would have then superseded General de Gaulle? (As Churchill was to say later, much later.) Well, *that* would have been nothing less than a disaster for the Allied cause! It would have meant exchanging, selling out for some ships and some territories, the sincerest friend England had ever had; the one, the only man who had come over immediately, thereby saving the honor of France, otherwise a nation disgraced, lost without him. Besides, one could count on his being unwilling to give up his place. For he had created it, not merely taken it, and he was the only one worthy of holding it through to the end, for the greater good and the glory of France, of England, and of democracy everywhere.

If it was true that the Commander-in-Chief of the French fleet and most of the officers of the French Navy and the French Army did not wish to place themselves under de Gaulle's orders, if it was true that the General himself was proving a hindrance in the rallying of recruits from France, then it was just too bad for the French Navy, too bad for the French Army! We would win without them! Even against them, if necessary.

In the other camp, clearly a minority, the Prime Minister was criticized for having forced upon the Royal Navy a task deemed repugnant. (As he himself said in issuing the orders, "You are charged with one of the most disagreeable tasks that a British admiral has ever been faced with. . . .") He was further reproached with having failed to take into account the psychology of French sailors, which is that of all sailors worthy of the name: none gives up his ship. If there really was the danger that the French fleet might not just hand itself over to the Germans but enter into an alliance with them, then Churchill had augmented, not diminished, that danger. For, as a matter of fact, he had succeeded in destroying or neutralizing no more than a small segment of the French fleet, while at the same time making the rest furiously, explosively anti-British.[1] His critics said too that he had perhaps ruined the chances for a return to the Allied side of the French armies of Africa and the Middle East once the war took a more favorable turn, and also, of course, of the powerful fleet,

[1] On July 8 the British did succeed in damaging the powerful new battleship *Richelieu* at Dakar with a hit by an aerial torpedo launched by a plane from the carrier HMS *Hermes*. The *Richelieu* could still use her fifteen-inch guns, as was soon to be demonstrated, but she could not be made fully operational anywhere south of Toulon and she had to be towed.

which was so sorely needed. Anybody who maintained that it was not needed had only to look at the dreadful straits Britain found herself in on the high seas, the pathetically meager escorts she was able to provide the ocean convoys that were her life. And this was so for many months.

Then, too, the minority held that it was gravely wrong to suggest, as so many people were doing, that General de Gaulle and his volunteers were the only Frenchmen who were friends of England and enemies of Hitler. Furthermore, Churchill's critics pointed out that he had, by this act of violence, all but shut off the flow of recruits from France. He had isolated de Gaulle from the French Army still further. And in one fell swoop, if it can be called that, he had eliminated for a long time, perhaps forever, any possibility that Admiral Darlan or any other officer high in the French command might one day, with arms and combatants, imitate the action of de Gaulle, might even take his place if the officer in question had more prestige and could bring into action a more numerous, more powerful, more effective military force. In other words, if his contribution was such that it could bring closer the day of victory.

In the opinion of people who felt this way, Churchill had, by the very fact of breaking off relations, automatically endowed General de Gaulle with a monopoly on Franco-British dealings. The General had become the sole French authority recognized by Great Britain. This meant that he was recognized, to all intents, as the sole representative of all France. For the Prime Minister to try in the future to assert the contrary would be to contradict himself.

And would de Gaulle turn out to be the incomparable friend of Britain that Churchill imagined him to be? Would he, in a liberated France, prove to be, as the Prime Minister thought, one soldier who would really respect civil and parliamentary liberties? And within the community of democratic nations, would the General be the ever-reliable ally Churchill envisaged? These and other doubts preyed on the minds of the little camp where opposition to Churchill was heard on this score. Apprehensions were felt, and voiced, concerning the cavalier way in which the General had overruled the advice given him by Lord Lloyd and by such sure friends of England as Torcy and Jean Monnet. Even then, there was a feeling in some quarters that in General de Gaulle's attitude toward Great Britain sentiments of suspicion and distrust might be stronger than friendship. Also, that he might have political ideas based on his well-known blueprints of military strategy, *and* that he might very well be harboring aspirations to the exercise of personal power not without precedent in French history.

Between these two extremes, there was, naturally, the great mass who thought that all this had no importance, because England would surely win the war, and then the French, the Belgians, the Dutch, the Danes, the Norwegians, the Czech, and all the peoples who had been overrun would again be happy, with governments of their own choosing.

End of July 1940

In the midst of these tragic events and of the various interpretations given them, I undertook to enlist in the Free French Naval Forces. But I wanted to do it without having to swear allegiance to the person of General de Gaulle.

At home I had to use extreme tact with Anne. Since the failure of our expedition to bring the baby from Brittany, she had again become deeply depressed. She kept saying that she wanted to go back to France. At the Embassy, where I was twiddling my thumbs, nearly everybody was packing up. None of them was very proud of it either. The general mood was far from comforting. Do not think that all the French who stayed in England were heroes, or that all those who went back to France were cowards, an idea that found some currency in certain French circles in London. It was impossible to generalize. One merchant remained in England so as not to leave his business; another went back to his in France. Some thought they would avoid the bombings by going; others thought that if they went back to France they would have to face the horrors of the Occupation. Anne wanted to go back for the baby and to nurse the wounded. I don't doubt that if she had gone she would eventually have enlisted in the Resistance, which would have been infinitely more dangerous than the bombing raids over London.

Some of the French naval officers who had come to Plymouth with their ships now wanted to return to France; after Mers-el-Kebir they were wild with fury at Churchill and de Gaulle. Then, too, there were the Fascist-minded who sincerely admired Marshal Pétain and could hardly wait to take the oath in his service. There were even a few of the Fascist-minded who thought they had good reason to stay on in England.

Questions of family played a part in many decisions. On one occasion General de Gaulle might very well have heard the remark of a simple soldier. The Chief of the Free French was that day haranguing some French soldiers who were being repatriated, urging them to follow his example and join his movement. Back in the rear of the ranks, a voice was raised: "Follow your example? It is easy for you to talk, sir. You managed to get your family to England. Mine is in Occupied France!" But the General seemed not to have heard.

Some stayed, only to run away later. A certain propagandist of the Free French cause went all the way to Scotland, with stomach cramps, when the first bombs began to fall. In contrast, our old and formidable friend, M. du Halgouet, returned to his native Brittany to confront the Germans. At the time of the liberation, I was not at all surprised to learn that he had succeeded in making life impossible for them in his part of the country, setting the SS against the Wehrmacht and vice versa: he had them shooting at each other. Paul Bret went to North Africa with the idea, which he carried out, of creating a news agency that would be as non-German and anti-German as possible. Soldiers like my friend

Brantes went back to France to constitute the Secret Army, and he, along with General Frère and General Verneau, were caught and executed by the Germans.

Many of those who stayed on in London or who came there to take civilian employment, a situation, or a sinecure were in no sense admirable. On the contrary, it was others who were admirable: men like Pierre Mendès-France, who turned down an invitation to be a minister in the Free French and enlisted as an aviator; or like Armand, who refused a diplomatic post to go to sea as a mere ensign and roll from scupper to scupper on one of those little corvettes on convoy duty. The most heroic of all were the men who shuttled between London and France on missions of espionage or for the Resistance.

There was an amusing case among those who took flight. This was a man with fine features, a pale complexion, and a most pitiful, frightened look. He begged for some sort of diplomatic assignment that would get him to America. At the Embassy, Castellane, who could occasionally be cruel, kept him treading water. But the man was capable of infinite patience. In the evening he would leave only when the offices were closed, and he would return first thing next morning and spend the whole day rooted to a divan waiting. Pranksters would go up to him and ask to see his cuff links, which the Queen of England had presented to him on the eve of our defeat, in witness to his fidelity to the Franco-English alliance. Later, in America, he was to become something of an apologist for Vichy. He is a well-known French writer.

In those last days of July, no bomb had yet fallen on London, but the Battle of Britain had begun. Just what was the Battle of Britain? Britain's lifeline was on the seas, and, in the months and years to come, a bitter, decisive battle was fought against German subs, German raiders, even against the giant *Bismarck*. For it was on this battle of the seas that the fate of Britain hinged. But at this moment everything depended on the Battle of Britain as it was fought in the skies, with the Royal Air Force pitted against Goering's giant and supposedly invincible *Luftwaffe*. Weird though it now seems, Hitler believed that with the French Army destroyed, and France prostrate in defeat, England in her turn would be sensible and ask for peace.

The same thing was thought at Tours and at Bordeaux. Thus it was that Hitler had nothing ready, God be thanked, to launch an all-out assault on England immediately after the Battle of France. He did not have command of the seas; he had to have at least command of the skies. Once the Royal Air Force was beaten, destroyed, the way would be clear for his paratroopers and for a complete blockade of British ports by mines dropped from the air and constantly replenished.

It is history that the *Luftwaffe* came within a hair of winning the Battle of Britain. If the English fighter squadrons had been moved to fields south of the Loire during the worst of the Battle of France, as General de Gaulle had gone to London to ask in Reynaud's name, the Royal Air Force could not possibly have held out. The fate of the world depended then on an infinitesimal number of fighter pilots. As Churchill, in his immortal words, put it: "Never in the field of human conflict was so much owed by so many to so few."

Whenever the words of the English Tacitus echo in my mind across the years, I find myself thinking of the courage it took for Torcy to tell Lord Lloyd that, in *his* shoes, he would not send the planes asked for by General Weygand to supply the Army of the North at the end of May, because of the inevitable losses in fighter planes needed to protect the bombers. He said this, as we now know, quite as much in the interest of France as in that of England.

We followed the Battle of Britain on the BBC and in the newspaper headlines: TEN ENEMY PLANES DESTROYED! Next day: TWENTY-THREE ENEMY PLANES DESTROYED! And the day after that: THIRTY-FOUR ENEMY PLANES DESTROYED! And so on. From time to time we had an unreal sort of vision of the struggle: lovely white contrails and puffs of smoke as ornamental as flowers against the incredible blue sky of that splendid summer of 1940.

With nothing to do, I went twice to the country. The first time it was to try to locate a cousin of mine who had been evacuated from Dunkirk. But, as it turned out, he had gone back to France before the armistice. The other time I went with Anne to visit some wounded Frenchmen in a hospital in Surrey. In that peaceful countryside, the preparations against invasion seemed altogether ridiculous: tree trunks blocking the roads, signposts taken down, the sentinels of the Home Guard, civilians, wearing steel helmets and armed with shotguns and hunting rifles! What was not ridiculous was the almost joyous determination one saw on every face; and the farmers' cottages transformed into blockhouses. Or the posters one read: *Every Englishman is today in the front lines!* LET EVERYONE KILL A HUN! And why not?

The English are a placid people, but beware of angering them. Deep in their natures is a strain of violence that, once unleashed, becomes implacable. When one saw the glint in people's eyes, one did not exactly envy the fate awaiting the invaders. What is there to killing a man once you get a sight on him? I am sure that our Mary could easily have taken care of three or four.

"Everyone can have his own," said the Prime Minister, as if he were granting a favor. Civilians as well as soldiers, he said, were to throw themselves on Nazi parachutists "with the greatest alacrity." So seriously did the people take this advice that many an RAF pilot who had to bail out and parchute on his own soil was faced with ugly crowds of housewives, farm workers, bus conductors, or their like, armed with meat cleavers, scythes, or whatever was at hand—until he could prove his identity. The best way to do this was to call out, and loudly, in basic Anglo-Saxon.

The Duke of Bedford betrayed his collector's passion when he ordered his gamekeepers to "bring them back alive." Londoners were quite ready to do battle in the streets. The vast capital, spreading over an area greater than that of any other capital in Europe, would certainly have been a prodigious Stalingrad. The invader floating down from the sky, or advancing by land, would have seen surge out of the ashes and the ruins of London a people in arms which, to use the Prime Minister's expression, would have "devoured" a German army.

Late in the day before the liner repatriating the diplomats was to sail, Anne, not quite looking at me, said, "I think now that I am staying." I took her in my arms and nothing more was said.

Anne and I had sold our car so as to make ourselves a little war chest. Castellane, when he found out, gave us one of his cars, a bright new one. That same day he refused severance pay to a secretary who had been with the Embassy for a decade or more. Margerie took care of her. Castellane had a heart of gold and would have done good works among the poor, if only he had known them.

For him the last weeks in London as chargé d'affaires were not a sinecure. Every day brought new incidents. The English behaved badly to the French sailors they had interned. How would we, the French, have behaved to English sailors if the situation had been reversed? I cannot say, but I do know that our attitude toward the Belgians after their king's capitulation was ignoble.

M. Corbin and M. Cambon did their best to help Castellane, plucking the thorns from his feet. At last came the day of departure. At seven that morning, Anne put on her best hat, and we went off to the little Addison Road station behind the Olympia from which the special boat train for Southampton was to leave.

"*Bon courage!*" those who were leaving called out as the wheels started to turn and the coaches glided slowly past us. "*Bon courage!*" called those who were staying. And who can say who had the most courage—those going home to France or those staying behind in London?

The train picked up speed and was soon only a red lantern, then faded from sight. As for us, Anne and I, we felt a new freedom. At last we were alone. We set off arm in arm, but swallowing hard. Back at the house it was: Mary, Mary, we no longer have any money; you must look for another place.

The next morning at ten we were off to Euston Station to bid farewell to M. Corbin. He had waited for the entire embassy to leave, helping out those who went and those who stayed. For the most Anglophile he found jobs of a kind they wanted. Louis Roché went to Ireland but lost no time in returning to London, with Pierre

Saffroy and Commander Lionel Bedin. These three were among the
first, after M. Cambon, to hand in their resignations. But it was
not to pass from one livery to the other. Louis Roché, for a long
time, and Pierre Saffroy, all through the war, preferred poverty to
the salaries they could have had in the service of General de
Gaulle. The hardest thing to bear was not being poor but, especially at first, being looked at askance by nearly everybody. By the
Free French, of course, but also by most of the English.

"What's this? You are not a Gaullist? But then you must be a
Pétainist? No? Then you are not on our side? You *say* you are? But
we are backing that wonderful General de Gaulle! Oh, you French
are so complicated! So hard to understand!" The easy way was to
pass oneself off as a little mad. A touch of madness is quite well
considered in England.

I neglected to note in my diary the dates on which the *Orduna*
left, and then, the day after, the Ambassador. But I remember the
hours. A bit before noon we were back at the house. We sat down
to a little council of war; we counted our sous. Mary indeed had to
leave. And Anne too, because for her the first thing was to get back
her strength, to go to the green countryside.

"We are expecting you tomorrow," a voice from the far reaches
of Scotland said to her. And the apartment? We would have to
sublease it. And permission from the owner? No matter, he was a
friend. He came by that very evening. "I won't hear of your giving
up the apartment. Keep it for the duration. We will settle our
accounts at the moment of our common victory!"

I insisted on subleasing. He insisted that we stay; we need pay
only at the war's end. But then he came forth with an unfortunate
idea. "My guess is that before the week is out General de Gaulle
will put you in a post of the highest importance. So don't worry!"

I was looking at Anne stretched out on the divan like Mme
Récamier, and I saw by her expression that no good would come of
this. If I had been smart, I would have run up a lightning rod; I
could have simply said, "We'll talk about it tomorrow." Instead, I
persisted in asking that we be allowed to sublet so as not to be a

burden to him. And he persisted in his generous refusal. Thereupon Anne took the floor. "But really," she said, "when a friend
asks a favor, it's the least you can do. What the devil . . . !"

Here was an instance when the music made the song. Anyway,
the friend who had been refusing us out of sheer generosity now
suddenly lost his temper. "If you want charity, why not ask your
. . . He is rich as Croesus."

At this point, Mme Récamier picked up her glass of whisky from
the coffee table by the divan and threw it, and after it another and
another, straight at the head of the proprietor, whose only fault
was unselfishness. He turned, drenched in whisky, and walked out
over pieces of broken crystal.

The incident was all the more regrettable because Scotch was
becoming scarce. There ensued some delicate negotiations, and
the bonds of friendship, soon to become affection, were renewed.
Subdued and repentant, Anne left for the Scottish countryside,
and I went to live at the Maison de l'Institut, at the corner of
Queen's Gate and Prince Consort Road, where I had boarded as a
student long before the war. Despite the headaches we had once
caused the director, Robert Loyauté Cru, he and I had become
friends. He made me welcome. We paid two shillings six for any
meals we had at the Maison. And it was not only I he welcomed
so warmly. He also had under his roof Raymond Aron, Robert
Hirsch, and the luckless Professor Dormoy of the École Polytechnique in Paris, who because he knew too much about certain
matters in his special field had been detained in England against
his will. There was Mme Dormoy, who was almost always in tears,
and there was Donald Monroe, a young man, a boy rather, whom
his mother and stepfather, on their departure from London, had
left under Anne's wing and mine.

There were others whose names I have forgotten. But I have not
forgotten Tobin, the butler, a long-time friend who had often
in our student days picked up the pieces after us. Now looking
most dignified in his tail coat, he would soon be going about
with a broom, sweeping up broken glass, for bombings were to
begin in earnest and with the first explosions the windows went.

Nor have I forgotten the housekeeper, whom we used to call "Mrs. Custard." She was terrified of mice and of ghosts but was dauntless under the bombs. They are all dead, all of them, Cru, the charming Donald, Tobin, Mrs. Custard, killed when a bomb fell on that beautiful dwelling and demolished it. But this was much later.

Now, at the end of July 1940, things were still quiet. After dinner, we played bridge. Raymond Aron was a crack player. But what we were really interested in was to get him to talk philosophy. Without ever being pedantic, he seemed always to maintain the high level of his thought. His conversation had a charm we could not tire of. He handled ideas as he handled cards at bridge, and took every trick. He recognized at once the talent of young Donald Monroe, whose short life was a poem—a brief lyric.

Now and then we talked politics. Nobody among us was a Gaullist except Cru. But even he sometimes made fun of the General and actually verged on impertinence when he complained that de Gaulle was making speeches instead of war. Oh yes, we did have a real Gaullist: he was Étienne Dennery, who became Director of Information, or something like it, with the General. Like Raymond Aron, Dennery was a product of the École Normale Supérieure, but he did not share Aron's ideas at all.

I still had nothing to do, which suited me. I felt free as never before in my life, but I was in danger of ceasing to be free at all: as I said, I was a reserve officer in the French Navy. But I had no wish to sign the oath to General de Gaulle, about which so much was being said, although I had yet to see it. I put myself down for the Home Guard, which was open to anybody: the famous agreements between de Gaulle and the English, which forbade Frenchmen to enlist in any of the English services, did not apply there. This still meant that I was doing nothing except making an appearance one night a week at an antiaircraft battery in south London. And we never had a chance to fire; German planes were not yet appearing over London. We had alerts, however. At that time the alarm was given when enemy planes crossed the coasts of Kent or Essex. In the daytime I took long walks in Chelsea, in Mayfair, in places of good repute or evil, looking about me with wide-open eyes. I felt then that the spectacle was soon to close: all that magnificence, wealth, decency, all those monstrosities too, those masterpieces of bad taste, the sordid streets, girls of every kind, good and bad, lily-fair complexions and the wrinkles of old age, churches and pubs and drunkards, the last lawns over which the last few children ran about in play; the children had come back but now were again being evacuated.

Once, feeling extravagant, I had dinner at a restaurant in Soho, starting home as soon as the sirens began to howl at the moon. On my way I looked in on bomb shelters. In the basement of a hotel, people of substance in pajamas, the women with their hair in curlers; in a cellar next door, the poor, very well organized, cooking a communal meal. When I reached the Maison de l'Institut, M. Cru, steel helmet on his head, proposed that I go up with him and share his duties as a roof watcher. I said I had letters to write. Actually I wrote only one, to Anne, telling her that I was still on vacation, which was all too true. To whom else would I have written? France seemed as far away as China. And even to America everything was heavily censored.

Pierre Maillaud asked me to join his news agency. He was very convincing, but I said no. Pierre Comert founded the daily paper *France*. I admired him but was not tempted. Again, I wanted to keep myself free to ship out. It seemed so much more invigorating than the staleness of life in London.

August 1940

Nevertheless, I was finally caught. This is how. In 1940 the Colonel—as his own children and I myself used to call him even before he actually attained the rank—was in London alone. One evening he asked me to come and see him. He told me that he, to use his own expression, had taken the plunge: he had joined de Gaulle's organization. There he did a job which he explained to me. I could give him a hand. "The load is too heavy. I can't carry it alone. Come and help me."

I asked him if I could be responsible only to him.

"Certainly," he said.

"To you alone?"

"To me alone. I have complete freedom to organize my department. I take with me whomever I wish. And if anybody tries to give you orders, directives, or whatever, he will have to deal with me."

I accepted, delighted to join the movement with this fine man to vouch for me and be my chief, without having had to sign an enlistment oath binding me to any one individual. He recounted his first experiences at Carlton Gardens. He said he knew that I had certain reservations about the General. He had once had them too, but now he had changed his opinion, completely. The personage in question, he said, was very different from what I imagined.

The really formidable beings are those one respects the most. For the Colonel I had not only respect but deep affection. He told me that General de Gaulle was a magnificent figure of a soldier. Sincerity itself, rectitude personified. So I thought he had political ambitions? How wrong I was! It was just the contrary: the General had a phobia about politicians, parliamentarians, whom he saw as middlemen and parasites standing between the citizenry and the state as in commerce they stood between producers and consumers.

But General de Gaulle, though pure, disinterested, clean, was not, for all that, simple-minded! On the contrary, his thoughts ran deep, and to discover his thoughts through the screen of his words was not always easy. This was the first time, but not the last, that I heard about the profound thoughts of the General and how they had to be distinguished from what was expressed by his lips.

While he talked, the Colonel had opened a bottle of Bordeaux to moisten the bread and cheese. And as the night grew older and we ate and drank, I found that the admiration of my future chief for the man he called *le Connétable*[1] was embarrassing me more and more. I felt guilty because I did not dare to contradict him, and I thought that my silence might pass for acquiescence. At last, I asked, "If you don't mind, Colonel, tell me how much you plan to pay me."

I couldn't have cared less about the money at such a moment, with our country overrun by the enemy. But I wanted to provoke an anticlimax of some kind, to underline in the clearest way possible, the heaviest-handed way even, that what was involved was simply an agreement between the Colonel and me, not an enlistment in the service of General de Gaulle.

I made my point. The Colonel by a gesture revealed how shocked he was by my question.

"I couldn't tell you. . . . It will of course be in keeping with your rank in the Reserve.[2] It won't be much. But you will have an expense account."

Finally he mentioned a sum that, if I remember rightly, came to about £50 a month. I said that was fine with me, and I took my leave until the morrow.

At eight-thirty next morning I was at the office at 4, Carlton Gardens. A plaque on the building indicated that here once had stood the town house of Lord Palmerston. From the roof, which was stepped back in terraces, one looked out over the Mall, with St. James's Park in front; to the left, the Admiralty Arch; and to the right, Buckingham Palace. A splendid view. The British government had given General de Gaulle the use of this requisitioned building for the duration of hostilities. In London, people quickly fell into the habit of saying "Carlton Gardens" when they wanted to designate what became in fact the headquarters of the future French government.

At the moment of my arrival, the building radiated joy because the financial problem had been settled at the same time as the question of official recognition. As early as the end of June, Gen-

[1] In France, in medieval times, the *connétable* was the head of the army. This name had been given de Gaulle in London by some of his own troops.
[2] Second lieutenant.

eral de Gaulle had been, in fact, "Chief of the Free French," but financially he was living from day to day, dependent on Churchill for everything, even his bread. Then, on August 7, he signed an agreement with the Prime Minister by the terms of which he could obtain the advances necessary for him and for his movement, which would be reimbursed eventually by France. From that day on, not only would the General have no more worries about money, but he would be empowered by the British government to enter into financial arrangements in the name of France. It would be hard to imagine more solid proof of the standing which was at that time officially accorded him.

In a *lettre d'envoi* accompanying the agreement of August 7, Churchill also repeated to de Gaulle what he had affirmed both before and since the French defeat, and most notably in his speech in the Commons the night before the General's broadcast appeal: that Great Britain would share with France all the benefits of victory and that France would be restored integrally in her independence and her greatness.[3]

---

[3] *Extracts from the Churchill–de Gaulle accord of August 7, 1940*

I

1. General de Gaulle is engaged in raising a French force composed of volunteers. This force, which includes naval, land and air units and scientific and technical personnel, will be organised and employed against the common enemies.

2. This force will never be required to take up arms against France.

III

4. General de Gaulle will be entitled to form a civil establishment. . . .

IV

1. Any expenditure incurred for the purpose of the constitution and maintenance of the French force under the provisions of this agreement will be met, in the first instance, by the appropriate Departments of His Majesty's Government in the United Kingdom, which will be entitled to exercise any necessary examination and audit.

Extract from Churchill's letter to General de Gaulle

London, 7 August 1940

". . . I would take this opportunity of stating that it is the determination of His Majesty's Government . . . to secure the full restoration of the independence and greatness of France . . ."

De Gaulle: *Memoirs*, Documents (1940–42), pp. 26–7.

To assume that France should consider herself obligated to General de Gaulle and to him alone for this promise by Great Britain is to offer a gratuitous insult to the value of the earlier promises made by the British. Besides, how could the British have had anything else in mind? Any theft from, or amputation of, the possessions of France would inevitably have thrown open to question the legitimacy of Britain's postwar holdings. One can admit, without in any way seeming to reflect on the sincerity of the British or on the worth of their promises, that of course it was very much in their interest at this moment in history to treat France so generously. But the General never ceased to suspect some devious design of the British by which they would profit by our misfortunes; "they might perhaps" be tempted by our overseas territories.[4]

The agreement of August 7 stipulated, finally, that the military forces established by the General could never "bear arms against France." [5] Not a single volunteer had any idea that the promise

[4] *The General's suspicions of English motives*

In drafting the August 7, 1940, agreement, the General writes, he had to bear in mind the possibilities both of victory and of defeat. Considering, "on the one hand the hypothesis that the fortunes of war might bring England to a compromise peace, and . . . on the other, that the British might perhaps be tempted by this or that overseas possession of ours, I insisted that Great Britain should guarantee the re-establishment of the frontiers of Metropolitan France and of the French Empire." The English agreed to "the integral restoration of the independence and greatness of France," but, he says, "without any commitment as regards the integrity of our territories." De Gaulle: *Memoirs*, I, p. 95.

[5] *Extracts from secret letters exchanged by Churchill and de Gaulle*

Churchill to de Gaulle, London, 7 August 1940: ". . . The article which specifies that your troops will not have to 'take up arms against France' must be interpreted as meaning a France free to choose her course without being under direct or indirect duress from Germany."

De Gaulle to Churchill, London, 7 August 1940: ". . . On the other hand, you point out that the fact that my troops will not have to 'take up arms against France' must be interpreted as meaning 'a France free to choose her course without being under direct or indirect duress from Germany.' "
De Gaulle: *Memoirs*, Documents (1940–42), pp. 26–7.

In his memoirs (Vol. I, p. 95), de Gaulle says about this accord: "I also had it laid down—not without objections on the part of the British—that in

thus worded was accompanied by a secret agreement, embodied in an exchange of letters, stipulating that what was meant by "France" was a "France free to choose her own course." That, needless to say, left out all of France and her empire under the rule of Marshal Pétain.

Naturally I knew nothing of any secret understanding. The General had not even let Admiral Muselier, his second in command, into the secret. I learned about it later, from the English.

The Colonel was not too pleased with the concept I had of my duties. I refused to handle anything of a political nature. I had disillusioned him, but he was indulgent. Nevertheless, I sensed that he was beginning to ask himself whether it would not be better, for me and for him, if some other job were found for me. Circulars were being sent around the offices, requesting personnel for all sorts of posts. One day I was asked to become a colonial administrator. That was the moment when, following the example of the Belgian Congo, a part of French Black Africa decided to go on with the war. Chad, the Cameroons, the Lower Congo, and Ubangi rallied to General de Gaulle. He had dispatched to that part of Africa Colonel de Larminat, Captain de Hauteclocque (better known later by his *nom de guerre*, General Leclerc), and René Pleven. As a reward to the Chad, the General cited it *à l'ordre de l'Empire* and declared that this territory "had shown that it remained *par excellence* a country of valiant Frenchmen." [6] This

no case would the volunteers 'bear arms against France.' That did not mean that they were never to fight against Frenchmen. The contrary, alas, had to be foreseen, Vichy being what it was and not being—far from it—France. But the clause aimed at guaranteeing that Allied military action, with which our own was merged, should not, even when it came up against the forces of official France, be used against the real France and injure its patrimony or its interests."

[6] ". . . I specify that the presence of French forces from one end of the Rhine to the other, the separation of the territories on the left bank of the Rhine and of the Ruhr Basin from what will be the German state, the independence of the Polish, Czech, Austrian and Balkan nations are conditions which France judges essential. . . . We are not distressed, moreover, by the likelihood that it will be up to us to bring some of them to realization, for we are 106 million men, united under the French flag, in immediate proximity to what concerns us most directly." De Gaulle: *Memoirs*, III, p. 96.

was at the time when he was accusing Marshal Pétain and his followers of the crime of handing over the empire to the Germans.
He said that France numbered more than a hundred million men.
At the liberation he declared that France still had a hundred million, quite enough to insure the presence of our troops from one
end of the Rhine to the other and the separation from Germany of
all the territory on the left bank of the river *and* the Ruhr besides.
His thinking in this respect had evolved notably.

In French Equatorial Africa there were all kinds of high posts to
fill because the governors and administrators who had not rallied to
the General had obviously fallen from grace. "But," I said on reading the circular, "I know nothing at all about Black Africa or about
its administration!"

"Oh, well," someone answered me, "you will learn! And then,
do you know what the salary of an administrator is? And the special overseas allowances? And the advantages? And the quarters?
And the service?"

"But," said I, "there is not a single German down there!" I was
creating a bad reputation for myself, I am sorry to say.

From time to time, the Colonel told me, "You must all the same
have an audience with the General."

"No, no, thanks anyhow, but I have already been presented."

"Yes, I know, but for our work, it would be more *correct* . . ."

"No, I assure you, I prefer to deal with you as we agreed. The
General has other fish to fry."

The truth is, I was afraid of meeting him. Sometimes I saw him
in the corridor, near the entrance to the building, or at the head of
the stairs on the second floor,[7] where his office was. I always managed to disappear. I had noticed that he had fallen into the habit,
in the building or outside it, of shaking hands as he passed. What
would I have done in such a case, if he had caught mine? The
prospect terrified me. A handshake binds; I did not wish to be
bound.

Nevertheless, during my sojourn at Carlton Gardens I found
myself one afternoon face to face with the General. I was returning

[7] What in England is called the first floor.

from lunch. There had been an alert. At the entrance to the building, the sentinel, with his helmet on, shouted: "Everybody to the shelter!"

"But," said I, "nothing seems to be falling."

"Orders from the General!"

"All right, then." I went down to the basement. There, seated on a sort of cot near the entrance to the shelter, was the General.

My fear that he would speak to me, or hold out his hand to me, won out over discipline. I beat a quick retreat into the corridor. The elevator was stopped because of the air raid, so I took to the stairs, three at a time. Nobody bothers to stop a man in uniform who seems to be on an urgent mission. Thus I reached the top floor and the terrace sparkling with sunshine. There I found a roof watcher and my friend Siriex, who was just as undisciplined as I. Next to us floated an enormous French flag. The sky was as pure as the sky over Athens.

Never had London known such a summer. Below us, St. James's Park lay in splendor. To the right, the royal gardens seemed a theater backdrop setting off Buckingham Palace. Very far off, to the left, down the Thames, clouds of black smoke rose from the docks which had been hit and above which, high in the sky, little silver butterflies turned, dived, chased each other, leaving behind them vapor trails of white against the blue. A fascinating spectacle that seemed some sort of game: it was the first Nazi bombing raid over London.

On August 15, the battle for Britain reached its height. On that day, one thousand planes were launched against England: Junkers, Heinkels, Messerschmitts, and Dorniers. Nearly three hundred were shot down. For the Germans, it did not seem to be a paying proposition. They had *not* won the battle for the mastery of the sky, and after that day they changed their strategy. The attacks were no longer directed against the RAF, to drive it from the skies, which they had not succeeded in doing. Henceforth they would begin a systematic destruction from the air.

September 1940

I managed somehow to hold on to my job until the end of August. On that date, General de Gaulle left England. Bound for where? I had no idea, thank heaven! I was perhaps the only man who knew nothing. It seems that most of the officers around me knew and also that in Vichy they were fully informed. Luckily for me, I seemed to inspire a certain lack of confidence. No one told me any state secrets, not even my Colonel, who was obviously troubled about my future in the business. Shortly after the General left on the great mission that was to remain a mystery to me until I read of its unhappy consequences, my Colonel called me in and remarked that, unlike a number of others in the building, I was not wearing the Cross of Lorraine.

This emblem had been invented, so to speak, by Admiral Muselier, and for a definite reason: there had to be some way at sea of distinguishing between a Vichy ship and one under his command, one of the Free French Naval Forces. The Admiral's father came from Lorraine, and so he got the idea of having his ships fly not only the traditional Tricolor but also a blue ensign with a Cross of Lorraine embroidered on it in red. The Reverend Father Thierry d'Argenlieu had been the Admiral's first chief of staff. An officer in the naval reserve until the war began in 1939, he had been known as Father Louis de la Trinité, Provincial of the Carmelites in France, but was now prominent among the Free French. It was he who proposed to de Gaulle that the Cross of Lorraine be adopted as the emblem of the whole movement. The General did just that, but nowhere does he give credit to Admiral Muselier, the first to fly it for, as I said, a purely practical purpose.

Surprised, I asked the Colonel, "Is it regulation to wear this in-signia on land *and* on British soil?"

He said no, it was not regulation, but he gave me to understand that my attitude was causing him a certain amount of trouble. I was really sorry, for his sake, and wished it was not he who had to answer for me.

Some days later he brought up the subject again.

"My boy," he said, "your situation here is not at all in order. And it's the same with Siriex. Neither of you has been to the Olympia. Now run over there and get it over with!"

The Olympia is to London what the Grand Palais is to Paris, and even uglier. It had been loaned to General de Gaulle as a military supply depot, a barracks, and a recruiting center. French sentinels stood at the entrance. My friend Siriex and I were shown to a room where a young medic in white blouse and kepi put us through a medical examination as thorough as any draftee ever got. Siriex was not too happy about it.

I said, "Let's not complain that they are being too military. I was afraid they wouldn't be military enough. Around me, at Carlton Gardens, I never hear them talk of anything but politics, colonial administration, salaries, canteens, mess, and promotion."

Once dressed again, we were directed down a long corridor im-provised out of raw lumber. At the end sat an orderly who asked us, "What branch of the service?" Siriex went to the right and I to the left, where I came to a kind of box in which a recruiting officer was seated behind an unpainted deal table. He asked me the usual questions—name, date and place of birth, rank in the reserve, and all that—and wrote down my answers on a sizable printed form. Upside down I read: ACTE D'ENGAGEMENT. "Aha!" I thought to my-self, "here it is at last, the famous enlistment oath!"

I noticed that the recruiting officer had two gold stripes on his sleeve which had been there a while and one that was quite new, which meant that he had been jumped in rank from ensign to lieu-tenant.

He asked, "How long in England?"

"Since the beginning of the war."

"What I want to know is when you last entered England."

I said that I had been there since my last round trip to France in March.

"So you were interned with all the others on July 3?"

No, I had never been interned. At this, he looked me up and down with an expression that seemed a blend of scorn and pity.

"Well, well! Nobody could say you came here all out of breath in your rush to answer the General's appeal! But now that you finally made it, sign this." Very sarcastic he was, and peremptory too. Maybe it was his new third stripe; I had only two.

I had thought a lot about this oath, so I took my time as I studied its wording. I noted that General de Gaulle was cited personally as Chief of the Free French Forces. And a man had to swear to serve with honor, fidelity, and discipline. In other words, he would be swearing to obey the orders of General de Gaulle himself, with honor, fidelity, and discipline, and not merely for the duration of the war, but also "three months afterward."

I put the form down and said, "This seems to be a personal oath of allegiance to General de Gaulle, cited by name—thus, to him personally. I'm not signing."

The newly promoted officer looked up in astonishment. "Then what the hell do you think you are doing here?" The tips of his ears seemed to be getting redder and redder. Raising an arm, he pointed to the door of his little box and roared, "Now b—r off!"

Without really thinking, I caught hold of his arm, shook him, and said, "You might try to learn some manners, you fat idiot." It was of course improper for me to call him *mon gros*, and all the more so as he was on the skinny side.

For a second I figured he was going to jump at me right across his little table. But he thought better of it. On his face now there was an expression of shock and amazement. I could only conclude that he was not a line officer or even a career officer. Outside, in the corridor, I waited a moment, thinking he might follow me out after all. But nobody appeared except my comrade Siriex. I asked him, "Did they pull the same trick on you?"

"What trick?"

"About signing the oath?" I was thinking that they might at least have posted it on the bulletin board, so that a man could see what he was expected to sign before he went to the Olympia, got undressed, examined, all that. I had the impression that Siriex might be thinking along the same lines, but, if so, he chose to keep it to himself. He simply said, "I take it that you did not sign. Right?"

"Right! But please don't spread it around Carlton Gardens."

"Naturally not! But, you know, I wonder if you are not being overly suspicious, overly pessimistic? I can't easily imagine that General de Gaulle would ever give an order that you could not, in good conscience, carry out."

"It's that I don't think I have any right to substitute General de Gaulle's conscience in place of my own." And I went on to say that, as I saw it, everything depended on the General, absolutely everything. There was no judiciary, no parliament, nothing—no guarantee at all. De Gaulle was the master, totally the master.

"But he himself is guarantee enough!"

"Not for me. I repeat: I don't think that any man can rightly hand over his conscience to another. *Or* ask another man to hand it over for him to take into his keeping!"

"That's your own interpretation."

"I think it is the right one, but if it is not, I will ask them to spell out exactly what safeguards they offer. They should find that easy enough. After all, when you enlist in the regular French Army or Navy, those safeguards are made so clear that even a peasant can understand them. In the meantime, keep this to yourself, *please.*"

"Not a word then. And good luck!"

On that we parted. I went back to the office as if nothing had happened. Actually nothing did happen for more than a week. The administrative officer had evidently neglected to make a report on me. But then came the day when somebody noticed that my enlistment papers had not been sent over from the Olympia. There was an inquiry. And that did it. I was summoned again to the Colonel's office. As always, his mood was paternal, but this time he was the angry father.

FORCES FRANÇAISES LIBRES

COPIE **ACTE D'ENGAGEMENT** COF

No. de l'engagement _____

Par devant nous, (1) _____

représentant le Général de Gaulle, Commandant en Chef les Forces Françaises Libres,

a comparu M. (2) _____ ●

　　　　　M. (2) _____ a déclaré :

—avoir pris connaissance du statut du personnel des Forces Françaises Libres ;

—s'engager à servir avec Honneur, Fidélité et Discipline dans les Forces Françaises Libres pour la durée de la guerre actuellement en cours plus trois mois.

Le présent engagement est définitif sous réserve :

　　　　　1° du résultat favorable de l'examen médical ;

　　　　　2° de l'accord de l'Etat Major Particulier du Général de Gaulle ;

lesquels devront être obtenus dans un délai maximum de 42 jours.

　　　　　A _____ le _____ 194

Lu et approuvé (3)

_____ | _____

L'engagé _____ | Le présent contrat est devenu définitif à

Signature de | la date du _____
deux témoins _____ | L'INTENDANT MILITAIRE

_____ | _____ ●

(1) nom de l'Intendant Militaire ou de l'Officier en faisant fonction.
(2) nom et prénoms de l'engagé.
(3) mention à porter en toutes lettres de la main de l'engagé.
(4) Grade et nom de l'Intendant ou de l'Officier en faisant fonction.

L'acte d'engagement est établi en deux exemplaires :
　　L'exemplaire blanc est à conserver par le Bureau des Effectifs.
　　L'exemplaire bleu est à remettre à l'engagé.

55.990

(23887) Wt.P.1913/119 10,000 (2 sorts) 3/43 .A.& E.W.Ltd. Gp.685

The enlistment oath

"Well, well, a fine thing I've heard! That you kicked up a terrific row: that you refused to sign the oath."

I swallowed. Such nerve as I possessed had failed me in the respect and affection I felt for him. But I was able to remind him of our understanding: I was to work under him to do a specified job at an agreed salary and was answerable to him and to no one else.

"So that was the point you were trying to make over there!" he said. He then tried to win me over, or, to put it more accurately, to convert me to the cause.

We took up again the question of the oath. Slapping the form with the back of his hand for emphasis, he said, "There is no doubt about it, your signature most certainly would bind you to obey the orders of 'the General, Commander-in-Chief of the Free French Forces'! But what greater moral security? Look, he knows better than any of us what must be done. He is our country's guiding light. He ranks first among all the *compagnons*, but they will share the eternal glory of being united with him. One with him, as he puts it, in *action*, in *sacrifice*, and in *hope*. But look on his face, my poor young friend," he said, pointing to the portrait of the General on the wall. "Oh, if only he himself were here! If only he could speak to you, say one word, just one! You would sign all right, and with both hands!"

As he said this, I could see his hopes revive. He would effect my salvation by waiting upon the General's return, when I would be exposed to the Presence. Meanwhile, he would have to take steps to save me from being purely and simply fired.

"To make quite sure they won't throw you out," said the good Colonel, "you must go straight off to see one of these three men!"

He gave me the names of the Triumvirs to whom the General in his absence had delegated his powers. The first was a certain Antoine, who went by the name of "Fontaine." He had been the business agent for a Belgian financier, Baron Empain. The second was Dewavrin, a young artillery officer who had been a captain during the campaign in Norway and was soon to be a major and then a colonel. He went by the name of "Passy." It was widely rumored that he and his associates in the Gaullist secret service had

belonged to La Cagoule.[1] All of them had followed his example
and, to protect their families in France, had taken the names of the
stations on the Paris Métro, on the Étoile–Porte d'Italie line—
names such as Bienvenue, Corvisar, Saint-Jacques. Whatever the
truth behind the rumor, I must here say that Colonel Passy was a
courageous, highly intelligent, dedicated man with ideas the exact
opposite of mine.

The third of the Triumvirs was in theory Admiral Muselier, but
in fact he was relegated to the handling of naval and military
affairs. The third man in the political and administrative hierarchy
of General de Gaulle was Professor René Cassin, who, by the way,
had not troubled to disguise his identity.

I was not a little intimidated, standing there before this eminent
professor. I felt a little as though I were in the presence of the
High Priest, perhaps the High Priest of Marduk, God of Babylon,
or the High Priest of the Temple of Jerusalem. It may have been
fortunate that he was not actually wearing the robes I imagined,
for he would surely have rent them asunder as he tried to make me
see the nature of my crime, the full horror of it. Then his voice
took on softer accents as he called upon me to purge my guilt, to
wash away the stain in forgiveness and in the joy of faith recovered.

---

[1] A *cagoule* is a hood worn by penitents and some friars. Les cagoulards, "The
Hooded Ones," was originally organized as a "protective service," with help
from the General Staff's Intelligence Service, to ferret out alleged Communists
in the Army. It became a haven for many kinds of counterrevolutionaries and
"anti-Communists," including Italian and German agents during the Popular
Front and the Spanish Civil War. Several assassinations were attributed to the
organization, notably that of the Roselli brothers, enemies of Mussolini. In the
fall of 1937, on the basis of forged papers portending an imminent Communist
take-over, the Cagoulards and the CSAR (Secret Committee for Revolutionary
Action), organized along military lines, evidently planned some sort of *coup
d'état*. The head of the French *Sûreté* said that in Paris alone they numbered
six to seven thousand men, armed by Italy. They had connections close to
Marshal Pétain and Franchet d'Esperey. There was never an effective investigation of them. Paul Reynaud, as Minister of Justice, was notably uninter-
ested. With the war, the Cagoulards split into two groups, one pro-Ally; the
other sold out to the New Order. The line of division was not always clear.
(Translator)

As I stood there, all but swamped by this flood of words, I found myself remembering my third year at the Lycée, when we were immersed in Racine and the student matinees at the Comédie Française.

What came to mind, the eye of the mind, let us say, was the fierce fourth act of *Athalie*, in which Joad in the full regalia of High Priest stands in the temple and proclaims that he has saved young Joas, the infant and only scion of the House of David, from the murderous designs of Athalie, true daughter of Jezebel. He has brought up the boy in the temple and now calls upon the faithful to give him their allegiance:

> ". . . But I see that you
> Already burn to follow me. Swear then, first,
> Upon this solemn book to live, to fight,
> And perish for this king whom heaven today
> Has given back to you." [2]

I tried to explain my reservations, but the professor only smiled tolerantly and proceeded to give me the benefit of a lecture on law. I cannot remember what he said, because I understood not a word of it. I did attempt to get the question back into focus by citing one concrete objection to the oath which had come to mind as I read the document for the first time. "So what it all adds up to, monsieur," I said, "is that if I refuse to obey some order from the General I am at one and the same time guilty of perjury, insubordination, and desertion. Right?"

The professor raised his arms to heaven. "But why the devil should it ever occur to you to refuse to obey an order from the General?"

For all the respect I felt was due Professor René Cassin, I was bold enough to point out that he had not answered my question. Whereupon, patiently and with the utmost kindness, he resumed

[2] *Racine: Five Plays*, translated by Kenneth Muir (New York: Hill & Wang; 1960).

his lecture on law just where he had left off. Again, I understood not a single word of what he was saying. He must have guessed this from my expression.

"Now, my friend," he said, "I have a lot of work to do. You have been given all the reassurance you asked for, so run along and sign the oath!"

"But, monsieur, I can't see that I have been given any reassurance at all. I haven't understood your reasoning."

"Well, then, what you had better understand," he said sharply, losing his patience at long last, "is that I have no time to waste on a junior officer who wants to make trouble!"

His tone now was not soothing, so I got up my courage and fired a personal question at him. "The wording of this enlistment oath —you seem to approve of it, monsieur. By any chance, was it you who drafted it?"

This might have made him really angry. But no, he got to his feet, raised, not his two arms as before, but only one, in a gesture of appeasement. After a moment's silence he said, more or less: "When your house is on fire, do you look to see whether the firemen are using filtered water to put out the blaze? We found ourselves in a situation of some urgency. We did the best we could. You mustn't attach importance to unimportant things."

"Good! Then I will not sign the paper, since you tell me that it doesn't matter."

"But that is not what I said! What matters is that you should behave like everybody else. How stubborn can a man be!"

Our discussion came to nothing. Nevertheless, I say again that Professor Cassin is a good and worthy man, and a most eminent man as well. And I admit that he too was bent on my salvation. When he let me go, he said, "The night brings good counsel. Go and think things over calmly. You are young. You have let your feelings run away with you. Come back and see me tomorrow. We will work it all out, and you, my boy, will remain in our ranks."

I did think things over, and next day I went back to see him full of hope.

"I will sign," I told him, "but I would like to write in, above my signature, the formula employed in the Navy, namely that I will undertake to obey any order that is given me 'for the good of the service and the success of the arms of France.' That is restrictive: for, if in good conscience a man considers that an order is not 'for the good of the service and the success of the arms of France,' he can most certainly be put in irons, but not for breaking his oath. He can be shot, but not as . . ."

The professor did not let me finish. Then I saw that the man before me was not the same as the night before. There had been a change. And what a change! The reason for it? I think I know it, but I have no evidence to put forward.

His voice was glacial as he bit off these words: "*You are to sign exactly the same oath as the others, you are not to add or subtract a single word!*"

I picked up my white cap from his mahogany console table and walked out of Carlton Gardens. It was September 20.

September 23–25, 1940

Some days later I was to learn, from the sorry outcome of his expedition, just where General de Gaulle had gone. It was to Dakar, accompanied by a formidable English fleet. He carried with him, he tells us in his memoirs, the fortunes of France. To use his own dramatic words: "Out in the open, in black night, on the swell of the ocean, a poor foreign ship with no guns [the Dutch liner *Westerland*], with all *lights extinguished*, was carrying the fortunes of France." [1] If his ship had gone to the bottom, and he with it, the fortunes of France would still lie there. As François Mauriac said of the General: "*Sa chance a été notre chance*"—"His fortune was our fortune."

[1] De Gaulle: *Memoirs*, I, p. 119.

At Dakar, however, fate or fortune—as you will—gave him the back of her hand.

In the early morning hours of September 23, Governor-General Pierre Boisson, holding the command at Dakar in the name of Marshal Pétain, learned from his radio that the base was about to be attacked, not by the Germans, needless to say, but by the British with a powerful naval squadron counting in it an aircraft carrier and transports with Free French and British troops. It was 6 a.m. when he heard this. General de Gaulle, speaking on the Dakar wave length from his "poor foreign ship," was summoning him to rally to Free France or to hand over his command *or* to face an all-out attack by "large Allied forces." The Governor declined to rally *or* to hand over Dakar to Free France and gave orders to fire on General de Gaulle's truce officers and to offer total resistance in the Marshal's name.[2]

Three days of intermittent battle followed, in which HMS *Resolution* was disabled by a torpedo, the Vichy French destroyer *Audacieux* and the submarines *Persée* and *Ajax* were sunk, still more damage was done to the *Richelieu*, and some hundred civilians were killed and two hundred wounded. Thereupon, the attack was called off.

[2] *General de Gaulle before Dakar, September 23, 1940*

"We are here to defend Dakar with you; we are here to bring food to Dakar," General de Gaulle quoted on leaflets dropped on Dakar.

(1) Over the radio, at 6 a.m., de Gaulle demanded to be allowed to land freely at Dakar and indicated that "if all goes well" the "powerful English squadron" and the "numerous British troops" which accompanied him would not open fire.

(2) At 7:07 a.m., he threatened that "if such opposition continues," the "enormous Allied Forces" with him would "enter into action."

(3) At 10:20 a.m., he issued the following ultimatum: "Free French Forces facing Dakar. The authorities at Dakar have refused to negotiate with the officers I sent them. The *Richelieu* and the Battery of Gorée have fired on the *Savorgnan de Brazza*, the *Commandant-Duboc*, and the *Commandant-Dominé*. The French ships and the troops which accompany me should return [sic] to Dakar and, if there is resistance, the large allied forces which follow me will take over matters on their own account."

Governor Boisson replied: "France entrusted Dakar to me. I will defend Dakar to the end. I leave you the responsibility for bloodshed."

The idea for this ill-fated expedition was General de Gaulle's, he tells us; it was late in July that he broached it to the Prime Minister, and on August 3 Churchill gave his approval. General de Gaulle had envisaged an attack by Free French forces overland, with troops landed at Conakry in French Guinea far to the south, which would advance through the interior along roads and a railway leading to the West African capital. But the British objected that this would mean immobilizing their covering warships for weeks, even months, in view of the obvious determination of the Vichy regime to defend its African possessions to the limits of its naval strength.

They would try it head-on then. Churchill was quick to see the advantages: Dakar, a huge prize in itself and a base for Britain's antisubmarine defense; the great battleship *Richelieu*, sorely needed with the Germans rushing to complete the *Bismarck* and the *Tirpitz*; the French, Belgian, and Polish gold bullion stored at Bamako, in the French Sudan; and French West Africa under Gaullist rule, a shield against German penetration from Dakar, about which the British governor of Nigeria had been having nightmares.

But would this adventure provoke Pétain into active hostilities? The Prime Minister has said that he felt in his fingertips that it would not. He later wrote that they "certainly had bad luck." Much of this bad luck came before Governor Boisson opened fire.

First, there had been a breakdown in security in bars and restaurants in Liverpool. Free French soldiers in tropical uniforms had openly raised their glasses in toasts to Dakar. Second, three Vichy French cruisers, fast, modern ten-thousand-ton vessels of the *Georges Leygues* class, and three light cruisers had slipped by Gibraltar, heading south. Though the British had been given advance notice by the Vichy attaché in Madrid, and by various secret agents, nothing was done to stop them. This was due to a series of incredible errors which later provoked a near scandal in the Admiralty, but by then the damage had been done. Joined by the *Primauguet* from Casablanca, the vessels put into Dakar, where they presumably landed marine gunners of undoubted loyalty to the Marshal to man the batteries, and then headed south, bound for

Libreville, to force the dissident colonies of Central Africa back
into line. They were intercepted by the British and turned back
but two cruisers went on to Casablanca. The other ships moored at
Dakar. Regardless of whether the Vichy French had been informed of the expedition in advance, they knew then.

Third, on the morning of September 23, when the Anglo-French
armada closed in on Dakar, not only was there no surprise but
there was no bright sunlit sea on which they could be viewed in all
their might by the citizenry and the garrison. There was a heavy
fog.

There was still another element, which was less bad luck than
miscalculation. Dakar was commanded by a very prickly customer.
Governor Boisson was a veteran of World War I, in which he had
lost a leg. He had been promoted to French West Africa after
being ousted from the French Congo by a Gaullist *coup*. Of the
extreme Right, he was, however, one of that breed of French
Rightists who could not bear the Germans. There were no Germans at all in Dakar, and this fact could have been attested to, as it
was shortly, by the new American Consul, who had arrived but had
not yet had time to report. Governor Boisson was deeply loyal to
Marshal Pétain and the whole Vichy concept. He knew full well
that a failure to put up a wholehearted defense to hold Dakar
would surely bring the Germans down into all of French North
Africa.

His reaction on hearing General de Gaulle's broadcast at six that
morning was predictable. He would not rally; he would not cede
his command; he would fight. British planes flew overhead dropping leaflets: *We have come to defend Dakar alongside you; we
have come with food supplies for Dakar*. He ordered the ack-ack
batteries to fire, and fire they did. Two naval launches flying white
flags entered the harbor with truce officers intending to hand the
Governor a written version of General de Gaulle's ultimatum. The
base commander, Admiral Landriau, who met them at the pier,
ordered them to leave and then, changing his mind, tried to have
them arrested. They leaped back into their launches and sped
away, followed by a burst of machine-gun fire, in which two of

them, Commandant d'Argenlieu and Commandant Perrin, were wounded.

General de Gaulle then broadcast in even more menacing terms. The *Richelieu,* the other warships in the harbor, and the forts opened fire. The British did not at first fire back, but when the HMS *Cumberland* was hit, Admiral Cunningham radioed: "Why are you firing on me? I am not firing on you." The answer was: "Retire to twenty miles' distance!" (Later, one of the English officers with the expedition remarked: "That is exactly what we would have answered in a comparable situation.")

The British thereupon fired several broadsides, but nobody on either side seemed to have much heart for this, the second armed clash between Frenchmen and Englishmen, counting Mers-el-Kebir, since Waterloo. Nevertheless, one French submarine was sunk, one destroyer was set on fire, and two British destroyers were damaged.

That night Churchill radioed from London: ". . . Stop at nothing!"

A new ultimatum next morning was rejected by the doughty Governor. Cannonades, exchanged in the fog, did a fair amount of damage. The *Richelieu* caught a fifteen-inch shell, the *Barham* was hit but not badly damaged, and a French submarine was forced to surface and surrender. On board Admiral Cunningham's flagship, the *Barham,* de Gaulle and the Admiral conferred that night. The General states in his memoirs[3] that they agreed to call off the attack and that the Admiral was to announce that he was halting the bombardment "at the request of General de Gaulle." But, during the night, the Admiral changed his mind, having received a fresh admonition from Churchill, who was worried about the political reactions in London and Washington to the triumphant broadcasts from Vichy and Berlin.[4]

The next morning, on the twenty-fifth, the fog was lifting, but the commander in Dakar put up a smoke screen which Churchill

[3] De Gaulle: *Memoirs*, I, p. 126.
[4] This is the version given by de Gaulle; it does not entirely check with Churchill's.

says "baffled our aim." Then the *Resolution* caught a torpedo from the French submarine *Bévesiers,* and, in danger of sinking, had to be taken in tow. Four planes from the *Ark Royal* were shot down.

From London came orders to break off. "It was obvious," wrote Churchill later, "that Dakar would be defended to the death." Looking back, one cannot help but feel that this should have been obvious all along. Says General de Gaulle: "Admiral Cunningham decided to cut the losses. I could not but agree." [5]

Vichy retaliated with a not overly zealous attack by air on Gibraltar, though not with a declaration of war. But, as Sir Samuel Hoare, the British Ambassador to Spain, pointed out to London, this was not what was wanted, to bring the war over Gibraltar.

The *Bévesiers* was commanded by an officer by the name of Lancelot. I mention this because he was later my commanding officer on the light cruiser *Le Terrible* in the naval operations covering the Allied landings in 1943, when he was of course under British orders. Introducing himself at Bizerte to Admiral Cunningham, he said, "I am the fellow who torpedoed the *Resolution.*"

"Good shot!" replied the Englishman.

General de Gaulle showed none of this spirit in his later dealings with Governor Boisson. In 1942, when the Allies landed in North Africa without General de Gaulle, the Governor received them with open arms, on Admiral Darlan's command. Subsequently, when de Gaulle came to power in Algiers and had Governor Boisson under his thumb, he had him thrown in prison. This was in spite of the vigorous protests of President Roosevelt and Churchill, who had both promised the Governor protection. All they could do for him was to have him given a more comfortable cell. I do not know whether he is still alive or died in disgrace.

---

[5] De Gaulle: *Memoirs,* I, p. 127.

"And I, in my narrow cabin, in a harbor crushed by the heat, was completing my education in what the reactions of fear could be, both among adversaries taking revenge for having felt it and among allies suddenly alarmed by a setback. . . . Admiral Cunningham told me expressly that we must give up the idea of resuming the affair in any way whatever." Ibid., pp. 128–30. (This statement does not coincide with the statement that the bombardment was stopped "at the request of General de Gaulle.")

October 1940

While all this was going on at Dakar, in London we had been experiencing some changes. The bombings had begun; by this I mean the bombings by night. The Germans were now attempting not only to destroy the great city but to break the nerve and courage of its people. Depriving them of sleep was one of the surest means to this end. Every night at dusk, and I mean absolutely every night, the sirens would wail, that "banshee wailing" Churchill complained about. Within thirty minutes, the bombs would begin to fall. Wave on wave of German planes came over, all night long, right until dawn. Looking back through my diary, I note with astonishment undiminished by the years that on *every night* from September 7 to November 3 an average of two hundred bombers were sent over London, there to drop their lethal cargoes. Every night great tongues of flames licked the clouds.

In the first weeks, the antiaircraft defense was not well organized. There were very few night fighters, and as radar was still in its early stages, they were not very effective. And there were not enough ack-ack batteries. Because of the raids on provincial cities, a high percentage of London's antiaircraft artillery had been sent to meet the need elsewhere. Only ninety-two guns were available throughout the whole vast area. There were nights when London simply had to take it without answering back. Even with the batteries they had, gunners were warned of the danger of bringing down their own night fighters. Then a wise decision was taken. The night fighters were not accomplishing much; therefore, they would be kept out of the way and the antiaircraft gunners would fire at will into the night sky even when they had no target in their sights or had not been advised of planes actually in their sectors. Within twenty-four hours, the number of batteries was doubled, and with English night fighters out of the way, they threw up a tremendous barrage. This may not have brought down so many German bombers, but the fearful uproar from the blazing guns proved to be something of a comfort to Londoners. At least they felt that they were no longer having to take it sitting down.

The news of the setback at Dakar came during the worst of this and was badly received in the Commons. The Members of Parliament had absolute freedom even in the midst of the war to criticize the way it was being conducted. And they were not exactly sparing in their use of this freedom, whether in the lobbies or in secret sessions or in public ones. What the devil was General de Gaulle doing at Dakar with a British fleet? The Germans were not there. Why did England want to run the risk of war with Marshal Pétain's France? Was England in need of still another enemy? Why another drama like Mers-el-Kebir, with elements of civil war to complicate it further? Could Hitler's wiliest agents dream of anything more delightful than to have the British and the French fleets destroying each other? And if the landing at Dakar had succeeded and had triggered—as it surely would have—a German invasion of all of French North Africa, what was Great Britain prepared to do about it? Were the British prepared even to fend off the Germans from their own White Cliffs? Furthermore, how had so many indiscretions been allowed to take place in advance of the expedition? Churchill's opposition, albeit a loyal one, here touched on a sensitive spot. Why not replace General de Gaulle with someone else? Why not, to be exact, replace him with a serious, highly esteemed French general with five stars to his credit who had just then reached London? He was General of the Army Georges Catroux and he had come from Indochina, where he had served as governor-general until the arrival of the Japanese and his replacement by Vichy. Obviously, he could not have been in England by June 17, the date on which General de Gaulle had made his historic decision "to climb to the heights." Was there not still time to entrust him with the task of creating a French army, just as Admiral Muselier was so successfully organizing the Free French Navy?

Churchill, however, was already committed to de Gaulle, and he would not abandon him. His sense of loyalty was absolute. All the responsibility for the setback at Dakar, he took on his own shoulders. When reproached with having involved himself too deeply with de Gaulle, Churchill answered that the General's conduct and bearing had been superb and "had made my confidence in him greater than ever." A number of Members of Parliament thought and said that Churchill was hurting himself by this attitude. They were apprehensive, many said, over the criteria on which the Prime Minister based a renewal of confidence in the General after the failure of the expedition, which they considered to have been in all respects ill-advised from the start.

Eyebrows were raised abroad, too. In Washington, Roosevelt took a highly critical view of both Churchill and de Gaulle, considering that the first had been too quick to commit himself and that the second had taken a plunge into "civil war." (These were his words.) The President was never to revise his unfavorable estimate of General de Gaulle, first formed after Dakar, nor was it ever to vary, regardless of the fluctuations during the next four years in the General's apparent chances for ultimate success in France.

As for General Catroux, he had just reached London. There he found waiting for him a letter from General de Gaulle.[1] This letter

---

[1] *Extract from General de Gaulle's letter to General Catroux*

29 August 1940

Mon Général:
    You cannot imagine with what joy I learned of your arrival . . . in the near future.
    . . . As soon as we are able to grapple with North Africa, "someone" will have to take it on. This someone will be you, *mon Général*, if you are willing.
    You know that the British Government, after having recognized me as "Leader of the Free French," has agreed in advance to deal with an "Overseas France Defence Council," should I form one, on all questions concerning the defence and economic life of our Empire. Such is in fact my intention. I ask you, *mon Général*, to agree to take the "North Africa" place on this Council.
    . . . As soon as we had a footing in Morocco, or in Algeria, could you perhaps . . . proceed to the spot, to administrate and command the Morocco-Algeria-Tunisia bloc? . . .
    You will form an opinion on Admiral Muselier. He has been criticised: he has his defects, but qualities also. At bottom he is a fine fellow. Obviously, I

is of special interest because it contains proof, if any is needed, that General de Gaulle never had, never would have, the slightest intention of giving way to any general officer senior to him or higher in rank. The mission he had conferred upon himself, he intended to direct himself until the end. General Catroux was reminded in this letter that Churchill had recognized de Gaulle as Chief of the Free French. The post offered General Catroux was a subordinate one; he was to become Administrator and Commander-in-Chief in North Africa, if and when these territories rallied to the cause of Free France.

What were General Catroux's personal reactions to all this? I would not attempt to define them. But Pierre Maillaud went to see him in London and asked what his relationship with General de Gaulle was to be. And General Catroux replied, "Collaboration, yes; subordination, no."

In the letter to General Catroux, General de Gaulle, referring to Admiral Muselier, said, "He is a fine fellow," and added: "Obviously, I would have preferred to see Darlan come over with his fleet." Admiral Darlan might have come over to the Allies sooner, with his entire fleet; however, those who knew him agree that the very prospect of being under General de Gaulle would have been sufficient to deter him.

Inevitably, as a result of Dakar, Free French volunteers began to complain that they had not joined up to square off against other Frenchmen. They were told in reply that the attack on Dakar had been due to "incessant infiltrations of Germans" and that the French authorities there had opened fire under German pressure (an affirmation dishonoring Governor Boisson). They were further informed that General de Gaulle had not wished to take part in any fighting, "to keep his promise to spare his soldiers any hostile action against fellow Frenchmen." The General took care not to reveal on this occasion the existence of the secret agreement.

---

would have preferred to see Darlan come over with his fleet, but Darlan did not come. . . .

De Gaulle: *Memoirs*, Documents (1940–42), pp. 33–4.

Throughout the war, every time I spoke to volunteers about the existence of this secret agreement, they accused me of spreading a monstrous calumny. Finally General de Gaulle himself published the text in his memoirs, when it became necessary for his explanation that he had waged war on other Frenchmen in Syria because they were not obeying the true France.[2]

Anne had been very happy when she learned that I had finally joined the ranks of *la France Libre,* as it was beginning to be called. At the start she did not adore the General either. But then she began to feel that he did us honor. She also thought his politics were not that bad: her ideas are of the Right, royalist for that mat-

---

[2] *How General de Gaulle's propaganda on the Dakar affair was presented*

A communiqué from the Free French Forces, published in *France,* September 27, 1940
  "The Headquarters of the Free French Forces informs us:
  'General de Gaulle knew that the great majority of the population was determined to join the cause of Free France. But for some time there was an incessant infiltration of Germans in Dakar . . . and so it was that General de Gaulle found himself suddenly faced with a new situation which provoked the combats in which he had not wished to participate in view of his promise that his men would not have to fight fellow French soldiers. It is known that, under pressure by the Germans, the authorities at Dakar opened fire. . . .
  '. . . The operation at Dakar proves clearly that if there is indeed a leader who is determined above all else not to shed French blood and to preserve his arms to fight Germany, it is General de Gaulle. . . .' "

Declaration on the radio by General de Gaulle's spokesman

  ". . . Father d'Argenlieu was leading this crusade as a priest, without arms, when he fell, gloriously wounded by hands that were seemingly French. We say 'seemingly French,' for who armed and commanded those sacrilegious hands? Germany. . . .
  "It would appear that new reprisals are being prepared to punish the Free French for safeguarding the Empire for France. So much the better for the victims! And so much the worse for those who judge complacently. . . ."
Published in *France,* September 27, 1940.

Declaration of General de Larminat, issued by General de Gaulle's headquarters

  ". . . You have been betrayed by Pierre Boisson. . . . Tomorrow you will be sold out to the Boches at X . . . like hogs at a fair." Published by *France,* Saturday, October 5, 1940.

ter. At length she and her brother became Gaullists. That gave the three of us material for conversation in case we ever ran short.

It also explains why Anne was so annoyed when she got my letter saying that I would no more sign an oath of allegiance to General de Gaulle than I would to Marshal Pétain, and was therefore leaving the Free French. After Dakar she wrote me, "It was on the day after Dakar that you should have left the movement, not the day before!" This goes to show once again that people react to the same things differently. Her letter crossed one from me in which I said that, luckily, I had left General de Gaulle's movement *before* the setback at Dakar. Immediately after Dakar it would have been difficult to leave, I thought.

"Really," she replied, "we don't have a single idea in common." This shows how in marriage one can avoid boredom.

Admiral Muselier made no effort to break with de Gaulle because of the Dakar fiasco, but he was thoroughly exasperated by it. He considered that the whole expedition had been badly organized to begin with. And furthermore he had been outraged to learn that de Gaulle, on his departure from London, had left the real authority at Carlton Gardens not to him, his second in command and a general officer, but to the Triumvirate which I have already mentioned. Then, too, Muselier had discovered that his movements were being watched by a certain Meffre, recently appointed Security Chief at Carlton Gardens, whom the Admiral considered a crook. Muselier had tried to get Colonel Passy to put him aside, but Passy continued to back the man. And Meffre, aware that the Admiral had tried to have him removed from his job, began preparing his vengeance.

Meanwhile, relations between the General and Admiral Muselier were turning quite sour, even at a distance. Instead of returning directly from Dakar, the General went to French Equatorial Africa. He then ordered the Admiral to join him there, instructing him to leave his command to a General Eon, who had just joined the cause. General Eon's is a name to remember; it will appear again in these pages. Admiral Muselier and General de Gaulle had an exchange of cables that from bittersweet turned poisonous.

"Your present attitude gives me no satisfaction whatsoever," the General cabled. The Admiral in turn sent on some disagreeable truths: *"Recruiting in both navies* [Navy and Merchant Marine] *has stopped completely since Dakar!"*

A rumor circulated briefly around London that Admiral Muselier was accepting volunteers in the Free French Naval Forces without having them sign the enlistment oath binding them to the person of General de Gaulle. I rushed over to the General Staff headquarters of the FNFL (*Forces Navales de Françaises Libres*), as they were called. The rumor turned out to be untrue; it originated in an intention the Admiral had been unable to carry out.

I then tried to enlist in the Royal Navy or in the Canadian Navy. It was then that I was told that General de Gaulle had prevailed upon Churchill to give instructions that no French citizen be allowed to join any of the armed services of the Commonwealth. Frenchmen of military age who were in Great Britain were therefore confronted with this very narrow option: either they signed an oath that engaged them personally and on their honor to obey any and all orders of General de Gaulle, *or* they renounced all hope of fighting the enemies of their country.

It was, I think, the obligation to sign this personal oath to the General that explains why the corps of Gaullist volunteers was the smallest of any occupied country. On land, it never reached 25,000 actual combatants, and of this number, fewer than six thousand were ever in action against the Germans, and that on one occasion only, at Bir Hakeim. It was finally in 1943 that the oath to all intents was abolished, when the Army of Africa, which numbered close to a quarter of a million men, went back into combat, and the Navy too. But the oath was still in effect for the Secret Army[3] in Occupied France.

[3] *Report from General Delestraint, Commanding the Secret Army, to the National Committee in London*

France, June 10, 1943

"I have the honour to inform you of the text of order . . . which I have just given to the Secret Army. . . . This conforms to the directives of General de Gaulle. . . .

"The Secret Army is an army of volunteers, but all the members must con-

There was nothing I could do but go back to the Home Guard, where one night a week I reported to an ack-ack battery in south London. The worst thing was getting there through squalid neighborhoods and, at all too frequent intervals, whole rows of working-class homes reduced to rubble. Once I was behind the sandbags around our battery, it was better. Everything was shipshape, and our people were in high spirits—working long hours, going without sleep, but turning up on schedule to man the guns. We would wait for the signal. Yellow alert: enemy planes over the coast. Red alert: sirens, searchlights jabbing at the night sky. A little to the south of us a battery would open fire; then two batteries. The beams of the searchlights would pick up nothing. The telephone would ring; we were to aim at such and such a sector in the sky. (This was before radar and other devices created by the "wizards," as Churchill called them, became available.)

There was a tonic in the bang-thump of the Bofors firing and the click of the warm cartridges falling into the net beneath. Cease-fire! Fire! A plane would be caught in the beam of our neighbors' searchlight. It would seem very far away. And it would be the only plane I saw! Then, at dawn, when the throbbing of the last enemy planes could be heard fading into the south and east, the meager breakfast—but what a delight—slices of bread with margarine, and tea served very strong, with milk, in unbreakable mugs. One experienced a kind of remorse—at having spent the night playing a cruel game with the Germans, at the expense of the civilians. Later, with radar, the AA batteries became really effective at night, as did also the British night fighters. But at first all we seemed to be able to do was make a frightful uproar—which was comforting to many, or so we heard.

The thunder of the bombardments echoing in Scotland brought Anne back to London. She seemed almost well again. Her return, while a joy, brought a new worry: the bombs. I left the Maison de

---

sider themselves to be bound by a formal engagement. Only their necessarily clandestine character prevents them from signing on with the Fighting French forces. . . ." De Gaulle: *War Memoirs, Documents* (1942–1944) (New York: Simon and Schuster; 1959), p. 185.

l'Institut, and the two of us put up at a pension at Queen's Gate. That same day, Donald Monroe went away as special correspondent for Pierre Maillaud's news agency and was good enough to leave Anne his little family of white mice.

"They are superb!" she exclaimed. "I have never seen such pretty mice! Look how they already crawl up my arm!" She had opened the door of their wood and glass house, and, of course, the mice took off. We spent part of the night looking for them all over our pension bedroom. One of them had climbed to the top of the drapes, onto a window. While we searched, the bombs whistled down, exploding in reverberant thunder. The antiaircraft batteries roared quite near. Up on the curtain pole where it had sought refuge, the mouse trembled, and so did we.

Several days later, our friend M. Cru let us have a magnificent double room at the Maison de l'Institut. It was on the top floor, which did not really make it any more dangerous but made us more aware of the danger because of the chunks of shrapnel from the ack-ack fire which from time to time clattered down on the roof. We spent our nights in a most ridiculous way. The sirens began to wail at six in the evening. For a little while, life seemed normal enough. There would be dinner, which we took in common in the dining room, served ceremoniously by Tobin. Then we went to talk or play cards. M. Cru would come down to ask for volunteers to watch for incendiaries. "Who wants to go up on the roof with me?" He did not have much luck. Finally he had to organize roof-watching shifts. Things might go well enough until ten or eleven in the evening. Then, if you weren't on watch, you could go to bed. But where? It all depended. Up in our room, if things seemed calm in the neighborhood, Anne would say, "Quick, to bed!" If at bedtime the raid was at its height, it would be, "Let's go down to the shelter." It was a most excellent shelter. Cru, a veteran of the 1914–1918 war, had ordered it built in the little garden adjoining the house. It was vast, had electric lights and bunks. But you froze down there. If, later on in the night, the raid appeared to have dwindled, Anne was apt to say, "I'm freezing to death, let's go back to the room." Then there would be a new wave of bombers over the neighborhood, and Anne would say timidly, "It's idiotic to risk getting killed out of sheer laziness." So down we would go again. Then, regularly with the first light of dawn, the sirens warbled the All Clear, the most ravishing of melodies. Then we would have a delicious hour of untroubled sleep. Safety is like everything else; it is appreciated only when it is in rare supply.

Anne's suggestion that it was idiotic to get oneself killed out of laziness found its justification later (when we were no longer in London), during the baby blitz of 1944, on the day when everybody in the Maison de l'Institut was killed. By then the raids were few and far between and nobody left his room when the sirens sounded, always hoping it was an alert of no importance. The shelter in the little garden was still intact the last time I went by the site where the Maison had once stood. The Maison was smashed to bits and in the rubble grew rosebay and spiked purple loosestrife.

The occasions when it was wiser to go down to the shelter were the exception. Most of the time during bombardments, which went on for weeks and months, the sensible thing was not to budge from where one happened to be. Otherwise fatigue, lack of sleep, and fear, with the usual side effects when one gives way to it, combined to give the enemy just what he was after.

On the subject of fear and the opposite side of the coin, courage, there was a passage in an English novel called *The Adventures of Brigadier Gérard*, by an author whose name escapes me, that delighted General Jackson. It concerns an extremely brave Frenchman taken prisoner in Spain during the Peninsular War, or, as we would say in France, during the First Empire. He was in England free on parole and was given to perpetrating such outrages as hunting foxes with a gun. He boasted like a Gascon. "When it comes to courage," he would say, "one people is just like another, except that the French are perhaps a little more courageous than the others."

What is undeniable is that not all races have courage of the same kind. I see more abnegation and fatalism in the Russian and also perhaps the German, more passion and individuality in the Italian, more honor in the Spaniard, more gaiety in the French, a fierce anger in the American, coolness and humor in the English. There is something comfortable in the courage of the English. Their recipe would be this: it is good to resist fear because fear is disagreeable and can be dangerous. It is good to practice courage because courage is agreeable and sometimes very useful. This English recipe for courage prescribes that you shave every day and brush your clothes and shine your shoes.

In the morning, after a hectic night with bombers overhead, it was surprising to go out and see how relatively light the damage had been after all the uproar. The milkman from United Dairies, in white smock with blue collar, would come along whistling, to leave the milk bottles on the doorsteps. Here and there there would be a bomb crater, a house or two gutted, broken glass on the sidewalk, a street closed off with a DETOUR sign—not much for all the dreadful din of the night. Passers-by might be red-eyed, but they would have a smile on their lips. *More and more open,* read a sign on a shop whose façade had fallen into the street. Houses that caught direct hits were quickly covered by wooden palisades, so that you might well think they were in process of construction, not in ruins. The dead were removed so rapidly that mornings I never once saw a body.

It still seems almost incredible to me. In London there were more than fifty thousand dead. Later, in Naples, where there were not so many, I arrived a month after the Allied landings, yet I still had to step over the dead in the street when I went out in the morning. In London the decency with which bodies were promptly covered and the speed with which ruins were cleared away or concealed behind wooden boardings, and the manner in which people hid their grief, are examples of what I mean when I say that English courage is comforting. Think of the porter outside the club, imperturbable and resplendent as always with gold braid. The doorman with white gloves at the restaurant held his blue umbrella over the ladies getting out of their cars, to protect them from the cold winter rains now beginning. There were also bombs and fragments of shrapnel, but, even under bombardment, why dispense with an umbrella when it rains? I have heard of Englishmen who carried umbrellas in the trenches in World War I. Why not? They exposed themselves to being killed just as much as their comrades.

Coming home from their jobs, workmen, clerks would wait quietly in long lines—sometimes in the hundreds—to take the bus. Night would be closing in. The sirens would begin to wail; in less than ten minutes the bombs would fall. But the people waiting stayed in line. A bus arrived. Those waiting for that particular bus would step forth and form a second queue to get on the bus. Those for whom there was no room went back to their places. No little tickets of priority, as we have in France at bus stops. And the cheats? There were some. When they were found out, nobody tried to inflict bodily punishment. Caught, the offender would walk away like a man who has made a mistake, rather than face the scornful faces. Usually there was silence, but now and then one heard a joke. It was rarely about the raid; more probably it was about *l'amour*, about women. "Up with the lark and to bed with the WREN" remained a favorite, even though somewhat time-worn. I once heard a bus conductor tell a soldier, "You can't see in the dark, but up ahead there you'll find a seat next to a pretty girl!" The soldier found himself sitting beside an elderly clergyman. As for the pretty girls, they had quite a time. As Ambassador Corbin remarked early in the war, the blackout gave the English a chance to be free, even audacious, in ways that once they would only risk across the Channel.

General de Gaulle, refusing to look on Dakar for what it was, had gone on to the Cameroons, already rallied to Free France, and there disembarked. At Douala, the capital, he made his entry in triumph. The entire population was in a state of euphoria, he reports in his memoirs.[4] "The moral unity of the Free French . . . was instantly apparent. . . . The enthusiastic emotion I had just encountered: I was to find it again, always, in all circumstances, as soon as the crowd was present. I must say that for me its result was to be a perpetual bondage. The fact of embodying for my comrades the fate of our cause, for the French multitude the symbol of its

[4] De Gaulle: *Memoirs*, I, pp. 130–1.

hope, and for foreigners the image of a France indomitable in the midst of her trials, was to dictate my bearing and to impose upon my personality an attitude I could never again change. For me this meant, without respite, a stubborn self-supervision as well as an extremely heavy yoke."

In London at this period, Churchill had several personal interviews with General Catroux and arranged for him to look in on Cairo.[5] By telegram, General de Gaulle promptly called the Prime Minister to order, reminding him that only the Chief of the Free French could send his subordinates off on missions, whatever their purpose. Churchill immediately made his excuses: he had no intention, he said, of violating the agreement. But this incident opened his eyes.

It was in the pages of *France*, which faithfully printed, in quotes, all statements handed it by Carlton Gardens, that we learned the results of de Gaulle's travels. From Fort-Lamy he took himself to Brazzaville and there ordered the military advance on Gabon. There were many casualties, but victory went to the Free French. In London the operation, applauded by most of the press and criticized by a minority of Members of Parliament, provoked a certain

---

[5] *General Catroux as an alternative trump*

"When he had arrived in London, after my departure from Africa, certain experts on ulterior motives imagined that the British would try to make themselves an alternate trump card out of this full general accustomed to big posts, while certain sticklers for etiquette wondered if he himself would consent to serve under a mere brigadier. He had seen Churchill more than once. . . . It did seem that the Prime Minister had in fact suggested to him that he take my place . . . with the classic objective of dividing in order to rule. A few days before Dakar, Churchill had all of a sudden telegraphed me that he was sending Catroux to Cairo to work upon the Levant. . . . I had reacted sharply, not against the idea, which certainly did not seem to me to be a bad one, but because the initiative required my approval first. Churchill had then given a satisfactory explanation, on the ground of urgency. . . . (Catroux reached Douala from Cairo). . . .

"I raised my glass in honour of this great leader for whom I always had feelings of deferential friendship. He answered . . . that he placed himself under my direction. . . . All those present recognized . . . that, for Catroux, de Gaulle was from now on outside the ladder of rank and invested with a duty that knew no hierarchy. . . ." De Gaulle: *Memoirs*, I, p. 133.

amount of off-the-record comment about the fact that among the dead and wounded there was not a single German or Italian soldier.

October 27, 1940

I was at Le Petit Club Français in St. James's Place when I heard a French broadcast on the BBC announcing that General de Gaulle had created from Léopoldville a Council for the Defense of the Empire, which was to save the colonies for France. The BBC then gave the text of an ordinance in which the General, making use of the royal "we," said he spoke in the name of the French people and of the French Empire, and announced that he intended henceforth to exercise all the powers of a chief of state *and* of a prime minister. He was to use these powers with the assistance of a Council of Empire, but in fact the Council was a mere extension of his own person, for he himself would appoint its members.[1]

[1] *General de Gaulle's Declaration from Brazzaville over the BBC, October 27, 1940*

"*Français,*

"... Taking official note of the fact that the Free French constitute henceforth the sole guarantee of *la patrie*, I, their chief, am today setting up a Council for Defense of the Empire. This Council will rule, in the name of France, over all French territories which are fighting or which will fight, with all the powers of a war government.

"French officers, French soldiers, French citizens, ignominious leaders are in the process of surrendering the French Empire intact. Up and to arms!"

Then de Gaulle read the first ordinance. (In French, *ordonnance* evokes the idea of orders on sovereign authority, such as the famous ordonnances of Charles X which precipitated the July Revolution, 1830, and the advent of Louis-Philippe.) This official text of the broadcast was communicated by the general headquarters of the Free French Forces in London to the newspaper *France* and was published by it, naturally without change. One needs only to consult the version published by General de Gaulle in his memoirs to see

The day after the ordinance was published, I went to see Torcy. When I tried to talk about General de Gaulle, I found the subject irritated him. He preferred to talk about Greece, which had just been invaded by Mussolini's troops. However, as I was getting ready to leave, he said, "Comert in his *France* published in full and at length the proclamation of General de Gaulle, his ordinance, and the communiqué from Carlton Gardens. Without any comment at all, Comert has adopted this policy: his paper is to print absolutely everything that General de Gaulle says. And that is the worst service he can render the General."

Pierre Comert, who came to London in June 1940, was the founder-director of *France*, which had begun to appear several weeks earlier and during the entire war would keep the French in England abreast of everything that concerned our country. Many Englishmen read it too. Now and then in the camps of the Free French it was banned.

Comert was a graduate of the École Normale Supérieure. A great friend of Torcy's, he was very like him in his rectitude and generosity, but in other respects was not like him at all. He was youthful in appearance, svelte, and elegant, in marked contrast to Torcy, who is tall, stooped, and dressed carelessly. He was lively and brilliant, and Torcy is sober and pensive. As I said, they were both very generous men, but generous in different ways. Pierre Comert wanted to believe in everybody, with a sort of deliberate suspension of his critical faculties. Thus he saw in General de Gaulle the same intentions that inspired Joan of Arc, who with her sword meant to

---

that it does not conform to the first official text of the broadcast, which went as follows:

"In the name of the people of the French Empire, we, General de Gaulle, Chief of the Free French, command:

"*Article I*—For as long as there shall not have been constituted a French government representing the French people normally and free of the enemy, the public powers will be exercised in all parts of the Empire liberated from enemy rules, as follows:

"*Article 2*—The authority appertaining to the Chief of State and the Council of Ministers will be exercised by the Chief of the Free French assisted by a Council of Defense created by him."

drive out the invader, crown the Dauphin, but not herself reign in any manner, shape, or form. She wanted only to go back to Domremy—remember?

"My poor Comert," Torcy used to say, "I suspect that you are due to be disillusioned." And disillusioned he was. For before long the General began to show that he was displeased with the newspaper and its director. He reproached Comert for defending such noxious and outdated ideas as the strict separation of the three powers—executive, legislative, and judicial; the total independence of the judiciary in whatever circumstances; and the notion of Liberty, Equality, and Fraternity. The General himself had deleted from all official documents of Free France the motto *Liberté, Egalité, Fraternité*—just as Marshal Pétain had done in Vichy, where the words were replaced by *Travail, Famille, Patrie.*

Comert had arrived from France with a staff of extremely able journalists, who stayed with him to edit the newspaper. I saw them often, and I count the friendship of Pierre Comert as one of the greatest pieces of good fortune that life has given me. His days in London were darkened by grief; his wife Janet MacWade, American by origin but French by marriage, had been interned in a German concentration camp. There was no news of her at all. When she was at long last freed, her health had been seriously affected.

End of October 1940

At the war's end, Pierre Comert presented me with a complete file of *France*. As a source of documentation on de Gaulle's activities, the file of *France* is all the more precious because the General was given to retouching his own texts now and then. He would cut out things that had appeared in the original or would introduce passages that had not appeared.

An example of the latter practice comes to mind, although in this case *France* was not involved. In his prewar book entitled **Vers** *l'Armée de métier* (*The Army of the Future*), the General called for the creation of a professional army and the massive employment of tanks; he was among the pioneers there. He did not, however, make any mention whatsoever, in his prewar text, of the tactic that was to give the Germans victory in the Battle of France: the *simultaneous use* of tanks and planes, the latter operating as dive bombers machine-gunning and bombing the adversary at the lowest possible level. It must be said that the English, themselves the inventors of the tank, did not think of this either. It was a German idea. However, in London, after the armistice, when the French Army had already been crushed, General de Gaulle brought out a new edition of his book in which he proceeded to say that, along with tanks, planes should be utilized, firing at almost point-blank range; *in other words, dive bombers.*

In the original edition, published in France in 1934, we read: ". . . Ground forces, particularly armored units, will receive valuable support from planes in the way of camouflage. Smoke released in the air will in minutes hide large ground areas, and the noise of the airplane engines will cover that made by the engines of the tanks.

"Inversely, cooperation with assault units will demand from the planes only a brief and concentrated effort. . . ." [1]

In the London edition, published, I repeat, after the defeat in France, where the German technique of combining tanks and Stuka attacks was used to frightful effect, we read: ". . . Ground forces, particularly the armoured units, will receive valuable support from the planes in the way of camouflage. Smoke released in the air will in minutes hide large ground areas, and the noise of the airplane engines will cover that made by the engines of the tanks. *But especially by themselves, attacking at close range and in depth, the planes become par excellence the arm whose lightning effects can best be combined with the capacities of the large mechanized units for breaking through and exploiting* [the breakthroughs]. . . .

[1] *Armée de métier*, p. 168.

"Inversely, cooperation with assault units will demand from the planes a brief and concentrated effort, *which is to say, that best suited to the character of the aerial army.* . . ." [2]

The English edition appeared in November 1940, and naturally, coming so soon after the Panzers had rolled back the Allied armies in France, it caused a considerable stir. As I remember, not one reviewer stumbled onto the difference between the new and the old edition: the addition of the seemingly prescient observation about the use of dive bombers. Quentin Reynolds was in London at that time, very much in London. In his *A London Diary*[3] he notes the impression the book made on him. "In the light of what had happened, it makes fascinating reading," he said, and repeated the notion then almost universally held: "No one read the book much—except the German High Command." Certainly the French General Staff should have taken it more seriously. As they should have taken, some ten years before, the same theory, then put forth by General Estienne. We should have had many more tanks and used them more intelligently.

The fact remains, however, that de Gaulle *did not* prescribe the use of dive bombers acting in concert with armored spearheads, and whatever the German command may have learned from him, it was not about the use of dive bombers along with Panzers. The General's willingness to add to his text, and thus, in retrospect, to enhance his already considerable reputation as a military genius and prophet besides, is interesting indeed. There is not the slightest hint in the English edition that the original French text has been improved upon.

This business of the ex post facto emendations to the text of *Vers l'Armée de métier* may strike some people as being of slight importance. They would be ignoring the danger facing the adherents of a corrupt form of Gaullism, a form de Gaulle himself could hardly fail to warn against. For the General, as everyone knows, is a

[2] Italics are the author's, and indicate the passages that first appeared in the London edition. (Translated here from the French of that edition.)

[3] Quentin Reynolds: *A London Diary* (New York: Random House; 1941), p. 210.

Catholic, was raised by priests, goes to Mass, and is a devout believer. He could scarcely fail to reprove the teachings of Father Molina and Father Escobar, which have been condemned by the Church. The practice of the doctrines preached by these two men is likewise contrary to the moral standards of our day. Few have done more harm to the public welfare by their deceptions than these Fathers.

And who were they? Father Escobar was a notable Spanish casuist of the early seventeenth century whose life work came to eighty-three volumes. As a member of the Society of Jesus, he labored so mightily and so well that for a long time the word "Jesuit" was a synonym for "hypocrite." He was one of the ablest proponents of the maxim that the end justifies the means. He was also an advocate of the doctrine of mental reservations, by virtue of which a Christian, for instance, to save his life when captured by Mohammedans, may swear, without sin, that he is embracing Islam. He swears, but, as he does so, he makes a mental reservation—crosses his fingers, so to speak. The morality of a given action lies then not in the deed but in the *moral intention*.

Father Luis Molina was also a Jesuit and taught at Évora and Coimbra. He was the author of the famous *La Concordia,* in which he sought to reconcile the Catholic doctrines of the efficacy of God's grace and of man's free will. His teachings were never condemned but they occasioned a heated dispute between the Jesuits, who sided with him, and the Dominicans. Later the Jansenists at Port-Royal took up the fight and soon found themselves under a thick barrage of fire, the Jesuits asserting all too effectively to Pope Urban VIII and his successor Innocent X that Jansenism was a form of Calvinism.

The young Blaise Pascal entered the lists in behalf of the Jansenists, championing their cause in his *Provincial Letters.* In perhaps the finest French prose ever written, he delivered a brilliant attack —sarcastic, stinging, and perhaps not altogether fair—on the extravagances of casuists such as Molina and Escobar, whose great talent was being devoted to the elaboration of specious subtleties in defense of wrong actions and wrong ideas.

Everyone who has read the *Letters* is familiar with Pascal's technique: A Parisian is writing to inquire how a man can get ahead in life by devious means, without, however, slipping into mortal sin. For instance, he wants to know how a man is to go about making others believe that he thinks the opposite of what he really thinks and is going to do the opposite of what he intends to do, all this without throwing himself open later to charges of having been guilty of deception.

Why, of course, he is told, by the doctrine of equivocations! His correspondent then goes on: "I would now say a little about the facilities we have devised for avoiding sin in worldly conversation and intrigue. One of the most embarrassing things is the need to refrain from lying, particularly when one is anxious to induce a belief in something that is false. In such cases, our doctrine of equivocations has been found to render admirable service. According to this doctrine, as Sanchez puts it, 'it is permitted to use ambiguous terms, leading people to understand them in another sense from that in which we understand them ourselves.'"

"I know that already, Father."

"We have published it so often that at long last, it seems, everybody knows of it. But do you know what is to be done when no equivocal words come to mind?"

"No, Father."

"I thought as much. This is something new, sir: I mean the doctrine of mental reservations. 'A man may swear,' as Sanchez says, 'that he never did such a thing (though he actually did it), meaning within himself that he did not do so on a certain day, or before he was born, or understanding any other circumstance, while the words which he employs have no such sense as would discover his meaning.' And this is very convenient in many cases, and quite innocent when necessary or conducive to one's health, honor, or advantage!

"Our doctors have taught, in the same passage, for the benefit of such as might not be expert in the use of these reservations, that no more is required of them, to avoid lying, than simply to say that 'they have not done' what they have done, provided 'they have, in general, the intention of giving their words the sense which a *crafty man* would give them.' "

. . . .

"And will you not also acknowledge that it would often prove very convenient to be absolved in conscience from keeping certain engagements one may have made?"

"The most convenient thing in the world!" answers the young Parisian.

"Listen, then to the general rule laid down by Escobar: 'Promises are not binding when the person, in making them, had no intention of binding himself. Now, it is seldom that anyone has this intention except if he confirms his promises by an oath or contract; so that when a man simply says, "I will do it," he means he will do it if he does not change his mind; for he does not wish, by saying that, to deprive himself of his liberty.' Escobar gives other rules in the same vein—you may consult them for yourself—and tells us, in conclusion, 'that all this is taken from Molina and our other writers, and is settled beyond all doubt.' "

Nothing is of timelier interest than these passages from the ninth of the *Provincial Letters*. The words have a political significance that could not have been foreseen in Pascal's time. Why? Because under a democratic system the people must be accurately informed if they are to exercise their powers of choice; if they are misinformed and deceived, the system breaks down. This should be self-evident.

Montesquieu put this idea in another way; he said that a despotic regime is based on fear, on force, and on the lie; that the absolute monarchy, if it has an aversion to the truth, if it lacks the motive power of virtue, had another, namely, honor; and that the democratic regime has need of a higher motivation, which is virtue.

The greatest of the more or less official French authors now alive is François Mauriac, who is at one and the same time a subtle casuist and a devout man. In patent contradiction of the ideal set forth by Montesquieu, he writes that "men must be deceived or at least misled, if they are to be saved." He asks himself whether the means employed in politics should not derive from the Christian conscience, and his answer is, indeed they should.

Right! Indeed they should! But the discrepancy between François Mauriac and Montesquieu is nevertheless striking and it bears directly on the question that the French people must answer. There cannot be two moralities, one that is permissible in the accumulation, in this world, of power and of honors and another to gain the Kingdom of Heaven.

Work, I was able to find easily enough: translations, articles for the papers, and broadcasts over the BBC twice weekly on the program called "Les Français parlent aux Français" (Frenchmen Speak to Frenchmen). This paid a guinea a minute, and a guinea of that time was worth two of today's. In other words, we had enough to live on. This was true of nearly all the French who found refuge in London. From every point of view—freedom, risks, rationing—we were privileged in respect to our compatriots at home. This realization suggested to me an article that I called "Les Privilégiés" (The Privileged), which ran in the newspaper *France*. An uproar ensued at Carlton Gardens. The Gaullists ensconced there liked to think of themselves as heroes, even as pariahs, which the General said they all were.

The truth of the matter is that the personnel at Carlton Gardens was very well paid and most admirably nourished. The mess, the canteens, the clubs of the Free French Forces enjoyed a deserved renown in London both as to quality and as to abundance. The salaries and expense accounts of the upper-ranks Gaullists permitted them to enjoy exquisite repasts in de luxe restaurants, nearly all of which were run by Frenchmen. The menus consisted of such unrationed items as game, caviar, *foie gras*, and champagne as long as there was any to be had. The Gaullists would invite each other to these places. Sometimes, ingenuously, they invited Englishmen, without realizing the reactions they thereby provoked.

Many an eyebrow was raised at the spectacle of these would-be ministers of some future French government having a high old time on borrowed money, pounds sterling that France would one day have to return, while rationing was so rigorous all around them in England and something very like famine prevailed in much of France. Torcy was sick with shame over it. He himself made a point of going only to working-class restaurants. "He's a penny-pincher," was the comment of certain Gaullists.

General de Gaulle, with more self-respect than was usually displayed by his associates, and also more intelligence, served his guests only the most frugal meals. The Operations Staff of our Navy likewise behaved with decency. The General, among his other qualities, had a sense of dignity. And so did his family. One never heard talk about Mme de Gaulle, who lived quietly with her daughters. Young Philippe de Gaulle was a student at the École Navale, or what in England substituted for it. When the General was in England, he spent his weekends with his family and in London lived at the Connaught, a quiet luxury hotel in Carlos Place near Grosvenor Square.

I was now making enough so that we were thinking of moving back to our apartment, when the English offered me a job with which went both food and a roof. At Woburn Abbey, where I had gone with my friend Voigt in May, the various services had been greatly expanded to keep pace with Hitler's conquests on the Continent. We had to keep up on information from Holland, Belgium, Denmark, Norway, and, most importantly, France. We also had to provide news for the peoples whose countries had been invaded. (What they were given in their own papers, now under Nazi inspiration, was of course poisoned, often very cleverly.) The BBC, in its broadcasts in the languages of the occupied countries, handled about three quarters of our total output. The rest went out in printed form. The Royal Air Force, on night flights once a week, was to drop a small newspaper over France. I was asked to work with them to edit this paper. Torcy thought I should accept the offer, and he had several suggestions to make.

"Try to restrict yourself to news only, in your newspaper," he said. "No interpretations! Our compatriots in France need to be *informed* on what is taking place outside. They don't have to be counseled or guided. And try not to let them pay you too high a salary."

"But I hadn't thought of accepting any salary. I make enough money at my other work."

"I would be surprised if they agreed to let you work for nothing," he said. "It is not the custom among the English except in charitable activities. They might suspect that by working without pay you hope to put over propaganda of some kind, and that is precisely what must be avoided."

As Torcy had predicted, the English would not permit me to work for them without a salary. But they did agree that it should be as low as possible; it was to be the same as the salary drawn by the most junior clerk in the Foreign Office, not a princely sum. Anne naturally went along with me, and she was permitted to work without pay. I found that my English colleagues readily agreed with me: the newspaper and the leaflets we would edit would contain news only. And I could feel free to give up the work whenever I wished, and could even leave England, which was important to me. The promise given me then was scrupulously observed later on. I had only to swear, on my honor, not to divulge any secret matters that might be confided to me. However, I did ask that the oath should not apply in my relations with Torcy; no objections were raised, for the English were as confident of him as of themselves. This did not mean, however, that they took his advice. At the Foreign Office they would have been happy to listen to him. But not at Downing Street. There was a certain coldness between Torcy's family and the Churchills, the result of an old quarrel going back to the days of World War I. Churchill had been taxed with something like frivolity for his role in the ill-fated attack on the Dardanelles, and the word or words then used in his regard still rankled. But what mattered most of all was that Churchill was a Gaullist. Gaullist Number One after de Gaulle himself. Torcy was definitely not a Gaullist.

It was equally agreed that I could spend two days a week in London, but I found that after several months I had to give up my work at the BBC; in fact, I quit broadcasting entirely, for reasons that will shortly appear. By virtue of my new job, then, we became, paradoxically, worse off financially than we had been before. We were, however, lodged and fed, and fed miserably. There was rationing, of course, and this, together with that inborn English genius for bad cooking, had literally hair-raising consequences. We were housed, not in the Abbey itself, but in a charming and much more modern and comfortable dependency called Maryland. The Duchess had built it as a model clinic for the wives of the tenantry, choosing a site surrounded by lawns, flowers, and rare trees. She was the Duchess of Bedford who in her own plane and at the age of eighty took off alone on a flight from which she never returned. No trace was found of her or of the plane. If I remember rightly, it was in August of that year, 1940, that the old Duke followed her in death. The government had taken the opportunity of his demise to requisition all of Woburn.

They had their motives. All the Russells are a bit peculiar, which is a well known fact of English life. But their peculiarity is, so to speak, alternating: one generation will be warlike, even actively bellicose, and the next pacifist. The old Duke, a veteran of service in India, was as military as they come, and during his long lifetime the Abbey was run like a barracks. In consequence, the new Duke was a conscientious objector.

As Marquess of Tavistock (the title borne by the eldest son), he had been in every kind of trouble imaginable during World War I. On succeeding to his father's title and estates late in the summer of 1940, he came out for an immediate peace with Hitler. By so doing, he ran the risk of being cut to pieces by his tenants, but not of going to prison. Opinions can be held freely in England, except when they are proclaimed in wartime by activists of one breed or another—Sir Oswald Mosley, for instance. Churchill did, however, express a desire to spare the new Duke of Bedford the horrors of war over England, and it was suggested that the Duke might profitably spend his time salmon fishing in Scotland, where he had holdings. Thus the government was able to lay its hands on the entire ducal property for the duration: the immense park, the Abbey itself and all of its dependencies, the Orangerie, the Chinese dairy, the farmhouses, and a number of cottages in the village of Woburn and in the surrounding countryside.

The new Duke of Bedford could not block the requisitioning of the Abbey, but he managed to keep the government from taking down and melting the handsome ornamental grilles around the square and dwellings in London that belong to the Bedford family. They were to be melted down and made into cannon. Today they still stand in Bedford Square, Russell Square, Tavistock Square, Woburn Place, and all the streets in the capital which bear any of the family's names. In 1940, when his father ascended to the dukedom, Lord Howland, as the grandson in the direct line of succession is called, became the Marquess of Tavistock. He took an exactly opposite stance and, despite his bad health, volunteered for the duration of the war and served until illness forced his discharge. There is also the celebrated cousin, the philosopher Bertrand Russell, the third Earl Russell, who is a descendant of the fourth Duke of Bedford and of the first Earl, Sir John Russell, the Victorian Prime Minister. He is not quite the most conventional Englishman of his time. As nearly everybody knows, he is a pacifist of the first water and counsels that in the event of an atomic war Great Britain should let itself be destroyed, or invaded anyway, in all humility, without the slightest resistance. Besides having a fine mind, he is a very attractive person.

When we left London in the brand-new car lent us by Castellane, I felt a little like a deserter. Exactly at the moment of our departure, in fact just as I was feeling around for the starter, there was an air raid. We tumbled out of the car and huddled together against the wall at the back of the garage. We had been warned that Woburn was extremely exposed and would become a prime target if the Germans ever found out what was going on there. Actually, I think they knew all the time, although they made very few attempts to bomb it. An error? Some of the evil tongues among us said that the pamphlets drafted there to shower on Germany were so poorly done that Goebbels found them useful to the Nazi cause and so prevailed upon his friend Goering not to bomb us out. This good-natured sally contained an element of truth, to the honor of the

English: they are not the gifted propagandists they are so often made out to be.

November 1940

General de Gaulle was still in Africa, but he was expected not to delay his return to England. However, before going back to beleaguered London, he took steps *on French soil*, as he stated so emphatically, to crown his labors as a Builder of Empire by creating a new decoration.[1] He did this "in the name of the French

---

1 *Ordinance creating the Order of Liberation*

In the name of the French People and Empire,
>   We, General de Gaulle,
>   Leader of the Free French,

Having regard to our Ordinance No. 1 of 27th October, 1940, organising the public authorities during the war and instituting an Empire Defence Council;

Having regard to our Ordinance No. 5 of 12th November, 1940, defining the conditions in which the decisions of the Leader of the Free French shall be taken;

Ordain:

Article the First. There is created an Order called "Order of Liberation," whose members shall bear the title of "Companions of Liberation."

This Order is intended to reward those military and civil individuals or collectivities that shall have distinguished themselves in the work of the liberation of France and of her Empire.

Article 2. The sole insignia of this Order is the Cross of Liberation.

Article 3. Admission into the Order of Liberation is pronounced by the Leader of the Free French.

Article 4. The procedure for applying the present Ordinance shall be settled by decree.

Article 5. The present Ordinance shall be promulgated in the *Journal officiel* of Free France and, provisionally, in the *Journal officiel* of French Equatorial Africa.

>   Done at Brazzaville,
>   16th November, 1940
>   C. de Gaulle

De Gaulle: *Memoirs*, Documents (1940–42), p. 65.

people and of the French Empire." Again, he employed the royal
"we"—or, in French, "*nous*": "We, General de Gaulle," etc.

The new decoration was to be known as the Ordre de la Libéra-
tion, and those who received this high distinction were to be
known as *Compagnons*—that is, "Companions," certainly not
"Comrades."

Like the *Légion d'honneur*, created by Napoleon, the Cross of
the Liberation was awarded to authentic heroes and also to loyal
servitors within the house, so to speak. The first category were most
certainly not impelled to perform their valorous deeds by the prospect of the medal, or cross, of the new order; as for the second
category, by their devotion they won it a hundred times over.

Toward the end of November the General left behind him the
African sun, the euphoria he had found at Douala, the "atmosphere of tense excitement" in the Chad, a land on which, he says
in his memoirs, "the beam of History has just lighted." [2] On his
arrival in London, he found the English capital sad; "fog had settled about men's minds." And furthermore, he said, "I found the
British strained and depressed." This could only have been by
comparison with sunny and euphoric Africa. In fact, for the first
time in nearly two months, there were nights without alerts; Londoners felt with satisfaction that they had won a battle. "London
can take it!" they said with understandable pride. They were sleeping better. The *Luftwaffe*, powerless to break their morale, now
went for provincial cities. On November 14, there was a bombing
raid on Coventry so terrible that as a result the word "Coventry-
ize" came into the English language.

Later I went to see those frightful ruins. It was there, even better
than in London, that I understood just what the courage of English workmen really was. Coventry is almost exclusively industrial, a
city of metalworkers and mechanics. The women had stayed with
their men, though the children had long since been sent to the
country, to Scotland, even to Canada. Coventry was a city in the
very front line: not one house was intact, not one had a whole pane

[2] De Gaulle: *Memoirs*, I, p. 131.

of glass. The population found itself deprived of everything essential to the happiness of an English workman: the well-kept home,
the coal fire in the grate, mutton or beef for dinner, potatoes, eggs,
bacon, cigarettes, strong tea with milk and sugar, beer and gin.
Working eight to twelve hours a day in the factories, these men
and women had little meat, and that was poor; one egg a week;
slices of bread with margarine with their weak tea, very lightly
sweetened. Cigarettes were rationed. The beer was weak. As for the
gin, one never found any that was mellow. The gin that was sold in
the bars tasted like ether and could make you blind. It was said
that prodigious quantities of whisky had been destroyed in the
raids and also that what was left was being exported to America for
the dollars. In London one could no longer find it by the bottle.
The "whisky" by the drink in the bars was raw and of dubious
origin, possibly distilled in the cellar.

These workmen and the world of junior clerks, employees, and
the like, who comprise three quarters of the English people,
suffered much more from rationing than the well-to-do middle
classes and the aristocracy—not because of the money, however,
but because they lacked imagination. A miner, the operator of a
lathe, an English mechanic seemed to have no idea that a hare can
be cooked deliciously, or that mushrooms gathered in the forests,
or fish caught in the rivers (salmon and trout, however, were game
only during the season, and one needed a fishing license), are all
edible. He did not realize that you can put oil in the skillet instead
of lard.

The English workmen whom I saw were for all their misery and
deprivation not at all downhearted. If General de Gaulle went
through a period of depression that winter of 1940–1 on coming
back from Africa, it may have been because of the difficulties he
found facing him in London. The honeymoon with Churchill was
over. The Prime Minister was to remain a loyal friend, but he was
no longer a confident admirer. He had forgiven the General for
having mistakenly believed that success was possible at Dakar, but
he was upset by the realization that he had so far misunderstood de

Gaulle as to believe that he would efface himself before a man as
distinguished as, for instance, General Catroux. Churchill seemed
now, belatedly, to have discovered that de Gaulle really was identi-
fying himself with France; this was, of course, not something new
in de Gaulle. He had already shown how he felt when he declined
to recognize Admiral Muselier's seniority.

At the end of September, Marshal Pétain's ambassador in
Madrid, Count de la Baume, called on his British opposite number, Sir Samuel Hoare (later Lord Templewood), with a proposal for partially lifting the blockade on food supplies from North
Africa to the Unoccupied Zone. He did so apparently under orders
from Baudouin, who was still the Marshal's Foreign Minister.
Along with this idea, the eventuality of France's reentering the war
on Britain's side was envisaged, albeit tenuously.

"If, he said, we would allow unoccupied France, that then
seemed on the verge of starvation," wrote Templewood later, "to
maintain a limited trade with North Africa, the French Government would give whatever guarantee we needed against re-export
of African imports to Germany. . . ." American supervision was
proposed, and the Vichy Ambassador further states that *if* the
Germans laid hands on these supplies, *then* the Vichy government
would escape to Morocco and resume the war. Templewood at this
time felt that "we had much better pretend that Pétain is still alive
and allow the strong currents of anti-German feeling in France to
gather strength behind this mummy. If we do not do this, we shall
see occupied France treated like Czechoslovakia and have more
incidents like Dakar . . ."

Would Pétain actually have followed through on this? I would
not attempt even to guess. Perhaps he would have delegated his
powers to someone else. But if he had failed to do that, his bad
faith would have been made patent.

On October 19, Templewood was authorized to discuss the pro-
posal further. Meanwhile Churchill had loyally consulted de
Gaulle and asked his advice on what the answer should be. The
General quickly declared that *even if* the Vichy government

should one day reenter the war, it must nevertheless not be considered the government of France. He went on to say that Marshal Pétain did not have sufficient prestige to bring the French into the fight again on the side of England. And then he proposed that if the English government did authorize food shipments, they should make a public declaration that they were doing so at the request of General de Gaulle.[3]

Nothing came of the proposal. Very shortly, Count de la Baume was replaced, and his chief, Baudouin, gave way to Pierre Laval. However, the British services were unfavorably impressed by de Gaulle's advice that a man of prestige would have to be found if the French people were to be encouraged to fight again, and also

[3] From London on October 3, 1940, Churchill cabled de Gaulle, who was in Lagos, about a proposal emanating from Vichy asking the British to relax their naval blockade on food shipments from French colonies to Unoccupied France via Mediterranean ports, as follows:

"(I) On October 1st the French Ambassador in Madrid gave to His Majesty's Ambassador a message from M. Baudouin for communication to His Majesty's Government.

"(II) The message was to the effect that if the French Government was not to be driven entirely into German hands Great Britain must allow supplies from French colonies to pass to unoccupied France. If these supplies were allowed, the French Government would be prepared to arrange any necessary supervision and would give a guarantee that neither supplies nor the equivalent in France would be seized by the Germans. If the Germans made an attempt to seize them the French Government would be transferred to Morocco and France would be once again united with the United Kingdom against Germany. . . ."

General de Gaulle's cable reply to Churchill

Lagos, October 3, 1940

". . . Even if the Vichy Government moved one day, either in whole or in part, to North Africa and proclaimed their will to take up the fight again, they could have neither authority nor effectiveness enough for waging war. . . .

". . . It would probably be preferable to suggest to the Vichy Government that direct supplies should be made through assistance organisations in the United States, provided that adequate control should be established. In this case and in accordance with a previous suggestion made by General de Gaulle, it would be advisable that the supply arrangements should be considered as having been agreed to at the request of General de Gaulle."

De Gaulle: *Memoirs,* Documents (1940–42), pp. 40–2.

by the condition he proposed to allowing food supplies to reach France—namely, that he personally be given the credit.

Roosevelt at this time was inclined to take a dim view of General de Gaulle, for the General wanted the President of the United States to recognize him as the English had done. But the President had already formed an impression that the General was a candidate for personal power and no democrat at all. Furthermore, the President and his State Department considered that the presence in Vichy of American diplomatic representation gave them an unequaled listening post and also some chance to hearten the out-and-out anti-German elements around the Marshal. Washington never at this time gave serious consideration to recognizing the General; the Vichy card was too important for them and for the English. And, even later, for a lengthy period after Marshal Pétain's eclipse, they were not happy about the General. Roosevelt never changed his mind about him.

At Carlton Gardens at about this time President Roosevelt was being pictured as an old fool who had let himself be taken in by Marshal Pétain. It is a mistake even to consider that the President was ever a partisan of Marshal Pétain's policy. But this idea has become fixed in many minds as almost a fact of history. It may take a long time for the truth to become clear.

And what is the truth? It is simple enough, really. Roosevelt and the American State Department were fully aware of the fact that Marshal Pétain and Admiral Darlan still had potentially decisive strength in their hands in the French fleet and the French bases, and they therefore undertook to maintain constant pressure on Vichy not to allow this power to be used to the benefit of Hitler and the detriment of the British and later the Anglo-American cause—constant pressure and, on occasion, direct threats. American influence, although many times more potent, was directed to identically the same ends as that exercised by the Canadian representatives in Vichy. The instructions laid down by Roosevelt and Cordell Hull, his Secretary of State, for Admiral Leahy, Ambassador in Vichy, are most enlightening. They were of course not made public at the time, but they have come out since in Cordell Hull's and Admiral Leahy's memoirs and in State Department documents.[4]

(Through Special Ambassador Biddle, the American government made its voice heard in these critical days. On June 18 Biddle handed Baudouin an exceedingly stiff note sent him by Hull at the direction of President Roosevelt. ". . . The President desires you to say that in the opinion of this Government, should the French Government, before concluding any armistice with the Germans, fail to see that the fleet is kept out of the hands of her opponents,

[4] *President Roosevelt's instructions to Admiral Leahy, American Ambassador to Vichy*

Washington, December 20, 1940

". . . I desire that you endeavor to cultivate as close relations with Marshal Pétain as may be possible. . . . You should endeavor to bring to Marshal Pétain's attention such acts done or contemplated in the name of France which you deem to be inimical to the interests of the United Sates.

"I have made it abundantly clear that the policy of this administration is to support in every way practicable those countries which are defending themselves against aggression . . .

"You will undoubtedly associate with high officers of the French Navy. I desire, therefore, that in your relations with such officers . . . you endeavor to convince them that to permit the use of the French Fleet or naval bases by Germany, or to attain German aims, would most certainly forfeit the friendship and good will of the United States. . . ." William D. Leahy: *I Was There* (New York: McGraw-Hill Book Co.; 1950), pp. 443, 444, 445.

Roosevelt's warning to Marshal Pétain

Telegram from Cordell Hull to H. Freeman Matthews, American chargé d'affaires in Vichy

Washington, October 25, 1940

". . . The government of the United States received from the Pétain Government during the first days it held office the most solemn assurances that the French Fleet would not be surrendered. If the French Government now permits the Germans to use the French Fleet in hostile operations against the British Fleet, such action would constitute a flagrant and deliberate breach of faith with the United States Government.

"Any agreement entered into between France and Germany which partook of the character above mentioned would most definitely wreck the traditional friendship between the French and American peoples . . . and would create a wave of bitter indignation against France on the part of American public opinion."

William L. Langer: *Our Vichy Gamble* (New York: Alfred A. Knopf; 1947), p. 97.

the French Government will fatally impair the preservation of the French Empire and the eventual restoration of French independence and autonomy. Furthermore, should the French Government fail to take these steps and permit the French Fleet to be surrendered to Germany, the French Government will permanently lose the friendship and good will of the Government of the United States." [5]) Ambassador Leahy had strict orders to dog the Marshal's every step and, when and if necessary, to threaten him in brutally undiplomatic fashion. He was also to encourage the many anti-German elements in the Vichy administration.

In this book I have no intention of violating my pledge concerning any wartime secrets that came to my attention in the two-odd years I worked with the English. Until 1944 I could not have mentioned Woburn Abbey. I could not even have said that I worked in a setting where there were black squirrels and bison; Woburn Park is the only place in England where these creatures are found. But before the end of the war the Abbey was evacuated by the Foreign Office and became a school for Wrens until the time it was returned to its proprietor, the twelfth Duke of Bedford. He was the conscientious objector, the advocate of a peaceful settlement with Hitler. The Duke, who would never have aimed his gun at another human being, died from an accidental gunshot wound in the woods of his place in Devonshire. I used to know him. He was a little mad but very gentle, kind to animals and to everybody but his son, the present Duke.

Anyway, the most important secrets that came to my attention had to do with military operations that are already, to this generation, ancient history. It goes without saying that preparations for the Dieppe raid and the landings in North Africa had to be kept secret, and the pamphlets that were to be dropped when the action began had to be prepared and printed under the most extreme safeguards. But these secrets ceased to be secrets once the events took place.

Secrets about the past have little interest except perhaps to pro-

[5] Cordell Hull: *Memoirs* (New York: Macmillan; 1957–58), Vol. I, p. 792.

fessional historians. That is one reason why the calumnies spread about President Roosevelt's attitude toward Vichy and de Gaulle could all too easily endure. In reality, the Americans showed themselves far more severe than General de Gaulle toward Frenchmen who had served under Marshal Pétain.

This American intransigence operated in a manner both comical and silly, after the Allied landing in North Africa, in respect to Couve de Murville. As Inspector of Finances, he had represented the Marshal on the Franco-German commission in Wiesbaden, where, with General Doyen, he put up a battle against each new demand by Hitler. The Americans, landing in North Africa, refused, in spite of the efforts of Robert Murphy, to have anything to do with him. Today, as everyone knows, General de Gaulle has him as his Minister of Foreign Affairs. (On the other hand, some of the American generals were very slow to take the measure of men like General Noguès, Admiral Michelier, and others who resisted the landings with all the force at their disposal *and* refused to obey Admiral Darlan's order to cease hostilities.)

At Woburn Abbey our life had nothing martial about it. We were not exposed to any danger save when we went down to London. I belonged to the local Home Guard. Had the Nazis come parachuting down, we would doubtless have had a lively time. But they did not come. My Home Guard duties were about as exacting as those of a forest or game warden in peacetime France. I was required to go on night patrol once a week, dawn patrol actually, rifle in hand, in the hope, always defrauded, of bagging a German paratrooper. We had another duty, "fire watching," at which everybody had to take a turn. This consisted of patrolling the rooftops to keep an eye out for incendiary bombs. For all able-bodied Englishmen, Churchill had revised the slogan "To the shelter"; it was now, "To the roof." The German incendiary bombs were small and light. Everybody, women included, was taught to run and pick the bombs up when they fell on his particular roof, to cover them with sand or throw them over the edge to the grounds, hopefully before they exploded. At Woburn, enemy planes passed overhead with their burdens of bombs, always going on to targets beyond us. But we had our practice exercises anyway, with the conscience the English bring to that kind of thing. Who knew when Marshal Goering's intelligence officers might decide that the time had come to wipe out our operation? We also went in for target practice, in the atmosphere of a country fair. Anne did her stint at fire watching, like everybody else. One day when there was a fairly serious bombing raid on us—it was late in the afternoon—she wanted to show off and so remained alone in the office where she worked at the Abbey (she did not work with my outfit). But when the bombs really began to fall, and not very far away, she hid under a table.

At Maryland, the day began at seven. Pink, the butler, would come in with two cups of strong tea, pull back the drapes, and, whatever the state of the weather outside, would announce that it was a fine day. If one objected that it seemed to be raining, his reply was inevitably, "Yes, at the moment, yes, but it will perhaps soon let up." He would then go and wake up our neighbors.

We then turned on the radio, which was on the night table between our beds: first the English news bulletin; then the broadcasts from France. We listened intently, our hearts in our throats, to the long lists that were still being broadcast at the beginning of that winter, of people who were looking for each other, calling for each other, after the terrible confusion of that summer of defeat. I would then get up and dress. Anne would stay abed, on the blessed order of the doctor, who had insisted that she not let herself get tired. From the window I could look out on the lake, which was already frozen over, on the turf, which that terribly cold winter of 1940-41 was so early covered with snow. I would watch the birds at their breakfast: Anne had hung outside our window a bag filled with food scraps and grain on which the tomtits already came to perch and feast happily. During the morning hour English bombers passed overhead, coming back from a night mission over the Continent. They landed on a neighboring airfield. In the park of the Abbey, fighter planes came down on the huge expanses of lawn. There were squadrons of them, the miraculous Spitfires. In the daytime they were concealed under the low-hanging branches of the oaks and the beech trees. At frequent intervals, on warning from the radar stations lining the entire length of the eastern and southern coasts of England, they would "scramble," as they said, and take off to the heights, from which they could dive on enemy bombers and hopefully too on enemy fighter escorts. They would stay in the air a half an hour or so and then come back. Between times, the pilots passed their hours just like the rest of us. And so it was that this strange war always bordered on peace: civilians were quite near to aerial combat, to the sights and sounds of it, without participating; combatants resumed an essentially civilian life ten minutes after a quick and always potentially murderous encounter in the air. From time to time a husband, a fiancé, a brother flew low over the Abbey and waggled his wings. Some even dropped in for a drink.

In addition to the birds, Anne numbered among her dependents her white mice, a whole family, or several families, lodged in little cage houses, all of them decendants of the pair given her by Donald Monroe. She shared her milk ration with them. When the patriarch of the little tribe died, there was a moment of sorrow and a burial in the ground under the snow. A wounded crow was cared for, but died, too. The misfortunes of animals seemed almost human in this inhuman war.

The early morning cup of tea is to encourage the English to get out of bed. Breakfast itself was served downstairs at eight o'clock. Long faces and silence, all part of the tradition. It is the one moment of the day when gaiety is in bad taste. We all ate our breakfasts over our mail, the newspapers, and the *Digest,* a bulletin mimeographed during the night which gave samplings from the various enemy broadcasts. At about a quarter past eight we heard an automobile horn in the driveway: the London car. There were actually several of these, which made the journey back and forth between Woburn and London. They were all either Rolls or Daimlers, all very big, old-fashioned and high, purchased from the Duke of Bedford and driven by elderly chauffeurs long in his service. There was an army of them, because the old Duke had preserved the customs of the stagecoach era even to the relays. At the relays, however, one changed not the horses but the automobiles. This is how it was managed: the old Duke always had four cars and eight chauffeurs, or four chauffeurs and four footmen, in London at his two huge town houses, all fully staffed though rarely used. When there was a guest to be called for and driven to Woburn, two cars appeared at his door, one for the master and the other for his valet, or for the lady and for her maid and the luggage. The two cars took off on the road for Woburn but halted at the old coach stop halfway there, at Hendon, as if they were horses out of breath and needing to be watered. There two more cars, two chauffeurs, and two footmen waited to finish the course. A total of four cars and eight persons, chauffeurs and footmen, were needed to convey a single guest one way; for a round trip, eight cars and sixteen persons. This system—most reliable, it seemed—was preserved until the old Duke's death in 1940. The Russells were chary of progress, although the old Duke did belatedly dispense with his horses in favor of the gasoline engine, once he was convinced that it had come to stay.

At eight-thirty another automobile horn sounded, along with a shout from under the windows of the dining room: "Anyone for the Abbey?" It would be one of the elderly chauffeurs with a voice like a beadle in a church. With no Rolls, he had been reduced to driving a mere station wagon called the utility, or the futility, wagon, which transported those who lodged at Maryland but had their offices at the Abbey. At this period, Anne and I were the only French nationals in the entire organization. Later Sylvain Mangeot came: a charming and gifted Englishman with a French father.

Anne worked at the Abbey, but only afternoons, with an Oxford professor who was thoroughly grounded in French and philosophy. I myself worked at Maryland along with two Englishmen, Terry and Tony. At the hour when the others set off in the cold for the Abbey, Tony, his feet snug in slippers, always had a satisfied smile on his face as Norman Cameron burned his mouth swallowing a last cup of hot tea and stammered out his frightful oaths. I then took a tray up to Anne, who had to be awakened a second time, and then went to work in the big common-room called the study.

Work went on until one o'clock, when our colleagues from the
Abbey came back and we had lunch, served by Pink transformed
into a sort of torturer; with his aides he submitted us to the worst
sort of torture, serving us what was certainly the most infamous
food in all England. I am convinced that the prisoners of the Germans got better treatment. There were twelve or fifteen of us at
the table, and we had to swallow what was served if we wanted to
stay alive. Most of us did. At four-thirty, work was again interrupted by the arrival of tea, served with saccharin. We took that in
the lounge, where we were distracted by the obeisances and the
circus tricks of a shepherd dog belonging to Mafalda. He per-
formed these canine servilities for a reward of bits of cake made
without sugar, without eggs, without butter, and without flour. I
felt that its base product must have been sawdust. But real sawdust? I wonder. The dog would eat as many of these as he was
given, but of course he never tasted them: he gobbled, the way
dogs do. Harold, who at thirty was the oldest among the Englishmen and consequently the boss at Maryland, had taught him to
bark furiously whenever anyone pointed at the Soviet Union on
the huge map of Europe affixed to the wall of the lounge. Harold
was known as the Playboy. As you might guess from his advanced
age, all the rest of us at Maryland had subaltern posts. In my job I
enjoyed an astonishing freedom. Most of our English colleagues
were there because they had been rejected for active service or
given medical discharges, or because they had some special accomplishment. Harold, for example, had been the highest paid make-
up man in Fleet Street before the war. Most of the girls were secretaries, or translators. There was a Belgian and an Austrian, both
well along in their forties, who were the only ones among us who
could be considered grown-up.

The English are what we in France would call *mondains* or, as
they would say, social. By this is meant that they like the society
of their own; society with a small "s," I should perhaps say. In time
of peace this can be tiresome, but in war it has a certain charm.
Every evening at seven we began taking our numbers for the bath-
room. It was unusual for the girls not to change their dresses and

for the men not to have made themselves "look respectable," as they put it, for dinner. The menu in the evening was quite as awful as at lunch and was to get worse and worse. The soup was what was least bad. As for the dessert, I never once tasted it. I had found a pretext for having to leave the table: it was to tune in on the French program of the BBC at 8:25. To this I owe the fact that I was not regularly taken ill.

It was usually toward the beginning of dinner that we would hear the planes above us. We could distinguish between English and German planes, especially bombers. The German bombers had an unmistakable (or so we hoped) double-pitched drone, a sort of two-level throb from their desynchronized engines. Thus we fell into the habit of saying, to reassure ourselves, I suppose: "It's one of ours!" One night Tony saw fit to add: "Famous last words!" That kind of remark can bring bad luck. But it did not.

At the approach of nine we all stopped talking and listened religiously for the nine bongs of Big Ben. After that came the news. It was not always terribly good during that fall and winter of the blitz. Neither was the news from France. After the news, the games and amusements of one kind or another began. Tangye would put on records of songs he liked and would then play each a dozen times until he had learned the words by heart. Of course it was exasperating, but no one objected. Norman played checkers with the Austrian or with the Belgian. Others went in for ping-pong, or darts, or cards. The girls outnumbered the men: there was a Mary, another Mary, and there was Rosemary. There was the beautiful Kay and the pretty Clara, Mafalda who had Italian blood, and Norman's wife Katherine, who had Russian blood. Anne went in for conversation rather than cards. One evening she chanced to be playing cards at a table where we had a guest, Sir Maurice Peterson, a former British Ambassador to Spain. The old monkey pretended to be hard of hearing, nearly blind, and to have all but lost his memory. Thanks to this bit of strategy, he won more money in two hours from Anne than I made in a month.

December 1940

As I said, our miniature newspaper for France was called the *Courrier de l'Air*. I was not hard put to find this name for it: I simply borrowed the name of the little paper that the French government, during the First World War, used to drop by balloon or plane over the occupied regions. At the outset there had been eight or ten days of fairly hot argument. I contended that we should not allow a single word of Gaullist propaganda either in the paper or in our French leaflets. My reason? They were dropped over France by the English; let General de Gaulle make his own propaganda. For the English to mix in it would be indecent. The English should avoid any appearance of sponsoring him, etc. These arguments were perhaps a bit specious, but they prevailed. I confined myself to straight news about the General, his movements, and his military exploits. There were hardly any.

I was thus freed from having to report the General's speeches— and he made a considerable number that autumn. One was especially for us, the Frenchmen of England. It was on December 19. He had invited us to the Hotel Savoy, which has a sizable hall. He praised to the skies those of us who were already at his side. Then he changed his tone and poured his scorn on the minority who were still reluctant to recognize him as their chief and their guide. He declared that there existed two courses of action, and two only, that of Vichy and his own. To be with him, with the Free French, was to be the honor and the soul of France. Not to be with him was, in the final analysis, to stand for capitulation to Hitler.

If these were indeed the alternatives, you can see that for those who, like me, did not want to sign the oath of enlistment to his

person, the simplest thing would have been to go and shoot ourselves at once.

General de Gaulle concluded his address by summoning us to
join him without reservations. In London, he told us, we had to set
an example, for the entire world was watching us. This last point
was perfectly true. The English were watching us, and at that
period, the fall of 1940, whoever was not with the good, the brave,
the pure General de Gaulle could only be, in the eyes of the great
mass of the British people, a disguised, undercover ally of Hitler's.

You can imagine just how agreeable it was in such circumstances
to have to say, however reluctantly, "No, I am not a Gaullist."

"What about Anne?"

"Ask her."

The truth is, she so wanted the General to live up to her illusions
about him that she was even more unhappy than I. She so craved
to admire him unreservedly, just as he asked! Eventually, after her
brother arrived, she did become a heartfelt Gaullist and went to
work on a voluntary basis for the Navy. But I am getting ahead of
myself.

As for me, I managed at Woburn to get along as I had already
done in London by seeming to be a bit off my head.

When Armand arrived, he proved very helpful to me. He would
say, "My brother-in-law? He's got a screw loose!"

Toward the end of that terrible year of 1940, the General began
making use of the device by which he was to bring into line not
only those Frenchmen free in foreign lands but even more effectively those who were not free, in France itself. He took them under his authority and issued orders to them. On December 26,
1940, he broadcast his instructions: at such and such an hour in
Occupied France (which was on Berlin time) and at such and such
an hour in Unoccupied France, nobody was to set foot out of
doors.[1] The order was repeated on the following days. This was the

[1] *Orders given by General de Gaulle to Frenchmen in France* (broadcast in
French by the BBC on successive days in late December 1940)

"On next January 1 [1941], from 14 to 16 hours in Occupied France, no
Frenchmen will appear on the streets of our towns and villages. There will
only be the enemy.

beginning of the series of plebiscites that would link the name of the General so closely with the spirit of resistance that the two words, Gaulle Resistance, would become synonymous. The hatred that sprouted in the very footsteps of the invader, the hope that would be born again in the hearts of Frenchmen with the first Allied victories—all this was to be embodied in one word: Gaullism.

The English services, Political Warfare and the like, did not encourage such plebiscites, unprotected by a secret ballot. As the English saw it, there was a tragic drawback: too soon the enemy's attention was focused on those who would resist. This seemed particularly to be feared in a nation which for centuries had not known slavery and so had not learned to dissimulate or even to conspire very successfully, which was all to its credit.

The General was careful not to call personally for acts of violence. One day, in fact, stunned and horrified by the amount of blood that was being shed to obtain pitifully small results, he would ask that no more Germans be killed. Neither did the General launch direct appeals for violence against the Pétainist French. But, on his orders, his lieutenants designated by name those persons who were to be shot down. They would say for example: Gendarme such-and-such on a certain day, in a certain place, handed over a patriot. To be shot down. How could they know that the very same gendarme had not also managed to save the lives of nine other patriots? How could they be certain that behind the accusation there was not some element of personal vengeance? Is it not evil, to sow hatred so blindly? You may ask if I am not exaggerating. Very well, have a look one day at the files of the BBC. Read the denunciations thus broadcast during the five minutes reserved for General de Gaulle or his spokesman. You will see whether there was constant incitement to vengeance or not. I was not surprised that at the liberation the purge in France was the bloodiest in all of Western Europe.

"On January 1, from 14 to 15 hours in Unoccupied France, and from 15 to 16 hours in Occupied France, all Frenchmen are to stay inside their homes or in other closed places."

The other side of the coin was that on the Gaullist radio from London any martyr of the Resistance became a Gaullist. One was not allowed to say, one was not even allowed to think that anyone could be against the invader and not be a Gaullist. By the robust definition arrived at by François Mauriac, General de Gaulle *was* France; to die for France, to die for de Gaulle was all the same thing. What's more, a man could be a Gaullist without knowing it.

In London the few non-Gaullist Frenchmen who could not possibly be considered soft on Hitler or soft on Vichy found themselves to be men without honor or simply ridiculous. For example, they said about Torcy that he had fallen into dementia praecox, or, to put it more crudely, senility. Of the non-Gaullist Jews, people began saying that they had fled France because they were afraid. (If so, why were they in London and not in New York?) It followed, of course, that anybody working with the British was a bad patriot, a British agent. Except for the official Gaullists broadcasting (men like Jean Oberlé), any non-Gaullist Frenchmen speaking over the BBC and paid by the English (such as Pierre Maillaud, Michel Saint-Denis, and many another) risked being labeled English agents. People would whisper: "He works for a foreign power." The same risk held for me, as will become apparent later.

Christmas came upon us and everyone did his best to make it a merry one. It was not easy, even though we did have, on Christmas morning, the blessed sound of church bells—blessed if perhaps incongruous in a nation so grimly beset and so savagely fighting back. It was a minor blessing no doubt, but we had not realized how much we had missed the bells, or rather how much we had dreaded to hear them, for when the invasion seemed imminent, from July on, the bells had been silenced, thenceforth to be rung only to signal that the Nazis were upon us. (They were, in fact, rung one nightmare day in the summer on a false alarm.) Nazi planes were still coming by the hundreds, ranging over all southern and western England. On December 20 and 21, Liverpool and the surrounding area were hit twice by a total of more than five hundred bombers. Manchester caught it next, almost on the eve of Christmas. In London things were relatively calm, but, though naturally none of us knew it, this quiet was to end, and terribly, within four days.

Grief had come to the families of a number of the girls and young women who worked with us at the Abbey and at Maryland. Nevertheless, they went into the woods to find holly and mistletoe. They stretched garlands of greenery and paper serpentines across the rooms. Greeting cards lined the mantels. Gift packages were all the more carefully wrapped because they contained little objects of no monetary value, which is the way it's done in England even in times of peace and prosperity. At the Abbey the professor with whom Anne worked staged a revue, which was to be followed by a ball.

Anne was to sing, but she had a bad throat, a very real bad throat. Seeing that I was upset, she looked after it and was well in time. It was to make me happy, or so I like to think, that she chose from her book not some royalist ditty like "O! Richard, O! mon roi," but "Les Trois Glorieuses," which was sung on the barricades of Paris in July 1830 during "the three glorious days" when Paris, goaded by the pigheadedness of Charles X, exploded and brought down the last of our Bourbon kings.

> On nous disait: soyons esclaves!
> Nous avons dit: soyons soldats!
> Soudain Paris, dans sa mémoire,
> A retrouvé son chant de gloire:
> En avant, marchons
> Contre leurs canons
> A travers le feu, le fer, le sang des bataillons . . .[2]

[2] They told us: you are slaves!
We said: let's be soldiers!
Suddenly Paris, in her memory,
Found again her song of glory:
Forward, let us march
Against their cannon
Through fire and steel, through the blood of the battalions.

After the last note there was silence, so surprised was everyone, and then thundering applause. She then launched into "Auprès de ma blonde." The English all knew this and with their inimitable accents joined in the refrain.

We had finally concluded that there would be no dancing. But this enforced abstention—continued later, by the way—was never really much liked. Gaiety and pleasures are an obligation for the English, particularly in trying times. In their eyes, this is considered hygienic, or so I imagine.

So passed Christmas.

On Saturday, December 28, General de Gaulle made a speech in his celebrated style. An anlysis of this style at its best will show that its special appeal lies in the use of a great many sentences beginning with the same words or phrases. This time the key phrase was "We proclaim." One of the passages that began with these words contained a curious and interesting hint—interesting not to me alone, as it soon became clear. "We proclaim that all French commanders, whatever may have been their faults, who decide to draw again the sword they have put back into the scabbard, will find us at their side without any desire to exclude anybody and without ambitions." (By *us*, General de Gaulle meant himself.) The meaning of this seemed not wholly clear to me. But maybe it was. Certainly "at their side" did not really mean "under their orders." And "without ambitions" did not exclude ambitions for France, the incarnation of which de Gaulle considered himself.

What was behind the curious declaration made at this moment? I was intrigued, and after asking a few questions here and there, I found out.

General Wavell had the Italians reeling through Libya. As an army, Graziani's forces had almost ceased to exist, after losing most of four divisions, 113,000 prisoners in all, and well over 700 guns. And Graziani was telling Rome he might have to withdraw as far as Tripoli.

Churchill, as he later wrote, "was most anxious to give Vichy its chance to profit by the favourable turn of events. There is no room in war for pique, spite, or rancour. The main objective must dominate all secondary causes of vexation." [3] Plans were afoot for an expeditionary force of six divisions, which, "if the French attitude should become favorable," would land in Morocco. The Prime Minister had sent messages to this effect to Marshal Pétain in Vichy and General Weygand in North Africa through the agency of Pierre Dupuy, the Canadian minister in Vichy. (The message destined for Weygand was sent him by hand from Vichy.) In essence, what Churchill had to say was that *if* the French government decided to cross over to North Africa, there to resume the war against Italy and Germany, Great Britain would immediately send "a strong and well-equipped Expeditionary Force of up to six divisions," to be supported by the Air Force, which had expanded, and by the fleet. "The command of the Mediterranean would be assured by the reunion of the British and French Fleets and by our own joint use of Moroccan and North African bases."

General Weygand had succeeded in rebuilding in North Africa an army with a potential of 250,000 men. But he was apprehensive —mistakenly, it was thought in London—lest his forces be brought back into combat too soon. Too soon in his mind meant at a moment when such action would only furnish Hitler with a pretext to pounce on North Africa. If this happened, Weygand felt certain that his renascent army would be crushed. (In view of the fact that the following months were to see Nazi armies rampaging through the Balkans into Greece as far as Crete, and Rommel stopped only miles from Cairo, General Weygand cannot be judged to have been overly pessimistic.) He believed that the French should wait upon an event that he considered as inevitable in the Second World War as in the First, namely the intervention of the United States.

On this question of General Weygand and North Africa, then and later, a revealing book is Ambassador Robert Murphy's *Diplomat among Warriors*, the story of his long career as "trouble shooter," which took him on presidential missions to Vichy, North Africa, Italy, Germany, and elsewhere during the war. Subse-

[3] Winston Churchill: *Their Finest Hour* (Boston: Houghton Mifflin; 1949), pp. 622–4.

quently he was the first postwar American ambassador to Japan and Assistant Secretary of State for United Nations Affairs. Murphy, who had had long experience in France, was at this time sent by President Roosevelt on a very special and delicate mission to French Africa. Like Admiral Leahy in Vichy, he was to try to stiffen the spirit of resistance to the Germans and to give discreet help. He discharged this sensitive role during and after the Allied landings in November 1942, by which time General Weygand had long since been removed from Africa at German insistence. In his book, Murphy tells how strongly anti-German the General and his entourage were. The situation was admittedly precarious, but, he says, "Weyland had infused new life and hope into the military group, reorganized it, made new plans, and carefully hoarded the meager supplies of ammunition and equipment. Many French officers were confident that they could defend at least some of the area indefinitely *if* the United States would supply them with the necessary equipment, petroleum, and other supplies. . . ." General Weygand said he hoped and was ready to believe that Hitler could be defeated, but he asked where the divisions were coming from. In 1940 nobody could say.

Murphy mentions one young diplomat on Weygand's staff, François de Rose, whom I referred to earlier as having left London in July 1940, only after serious hesitations. In my opinion he succeeded in the long run in doing a far better job in Algiers helping to rebuild the Army than would have been possible if he had remained in London as a diplomat in General de Gaulle's service. It was from François that Murphy learned of the Prime Minister's message to Weygand. The General forwarded it to Vichy, only to learn that the Marshal had already received it but had not been told that it was being sent to Africa too.

"This confirms my distrust of Churchill's judgment," said Weygand. He also believed that Churchill and General de Gaulle had been "inexcusably rash" in their attempt to capture Dakar. He considered French Africa his country's sole remaining trump. "A premature move could easily lead to a German blockade of the western Mediterranean."

Murphy further writes that General Weygand was dogged by serious apprehensions. Nothing must be done to arouse German suspicions, already high. When Weygand received Churchill's message, he thought it generous but imprudent. He and Murphy now shared a new anxiety, that their efforts to rebuild the French African Army in expectation of American intervention in the future might produce unwanted publicity. If Churchill knew about it, wouldn't he mention it to de Gaulle? If de Gaulle talked about it over the radio, wouldn't that put Weygand in danger by directing German attention to his efforts? And would not Hitler demand Weygand's removal?

There was another factor: Weygand was not the man to receive such a proposition from Churchill. His was a nature constantly tormented by scruples. He detested Pétain almost by inheritance, one might say, since he himself was one of Marshal Foch's loyal crew. But Pétain was then his superior and it was out of loyalty to his superior that he sent the letter on to Vichy.

Another case of loyalty: Churchill told everything, or nearly everything, to General de Gaulle. He told him that he knew from British agents in Tangiers that General Weygand was stealthily preparing an army destined one day to resume combat. (This was confirmed for me by de Gaulle's representative in Tangiers at that time, Commandant Luizet.)

Now consider General de Gaulle's reaction. Everything pointed in one direction: General Weygand was engaged in an enterprise which, on the military level at least, was parallel to the patriotic efforts of General de Gaulle. Thereupon de Gaulle came forth with the broadcast I have mentioned. Was Weygand grateful to him? Not in the least! He was furious. Some of his people even went so far as to speak of sabotage. They found it difficult to believe, Murphy said, that the radio pronouncements from London —there were more of them later—did not constitute "a deliberate attempt to sabotage their efforts. . . . Some even speculated that this might be a subtle de Gaulle scheme to undermine Weygand's position and force his departure under Axis pressure, which later did occur."

General Weygand indeed considered that he had been publicly compromised by de Gaulle's reference to a sword blade being drawn from the scabbard once again. He was more sure than ever that the Germans would demand that Vichy clip his ears.

Neither, his nature being what it was, could he discern any evidence of generous or noble intent in the letter that General de Gaulle sent him two months later, on February 24, in which de Gaulle said, "I propose to you that we join together." The letter ended on these words: "If your answer is yes, I assure you of my respect." Far from leaping happily at this offer, Weygand was angry. He felt that the closing words were, as he later wrote, *rude*.

The day would come at last when Weygand would be recalled from Africa as the result of dire German threats to Vichy (in November 1941). And later, at the time of the Allied landing in North Africa, he was arrested and jailed. On that day Torcy, who had passed some rather severe judgments on General Weygand's many hesitations, said to me, "There we have it, an end to all his troubles with his conscience!"

At Carlton Gardens I had an old friend, an ardent Gaullist, whom I used to call the Porte-pensée. And why not? There was the Porte-parole, or "Spokesman." This friend always seemed to be able to enlighten me on the General's deepest thoughts, so I dubbed him the *Porte-pensée*. (I know that this comes out clumsily in English as "Thoughtsman," but the meaning seems clear enough.) Actually I don't think he was particularly well informed, but he had both intuition and judgment, two precious qualities when joined together. One day I put this question to him: "If General Weygand had accepted the offer of 'union,' would de Gaulle really have surrendered first place to him, in consideration of the fact that Weygand, his senior by decades and a former commander-in-chief, would bring with him all of North Africa and a real, live army?"

My friend looked at me, pity in his eyes. "What a way to talk! It's idiotic! *Surrendering a place*—for heaven's sake! There is no question of any *place*. General de Gaulle has *a mission*. His *mission* is to assume, to incarnate France in his own person. Look, you don't surrender a *mission* as you would a *place*. Can you imagine Joan of Arc surrendering her *mission*, to crown the Dauphin and all that? The General will render an account of his mission to the French people, once he has fulfilled it. And it will be the French people and only the French people who can relieve him of it!"

"Yes, I see. And my guess is that the French people will never relieve him of it."

"Fine! If you think that, come join us right away."

"No, not right away, and not later on either, thank you."

Then we fell to quarreling, our old quarrel in our friendly way. I never approved of my friend's course of action, but I always thought him astonishingly right in his predictions, almost clairvoyant, in fact.

The General was to go to the country that weekend, but he had two things to do before leaving. One was to broadcast to France on the twenty-eighth repeating his commands to the luckless Frenchmen there to hold that "immense plebiscite of silence" on the first day of 1941. Then he had to confer with Commandant Meffre. This he did without informing his second-in-command, Admiral Muselier, who had demanded that Meffre be fired from his job as chief of security at Carlton Gardens. On the General's return from Africa, Admiral Muselier had complained to him of Meffre's conduct. On December 23, the Admiral's Chief of Naval Operations, Captain Moullec, had filed an official complaint with the General: Meffre had conducted a clandestine search of the Captain's hotel room and had removed certain personal effects. The General agreed to take disciplinary action immediately.

In his memoirs,[4] Admiral Muselier goes into detail, referring to both Moullec and Meffre by their wartime cover names. "The General formally promised Moret [Moullec] to take the necessary punitive action against Howard [Meffre]. Needless to say, he did not keep his word.

"A few days later, I myself intervened and, despite objections from Passy and Fontaine, obtained a promise that Howard [Meffre]

[4] Émile Henri Muselier: *De Gaulle contre le Gaullisme* (Paris: Editions du Chêne; 1946).

would be relieved of his functions. Designated for service in Africa, he pretended sickness and managed to bring on conjunctivitis. Thus he did not leave. I renewed my efforts with the General, who then promised me that Howard [Meffre] would finally give up his functions at Carlton Gardens on December 25." But, on that date, Meffre was busily engaged in working out the details of an intrigue which would send Admiral Muselier to prison.

"On December 27, without saying anything to me, General de Gaulle agreed to receive the man. On that occasion Howard warned him that there were in existence certain grave charges against me; de Gaulle let him go ahead and, on December 31, at the moment of the *dénouement*, left London for forty-eight hours." Needless to say, at that moment the Admiral had no intimation of the conspiracy against him.

1941

January 1–2, 1941

New Year's Day is not a holiday in England. It was on a Wednesday, and I was in London, as was my custom in the middle of the week. The damage done to the City by the Nazi fire raid of the night of Sunday, the twenty-ninth, was fearful. It had been a nightmare. When I reached Fleet Street and looked up Ludgate Hill, I was awed by what I saw. There stood St. Paul's as no one in centuries had seen it, fully exposed to view; it was now no longer obstructed, half to two thirds hidden, by the clutter of buildings old and new in the foreground. All around Wren's masterwork there were blackened, still smoking ruins where nearly a square mile of the City of London had been obliterated. Londoners, who had seen a lot since the blitz began, would never forget that night. The official count gave the number of fires started by incendiary bombs as near fifteen hundred. They were already calling it the "Second Great Fire of London." The twenty-four-inch water main from the Thames had been broken by high-explosive bombs. Although St. Paul's could now be seen in its intended majesty, barely damaged though smoke-stained, one was sickened to learn that eight of Wren's smaller churches had been hit that night. The Guildhall was severely damaged, and much else.

Nobody then was quite sure how St. Paul's had escaped destruction. A rain of incendiaries had been seen to strike the dome and bounce off. I was told that actually a team of fire watchers had pledged themselves to save the cathedral from fire. Running on the roof up to the incendiary bombs as they fell, they picked them up and threw them into the street below—all save one. This one had burned halfway through the lead covering of the dome, and just when the frantic firemen and the wardens were expecting it to set fire to the building, it fell off and down onto the gallery. Understandably, there were many who considered the salvation of St. Paul's miraculous and who thought of it also as an omen of victory to come. But Britain was a long way from victory in January 1941. Churchill visited the City that Monday. The houses were still on fire. A woman asked him: "When will this war be over?" He answered: "When we've defeated them."

On Thursday morning I went back to Woburn. Only later did I learn that at about the hour when I was leaving town a mysterious affair was to break open like an abscess in the little world of the Free French. It involved Admiral Muselier. The Admiral was taken into custody at his home in London and was then led off to Scotland Yard. On what charge? At the moment, the nature of the charge was not revealed to him. It was treason.

Here I will go back a little—to the conversation between General de Gaulle and Commandant Meffre, alias Howard, whom the General had promoted to the rank of Chief of Security for the Free French. What else did Meffre tell the General? The General nowhere gives us any clue. Did Meffre tell him that the charge pending against Muselier was treason and that the British Intelligence Service was at that moment preparing to arrest him? If he did, one must assume that the General would have warned Admiral Muselier, who was, after all, his number-one associate in the Free French organization and the chief commander of what was by far the largest, most active fighting unit under the Free French flag, namely its Navy. But the General made no effort to see Muselier that night or the next day, when he left for his country place at Ellesmere in Shropshire, just south of Liverpool. De Gaulle was still there on the evening of New Year's Day when he had a call from London. The Secretary of State for Foreign Affairs wanted to speak to him: Eden himself was on the telephone. He said that a very grave, very urgent matter had arisen which demanded the General's immediate return to London.

Did Eden say what this urgent matter was? I have no way of knowing, and I must here confess that many aspects of this affair are still quite unclear to me, or perhaps I should say shrouded in mystery. In fifty years it may all be brought to light. If so, it should fill an entire volume and will be fascinating to amateurs of espionage literature. Nothing will be missing from it, not even the love angle, for there will be an amorous intrigue involving the beautiful Miss Trevelyan. There will even be a duel, or almost a duel, which a Brazilian diplomat, affianced to a Mlle d'Anjou, was determined to fight with a French officer, a certain Captain de Soubeyran. Then there will be the deportation of Captain de Soubeyran, on the orders of General de Gaulle no less, to a prison camp in Africa. And the arrest of two ladies of immaculate reputations, Mme la generale Nicolle and Mlle Terré.

I can't go into these details now, but want simply to suggest to some film director of the future that here is quite a movie to make, against the background of wartime London under the bombs, and with Scotland Yard, always reliably sinister in films. What about the role of the General? That is the question: how to stage *Hamlet* without the Prince?

General de Gaulle was fifty years old at the time; he would be fifty-one on November 22. I vividly recall him as I used to see him in the partial intimacy of the first-floor landing, or in the corridors at Carlton Gardens, in some club or other, or at a reception; sometimes at a distance, on the big public occasions. But, no matter how, he was curiously the same always. I mean to say, he was always on his guard, always official. Enough to make one believe that he was also like that in the solitude of his bedroom, standing in front of the mirrored wardrobe.

He was strikingly tall for a Frenchman, of course. But more especially, he was oddly proportioned, with a pale face and a head that seemed small in relation to his body, and the chest almost squared, like a wooden idol's. When standing, he held himself like a statue. A former classmate at the École de guerre, Captain Laffargue, has already remarked this: "He held himself very stiffly when he walked, very serious, with a kind of swagger as if he were propelling along his own statue." But in walking he resolutely threw out his abdomen, rather than his chest. His arms hung down at his sides, his slender wrists almost reaching the edge of his khaki tunic.

When seated and talking, he had a way of clasping and unclasping his hands, as if passing an argument from left to right, and then, having done this, he would open his hands and raise his innocent palms heavenward.

His hair was at that time dark and combed rather low over the narrow forehead, parted neatly on the left. His long heavy eyelids opened when he became animated, to disclose small round eyes set very close together. The gaze from those eyes was distant, letting no thought filter through, but they inspired some people with a sudden immense confidence—such was the case with Winston Churchill, as it is today with millions and millions of others. But they aroused in some an uncontrollable mistrust. The ears, large, standing out from the head, suddenly became very noticeable when he donned his kepi. The lower part of the face was heavy, fixed, expressionless. The absence of a chin took on its true significance only in relation to the mouth, disdainful yet engaging, and in relation to the impressive nose. The Prince de Condé looked something like this, as do certain fish; one might say it is the look of conquerors.

In 1941 that mouth was surmounted by a minuscule black mustache, cut short, an item much discussed by his adorers. Some wanted the General to sacrifice it—because Hitler wore one, and Charlie Chaplin. Others said that the General ought to preserve it, if he was to remain faithful to his image, his personage.

The General's voice and the words it measured out, and the rare gestures that punctuated it, and the expression of the eyes that accompanied it had the most contradictory effects upon his listeners. Most of them were, like Churchill, immediately subjugated by the accent of sincerity of this Frenchman who represented for them the heroic figures of the almost legendary Roland, or Bayard *Sans Peur et sans Reproche,* and of all the great paladins of French history. The English also saw in him the Frenchman grateful to the Allies who were going to save our country. Others—and to tell the truth, they were very rare—had an opposite reaction. The same voice, attitudes, gaze, words inspired mistrust.

But to everyone, admirers and detractors alike, the General seemed to be like a man playing a role. So he always seemed to me. All his words sounded as if prepared in advance, learned by heart. Yes, from morning to night, Charles de Gaulle never stopped playing the part of Charles de Gaulle.

To return to the telephone conversation on January 1 between Eden in London and de Gaulle in his Shropshire retreat: would the General now snatch up his kepi and rush to London while there was still time to ward off the catastrophe? (By that, I mean the ignominious arrest of Admiral Muselier.) Would he make every effort to warn the Admiral? Perhaps Eden did tell him on the telephone of the danger hanging over the Admiral. Whatever was said or not said, the General did not leave the country until January 2.

Admiral Muselier told me later that the English authorities had sounded a warning not only to the General but also to his Chief of Staff at Carlton Gardens, Lieutenant Colonel Angenot. According to Muselier, they told Angenot exactly what it was all about, whereupon Angenot had telephoned de Gaulle immediately to inform him. Admiral Muselier says this in his book; de Gaulle has said that Angenot told him nothing.

Very early on the morning of January 2 the Admiral, who had no reason to suspect anything, came back to London. He had been at Windsor taking part in a benefit for the British Red Cross. When he reached his home at 49, Hallam Street at 9:30 a.m., he found two inspectors waiting to arrest him. They said that they did not know on what charges. The Admiral knew even less. He changed into civilian clothes, not wishing to disgrace his uniform when, to any passer-by, he was obviously under arrest. It was a very cold morning. He put on his overcoat with the brass buttons of the French Navy but no insignia and went with his escort to Scotland Yard, where he was placed under the guard of a series of inspectors who were relieved every hour. No one told him why he was arrested. At one o'clock they brought him lunch.

Why was he made to wait like his? I can offer a suggestion that is little more than a theory. But before I do, I will return to certain facts. General de Gaulle reached London that same morning and went to the Foreign Office, where Eden was impatiently waiting for him. The Secretary of State, obviously very distressed, came out with it: Admiral Muselier faced a charge of treason. He was supposed to have tried to send advance warning about the Dakar expedition to Vichy, and he was supposed to be now engaged in a plot to hand over the submarine *Surcouf* to Admiral Darlan. For his services he was said to have received £2,000 from Vichy agents, and was thought to be expecting even more money as his price for blocking any further enlistments in the Free French Naval Forces.

The General asked to be told the grounds for these charges. Eden replied that they were based on certain letters signed by General Rozoy, Chief of the French Air Mission before the armistice, who had only recently been repatriated to France. The letters were typed on the stationery of the French Consulate in London, where a representative of Vichy was still in charge. Eden produced them for the General to examine and then asked what the General thought—asked it with apprehension tempered by hope. He anticipated a violent outburst: "What's this! You dare to lay a finger on Admiral Muselier, my chief associate? How could you even suspect him?" Such an outburst would indeed have implied that in General de Gaulle's opinion the Admiral could not possibly be suspected of treason. The Secretary of State for Foreign Affairs even expected an ultimatum from the General: "If you do not immediately release Admiral Muselier, I will sleep in prison too tonight. And that will mean a break between you, the English, and the Free French!"

We know how the General is when his prerogatives and national honor are in question, how intransigent he can be. We know that later he often threatened to break off relations with the English over incidents involving his honor to a lesser degree than this. But here his reaction was not at all like that. He only said that he was thunderstruck, that this could only be the result of some huge error, that the whole thing was most extraordinary, that he would make inquiries and would reflect on the matter, meanwhile treating it "with every possible reserve." [1]

Make inquiries, reflect? After being told that his second-in-command was an ignoble traitor? Now it was Eden's turn to be thunderstruck. Was this *all* the General had to say? If so, he seemed to be admitting that the charges might have a foundation in fact. He asked for time to conduct an inquiry? He neither threatened to break off relations nor asked to join the Admiral in prison? He did not even offer his word as bond for the Admiral? Then there was no longer any reason for hesitation. The arrest must be confirmed and the Admiral, until then merely detained, must be moved to a prison cell. As soon as General de Gaulle left the Foreign Office, the order was indeed given to the Yard next door.

The reason for keeping the Admiral waiting so long could only be this: Eden must have hoped that after his talk with de Gaulle there would be no need to go to such extremes. Disappointed, he could do nothing but allow the case to take its normal course, normal insofar as a charge of treason could be normal.

Admiral Muselier often told me how things went with him during his ordeal. As he related it all in his book,[2] I will here hold to the bare essentials. At the beginning of the afternoon he was taken to Pentonville Prison and thrown into a cell like any felon. He still had not been told the nature of the charges against him, but he had been informed that he was there by virtue of an order of incarceration for the duration of the war. He was searched thoroughly and submitted to the most basic kind of medical examination. The doctor, a callous sort, ignored a far from invisible wound dating from World War I and managed thereby to inflict considerable pain. He considered the man a traitor, a dangerous spy, perhaps even a criminal facing the gravest of charges. The Admiral was wearing civilian clothes, so he attempted to enlighten the hard-

[1] ". . . After forty-eight hours of inquiry and reflection, I went to see the British Minister and said to him, 'The documents are ultra-suspect . . . !' " De Gaulle: *Memoirs*, I, p. 147.

[2] Muselier: *De Gaulle contre le Gaullisme*.

handed practitioner. "I trust you are aware that I am a French admiral, and I am a wounded veteran of World War I."

"If you were an admiral, you would not be here!"

The luncheon General de Gaulle was attending that day was a large function being given at Lancaster House for the Allied commanders by the Secretary of War. Admiral Muselier had been invited, along with his Chief of Staff, Captain Moullec. Moullec, who had not seen the Admiral the whole morning—for good reason, as we know—decided to go directly to Lancaster House, expecting to meet Muselier there. He arrived early and, on consulting the seating arrangements, noticed that the Admiral's name had been covered over by a card, evidently at the last minute. Commander Lacy, an English liaison officer, informed him of developments. The Admiral had been arrested on a charge of treason. At this very moment the General arrived. When Captain Moullec presented himself, the General said, in a voice loud enough to be heard by others: "Well! well! Captain, it's a fine thing I've just heard about your admiral!"

Captain Moullec protested. There must be some mistake!

"Come to my office after this luncheon, and I will show you photocopies of the incriminating letters found by the British services."

When the luncheon was over, Moullec went up to General Spears and Major Morton. "I have no facts to go on," he told them, "but I can assure you that your government is making a serious mistake."

General Spears remained silent, but Major Morton answered sharply. "We have documentary proof. And our services know their business."

The Captain then went to Carlton Gardens as instructed. He arrived at the same moment as the General and followed him into his office. The General took five photographs from a briefcase and handed them over for Moullec's inspection.

"Well, what do you say to these?"

Captain Moullec scanned the supposedly incriminating letters, noting that they bore the signature of General Rozoy of the French Air Force, now back in France. "What do I say? I say they are false! Spurious! Forgeries! Any word you like for an obvious plant!"

"Why, may I ask?"

Captain Moullec's answer was blunt. He did not know General Rozoy personally, but, from all reports, Rozoy was an able officer brevetted to the General Staff. He would never have put his name to such letters. They were on the official letterhead of the French Consulate; the Consul would never have allowed his official stationery to be put to such use. Furthermore, even a cursory inspection of the wording of the supposed letters revealed errors, violations of General Staff usage. "They jump right off the page, to the eyes of any man who knows such usage. Procedures that are elementary to anyone with General Staff training!"

"Hum! . . . Why don't you go and reflect further on this matter and note down any observations you may have made about these documents? I will call you toward the end of the afternoon."

I should perhaps explain just what kind of man the General was faced with. Captain Moullec was a type of officer uncommon in the French Navy. First of all, he was a republican in an officers corps in which many reeked of the ideas of the Action Française and other groups of the extreme Right. It was not by accident that the Navy, in the years before the war, was affectionately dubbed "La Royale" (a pun, too, on the fact that the French Admiralty has its seat on the rue Royale, in Paris). In the time of the Third Republic, Admiral Darlan was called upon to reprimand Admiral Platon because he persisted in displaying in his cabin a large autographed portrait of Charles Maurras, the royalist firebrand.

Moullec was a Leftist. Not the subversive Left, however; in France in the years between the wars, subversion was at least as frequently to be found on the Right. He had another characteristic that set him apart from his fellows in the Navy: he placed the interests of the service above the interests of his chiefs; and he placed the nation above the Navy. This sort of thinking was considered very close to subversion by most of the officers I have known. They sincerely believed that they were best serving the interests of the Navy when they were loyally serving their particular chief. Our Navy was full of officers of the sect known as ADD (*les Amis de Darlan*). They were likewise convinced that they were best serving the nation when they placed the Navy slightly above it. Few of them had any doubts about their capacity to lead the nation, the better to cleanse and regenerate it. And so it naturally came about that under the regime of Marshal Pétain two admirals, Darlan and Platon, were ministers; another was governor of Indochina; an admiral was resident-general in Tunisia; another was high commissioner in the Antilles; still another, prefect of police in Paris; and an admiral was director of the École Nationale de Police. I couldn't even try to guess how many became prefects under Vichy.

Captain Moullec, then, differed radically from the usual officer of the French Navy. He even went so far as to insist that the ships of the Navy belonged not to the admirals, but to the country. His judgments in any matter were based on a fair assessment of the evidence, not on friendship, not on *camaraderie*. I hardly need to say that he was not of the ADD. He was, in fact, on rather bad terms with Admiral Darlan, a genial, back-slapping sort. The Captain, on the other hand, was rather reserved. He was not overly loved in the Navy.

By this time the friends of the Admiral were busy in his behalf. Captain Moullec had spread the word, and the members of the Admiral's staff at Westminster House, without exception, were active. So were the officers of the British Admiralty who were acquainted with Admiral Muselier or who knew his reputation as chief of that exemplary Free French Navy. Among his English friends was Mr. Alexander, First Lord of the Admiralty, and Sir Dudley Pound, First Sea Lord, not such bad friends to have in a crisis. Then, too, there was Admiral Dickens, who demanded to see Muselier, and threw his arms around him. Not for one second did Admiral Dickens doubt his French colleague's loyalty.

Moullec realized of course that General de Gaulle was the man to convince of the Admiral's innocence, for, given the General's special standing with the British, he would only have to give his word and Admiral Muselier would be freed at once. After a quick search, then, the Captain got together a sheaf of documents; he suspected that personal vengeance was at the bottom of the whole affair. Who had a motive for revenge against the Admiral? Meffre, obviously: an extremely able, devious fellow, capable of anything. Spurious letters? All in the day's work for a man like him.

At six that evening, Captain Moullec was again in the General's office and gave him his detailed observations: "Gross errors in the texts in obvious contravention of General Staff technique. . . . Inconsistent with the truth in many points. . . . Information at variance with the chronology of events of September and October 1940. Psychologically unlikely, out of character. . . ." The Captain concluded his analysis by observing that a thousand suppositions could be made about the Admiral but that one hypothesis was absolutely out of the question: treason.

"General," he said, "if you were to tell me that Admiral Muselier had tried to lead the Prime Minister's wife astray, I would say, 'Maybe.' But treason? Preposterous!"

The General seemed impervious to all the arguments, however. Captain Moullec had his full share of self-control, but this was too much. "Come, General, the hours slip by and we have done nothing to protest the ignoble treatment of the Admiral, who, after all, does command the Free French Naval Forces."

The General's temper, or anyway his voice, began to rise. Addressing the Captain by his *nom de guerre*, he said, "Moret, leave the room or I will send you to keep your admiral company!"

If this threat was meant to silence Moullec, it failed. General de Gaulle had to be brought around to see the light, or to admit that he saw it. The Captain proceeded to call together the senior officers of the Free French Naval Forces then in London, Captains Auboyneau, Gayral, Ortoli, and Wietzel. They agreed to consolidate their efforts.

At eight o'clock that evening, January 2, Moullec returned to his hotel, the Cumberland, where he was living after having been bombed out of three previous abodes. It was in his room at the Cumberland that before the holidays his effects had been searched by a Sergeant Colin, a man on Meffre's security staff at Carlton Gardens. Incidentally, some gold jewelry and two sovereigns had disappeared during this search. As he entered his room now, Captain Moullec noted that an English detective in plain clothes was standing in the hall at a discreet distance from his door. Evidently the General was not merely being caustic when he threatened to send him to join his admiral in prison.

January 1941

If the Captain had a bad night, so did the General. At three in the morning, he telephoned Moullec. "Moret," he said in gentler tones than he had used earlier, "I have come to the conclusion that these letters are indeed forgeries."

"But, General, it took you all of fifteen hours to reach that conclusion!" The General chose to ignore this nuance of insolence.

The Operations officers at Westminster House believed that the General, finally convinced that the charges were based on fabrications, would go to see Eden at the earliest. In their imagination they saw him making an indignant scene at the Foreign Office, passionately summoning Eden to release his second-in-command. Knowing the General, they could all but hear him: "An error of the grossest kind! Keep Admiral Muselier in prison one minute more, and I will break off relations with the British government. I will go to prison myself and join him!"

The English would of course be obliged to release Muselier. The General would give his word as bond. He would say, "Hand Admiral Muselier over to me! I will keep him at my side while you decide that the charges are based on forged documents." What else could the English do?

But the General proceeded otherwise. He contented himself

with informing Eden that there was nothing against the Admiral but the documents in question, which were supposed to have emanated from the Consulate—the old Vichy Consulate, now closed—and were signed by a general now in France and must therefore be considered "highly suspect." Now, to anyone who knew—and many did by this time—that the perpetrator of the plot was not in France but very much in London, and not so very far from Carlton Gardens, this seemed a little off the mark. Anyway, if a document is a forgery, one does not describe it merely as "highly suspect."

It was not until January 8, six days after the arrest, that General de Gaulle decided that the time had come to go to the mat for his Admiral. Now he threatened to sever relations, in a prickly sort of statement. Meanwhile, it was the British Admiralty, not the General, which made itself responsible for Admiral Muselier. They found that he had been badly treated, that one of the wardens had tried to tear the buttons off his greatcoat and that, when the Admiral had protested, he had made an insulting gesture as of a noose around the neck. And the Admiral had developed an infection in the lungs. He was moved to the Naval College in Greenwich. A stream of British officers came to call, showering attentions on him. It was observed that among the callers there was no French General named de Gaulle.

On January 6, two days before the General got around to sending his ultimatum to Eden, the Admiral was taken back to Scotland Yard. That ugly structure by the Thames below Whitehall had been made uglier still by the war: sandbags were piled high against the outer walls. But inside it was as spotless as a hospital. The walls were painted aquamarine; the brass doorknobs shone like gold, and like anthracite the big black shoes by which one can identify an English policeman.

Commander Younger of the Yard at long last showed the Admiral the letters on Consulate paper which caused his arrest. After merely a glance, Muselier said, "But it's an obvious forgery! Kindly bring in one of your specialists in counterespionage and have him look these over in my presence."

There was no shortage of such experts at the Yard. The one

chosen arrived and found that there was no need for lengthy inspection of the incriminating documents. He handed them back. "Yes, indeed," he said, "these are forgeries, and forgeries of the most inept kind!"

"But, but . . ." stammered Commander Younger, red in the face.

So the experts confounded the unhappy Commander; this fox, contrary to Major Morton's expressed opinion, turned out not to know his job very well after all!

The Admiral laughed for the first time since his arrest. His formal release would come two days hence.

During this confrontation, General de Gaulle was in the next room. The Admiral went in to find him. The General was extremely affable, even cordial, but the Admiral was glacial. When the General stated that he never for one minute doubted the Admiral's innocence, Muselier raised his eyebrows and asked: "Never? When Moullec went to prove it to you, I seem to have heard that you threatened to send him to join his admiral in prison!"

The exchange was brief. When the two men left the Yard, a number of persons were struck by the worried look on the General's face and by something very much like scorn on the Admiral's. The General went straight off to Churchill to demand an apology for himself as chief of the Free French. The Admiral was himself soon to receive the excuses of the English government and an invitation to dinner from the Prime Minister and Mrs. Churchill, and be granted an audience with the king. Eden in his letter of apology said, ". . . His Majesty's Government have satisfied themselves that the documents, which at first appeared to cast suspicion on you, are spurious. . . . His Majesty's Government looks forward to continuing their collaboration with yourself and with the Free French Naval Forces under your command, which are rendering such signal services to the Allied cause. . . ." In truth, in this darkest moment England was fighting for her life on the seas as well as in the skies. With the Mediterranean all but closed to them, convoys for Egypt and the East had to go around the Cape of Good Hope. Nazi submarines were operating effectively out of

Atlantic bases on the French coast, and surreptitiously out of Spanish ports, notably in the Canaries and far down the coast of Africa.

The Royal Navy placed a high value on the courage and the dash
of the French. Operating mostly in corvettes, they were equipped
with all the new antisubmarine wizardry as it developed, asdic, radar, etc. General de Gaulle was much later to express great pride in
his fleet. But at this moment he considered that the British were
overdoing things with Muselier. In his memoirs he states that
Churchill and Eden, "obviously much put out," expressed their
promise to repair, "in regard to Muselier, the insult which had
been done him. I must say this promise was kept. Indeed, the reciprocal change of attitude on the part of the British and of the
Admiral was so complete that it soon turned out to be excessive. . . ." [1]

General de Gaulle's ill humor can be easily understood. The
great espionage scandal within his own ranks, which turned out not
to be espionage at all but something else, did not end to his credit.
While the public heard nothing of this at the time, word of it
seeped down from the Cabinet through the services and even to
New York and Washington. Opinions expressed regarding the
General's conduct in the affair were not flattering. Within a
month, Churchill found it expedient to warn his services generally
that they must stop giving General de Gaulle the cold shoulder.

Another consequence of Admiral Muselier's ordeal was a growing misunderstanding between Carlton Gardens and Westminster
House, headquarters of the Free French Navy. This reached the
proportions of hate. The Admiral talked to me of this development
and mentioned something that was said at this time by some
hothead at Carlton Gardens: "We did not get your admiral's scalp,
but next time around count on us not to bungle the job."

In the *Courrier de l'Air* I did not fail to report, and prominently,
as you can imagine, the military exploits of the Free French Forces.
Ever since Sidi Barrâni, in the autumn of 1940, French volunteers

[1] De Gaulle: *Memoirs,* I, p. 148.

of French as well as colonial (mostly African) origin took part in operations in Libya. Their presence was mentioned at Sollum and at Bardia, and they played a part in the capture of Tobruk in the third week of January 1941. Lieutenant Colonel Colonna d'Ornano, who had set out in January with a group from the Camel Corps (*méharistes*), after a five hundred kilometer journey across the desert had attacked Murzuch, capital of the Tripolitanian oases of the Fezzan, with the help of a British patrol from the Nile. (The Italian post at Murzuch was some 550 miles due south of Tripoli.) "The air base was taken, the hangars, planes and repair shops burned. The Italian garrison, hysterical, took refuge in the fort, leaving prisoners behind. The Lieutenant Colonel met a glorious death at the head of his troops." Such was the text I gave in the *Courrier de l'Air* on the basis of communiqués from Carlton Gardens. Some weeks later, still following the Gaullist communiqués, I announced that toward the end of February Colonel Leclerc with a motorized column accompanied by planes had "victoriously fought the Italians in the heart of the Cufra Oases in Italian Libya, thus accomplishing a desert raid of over one thousand kilometers from his base in the Chad. The enemy surrendered." One must therefore assume that the first "capture" was incomplete.

To the news from Carlton Gardens about the heroic actions of the Free French Forces on land, I added the news—these bulletins were more accurate—about the Free French Navy. Two ships had been lost in action: the *Poulmic*, a patrol trawler, and the submarine *Narval*, which had mysteriously disappeared without a trace while on duty in the Mediterranean. Naturally I also printed the declarations made by General de Gaulle about the various actions.

"I, their chief, state that the exploits of our soldiers at Tobruk, at Murzuch, at Kassala, cruises like that of our *Narval*, aerial actions like those of our aviators in the skies of Libya and Abyssinia, are of those pure pages of glory that your children will recount to their children with pride."

One was frequently given the impression that the General disposed of a real army and that the victories he kept announcing were on a major scale. François Mauriac has since explained why this had to be: "The General simply overestimated the forces at his disposal for the purpose of his cause."

I went twice a week to Carlton Gardens to ask for news to publish in my little paper—which, don't forget, was to be read in France—about the military actions of the Free French Forces. At first I used to see my friend Siriex. As long as he was there, he was the one who gave me the news—when there were any. With him I got along marvelously. There was a good deal of sparring, but we always parted on good terms. I would then go upstairs. Sometimes, on the stairs, I would catch sight of the General; but, heaven be thanked, he now seemed to have forgotten who I was. I would then go in to call on René Pleven. With him, things never went so easily. He would say something like, "From the heights of your balcony, you look down on us, the Gaullists, with scorn. But, while you keep count of the attacks on us, we ourselves are the dead and wounded!" Of course he did not mean to suggest that he personally was either dead or wounded.

Pleven upset me when he talked like that. He was a friend of prewar days. At the moment of the shameful surrender at Munich, and afterwards, he seemed most sympathetic to me. But now he was inclined to judge me more and more severely. He thought me very wrong for not having signed the Gaullist enlistment oath, wrong for thinking that General de Gaulle aspired to the personal exercise of power in France, and wrong for reproaching him with spending more time fighting Vichy than fighting the Germans and the Italians. On several occasions he felt it necessary to inform me that the General was not at all happy about my little sheet. Or about the pamphlets produced by the English at Woburn. I could well believe it. The General would have preferred to have us back his appeals for violence against Vichy. Once Pleven made this pronouncement, which I repeat textually: "The French people are asleep. They must be awakened! They need a touch of the whip."

Need I say that when he talked like that it was not because he was ill-natured? I cannot envisage him with a whip in his hand. Nevertheless, it was clear that he was rather inclined to violence, on the part of others. I thought what he said on this occasion revolting. Our conversation came to a bad end. And when Anne heard about it, I was severely scolded.

February 1941

Mornings, when I reached London, I went first to see Torcy. From Bush House, where the Rolls or the Daimler from Woburn dropped me, I took the Underground. I came up through the old wooden station of South Kensington, decrepit and fragile, with its little shops where you could still whiff the peculiar smell of all those prewar stations, a mixture of the ozone released by electric sparks, of coal, fruits, flowers, disinfectants, and tobacco.

Torcy had leased three rooms in a nearby house for the duration. I would find him on the second floor in what he called his office. Very few books. I suspect that he often reread the same ones. And why not, when one has one's favorite books at hand? He passed as caring little for the social world, but he was much sought after, and was courteous and modest to a degree. His judgment was both respected and feared. And he had more sense in his little finger than there was to be found in all the great brains of Carlton Gardens. Try to picture him: tall, slightly stooped, his suits loose, comfortable, always a black or a dark gray—the general effect being that of a man who did not wish to look out of place but who clearly would not go out of his way to please. Topping that long body, a head as French as those of the sculptures on the portals of our cathedrals; the forehead high and slightly receding; his eyes light and deep-set; the nose prominent. The lower part of the face was firm and a little sad. Around his mouth a little smile was apt to play in which one could read both kindness and skepticism. In his expression there was an ever present politeness, and a slight absent-mindedness. He had the manners of a gentleman and the look of a peasant when he is accused of playing the fool. More than one vain and feather-headed individual let himself be taken in by Torcy's looks and manner.

He was given to saying that events carry more weight than men do. This came as a surprise from a man who never bent before the force of things and who had respect for only the choicest minds. He often said that there is no changing men. His English friends were distressed to hear him say this: they greatly hoped that he would make himself available to General de Gaulle, so that, near him, he could work a change in him. They had also hoped, before the war, to be able to reform, to soften, to mellow certain individuals powerful in Europe who were clearly—to all who had eyes to see—destined to bring misery to the world. One is inclined to think of the English as realists, but there is no denying that, faced with some possibility of modifying human nature, they can be wildly romantic. They can be equally so in their belief in chance. "Something will turn up," said Mr. Micawber.

In this respect there comes to mind an episode that gives a clearer picture of Torcy than I have been able to paint. It was, I believe, in 1937. There was then at the German Embassy a minister-counselor named Dr. Theodor Kordt. He was a Prussian, with spectacles, very small and very patriotic. He did not like Hitler. Nevertheless he hoped, like Neville Chamberlain, that Hitler would change. Pierre Maillaud used to see this diplomat frequently and got an idea to introduce him to Torcy, who, however, was not much interested. Maillaud insisted, and at length a luncheon was arranged. There were four of us: Dr. Kordt, Maillaud, Torcy, and I. From the hors d'oeuvres on, the Doktor wanted to talk politics. Torcy did not rise to the bait. He chose instead to talk about such things as the weather. Ten times at least the Prussian returned to the charge, and always with the same theme: Hitler was difficult, but if his demands were satisfied, he would then, like any man who has dined fully and well, doze off and become quiet, quite peaceful and easy to handle. Torcy still made no reply. Over coffee, the doctor, a model of perseverance, returned to the charge. Then it was that Torcy, taking from its yellow package one of those miserable French cigarettes we used to call Élégantes, chose to speak: "Now, if you would care to listen, Monsieur Kordt, I would like to tell you an anecdote. This is rarely done in our line of work any more, but please do me the honor of listening to it. I heard it from one of my great-aunts, and she heard it from her father. So, as you see, it dates back, but not to yesterday. That great-great-uncle of mine was an officer under Napoleon, who was then known as Bonaparte. It was during the campaign in Italy. Bonaparte was in the habit of gathering his young officers together on the eve of a battle to distract them. Together they would work out problems in mathematics or play billiards. On the evening in question, having thus amused himself, Bonaparte said: 'Now, messieurs, you should go to bed. I will expect you up at dawn when we go into battle. I think I should tell you that it will not go easily. There will be three Austrians to each Frenchman. But we will win. When we have won, however, that will not be the end. For there will be another battle. We will win that one, too. And tonight I want to reveal to you that my destiny is to go always from battle to victory, from victory to battle, from battle to victory, from victory to battle.' There you have your story, Monsieur Kordt." Now it was the Prussian's turn to be silent.

Torcy, as I have already implied, did not have much interest in having people talk to him about General de Gaulle. "Churchill has taken him up on his crupper, and nothing we can say will change things in the slightest. When Churchill wants to get rid of him, it will be too late: by then the General will have been adopted by the English and French peoples. Poor France! The defeat. Then Pétain. And afterwards General de Gaulle. It's very sad. Now get along with you. Back to work."

On leaving, Torcy and I went nearby to the offices of the magazine *La France Libre*, which had been set up in quarters loaned by the Institut Français. The founder and the moving spirit of this publication was André Labarthe. Hair unruly, voice and cheeks cavernous, eyes feverishly bright, he was always enthusiastic or indignant over something. When he was there, I mean; because more often than not, he was out. But one could always find Raymond Aron. Though his title was editorial secretary, he was in reality editor-in-chief. To my eyes he was the philosopher as described by La Bruyère, and Socratic besides: in every issue, the most interesting article was the one extracted by him, if not from a slave, from the Slav, an immense Slav called Staro. Staro was a genius at strategy, but he could not express himself in any known language. He would be locked in a room with Aron, gynecologist par excellence, who after two or three hours of Socratic questioning would bring forth the clearest, most intelligent, most prophetic analysis of military operations of any appearing anywhere that I knew of. At the War Office they looked forward impatiently to this monthly article; they would send over for the proofs.

Another personage on *La France Libre* was Mme Lecoutre, who managed the business office, where everything went as if by magic in the midst of what appeared to be wild disorder. Funds to keep the magazine going were raised behind the scenes by Mme Michaelis. In spite of every imaginable difficulty, the review was a remarkable success. Early in the game André Labarthe had been at Carlton Gardens, but while General de Gaulle was sailing off to Dakar, he had crossed swords with the Right-wing elements there. Labarthe was more or less on the Left. (In the spectrum of French politics, Right and Left do not coincide at all accurately with the Anglo-Saxon use of these always tricky words.) Once out of Gaullist headquarters, he founded *La France Libre.* He always said that it was from this review that General de Gaulle had appropriated, or perhaps it would be better to say borrowed, the name of his movement. Actually the General was later to discard the name because it connoted a limitation of his authority to the French outside France. That was when he changed it to "Fighting France" (*La France Combattante*), by which it was implied that the General commanded not only those Frenchmen who found themselves free outside France but also those who were fighting in the Resistance within France.

Relations between the General and Labarthe were at first of a not overly benevolent neutrality. When the review was getting started, Labarthe asked the General to write an article describing the crisis within the French government just before the armistice. The General answered in the negative; his letter was published in the February number. He begged off regretfully, but he wanted nevertheless to render homage to Paul Reynaud, who had never ceased, he affirmed, to work and to act for the honor and in the interests of France. This was a point of view not universally shared then and even less so today.

The General ended his letter with the ritual expression of good wishes for the review and with what appeared to be a warm "assurance of his sincere friendship." This friendship, if it was that, was later to be severely strained. In the end the General decided to ban Labarthe's review from all the military camps in England and from the territories in Africa and elsewhere which were under his control. This ban was invoked, I believe, because of an article which, when read with attention, demonstrated that General de Gaulle as a strategist had been guilty of a serious error in so completely overlooking the role of combat aviation in modern warfare. In the long run, Labarthe and his whole staff became extremely anti-Gaullist. I now and then arrived at the offices of *La France Libre* with a little job of work under my arm. Raymond Aron was strict. I would bring him book reviews and he would often turn them down on the grounds that they were too violent.

In some areas he let me have my way. It was thus that I wrote a critical analysis of a book called, I believe, *A travers le désastre*,[1] in

---

[1] "Here we find André Maurois analyzing the causes of the war, the responsibility for which he attributes to Great Britain. There was of course a certain Hitler, *but* if Georges Bonnet had been listened to . . . everything would have worked out all right. . . . Bonnet's efforts were unavailing; Great Britain would not bend. Public opinion was impatient. The British Prime Minister ran the risk of being toppled by a ground swell in the House of Commons. Thus, Great Britain declared war. This was six hours before France, where Bonnet had procured the delay. . . . Here also we have the theme of the Anglophobe propaganda which Maurois had adopted for his own. . . . In taking sides against a country without which he would have remained in obscurity (his first success was in his work in Anglo-French liaison in World War I), in denying his origins at the time when his co-religionists are suffering persecution, in courting the champions of Hitlerism, André Maurois has lost the es-

which André Maurois imputed British responsibility for the war. This piece appeared in *La France Libre,* but I signed it not with my own name but with a pseudonym. I bring this up because General de Gaulle had me accused in 1943 in Algiers, when I was director of Radio-Algiers, of having given Maurois time to speak over the air. As a matter of fact, Maurois's tenderness toward the Marshal and the whole defeatist crowd had prompted me to refuse him time. It was Commander, later Admiral Barjot who raised the ban during my absence in Morocco. I admire André Maurois's talent, but I felt no sympathy for his attitudes during the war. I was glad that he was able to get away to the United States, but his ideals were never mine.

Every time I went down to London I paid a visit to the remarkable staff that Pierre Comert had gathered around him on his newspaper *France.* Their offices were on the top floor of the Reuter building in Fleet Street. From its windows, one had an admirable view of the City and of the bombardments. From there I saw the smoking ruins of the lovely church of St. Bride's after the great fire bombing on December 29. Comert and his associates had felt the heat of the flames, which had all but licked their windowpanes. In the office were Louis Lévy, Marcel Hoden, and two top-ranking journalists, Georges and Charles Gombault, who are as esteemed today in Paris as they were then.

Pierre Maillaud's press service was two floors down. The General had tried to take over this agency, which was first called L'Agence LEF (Liberté, Egalité, Fraternité) and later AFI (Agence Française Indépendante), but Maillaud did not want him to have it. He later told me how he fended de Gaulle off. The agency, he explained, could exist only with the cooperation of the English and thanks to the use of material supplied by Reuter's. To operate an agency without this help, Maillaud told the General, would require capital. He gave an estimate of how much, a really astronomical figure. The General let the idea drop.

---

teem of Frenchmen who value sincerity, rectitude, courage and fidelity even more than talent." *La France Libre,* January 29, 1941.

I also often went to *The Times,* to ask Iverach M—'s advice. He is the most intelligent, talented, and sensible English journalist I know. Then in the evening, before going to bed at the Maison de l'Institut, we sometimes had dinner at Le Petit Club Français. It was in the basement of a house on St. James's Place. The celebrated Olwen had founded it, I think. In any case, she was its moving spirit. Gossip had it that she belonged to the Intelligence service. But there was no place in London where people spoke their minds more freely. Nearly everyone there was Gaullist, but of two different breeds: those who fought and those who politicked; the combatants and the Carltonians—breeds as different as bulls from steers. The Carltonians complimented the combatants on their exploits with a tendency to exaggeration. The combatants, who spoke modestly of action they had seen, were given to sticking *banderillas* into the backs of the Carltonians, who naturally did not react since they were steers. This spectacle was worth the price of admission, not so much for the skill shown by the *banderilleros,* as for that shown by the incense bearers; the dexterity with which they would swing the censers, making them clink against their chains, made one think that they had perhaps been acolytes in their youth.

What was the Carltonian brand of Gaullism? The definition was simple: it was the undertaking of certain men to preside over the government of France when the Allied victory became a fact, and thenceforth to insure her government. In this undertaking they were certain of success. But, in my opinion, they could not be sure that their procedures would not come as a huge surprise to the Gaullists inside France. The paradox that I claimed was in the cards was that the Pétainists in France would become Gaullists and the Gaullists in France would become anti-Gaullists.

If I had a bottle of champagne for every person I offered to bet on this point at Le Petit Club, I could drown for ten years my sorrow at seeing the majority of my fellow countrymen declare themselves in favor of the personal exercise of power. "The most personal that France has ever known," says François Mauriac, who is very pleased that it should be so. If at eight twenty-five the General spoke in person over the radio, the Carltonian Gaullists and the combatant Gaullists were unanimous in crying out, "*Vive le Grand Charles.*" How could it have been otherwise? The combatants had all signed the oath on enlisting and they obviously did not wish to admit that they were wrong in having done so. Furthermore, what pleased them in the movement they attributed to the General, and what displeased them they blamed on the entourage. This always happens in regimes in which one person rules supreme. And here is one of the reasons why there are not ten of us, perhaps not even five, from among the French who were in London during the last war, who can write about what we saw there. Write about it, I mean, with full intellectual and moral freedom.

Since the claim I am here advancing is not exactly self-evident, it calls for some elaboration. First, there were very few of us who kept apart, within our own small circle. As for the Gaullists who signed that very special oath in London, they would particularly not want to go back on that chapter of their past now, considering that they were hailed as heroes on their return to France in the General's train. They prefer to think that it is the General who has changed. There they are mistaken: he has not changed, unless it is that he has acquired a certain mastery over problems and that he has made connections that he did not then enjoy. Even in France, how many Gaullists would today admit that they had made a mistake? And could it be said that the heroes of that time had made a mistake? Jean Moulin, who lies in the Panthéon, a hero of the Resistance, symbolizes them all. Did he wish for and work for a regime such as we have today? Obviously I cannot say. As for his comrades, can they now say, "We were wrong"? That would be to abjure, to renounce the faith of those days.

Of those rare Frenchmen in London who were not Gaullists, some, like Torcy, maintain a disdainful silence. Others, like Pierre Comert, have gone to their graves. Of course Pierre Comert, Torcy, and some few others who for reasons of age or health were not able to fight did not have to resolve for themselves the ordeal of the Gaullist enlistment oath. There were others who had no military aptitudes but who were, for all that, nonetheless courageous under the bombardments.

The reputation I had (and rather encouraged) of being an odd-ball, but fundamentally not such a bad fellow, enabled me for quite some time to air my criticisms of General de Gaulle at Le Petit Club. But there came the day, inevitably, when I went too far and I had to give up going to that agreeable little dive where the good Olwen reigned like the sybil on her stool.

The disputes with the Gaullists all centered on the Resistance; to be exact, on three questions:

(1) Did anyone have the right to encourage the Resistance inside France to take risks that he himself did not share?

(2) Was it in the interest of the cause that some men should be sent to their deaths because "the blood of the martyrs is the seed of the Church"?

(3) As for the information reaching the Bureau Central de Renseignement et d'Action (BCRA), was it accurate enough to base on it orders to the Resistance to kill perons designated as collaborators by this London bureau, which was directed by a colonel of the extreme Right?

I would sometimes go so far as to claim that the BCRA, under the command of Colonel Passy, numbered in its ranks, along with some pure, unselfish, disinterested heroes, certain Cagoulards whose objective was to set up in France at the liberation a personal and authoritarian regime. You can easily see that ideas like this would surely get me excommunicated. That is, in fact, what happened, to Anne's great regret. She would have preferred not to be exiled from this Gaullist milieu with which we had so many ties of affection. On one occasion, however, she did back me to the limit against an embattled Gaullist. This important man from Carlton Gardens, whose name I shall not give now that he is dead (of natural causes), was holding forth in his cold and bitter manner. Finally he said, "In France, blood must be shed!" The setting for this little quarrel was not Le Petit Club but L'Ecu de France, where he was dining and dining very well too, and where I happened to be waiting for Pierre Maillaud, who had been good enough to invite me for dinner. I seem to remember that I then picked up a knife from the table and said, "Here you are! All you have to do is to go to France, and with this simple table knife you ought to be able to kill at least one German. Then blood will be shed, his and yours. If you want a Lysander to carry you over at night and land you in some field, let me know. I will speak to English friends. Or perhaps you would prefer to be dropped by parachute? I can arrange that too." After this exchange, my relations with the gentleman were a bit strained.

With Maurice Schumann, the Porte-parole, it was possible to express oneself more or less freely. But only more or less. It wasn't wise to go too far with him. There were subjects about which one could not make jokes, however innocent, with him. One day I made some remark about the General that must have been a little out of order. (I vaguely remember that it had to do with the famous General Trochu in the last days of the Third Empire. He was a voluble fellow who wrote a much-read pamphlet on the French army, made speeches, but, as military governor of Paris after Sedan, somehow never got to meet the Prussians in combat.) Whatever it was, Schumann did not like it and said, "You have wounded me!" So I applied bandages. In truth, I am very fond of him. I have heard various people express doubts about his sincerity; they could not be more mistaken. Maurice Schumann is a sincere man. He is absolutely sincere about each successive conviction. Take his previous "antimilitarism." He was not the only man, Lord knows, to have changed his mind. And whatever he is saying at any given moment, he believes. Just as his convictions succeed one another, so do his sincerities.

No matter what he did, he did it always in the service of what he considered to be a high cause. If ever he had to lop off a diseased branch, it would of course be to save the tree. There is the great religious order in which whatever is done is *ad majorem Dei gloriam,* to the greater glory of God. With Schumann, it was *ad majorem Gaullie gloriam,* to the greater glory of de Gaulle. Then, of course, he was not free; one has always to come back to that. With a man like Schumann, the oath counted. As Porte-parole, he was ordered to speak the Word and he spoke it—without argument, as if it were scripture.

Something can be said in Maurice Schumann's favor that cannot be said about all of his colleagues at Carlton Gardens: he was always entirely disinterested and he would accept no new stripes. Until the end, he remained Lieutenant Schumann. By temperament he was prey to anxiety, and he had the look of a man who hungered for the truth. And the truth he had found, as I suggested, in many quarters successively: he had been a pacifist and a disciple of Alain, then an admirer of Léon Blum, then one of Cardinal Verdier's ecstatic penitents. And now he was of the elect company of the General. To each of these phases he had brought the same ardor, the same faith, and the same intransigence.

When I say that I like Schumann I do not mean to suggest that I approve his role in France any more than I liked it in London. For example, I felt that in London he had been, however sincerely, a most unfortunate influence on Simone Weil, *la petite Weil,* as we called her in college.[2] After escaping from France in 1942, she had gone to New York and then come to London to join General de Gaulle. From Maurice Schumann she had caught the conviction that the General was the very model of a democrat and that he would abandon politics once France was liberated. Poor little Weil, who so strongly condemned the personal exercise of power in all its forms; at Carlton Garden they had her write down her thoughts on the ideal society that she hoped to see established in France. She was never to see the reality of 1944 and after, for she died pitifully young in London in 1943.

The propaganda of Carlton Gardens in England was of such a nature that it almost persuaded the English that without General de Gaulle the French would have crawled at Hitler's feet. I can think back on a little scene that took place at Maryland soon after Anne and I arrived at Woburn. One of our English visitors, who had been taking the Gaullist line a little too seriously, saw fit to exclaim: "How sad it is to think that the entire French people are ready to make friends with Hitler! With that wicked man! And what a relief it is, madame, to see that there are still some few

---

[2] Her books, all published posthumously, have given her a deserved renown in the world of letters, or perhaps more accurately, of philosophy. (Translator)

Frenchmen and Frenchwomen like yourselves who have listened to the words of General de Gaulle and have remained faithful to the English alliance!" For a moment I thought this would-be flatterer was going to get a glass of whisky full in the face. But there was no glass within reach of the gentle Anne. When the visitor left, Norman Cameron tried to console her, stammering out some unintelligible words. That night he wrote a poem for her which she found next morning under her plate. He called it "The Invader." Here are several lines from it:

> Our shops and farms wide open lie;
> Still the invader feels a lack . . .
> He calls for worship and amaze;
> We give him yes-men in a row . . .
> "Love me," he bids. We offer him
> The slack embraces of a whore . . .
> Invader-outcast of all lands,
> He lives condemned to gorge and crave,
> To foul his feast with his own hands,
> At once the oppressor and the slave.

So it was that we discovered that Norman was a poet. He had done a brilliant translation of Rimbaud's *Le Bateau Ivre*. Later he and Anne put the letters of Stendhal into English and rendered François Villon in Elizabethan verse. Norman was a huge chap, six feet six in height, careless in his dress, hair never combed, and with the politest, most aristocratic manners. On our arrival, he welcomed us as if we were guests long and impatiently awaited. He had such a gift for hospitality and was so gracious that one was warmed by the mere offering of a cigarette or of a chair. Anne he treated like a princess in exile, which sometimes went down badly with his young wife, Russian in origin, whom he called "my lamb" though actually she was a tigress when she thought she had reason for jealousy.

"The English are good fellows," Norman said once (he was Scottish). "They always have the best intentions, but, between us, they are often awkward." He was referring to the visitor who had considered us exceptional among the French because we were not wagging our tails at Hitler's heel. Here it must be said that one of our minor, very minor trials, during our years in England stemmed from the occasional efforts of Englishmen to give us lessons in patriotism. There comes to mind an incident dating back to the French Revolution. An English frigate had captured a French transport returning from l'Île Bourbon (today La Réunion) which had aboard it a Marquis de Montrond. He introduced himself, and the commander of the frigate invited him to dine in the captain's cabin. Seating him on his right, he proposed a toast. "France," he said, "has become a country of brigands, but"—raising his glass and smiling at his guest—"there are some exceptions." The Marquis de Montrond got to his feet and replied, "To be aboard an English warship is to be already in England, a country comprised only of gentlemen, with"—raising his glass and smiling at his host—"some exceptions." The simple truth is that lessons in patriotism go down badly, even among citizens of the same country. When some Englishman tendered such lessons to us, I could only smile politely and wonder just how he would take it if I were to tell him where *his* duty lay as a patriotic Englishman.

At this late date, it is hardly indiscreet to reveal that the British Department of Economic Warfare was busy devising ways and means of disrupting German transportation in Occupied France. On one occasion, somebody proposed dropping pamphlets over France calling upon French patriots to take part in the destruction of rolling stocks, railway tracks, and the like. I said that I could not bring myself to prepare any such pamphlets, and I explained why. The subject was never raised again. And no such pamphlets were drafted either by me or by others. I give this as an example—and I could give twenty more—of how the English would respect the freedom of Frenchmen in exile and would not encourage the peoples of the occupied countries to take risks too soon—the kind of risk that I liked to call "telecommanded." Some Gaullists were specialists at "telecommanding" their countrymen to risk their lives, and far too soon.

The Resistance in France was both heroic and extremely useful. But premature acts of resistance, I felt, had two serious drawbacks: first, they kept the Germans on their toes, which was fine *for them*; and second, such acts, usually not too damaging to the enemy (a cut telegraph wire can be quickly repaired, and so can a railway line), allowed the Gestapo to discover, to deport, to kill tens of thousands, perhaps even hundreds of thousands, of men and women whose efforts would have been infinitely more useful at the right moment. To me, it seems that open resistance should not have been encouraged until the very moment when the Allies were about to disembark on French shores. (I believe that General Eisenhower said something to this effect over the radio at the moment of the actual landings in Normandy, in June 1944.) And not an hour before. In fact, just one minute before would have been the ideal. It also seems to me that action should have been taken whenever possible by individuals, so as to avoid increasing the risk because of the possibility of betrayal. In the event of discovery, too, the reprisals would be limited to very small groups. Personally, if I had been able to play any part in the Resistance, I think I would have acted entirely on my own, without confiding anything to anybody.

From every point of view, those of us French who remained abroad were in every sense privileged. And it is of course astounding that the roles were in the end so far reversed that it was the French from outside, those who succeeded in escaping, who took over the government of France.

March 1941

Toward the middle of March, the General went back to Africa. Before taking his plane, he called together all the French in London and made us a speech. "This gathering of several thousand good Frenchmen and Frenchwomen, some for the sole motive that they find here and share the same emotion. . . ." The entire hall vibrated in unison. These meetings were most impressive. (Before the war, I had somehow associated them with what was then being called "the wave of the future," and I can remember the thundering applause, the orchestrated cheering coming over the air from countries that boded no good to French democracy or democracy anywhere.)

A part of the General's speech had to do with the Empire. That had been the General's dominant theme during the month of February, and the English had recognized his Committee of Defense for the Empire. At this time General de Gaulle would not have admitted that any of the overseas territories would not belong forever to France. Even in his celebrated speech at Brazzaville, he reaffirmed essentially the merits of colonialism. In London the General had had reprinted some of his earlier writings on the French colonies. He prescribed the use of force to maintain our domination until the day when, as he said, the colonial peoples, *still badly informed,* would *frankly accept union.*[1]

[1] *General de Gaulle's ideas on colonialism*

"While, under the protection of our shield, wealth, education, and liberty are spreading in these countries (the colonies), we see coming into being there currents of ideas, of passions, and of interests the manifest aim of which is to put an end to our domination." To maintain French domination, he prescribed the use of force for as long as might be necessary, until "wisdom is acquired by the elite" of the various colonies and "a spirit of loyalty by the masses." Then "we will see populations now reluctantly resigned to the tie with us accept it frankly. But, until that comes about, let us remain the masters lest everything be lost." From *The Army of the Future,* as reedited in London during the war.

The French must put no trust in natives to govern the Empire, however. ". . . Although the devotion of auxiliary troops is an almost intact treasure, it would be henceforward impolitic to make them the sole source of our authority. France would be imprudent to rely entirely on native troops to protect the Empire. But from the moment that a body of men of our own is created—our own men, but professionals and thus willing to undertake campaigns in faraway places and removed from the competition for votes; and if from time to time we show these fine troops in carefully selected regions—we will be well enough prepared, in the event unpleasant developments render the native troops less likely of success." From *The Army of the Future.*

He then showed not the slightest confidence in natives when it came to filling the larger part of the posts of command in the territories that had rallied to his cause. Whence came the need to find among the French in London, or those who later arrived in London, a whole corps of colonial administrators. Of course, this inevitably reduced the number of men in combat service. But what mattered above all else, they were saying at Carlton Gardens, was to "preserve the Empire" that Vichy was supposed to surrender. The good Professor René Cassin dwelt on this in his speeches, he too saying, "Marshal Pétain is selling off the Empire." In another speech he said, "Our colonies are ours, only ours!"

In view of the fact that General de Gaulle was decidedly committing himself to a career as a statesman, some of the English set themselves the task of discovering just what his political ideas might be. Several of these men, who were highly placed in the English government but did not necessarily share the opinions of the Prime Minister on personalities, on de Gaulle for instance, went to see Torcy. They had known him a long time and had complete confidence in his judgment.

"What are the General's ideas?"

"Ideas? Why, he has none."

"What? We meant his political doctrine."

"He has none. His ambition—we know what his ambition is. But his ideas? None!"

Torcy's friends were skeptical. When they persisted that the General had to have *some* ideas, and, whatever they were, they wanted to be informed about them, Torcy patiently explained: "Listen, if you want to learn for yourselves that General de Gaulle has no doctrine of any kind, try an experiment. Invite him to luncheon or dinner. Let one of you launch into some subject or other: for example, let him declare that he favors free trade. Or, on the contrary, that he believes in a managed economy. What the subject is doesn't matter. You will see that the General will give forth with some masterly affirmations in his support. Then let another of you continue with the same argument, whatever it may be. The General will become still more eloquent in agreement. Now, when the third man among you gets his chance to speak, let him say, 'I do not share your opinion, for this or that reason.' Then the first man who loosed the rabbit down the track will say, 'Come to think of it, your objections are worthy of consideration.' Then I'll wager you will find yourself face to face with a General de Gaulle who will extricate himself by a series of peremptory ambiguities. He will back and fill, but always in a tone of authority. Choose any subject you like: the urgency of dividing conquered Germany into slices like sausage, or, on the contrary, the importance of a united Germany allied with France. Say that you look to the return of the monarchy in France, *or* of a parliamentary republic. Do not be shy in your choice of vast ideas."

The experiment did take place. And it went along just as Torcy had foreseen. The three Englishmen were flabbergasted. Afterward they said to Torcy, "That man is not a politician; he's an advocate, a lawyer!"

"There I think you are wrong," Torcy said. "He will reign in France."

On the eve of flying off to Africa and Egypt, General de Gaulle received the diplomatic correspondents of the English press. He assured them that, according to irrefutable testimony, the Germans were infiltrating Morocco, Algeria, French West Africa.[2] (Robert Murphy, who was there, was saying the exact opposite.)

From London, the General flew first to Khartoum. He wanted to get his hands on Djibouti, then still under Vichy control. But how? It was really quite simple: this port and the area surrounding it depended entirely on the sea for their supplies. One had only to set up a blockade, and when the French were hungry enough, they would surrender. To starve them into surrender, however, the co-operation of the British fleet would be needed.

The General thereupon instructed his local representative, Gaston Palewski, to obtain British cooperation. Palewski, a man of deep loyalties, once the intimate collaborator of Paul Reynaud and

[2] *General de Gaulle's statement to the English press*

"Nazi infiltrations at Casablanca, Dakar, and in Algeria are demonstrated by evidence from indisputable sources." Quoted in *France*, March 13, 1941.

later an equally faithful associate of the General's, was not able to persuade the English. But the General bore him no grudge. Later, in fact, he made him director of his secretariat. De Gaulle had fully understood that Palewski's failure here was due not to a lack of effort or ingenuity on his part but to British bad faith, particularly that of the Admiralty. The General believed, and so wrote in his memoirs,[3] that by keeping the French "passive and impotent," England would have the whole area around the sources of the Nile, Abyssinia, Eritrea, Somaliland, and the Sudan. So why bother to help with Djibouti? Thus the Vichy authorities were able for two years more to feed the colony and maintain it "in pernicious obedience." Some day, I feel sure, a scholar will do a study of General de Gaulle's powers of prophecy. He is sure to take note of this passage in the memoirs.

The First Lord of the Admiralty, Mr. Alexander, was a member of the Labor Party. He was not enamored of General de Gaulle, especially since the Muselier "espionage" affair. It was rumored in London that Alexander considered General de Gaulle and Marshal Pétain as like as two peas in a pod.

The Navy in England was by far the most democratic of the three services. This always came as a surprise to French sailors; with us, it was just the contrary. The explanation lay, I think, in the fact that the English Navy had its roots deep in the country. There were few families on the British isles who had not had one or several of their own at sea; in France this would be rather the exception. The Navy was to England what the infantry was to France.

[3] De Gaulle: *Memoirs*, I, p. 169.

Spring, 1941

Under our windows at Maryland, the snow on the lawns held on until very late. Then suddenly spring arrived. All the English say about the splendor and freshness of their spring is true. In spite of the bombings which had pitted the capital with blackened ruins, the parks of London came all of a sudden ablaze with daffodils, their clear yellow like new-minted gold and most luxurious in effect. At Woburn Abbey the stags, having completed their annual tournaments, went to bathe in the lakes. The Reeves' pheasants trailed their brilliant tail feathers through the brush. The swans—white swans, black swans, red swans—promenaded their little families of cygnets around and about the thirteen lakes of the domain. Perversely, all these were portents of the probable arrival of the invaders. What they had not dared to try in the autumn, they might now be going to try in the spring. *"Nous attendons toujours les Allemands; les poissons aussi,"* Churchill had said, in French. The truth is that we thought it rather more likely that they would fall from the sky like a cloud of locusts. At Woburn the Intelligence experts forecast that the first assault might bring a quarter of a million Germans, or even half a million. Mortals began to appear more mortal still. The little lambs, born yesterday in the fields, seemed more fragile than in other springtimes. Our patrol at dawn became more serious. But I myself never ran into anything but mushrooms.

On patrol, we went by two's. My companion was often Terry, chief of the French section. He did not live in Maryland; one of the lucky ones with a family, he had lodgings in what we called the farms, where they ate much better than at the Abbey or at Maryland. Another frequent companion of mine on patrol was Norman

Cameron. Or it was one of the gamekeepers who lived on the domain. These keepers were all too old for the army, but they were remarkably good shots. The old Duke demanded that of his men. He himself, in the days when he was still able to hunt, never winged a bird. When he was in any doubt about a shot, he did not pull the trigger.

If a guest winged a partridge and the dogs did not bring it in, the guards were sent to find it if it took the entire evening and the whole night. Until it was found, nobody on the domain was allowed to fire a shot. On one unlucky occasion during a partridge shoot, one of the guests saw a large bird coming straight at him with the speed of an arrow, so he fired and proudly brought it down. He had succeeded in bagging one of those outsized parrots from India which are among the most beautiful and swiftest birds on earth. The Duke was in a fury and decided to have no more partridge shoots. The result was a population explosion among the partridges, and then an epidemic from which nearly all the common or gray partridges died. Only the red-legged partridges remained, the kind the English call French because they remind one of the red pantaloons worn by the French infantry before World War I. The epidemic occurred four years before our arrival; meanwhile, the gray partridges were prospering again.

One might think it surprising that our fare at Woburn was so mediocre (I am trying to be complimentary) in a region swarming with game of all kinds. But this was England; and rules were rules, and although game was not rationed, eating it was frowned upon. I suppose that this could be called English hypocrisy. I confess that later, when Anne and I had returned to London, the gamekeepers with whom I had made friends gave us partridge, pheasant, rabbit, and even venison filets in exchange for cartridges, a supply of which I had put in before the war. It was with not the slightest scruple that we sat down to these delicacies.

Earlier that spring, Harold the Playboy, the head of the house, was called to the office of the director. When he came back, he had such a worried look that we at first thought he'd had a reprimand. But it wasn't that. He went off to find Kay, the ravishing secretary whose young husband was a fighter pilot. "My dear Kay," he said gently, "I would like to talk to you a moment." He led her to her room. This was so unusual that she began to understand.

"Is it John?" she asked.

"Dear Kay, do sit down. I have something to tell you that is bad."

She did not sit; she simply fell, crumpled to the floor. Harold tried to catch her in his arms, but she struck her head on a corner of the bed. That night at the table she had a little cut which later would be no more than a thin line. Henceforth for all her days she would bear the scar of her husband's death, a white line, on her temple.

We had our sorrows. We the French could not bear to think of our million and a half prisoners in German hands. And the others whose countries had been overrun could only hope against hope. Everything considered, we made the best of it. There were even moments of gaiety. Anne began calling me *Monsieur le vilain*, which comes out in English as "scoundrel" or "rascal." Kay, who had buried her grief deep within her, joined in and got the others to do the same. There were never any quarrels. Jealousies there were—inevitable with so few young men and, between the Abbey and Maryland, so many pretty girls.

The queen of the secretaries at the Abbey was Doris, who later married a French sailor in Africa. At Maryland, one of our two Marys already had a husband. The other married my friend Paniguian. Rosemary left us to join the Wrens and then she too married a sailor, this one English. We ran into them in Algiers in 1943. In addition to the secretaries, we had our girl chauffeurs, all in uniform; we called them "the mechanized beauties."

The war off in the distance and on the seas was going none too well. In Libya, General Rommel, dispatched to the rescue of Mussolini's legions, was forcing the English to retreat. *Il Duce* had had a shellacking in Greece—which is to the honor of the Greeks but also, to my way of thinking, of the Italians; if I had been Italian, I would have most certainly deserted. In Greece too, Hitler had to go to the rescue, and the situation was reversed. The English, who

had sent in an expeditionary force, had to pull out. And then they
had to leave Crete, where the New Zealanders were heroic in vain
and the Navy superb; once again, this was an evacuation. And, as
Churchill had said earlier, wars are not won by evacuations. After
this Dunkirk, Admiral Cunningham had under his command in
the Mediterranean only two battleships and three cruisers to match
against Mussolini's entire fleet. Three English cruisers and six destroyers had been sunk. Two battleships, *Warspite* and *Barham*, as
well as the carrier *Formidable*, had been seriously damaged.

In sailors' families throughout Britain, tears were shed every day,
in private. In the cavalry, losses were figured in terms of sabers
or of horses; in the Navy and the Merchant Marine, in tons. England lost more than 300,000 tons in January, more than 400,000 in
February, more than 500,000 in March, and more than 600,000 in
April. Losses in lives were not tabulated, at least not for public
consumption, but they were heavy indeed.

But nobody wore mourning.

The German Army, a little behind Hitler's schedule but in no
wise fatigued by its efforts in the Balkans, Greece, and Africa, was
massing on the frontiers of Russia. That should have reassured us.
But not so; the apprehension of the War Office grew apace. The
belief commonly held was that, before launching his great assault
on England, Hitler wished to do away once and for all with the potential menace of the Soviets at his back. It was generally thought
that he would finish off the Russians in six weeks or so. *Then* England would have to bear the brunt of the German might. The
Americans, whom I seemed to be seeing more and more often in
London, and the English too, did their best to warn Stalin of the
danger. These warnings had the opposite effect. There are some
great liars who get their just deserts when nobody believes them any
more. But there is another kind of liar who no longer believes anybody; in the habit of deceiving people, such liars as these believe
that everybody is out to deceive them. Through skepticism, they
became naïve. Stalin was such a one.

To quote the great Cardinal de Retz: "The most distrustful persons are often the biggest dupes."

May 1941

Several weeks had passed without a bombing raid on London. There had been a very bad one on the night of April 16–17, with seven hundred German bombers coming over during eight long hours. More than a thousand people had been killed, and two thousand badly hurt. On May 8 we heard with dismay the German announcement that they had destroyed the Rolls-Royce works at Derby. It turned out that they had made a mistake, a mistake induced, as we later learned, by the new British device for "bending" their directional beam; unknowingly, they dropped their bombs in open country, killing two chickens.

But on the night of Saturday, May 10–11, there had been a tremendous attack, the heaviest and most destructive of the night raids since the great fire raid in the week of Christmas to New Year's. Although nobody could then know it, it was the last such raid.

Anne and I were not there on Saturday night. We were coming in very early on Sunday morning from Woburn when, miles out of London, we found ourselves in a thick pall of smoke that blacked out the rising sun (we had left very early from Woburn). From the darkened sky there filtered down a flurry of charred paper. Later we learned that this came from a huge fire in the building in the City where the Sunday newspapers had been stacked for delivery.

We soon heard the story. During the night the German bombers had flown over London in relays, with incendiary bombs for the most part, knocking out five docks, scores of factories, and blocking all the main railway stations. The casualty list was well over 3,000 dead or wounded. And that was the night the House of Commons, as the British said at the time, "copped it." One bomb left it a blackened ruin, and so it stood for years, as a reminder. Luckily, no one was in it at the time.

In our little car we felt our way that dark morning the length of Green Park to Wellington Barracks, where Admiral Muselier (General de Gaulle was still in Africa) was reviewing the Free French troops. Afterward we might have gone to Westminster Cathedral, to the mass in memory of Joan of Arc, whose feast day it was. We went home instead to see what had happened to our apartment. It was intact, although an entire building at the corner of the square had been obliterated by one of those magnetic naval mines, called "land mines" by Londoners, which the Germans were dropping by parachute. Our building was barely damaged, but the apartment presented quite a sight. A huge wall mirror, some eight feet wide and a good six feet tall, had been torn from the wall by the outdraft following the land mine's explosion, and had been smashed to bits against the opposite wall. Our tenants had been wise enough to spend the night in the shelter and hadn't even a scratch.

Anne and I went into the City of London, which from a distance seemed one vast bonfire. It was the very image of hell. The sun could not be seen at all. Against the sky-high curtain of black velvet, geysers composed of millions of sparks shot up from time to time as another burnt-out building fell in upon itself. One dared not get too near for fear of collapsing walls and the infernal heat that the still-burning buildings gave off. At the height of the fire it was ebb tide on the Thames, and that, along with the fact that some water mains were smashed, mostly by direct hits on the pavements above them, meant that the firemen did not have water enough for their hoses. They would get trickles of mud. Now, at high tide, they were dipping water out of the river and carrying it in barrels and buckets in trucks. The buckets and the trucks, against the immensity of the disaster, had about them something derisory, obstinate, and indomitable. Hundreds of fires were still out of control. Some were still burning as late as Tuesday.

The disaster of that bombing raid was so great that one was

numbed by it. Or almost. But there crept in beneath the numbness a twinge of selfish personal loss. Over what? Our mirror? No. But Dunhill's shop in Jermyn Street, beloved by every smoker, had been snuffed out. And then we saw that Wren's lovely St. Clement Danes had been hit. Again, a small private grief for anyone who had been raised on English nursery rhymes, as I had been.

> Oranges and lemons,
> Say the bells of St. Clement's . . .

The bells of St. Clement's would be saying nothing for quite some time. Even Big Ben was thrown out of kilter for a little while. Not for long, though: the English wouldn't stand for that. There were limits, as the charwoman said, to what that "narsty man" should be allowed. I read about her in the English papers. She and her crippled son Alfie had been bombed out of their little house. "When he tykes after the loikes of me and Alfie, he's going too far, that narsty man!" And so he was.

It was a truly fantastic day. Reichsführer's deputy Rudolf Hess had landed in Scotland, on that mysterious mission that was never to be fully explained. He had come to see the Duke of Hamilton, who was, needless to say, appalled. He also had some other dukes on his list, including of course the Duke of Bedford.

We had no way of knowing that this greatest raid was to be the last. Only Adolf Hitler and his clique knew it then; and why. It was for the British people a very painful moment. They, all alone, had stood up to so much. Now it seemed that the bombings would go on and on until there was not a building left. The English were bone-tired. And they saw no light at the end of the tunnel.

Then, on May 24, England's cup of woe was filled to overflowing when she lost the HMS *Hood*, the fastest and most heavily armored of her battle cruisers. She had joined in the chase after the *Bismarck* when the world's biggest battleship finally nosed out of her hiding place in a Norwegian fjord. A shell from the *Bismarck*'s fifth salvo struck, it seems, in the lightly armored spot between her funnels, plunged into her vitals, and the great ship blew up. In a matter of minutes, there was over the sea nothing but a column of smoke. Of the 1,500 men of her complement, three survived.

Churchill had some rough times in the House of Commons. The feeling about him at this bad moment in the war was perhaps best expressed by Margot Asquith, Lady Oxford, the highly vocal widow of the great World War I prime minister, when she said, "Do you know what my husband would say to Mr. Churchill if my husband were alive now? Mr. Asquith would say, 'I don't admire you, Mr. Churchill, for your oratory, though it is inspired. I don't admire you for your wartime leadership, though it often reflects true greatness. I don't admire you for your mastery of the House of Commons, not even for your paintings and your bricklaying. But I admire you, Mr. Churchill, for your robust good spirits when times are black.' "

June 1941

It was at this precise time, when Churchill had so many worries, that General de Gaulle urged his plan for the opening of a new front. Against the Germans? Against the Italians? Not at all. Against General Dentz in Syria and Lebanon. General Dentz owed allegiance to Marshal Pétain.

This whole business was extremely complex. I will try here to reduce it to its essentials. Syria and Lebanon had been under French mandate since the end of World War I. In principle, they were to continue so until the French parliament had ratified the agreement, signed before World War II, to make them independent.

To carry out his project, the General had need of British help for the simple reason that General Dentz commanded 30,000 fighting men, against whom the 6,000 Free French could not have gone far. The British answer, after a series of hot exchanges between Churchill and General Sir Archibald Wavell, British Middle East commander, was this: yes, we will gladly help you, but on two conditions. First, we must make certain of the presence or the imminent arrival of the Germans in Syria and in Lebanon; otherwise, it would be best to leave the Vichy French alone. Second, in the name of France, since you represent France, you are to grant independence to the two countries, grant it now. We have no wish to lend a hand to an operation that would only confirm the dependence of Syria and Lebanon. We favor independence for all Arab countries in the Middle East, including those which have hitherto been in French custody.

The General was embarrassed by these conditions. If he granted independence at that time, he would surely be accused of alienating part of the French empire in flagrant contradiction of his slogan: "Vichy is surrendering the Empire; General de Gaulle is saving the Empire." If he argued that he did not have the powers necessary to grant Syria and Lebanon their independence, how could he continue to claim that he incarnated France? What would be a solution for him? Why, the answer is simple enough: proclaim independence *now*; there are ways of drafting a declaration.

Was Hitler informed of de Gaulle's determination to enter Syria? To me that seems probable; in London it was being talked about openly. You can imagine how Hitler would enjoy the thought of a battle between Frenchmen, with the English mixed up in it as well. For the Germans, that would be a highly profitable operation with no investment, and without casualties of any kind. Furthermore, Hitler might have wished to use it as a red herring while he sent his armies against Russia.[1]

[1] ". . . We could not think of entering Syria unless the enemy himself was setting foot there." De Gaulle: *Memoirs*, I, p. 174.

"The memories evoked in me by the campaign we had been obliged to open were cruel ones. . . . But the tighter sorrow gripped, the firmer I grew in

A rebellion in Iraq, directed by Rashid Ali and promoted by the Germans, at that moment threatened Basra and the English oil supplies. Hitler sent Rashid Ali arms transported by German planes, which landed, enroute, on airfields in Syria, with the authorization of Vichy. They did no more than land and take off. The Germans arranged for false news reports which were spread in Lisbon and in Ankara, from where they were picked up and sent straight to London. The burden of these dispatches was that German armored divisions were about to land in Syria.

I remember clearly walking down Charing Cross Road with Torcy after lunching on lima beans cooked in rancid oil in a frightful Greek restaurant in Shaftesbury Avenue. We came to the corner of St. Martin-in-the-Fields and Duncannon Street, and saw the enormous black headlines of an *Evening Standard* poster: TWO PANZER DIVISIONS LANDING IN SYRIA.

I can still see Torcy as if it were yesterday, pointing to the poster and saying, "I am sure that is false." It was, in fact, false. That same afternoon, on my way to Fitzmaurice Place to meet the automobile that would drive me back to Woburn, I met one of General de Gaulle's commissioners, who was to take the same car. He had managed to be invited to Woburn, in principle once a week, to present the General's viewpoint, though in a setting apart from the Abbey itself and the offices. In other words, his function at Woburn was, hopefully, to counter my nefarious influence.

As the car started off, he spread out the *Evening Standard* and, slapping the headline with the back of his hand, said, "How about that! There we have it! Two armored divisions!"

"I saw Torcy just now, and he said categorically, 'I am sure that is false!'"

---

the determination to go through with it. The same was true, indeed, of the soldiers of Free France, of whom, practically speaking, none was to weaken." De Gaulle: *Memoirs*, I, pp. 184–5.

"On June 22 . . . Hitler launched his armies in the direction of Moscow. He had an obvious interest in the largest possible fraction of the forces opposed to him being tied up in Africa and Syria." De Gaulle: *Memoirs*, I, p. 187.

"And I am just as sure that it is true! Torcy has lost his judgment. He is failing visibly."

"Just how would you know that? You never see him. When you or any of your Gaullist friends so much as get a glimpse of him, you hurry off to cross to the other side of the street."

In response to the reports that the Germans were about to arrive there, Churchill decided to intervene in Syria and Lebanon. You will recall that de Gaulle, in order to obtain British agreement for his plan, had promised independence. Now the British said, "We will add our guarantee to your promises."

"Oh, no!" replied de Gaulle. "My word is enough!"

"We prefer to give ours, too."

"That is so you yourselves can benefit from the operation!" countered the General. "It is to win the favorable opinion of the population. You want to take the place of France in the Middle East."

"No, not at all!" objected the English. "On the contrary, we have decided to proclaim that we have no designs on Syria and Lebanon. But if you enter the country with the help of British arms, we want it to be with our guarantee of independence also. Otherwise, don't count on us. It is up to you to decide."

The General agreed. But the campaign opened in an atmosphere of mutual distrust and suspicion. The General was not at all convinced that the English had no designs on Syria, and the English doubted the value of Free French military help in the campaign. De Gaulle instructed General Catroux to issue a proclamation that began and ended with the words: *"France declares you independent!"* But buried in the text was a sentence indicating that before independence became effective there would be a formality to fulfill, a treaty to negotiate and sign.[2]

[2] *Proclamation of General Catroux in the name of General de Gaulle* (Published in *France*, London, June 9, 1941; but not included in General de Gaulle's *Memoirs*.)

Inhabitants of Syria and Lebanon!
At the moment when the forces of Free France, united with forces of the British Empire, its ally, are entering your territory, I declare that I am assum-

The inhabitants of Syria and Lebanon distinctly heard General Catroux declare in General de Gaulle's name: "I proclaim you free and independent." They also heard him say: "A great hour in your history has sounded. France declares you independent through the voice of her sons who are fighting for her life and for the liberty of the world." They, not unnaturally, considered that the proclama-

---

ing the powers, the responsibilities, and the duties of representative of France in the Middle East.

I do this in the name of Free France, which identifies itself with the traditional and the real France in the name of its chief, General de Gaulle.

In this capacity, I come to put an end to the mandate and proclaim you free and independent.

You will henceforth be sovereign and independent peoples, and you may either constitute yourselves into separate states or unite in a single state. . . . In either case, your independence and your sovereign status will be guaranteed by a treaty defining our reciprocal relations. . . . This treaty will be negotiated as soon as possible between your representatives and myself. Pending this, our mutual situation will be one of complete unity for the purpose of achieving an ideal and our common objectives.

Inhabitants of Syria and Lebanon, my declaration assures you that if the Free French and the British forces are crossing your territory, it is not to take away your liberty, but to assure it. It is to drive out of Syria the troops of Hitler. It is to prevent the Middle East becoming an enemy base to be used against the English and against ourselves.

Inhabitants of Syria and the Middle East, if you answer our appeal, if you rally to us, know that the British government, in agreement with Free France, has promised to grant you all the advantages enjoyed by free countries associated with us. Thus, the blockade will be lifted and you will immediately enter into relations with the Sterling block, which will open vast possibilities for your imports and exports. You will be able to buy and sell freely in all the free countries.

Inhabitants of Syria and Lebanon, a great hour in your history has sounded. France declares you independent through the voice of her sons who are fighting for her life and for the liberty of the world.

Extract on Syria from Dictionnaire Larousse, *postwar edition*

". . . Despite having recognized the independence of Syria and Lebanon, France reserved for itself the maintenance of order in the Middle East, for reasons of military security, necessary to the conduct of operations in the war. Only with great uneasiness did Syria and Lebanon bear this restriction, and the disembarkation of new French troops was the occasion for bloody incidents (May–June 1945), in the course of which British troops were called upon to intervene in spite of French protests."

tion meant what it said, that they were then and there independent. The verbs in the Catroux proclamation were not in the future tense. Neither were they conditional. The present tense exclusively was employed. So the Syrians and the Lebanese believed that they were to become independent as of *now*.

It was on a Sunday (another historic Sunday), the eighth of June, that the troops of General de Gaulle crossed into Syria. The unlucky Free French, worthy of a better cause and of another enemy, were met by heavy fire from the forces of Vichy, who were the more exasperated because de Gaulle said he was rescuing them from the Germans when they had not seen even the shadow of a Nazi soldier. General Dentz, a solid fellow, administered a licking to General Legentilhomme. The British Middle East commander, General Wavell, had to send reinforcements, and finally, on June 21, it was the Australians who took Damascus. General de Gaulle made his entry into the city on June 23. That same night the Nazi planes came over and bombed the city: Germans at last, but in the skies overhead.

The victory over the army of Vichy was won by British troops, five or six times more numerous than the Free French. General Dentz thereupon addressed himself to the English, not to General de Gaulle, to negotiate an armistice. His reason was other than military: he could not stand the sight of the Chief of the Free French even in a painting on the wall! The Vichy troops didn't like de Gaulle. Only 2,000 out of Dentz's 20,000 rallied to Free France; they could not understand why they were accused of welcoming Germans to Syria.

General de Gaulle was far from pleased that it was not to him but to the English that Dentz surrendered. And the Lord only knew what the English would conclude in the way of an armistice!

The General's apprehensions were borne out. The so-called Acre convention ran counter to all his ideas; and this in spite of his having warned Churchill on June 28 (as he says in his memoirs, Vol. 1, pp. 189–208) "of the extreme importance which England's behaviour towards us in the Middle East would have from the point of view of our alliance." The convention, he said, in form and substance "went beyond my worst fears." He refused to recognize it and withdrew to his tent—all the way to Brazzaville. This action he attempted to explain: "My only means of limiting the damage was to gain space and height, to reach some cloud and from there swoop down upon a convention which would not bind me, and which I could tear up as far as I could."

The English, he thought, had "ulterior motives." They wanted Syria for themselves. He thereupon telegraphed Churchill declaring that the convention was "extremely painful to our dignity" and threatening to break relations. Churchill was irked. If he handed over Syria and Lebanon to General de Gaulle, what would happen to the promised independence which Great Britain had guaranteed? Would it be honored immediately? To express any doubts on this subject would be to insult General de Gaulle; on the other hand, if the General followed through on his threat to break relations, what would be the consequences to him, Churchill?

It would have been easy to justify his attitude: he had only to reveal the facts in their entirety. If all the facts, such as I have tried to present them here, had been made public in England, General de Gaulle would have had to pack up and move to Brazzaville for good. Some members of the entourage in London were afraid that this would in fact happen. But the General knew better; he knew that *Churchill could not break off with him!* Why? For friendship's sake? No, even if this friendship did indeed exist. The reason was simply that Churchill could not divulge to the English people the full record of the Free French leader's behavior to him and to the British government. For it was Churchill who had chosen General de Gaulle—who, so to speak, underwrote him before the country.

The press would ask, public opinion would ask, and, most important of all, Members of Parliament would ask how the Prime Minister could have made such a mistake about the man. On how many disastrous undertakings, beginning with Mers-el-Kebir and Dakar, had Churchill not embarked? And why was he revealing the truth about the relationship with General de Gaulle so belatedly? Why had he for so long proclaimed General de Gaulle to be England's best friend?

Very well, the independence of Syria and Lebanon could wait. Grant General de Gaulle what he wants! Such were Churchill's orders. Anything would be preferable to a break.

Take note of General de Gaulle's technique. It would serve him again. And each time he would win because each time it would be even more difficult for Churchill to confess before Parliament and the country that he had made an error which the Opposition already considered serious and of lasting consequences. Later, even with Roosevelt's help, he could not do it.

Do not think that Churchill no longer entertained feelings of friendship for the General: Churchill's friendship, as I have said, was (at this time and all through his career) in no way affected by the attitudes of the friends who were its recipients. As with love, it would grow stronger in the face of obstacles. In this attitude of friendship through thick and thin there was, of course, an element of pride.

As for General de Gaulle, he had no reason, in my opinion, to fear the consequences of public clashes with the Prime Minister on matters of policy. First, because he had courage. And then, too, he knew that Churchill could not disavow him, could not repudiate him—for one reason above all, that the popularity of the Free French leader inside France would inevitably be reinforced, immeasurably so, by any disavowal or repudiation. Churchill said just that one day when he accused de Gaulle of deliberately provoking open quarrels. General de Gaulle reports this odious accusation in his memoirs. But it was qualified by the Prime Minister's admission that the General could not afford to let himself appear to French eyes as a puppet of the country that had given him asylum and had also subsidized him so generously.

If the General, far from appearing a too docile ally, passed for extremely prickly and difficult, and capable of attributing to the English first and then to the Americans fell designs against the interests of France, it was because he was following the dictates of his conscience. He was willing to offer public opposition to the Prime Minister and later to the President of the United States because he really believed that the British, as he says in his memoirs apropos of Syria, entertained "malevolent designs" and that the Americans wished to impose their will on the world—a sentiment he has repeatedly put into bitter words. Then, too, he proceeded, however unwittingly, to play up to the xenophobic sentiment so widely prevalent in France among the *petits bourgeois* of a generation that I like to think is rapidly fading away. This xenophobia in our country seems to apply particularly to those who are labeled "Anglo-Saxon," as if there really were such a race.

During the war I knew any number of my compatriots who were persuaded that the Americans meant to steal Casablanca from us, to cite but one example, and that the English meant to snaffle Bizerte. These were not just "little people" of the kind who might be expected to nurture xenophobic prejudices; all too frequently they were officers in the French Navy from upper-middle class families, and they were perfectly sincere in this.

Here is the heart of the matter. If one overlooks this, it is all too easy to miss one of the fundamental reasons for General de Gaulle's success—a reason that is operative to this day. François Mauriac did not overlook it in his book *De Gaulle*,[3] which is so useful to an understanding of the General and his admirers. In fact, he accords the highest marks to the Chief of the Free French precisely because the President of the United States disliked and distrusted him. To cite Mauriac's own words, he offers up praise to the General because he, the General, was the adversary "whom President Roosevelt, from the very first day, sought to push aside, and whom he tried to overcome right up to the end. And not only Roosevelt but Churchill himself, despite a friendship that was doubtless sincere."

[3] François Mauriac: *De Gaulle* (Paris: Grasset; 1964) (New York: Doubleday; 1966).

Summer, 1941

On the morning of Sunday, June 22, Pink came into our room as usual and went through his ritual. He put a cup of tea on the night table at the head of each bed, drew the blinds, and delivered his report on the weather.

"A fine morning, sir. The sun is shining and the birds are singing."

He always said "sir," as if Anne were not there. Anyway, she was nearly always still asleep or pretending to be. On this particular morning, Pink said: "Did you hear the BBC at seven o'clock, sir?"

"No, Pink, is there any news?"

"News which I suppose would interest you, sir. Mr. Hitler has entered Russia. He has declared war on the Russians, Mr. Hitler has, sir."

"Very bad news for them, Pink."

"Very unpleasant news for the Russians, sir. And very pleasant for us, wouldn't you say?"

"Indeed, indeed, Pink."

I went downstairs with some speed. Maryland was barely awake: on Sundays we had breakfast later than on weekdays. Norman was humming as he stood by the window looking out at the bright yellow jonquils that made us all hunger for the eggs we did not get. "The Playboy," he said, "is going to have a devil of a time keeping Mafalda's dog from barking at the wall map of Russia, after all the trouble he had teaching him the trick!"

Georges did not, like Pink, suppose that the news was very pleasant for us. His was the official view, that of the War Office: "Give him six weeks and Hitler will have brought down the Russian bear, skinned it, and cut it up for the market. He is a most distinguished butcher, that Hitler. He will cut it into steaks, roasts, and boiling meat. When that's over, he will send all his planes and all his parachutists right on our backs. He would have done it sooner, but he had to get rid of that bear. Yes, in less than two months I think that we will be able to close up this damned shop here and kill some jerrys instead of showering him with the damned propaganda from this damned printing shop."

The words of the honorable Pink and of the official Georges give a fair idea of the contradictory opinions held by the public and the experts on that astonishing day. For the English people, by and large, the German attack on Russia came as a happy surprise: Hitler had taken on another enemy, and one on which they had not counted. For the strategists of Whitehall, it was a catastrophe that they had of course foreseen. Up until then, the Russian Army and the Russian Air Force had constituted a power-in-being at Hitler's back which kept him from making an all-out attack to the west. Once this menace to the east of him was crushed, he would really pounce on England with everything he had.

That Sunday morning I met only two men, apart from Pink, who proved to be clairvoyant. One was Brigadier-General Skaife, and the other, Paniguian. Brigadier Skaife had been British military attaché in Moscow. His reports sent to London described the formidable strength of the Red Army. However, when the War Office saw that this same Red Army in 1939 was held in check by little Finland, they lost no time bringing the Brigadier home. Clearly the man must be mad. So they palmed him off on the Foreign Office, naturally as an expert on Russian affairs—the sort of trick one department will play on another. He finally reached us at Woburn Abbey—the ultimate in disgrace. He did nothing but play golf and read, with close attention, every scrap of information coming out of Russia.

On that June 22 the Brigadier was beaming. Hitler was done for, he said to anybody who would listen. And we asked nothing better than to listen. He put on such a startling imitation of a Russian soldier that we had him repeat it for us the next day. The second performance took place in a one-time carriage house that had been transformed into a lecture hall. He marched back and forth, up and down, in the Red Army's variant of the goose step. He wore his usual dress shoes but managed somehow to give the impression that he had boots on weighing four pounds each. At each ponderous, formal step he would roar something like, *"Broum! broum! broum!"* Then he gave us a vivid description of the enormous Russian tanks going into action, and of Russian artillery, mechanized and horse-drawn, wave on wave of it. His euphoria of that day was marred by one thought, and only one. He took me aside and whispered, "Hitler is done for, without a doubt. But Stalin, he will be saved!" One can't have everything.

The other one among us who immediately understood what the German attack on Russia meant to us all was my friend Pan, Armenian by birth, English by naturalization, very intelligent and admired by us all. He too had an imitation for us, of a Red Army general he had known in Rumania I think, who used to name off for him in French the great rivers of Russia, starting in the west and moving east, his voice swelling in volume from river to river: *"Bon fleuve Dniester! Bon fleuve Niémen!* Excellent, excellent *fleuve Dniéper! Mais Volga! Volga:* IMPASSABLE!"

That night nobody came late to the lounge. We had all taken our places around the radio set, and our stenographers had their pads ready to take down the speech the Prime Minister was to pronounce. The text, prepared at the last moment, had not yet reached us by the private Foreign Office wire. Big Ben's bronze voice came over the air waves, nine heavy bongs. The BBC broadcaster read the evening news bulletins, and the news was very bad, as usual at that period in the war. Then Churchill was announced. From the loud-speaker we heard a slight coughing, a clearing of the throat, and then that voice, deep, friendly, and warm, in the momentous words: "But now I have to declare the decision of His Majesty's Government. . . . And that we must speak of now, at once, without a day's delay. . . . We have but one aim and one single, irrevocable purpose. We are resolved to destroy Hitler and every vestige of the Nazi regime. . . . It follows, therefore, that we shall give whatever help we can to Russia and to the Russian people.

"The Russian danger is, therefore, our danger, and the danger of the United States, just as the cause of any Russian fighting for his hearth and home is the cause of the free men and free peoples in every quarter of the globe."

In London the next day, I went to Carlton Gardens. I wanted to know, for the *Courrier de l'Air,* which the RAF was about to rain down over France, whether General de Gaulle, like Churchill, had made a statement on the sensational new turn in the war.

"Have you any news from the General?" I asked.

"Yes, great news! He has made his entry into the capital."

"The capital? What capital?"

"Damascus, of course!"

To my questions about Russia, the answers were about Syria. There was much talk of *perfidy*—not Hitler's *perfidy,* but the *perfidy* of the English. For months, for years, the representatives of General de Gaulle and the British agents, led by General Spears, would be pulling each other's hair over the state of the Middle East. Their wrangling—wherein perfidy sometimes did genuinely play a part—got nearly out of bounds at times, with threats and counterthreats of war. There was a dispute over the country of the Druses, those stiff-necked, industrious people in southern Syria. "If we have to fight you," said the English general to the Gaullist general, "we are ready to do it!" If these furious voices had reached Hitler's ears above the uproar from the Russian front and other fronts, how sweet they would have sounded to him! They were still to be heard long after his death in 1945.[1]

Torcy occasionally used to say, "These quarrels will have as an

[1] "Then, on June 4 [1945] I sent for the British ambassador, asked him to sit down, and said, 'We are not, I admit, in a position to open hostilities against you at the present time. But you have insulted France and betrayed the West. This cannot be forgotten.' Duff Cooper stood up and walked out." De Gaulle: *Memoirs,* III, p. 221.

end result our being thrown out, all of us, English and French. And that will not be for the greater good of the Arabs either. Our two old countries ought never to quarrel in front of the Arabs, ought never to appear the one apart from the other. Every time the English try to carry on a uniquely English policy out there, it fails. Every time we try to follow a uniquely French policy, it fails. The tête-à-tête with the Arab can be fatal. You will see that General de Gaulle, in wanting France, and France alone, in what he persists in calling 'the Empire,' will lose everything. That will be a misfortune for the Arabs. Once they have kicked us out the door, they will reestablish states of servitude among themselves which will set them centuries back in time. It is true that we French are not exactly qualified to give lessons to them; if we show ourselves incapable of handling our own affairs, why should we want to handle theirs?"

He talked to me like that twenty years before we were shown the door in Algeria. Fifty years ago his father, one of the truly great diplomats of the Third Republic, said, when he was in Algeria: "I don't want a French university here. I don't want French barracks. Our children should go to France to study, our young men should do their military service in France. If not, eventually there will be something like two Frances and we will head straight toward catastrophe. The natives will suffer, and we will too."

It was some time after Churchill's forthright statement that General de Gaulle got around to taking a position publicly on the German-Russian War. He followed close in Churchill's footsteps then, but very soon he was to catch up with him and pass him by. He began to talk in terms of "our dear and powerful Russia," and "our cherished unions [syndicates]." He was quick to realize that after the German onslaught the French Communists, released from the paralysis of their party line of 1939–41, would become furiously active in the Resistance and soon would be setting the pace. The General went to work on them with his usual intelligence and brought them over to his side, offering them places in his embryo government. This worked well enough in France. But in a foreign-policy fling the General stubbed his toe, so to speak. He had an idea that he could use Stalin as a sort of counterweight to the "Anglo-Saxons." This phantasy he described as "playing the Russian card." But, for all his pains, he only got a show of scorn from Stalin. Stalin did not want him at Teheran. And he was not present at Yalta to hear Stalin deny the French any part in the occupation of Germany—until Churchill and Roosevelt made his case for him. Then, too, at Yalta the partition of Poland, at that time totally under the Red Army, was agreed to in effect, and no one troubled to consult the General, who had very strong ideas on the Polish question. So did many other people, including the Polish government in exile and the Polish armies fighting alongside the Allies. But nobody seemed disposed at the time to argue with the Red Army.

The General returned to London on September 1. His epistolary relations with Churchill were strained almost to the breaking point. His Free French advisers in London had been alarmed by the General's tone, but their respectful efforts to persuade him not to do the irreparable had been furiously rebuffed. He was accusing English agents in the Middle East of affronts of every sort, and not always without cause. To him the most odious offense had been the efforts on their part to oblige him to grant independence immediately or in the very near future to Syria and to Lebanon. "They are trying to supplant us in the Middle East!" This was his theme, and I must concede that in this instance he was right. There is no doubt that British agents, swarming there, had been ordered by Churchill to cease trying to dislodge their French allies, but in Arab countries English functionaries easily caught a local fever that might be called Lawrencitis. This malady paralyzed its victims' obedience reflexes. The cure was well known, at least it had been in the past. Local treatment was always contraindicated. London was the place to look to; the Foreign Secretary or, better still, the Prime Minister must be told that the complainant did not for one second doubt that the promises the British had made would be kept but that meanwhile their feverish agents must be curbed.

General de Gaulle, disregarding the pleas of his subordinates in the British capital, took quite another line: he questioned the good faith and sincerity of the British. And this threw Churchill into such a state of indignation that he declined to see the General at the time of his return to London. He made him wait fifteen days. Meanwhile, on September 9, the Prime Minister made a statement, before the House of Commons, concerning Syria and Lebanon. The third of its three points contained a concession to the General: England admitted that Syria was not to be granted independence before the end of the war. But the Syrians were to be given increasing opportunities to administer their own affairs.

The other two points were, first, that British troops had provided the major effort, with four divisions to the six battalions of Free French; and, second, that Great Britain had no political ambitions in Syria or Lebanon. She had no desire or intention to take the place of France.

Finally, on September 15, Churchill received General de Gaulle. The first part of their conversation was stormy. The two men did not understand each other. They never would. Churchill took it hard that the General should attribute to him, among other devious designs, the ambition to supplant the French in Syria after he, Churchill, had solemnly affirmed the contrary. He was beside himself in the face of this challenge by his *protégé*, General de Gaulle, to his sincerity and to his word.[2] However, toward the end of the conversation the two men changed the subject, wished each other well, and parted on a handshake.

But misgivings persisted. Churchill, quite seriously disturbed and worried, and having, as he put it, other fish to fry besides the affairs of Carlton Gardens, handed the whole thing over to Anthony Eden, then Foreign Secretary. Eden's exchanges with General de Gaulle were less cordial and also less violent than the Prime Minis-

---

[2] ". . . Mr. Churchill, each time we came into collision on account of the interests for which we were respectively responsible, treated our disagreement as a personal thing. He was hurt by it and grieved, in proportion to the friendship which bound us to each other. This attitude of mind and sentiment, added to the devices of his political tactics, plunged him into fits of anger which gave our relationship some rude shocks." De Gaulle: *Memoirs,* I, pp. 231–2.

ter's. Nevertheless, it was to Eden that the General was reputed to have declared one day, not that he was Joan of Arc, as was said later in France, but: "You have already burned Joan of Arc and now you want to burn me!"

This was how it was told around the clubs, but I cannot say whether it was true or false, not having heard it, as you might guess, from Eden personally. An old member of one of the clubs, who was on intimate terms with the Foreign Secretary, said that Eden's response to the General's remarkable accusation should have been: "Suppose that we were to burn you at the stake as we burned Joan of Arc, what, in these circumstances, would Madame de Gaulle's position become?"

That summer of 1941 we spent watching the map of the Soviet Union and trying to understand and to report on in our little *Courrier de l'Air* the advance of Hitler's three armies plunging deep into Russia. The Nazis' systematic massacre of prisoners and of conquered populations aroused in Russian hearts a fierce courage born of despair, of indignation, and of faith, and a welling up of the deep springs of Russian patriotism. The fanatical spirit of sacrifice shown by the German soldier was more than matched by the stoic courage of the Russian. The fascinating, yet horrid spectacle of the Germans hurling themselves into combat to the cry of "Heil Hitler!" was to continue for months and even years. The thought of men reduced in our century in Europe to such total denial of individual conscience was enough to bring on spells of the bitterest melancholy.

Nevertheless, we were gay, had to be gay, during that nightmare summer. Looking at it selfishly—and how else?—one had to admit that the war was not going as badly as we had feared. Everybody sensed that American intervention was only a matter of time. Roosevelt saw to it that American supplies passed under the very noses of the German U-boats, all but inviting them to fire their torpedoes. He arranged a rendezvous in the North Atlantic off Argentia in Newfoundland in August with Churchill, the President aboard the cruiser *Augusta,* the Prime Minister aboard the great *Prince of Wales* which was so soon to go to her end in the Far East in a new phase of the war that was then still over the horizon. The Prime Minister took along his chiefs of staff, and the President was accompanied by a large number of military and civilian advisers. Much more than the Atlantic Charter came out of this meeting. When an exuberant Churchill returned to England, people's hearts were lifted to hear him say in a broadcast, jauntily, as if it were an afterthought: "Some American destroyers happened to be going the same way too, so we made a goodly company at sea together." The Americans, then, were learning to cope with U-boats! There was deep interest also in the report of the lesson read aboard the *Prince of Wales,* attended by the entire Anglo-American party. It was from the first chapter of Joshua: "There shall not any man be able to stand before thee in all the days of thy life: as I was with Moses, so will I be with thee: I will not fail thee nor forsake thee. Be strong and of good courage. . . ." Many a Gaullist was bewildered by these words from Joshua as they were used on that occasion by two men who, for all their differences of character and of interests and their many disagreements, were to remain staunch friends and loyal allies.

In the war on the seas, there was a development of immense importance: for the first time, new ships fresh out of the dockyards surpassed in tonnage those sunk by submarines and the Nazi planes.

Anne and I had personal reasons for happiness: we had just had word from our parents and now knew that our baby was in safe hands. My brothers had managed to get to North Africa and wrote from Casablanca asking if I advised them to come to England. I replied that if they did not want to sign the oath to General de Gaulle's person, they would stand a better chance of seeing action by staying where they were.

One of my letters, entrusted to the Foreign Office, was turned over to an intelligence agent who was a Gaullist (there were many more English Gaullists than people today realize), who put my signature to a use that I can only call disloyal, and leave it at that.

One day I asked Norman Cameron, with whom we had become close friends, why he had been so very nice to Anne and me from the day of our arrival a year before. "Because you seemed so unhappy," he said. I would not have thought that. But now that I recall that period of my life, I can see that perhaps we did seem sad. After all, we were far from our country in its plight, we were without news, rereading old letters and making little jokes so as not to cry. We had failed in our attempt to bring the baby out of France; we had lost our reputation among the French Gaullists; we were considered out of our minds by the English because we were not Gaullists. Yes, I can see how Norman might have thought that.

Autumn, 1941

From my diary, I see that Anne and I took a five-day vacation at Saint Ives, almost at the tip of Cornwall. The moment you cross the Devon, you leave England behind. You are in a foreign land. And we found it delicious. We could imagine ourselves in Brittany. And we partook heartily of forbidden fruit: fishermen took us out in the Bay of Saint Ives to look for mackerel.

In my notes I find other memories that have nothing to do with politics or the war, so you will be spared them. Since the beginning of Hitler's offensive against the Soviet Union, the bombing raids over London had ceased. Mme Maisky, the wife of the Soviet Ambassador, actually destroyed their air-raid shelter. She was wrong; later there was the baby blitz, not to mention the V-1 and V-2 rockets. But, save for the raging battle of the Atlantic, notably in the western approaches, the war had now moved elsewhere. Britain herself was no longer in the front line. We knew our fate was being decided along the vast, flaming, still constantly receding battle line to the East, where the Germans were locked in mortal combat with the Russians in a front extending from the Gulf of Finland to the Black Sea. Very soon the cold and the snow would come. No Frenchman familiar since childhood with the catastrophe dealt out by General Winter to the Grande Armée of Napoleon had to be reminded of the inexorable approach of the new ally.

Winter, 1941

General de Gaulle had an idea: it was to take possession in the name of Free France of Saint Pierre and Miquelon, two tiny islands off the southern coast of Newfoundland. They had been French since the seventeenth century, and the haunt of fishermen, mostly Bretons, who worked the Grand Banks.

The General broached the matter to the English. He had to do this because Saint Pierre and Miquelon could only be taken from the sea, and all the ships of the Free French Naval Forces were under British orders. At first, neither the Admiralty nor the Prime Minister raised any objections. The experts said the operation was not of prime importance but the wireless station on Saint Pierre broadcasting weather reports might possibly prove useful to German submarines in wait for the convoys that regularly passed through those waters.[1]

---

[1] Ironically, once the station was in Gaullist or, in a manner of speaking, Allied hands, torpedoings increased catastrophically, not only in the North but all up and down the Atlantic coast. With America's entry into the war, U-boats became active in American and Caribbean and South American waters as well. In the weeks between January 12 and February 6, 1942, there was an estimated total of 259,311 tons of shipping torpedoed in the Western Atlantic. And the figure was to go up and up. From this, one must assume that whatever the potential danger of the Saint Pierre–Miquelon station, the Germans did not need it.

Admiral Muselier was consulted and was delighted with the idea, the more so because there was no prospect of French blood being shed; the islands had no defenses, and sentiment among the population was reported to be overwhelmingly hostile to Vichy. *But*, Churchill said, the Canadians and the Americans must first be consulted. Washington's response was emphatic: Saint Pierre and Miquelon were absolutely not to be touched. There was an agreement between the American government and Admiral Robert, commander of the sizable French squadron in the Antilles. The Admiral, who ruled in Marshal Pétain's name in Martinique, had promised to observe a benevolent neutrality toward England on condition that the *status quo* be preserved in respect to the islands under his command until the reentry of France into the war. Saint Pierre and Miquelon fell within his domain. The agreement with him must not be jeopardized, concluded Washington. Antagonizing the powerful French fleet would compromise the landings envisaged for some future date in North Africa—and all for two barren little islands of no strategic importance. Churchill was immediately convinced of the wisdom of the American position, and he exacted from General de Gaulle a promise that, in these circumstances, the expedition on Saint Pierre and Miquelon would not take place.

General de Gaulle, however, allowed Admiral Muselier to believe that Churchill had given his consent and that the Admiral was to proceed, although with the greatest secrecy. For, the General said, Churchill did not wish it to appear to the Americans that he had given his approval in the face of their unfavorable reply. Admiral Muselier did not have to be told twice. On November 24, at Greenock in Scotland, he embarked joyously on the corvette *Lobelia*. With him he took Commander Héron de Villefosse and his aide-de-camp, Savary. They were supposed to be going to Canada; there was of course no mention of Saint Pierre. They were in fact going first to Halifax, where the Admiral was to inspect the submarine *Surcouf* and the Free French corvettes engaged in convoy duty in the North Atlantic.

The story of this expedition has been told by Commander de

Villefosse in a book entitled *Souvenirs d'un Marin de la France Libre*, now out of print and difficult to find. Both he and Admiral Muselier, who were to become close and respected friends of mine, spoke to me often of this affair, which was to have a number of consequences, among them the rallying of Saint Pierre to the side of Free France and the resignation of Admiral Muselier, who felt that he had been the victim of an unbelievable series of deceptions on the part of General de Gaulle.

The weather on their departure was so frightful that the *Lobelia* was damaged and had to put in at Oban, on the Firth of Lorne. "You were warned, Admiral," the English officers there told him, "not to set out for Canada in a corvette at this time of year. Are you sure you would not prefer to make the crossing on an English cruiser? Or by plane?"

"No, no," was the answer. "I will make the necessary repairs and continue on this corvette."

The corvettes of the Flower class, British-built, were the smallest escort craft in the North Atlantic—tonnage, 1,000; overall length, 200 feet. They were broad and had a low, thick funnel, a high fo'c'sle, and a whalerlike stern. They were not pretty. Someone described them as a "floating platform for depth charges." They also had a four-inch popgun forward, and they could be built quickly and cost less than any other escort vessel imaginable. In the wild seas of the North Atlantic, they were tossed around like toys; a 45-degree roll was considered fairly normal. (It was said they would roll on wet grass.) Later the larger frigate type was designed.

The warning of the British at Oban came close to fulfillment. The *Renoncule* all but foundered. Halfway across the Atlantic, the Admiral found it advisable to move from the *Lobelia* to the *Mimosa*, crossing from one to the other in a ship's boat in mountainous seas. The little Free French squadron was two days out of Newfoundland when sensational news reached Muselier over the *Mimosa*'s radio. Once again the war had come to one of what Churchill called its "grand climacterics." The date was December 7, 1947.

December 7, 1941

This historic date also fell on a Sunday. The Japanese had struck their surprise blow at the American fleet in Pearl Harbor; they had bombed Manila, attacked Hong Kong, and had begun their remorseless sweep through Southeast Asia.

It was 8:30 in the evening at Maryland—or should I say, Woburn Abbey?—when the telephone brought us the news. President Roosevelt had ordered general mobilization. We did not know it then, of course, but when Winston Churchill, dining with Ambassadors Winant and Harriman, heard the BBC bulletin, he decided to call the Foreign Office to order a declaration of war "within the minute." Winant advised him to call the White House to find out for sure. Call he did, to be told by Roosevelt, "We are all in the same boat now." Both the United States and Great Britain declared war the next day.

The news was black and would be blacker, but we realized now, for the first time, really, that the war surely would be won. Any fears we might have had in the recesses of our minds that the American might would be mobilized primarily, or even exclusively, in the Pacific were swept away when Germany and Italy honored their pledge to the Japanese by declaring war on the United States. Our reaction was joyous, and I confess it. None of us thought to say, "The poor Americans!" We really did not even think it. Now, after a quarter of a century, I am still of the opinion that it would have been an incalculable misfortune for the Americans, as for the rest of us, if they had not been thus precipitated into the war.

Scarcely had we heard the news than we were set to work to prepare leaflets to be dropped over France informing our compatriots of this latest development. They would have heard it over the Axis and Vichy radios, but we wanted them to know of President Roosevelt's promise that the American people would fight until victory was won over the Nazis and the Italian Fascists as well as the Japanese. All but the most purblind among them must really have known it anyway. It was all very well for Hitler to say that the Americans "can't stick in a crisis." Just how wrong he and the other prophets of the New Order were, would become apparent in not too many months.

We got very little sleep at Maryland that night. On board the *Mimosa*, battling the tempest, plunging, rolling, advancing painfully, they could have got very little sleep either. They had heard the news of Pearl Harbor too, and next morning, according to Commander de Villefosse's subsequent account: "We were on the bridge together, the Admiral, Savary, and I. We had had the night in which to think things over, and now we found ourselves spontaneously prey to the same fear and shouting it to each other above the gale, 'But this changes everything!' "

December 1941

It changed everything because the Americans had now become our allies. There was no longer any question of acting without their approval. So, on his arrival in Canada, the Admiral sought out the American representative in Ottawa. Already on December 4 the Canadians had informed Washington that London was proposing Free French occupation of the islands and that they disapproved. Washington's answer to the Admiral's query from Ottawa was prompt and clear: Impossible! The American refusal was motivated by the existence of a secret project for landing in French North Africa at some not too distant date. This plan presupposed that the French North African Army, and if possible the entire French fleet, would come over to the Allies. And with it, of course, Admiral Robert's squadron in the Antilles, which guarded Saint Pierre and Miquelon, would come back into the war. These great hopes could not be jeopardized just to give General de Gaulle the satisfaction of winning a plebiscite on two small islands.

Needless to say, Roosevelt had not instructed his minister in Ottawa, Mr. Moffat, to explain this project to Admiral Muselier, for the Admiral would have felt bound to inform General de Gaulle. Moffat confined himself to informing the Admiral that, for reasons of overriding importance, the operation must not take place. According to the American State Department, Moffat did tell the Admiral that occupation of the islands by Canada would be the best solution. Thereupon the Admiral "expressed bitter disappointment and said that he felt that the American government was making a mistake but that he would of course not proceed to the occupation." Immediately after this, the State Department was informed by the Canadians that they had dropped their own plans for taking control of the islands, due to British objections.

After seeing Moffat, the Admiral cabled General de Gaulle to ask that the date for carrying out his orders be postponed pending negotiations with the Allies, since the expedition did not have American approval. On December 17 the Foreign Office cabled Washington that the President's views had been made known to de Gaulle, "who agreed that the proposed action should *not* (repeat *not*) now be undertaken." However, on that same date the General cabled Muselier urging him to act without reference to the Allied powers. He stated that he was assuming "full responsibility on your behalf in this matter."

Then, on December 18, he ordered the action in unmistakable terms. His cable read, "We have, as you requested, consulted the British and American governments. We are informed reliably that the Canadians intend themselves to destroy the wireless station of Saint Pierre and Miquelon. Under these circumstances, I command you to rally Saint Pierre and Miquelon by your own means and without saying anything to foreigners. I assume the entire responsibility for this operation, which has become indispensable in order for France to keep her possessions. Signed: General de Gaulle." At the same time, Admiral Muselier received a cable from his chief of staff, Captain Moullec, reading, "The Foreign Office informs us that the President of the United States is categorically opposed to the scheduled operation." Faced with these contradictory cables, the Admiral preferred to believe Captain Moullec's account. Furthermore, he did not consider the operation indispensable to save Saint Pierre and Miquelon for France. He was convinced that the Allies had no wish to take over the islands for themselves, even if they decided to destroy the wireless station. But he was disturbed by the order contained in the General's cable. Was he to obey or disobey? If he obeyed General de Gaulle, he would be disobeying his commander-in-chief, for his commander-in-chief on the seas was British. Moreover, he would have to deceive his commander-in-chief, leading him to believe that the ships were not bound for Saint Pierre. Thus, to obey the General was to incur the consequences of disobedience and deception in respect to the commander-in-chief. Henceforth, what would the word of the Chief of the Free French Navy be worth at the British Admiralty?

To obey the General was to run counter to the wish categorically expressed by the new ally, the United States of America. And there would be consequences there too. The President of the United States, already on his guard against General de Gaulle, would never again place any confidence in the Free French Forces. He would not permit them henceforth to participate in Allied operations.

But disobeying the General was insubordination, it was a breach of military discipline and, in a sense, dishonor, not to mention any other counts that could be charged to him. Put yourself in the Admiral's shoes. What would you have done? There is no easy answer.

This, however, was the course of action Admiral Muselier decided upon: He would obey the General; he would disobey the British commander-in-chief, deceive him, in fact, and go against the expressed wishes of the Allies. *But* once he had carried out the General's orders and completed the operation, he would hand in his resignation as Commissioner of the Navy on the French National

Committee, to demonstrate that he was disassociating himself politically from General de Gaulle.

The previous September, General de Gaulle had set up the National Committee as the embryo of an eventual government. The "Ministers" would be known as "Commissioners." General de Gaulle chose them, and General de Gaulle could dismiss them. René Pleven became Commissioner of Economic Affairs, Finances, and Colonies; Maurice Dejean, Commissioner of Foreign Affairs; Admiral Muselier, Commissioner of the Navy and Merchant Marine; General Legentilhomme, Commissioner of War; Professor Cassin, Commissioner of Justice; André Deithelm, Commissioner of the Interior, Labor, and of Information; and General Vallin, Air Commissioner. In principle, this committee met once a week, like a council of ministers. By resigning from it, Admiral Muselier counted on showing, for all to see, that he was no longer politically dependent on General de Gaulle. He would stay on simply as Chief of the Free French Navy, and only that, under the orders of the Supreme Inter-allied Command.

It was on Christmas Eve that Admiral Muselier arrived off Saint Pierre with the submarine *Surcouf*, then the largest in the world, and the corvettes *Mimosa, Aconit,* and *Alysse.* He handled the affair admirably. The correspondent for *The New York Times,* Ira Wolfert, who was there, reported on Christmas morning that the Free French had been warmly received. "A little less than half an hour after the first sailor jumped ashore, the islands had been secured in a military sense. Not a shot was fired; the Admiral's Chief of Staff [Villefosse] was able to report that not a drop of blood had been shed." Next day a plebiscite was held, and an overwhelming majority was obtained—98 percent—in favor of Free France.

The landings were actually taking place while President Roosevelt and the British Prime Minister were lighting the Christmas tree on the White House lawn. American public reaction was by and large enthusiastic. *The New York Times* thought the incident "picturesque, but as an act of policy [it] seems to have been a blunder." So it seemed to Washington, where the news from Saint Pierre aroused the anger, one might almost say the fury, of Secretary of State Cordell Hull. On Christmas Day, Hull issued a blistering statement referring to the "so-called Free French ships"; it gained him more than his share of the headlines at a time when disaster flamed from nearly all fronts, old and new. He termed their exploit "an arbitrary action contrary to the agreement of all parties concerned and certainly without the prior knowledge or consent in any sense of the United States Government." [1]

Hull's reference to the "so-called Free French" seemed particularly unfortunate. It was never to be forgiven him by even the most pro-American among those who fought for Free France, or by the very large and vocal sector of American opinion which had become thoroughly disgusted with Vichy. Naturally, there were dramatic protests from Admiral Robert in Martinique. In Vichy, Admiral Darlan told Admiral Leahy that the Germans were using the incident as "an argument for the entry of Axis troops into French North Africa so that they might protect it against a similar invasion." [2]

Roosevelt was at first less severe than the Secretary of State; less severe, perhaps, even than Churchill, who was in Washington. Churchill was perturbed, even humiliated; for he had told the President that General de Gaulle had given his word not to take the islands. And Roosevelt, who had no liking for the General, had waxed ironic. "You see," he said, "I was not wrong about him."

Later Hull was to go even further; to Sir Ronald Campbell, Counselor to the British Embassy, he said, "I wonder whether the British are more interested in a dozen or so Free Frenchmen, who seized these islands, and the capital they can make out of it primarily at the expense of the United States Government, than they are in Singapore and in the World War situation itself. I have neither seen nor heard of anything from a British spokesman in the last few days that would indicate to me that there existed a World War compared with the Saint Pierre-Miquelon situation." [3]

Looking back on this incredible incident, one cannot help but

[1] Hull: *Memoirs*, Vol. II, p. 1130 ff.
[2] Ibid.
[3] Ibid., p. 1136.

wonder whether the Secretary of State foresaw the prodigious growth of the Gaullist myth in France, to which the Saint Pierre–Miquelon affair undoubtedly contributed. There is reason to think that President Roosevelt thought the Secretary was going too far. Within a matter of weeks, he would be advising him, or, to put it more accurately, ordering him to drop the whole business.

Very soon Roosevelt too was to show his temper, as when he warned Churchill that he might very well send the USS *Arkansas* to throw the Free French off their little islands.[4] It is quite likely that it was indeed at this time that Roosevelt gave up his "French plan." He had hoped to do what he could to see that France should play a major role in a liberated Europe. But with General de Gaulle at the head of French affairs, the President had second thoughts. He would go on refusing to recognize the General as chief of the French government until the French people had accepted him as such. He knew what this attitude would cost him: he was already being criticized by the Free French, by the French Resistance, by English public opinion, and likewise by the majority of American opinion. But he preferred this burden of unpopularity to the burden he would have on his conscience if he recognized General de Gaulle in his self-proclaimed role. That would have been to recommend to the French people, to the Americans, to the entire world a man he thought little good of and much that was bad.

From London on December 29 the General sent Admiral Muselier on his remote islet a cable that in four short lines made two interesting points: ". . . I am informing you that the English are satisfied with our action for reasons of maritime security and because of its effect on the danger from the Americans to the British possessions in America." On that same day Churchill was reaffirming to President Roosevelt his disavowal of this selfsame action. And, needless to say, the Americans had then as now not the slightest intention of appropriating British possessions.

We celebrated Christmas in London as guests of Commander

[4] Robert E. Sherwood: *Roosevelt and Hopkins* (New York: Harper & Bros.; 1948), p. 489.

Bedin. He was enrolled in the Free French Naval Forces but was
disgusted and on the point of leaving. Naturally we talked a lot
that night about Saint Pierre. André Labarthe was beside himself.
He said that Admiral Muselier had acted like a child, that he had
fallen into a trap, that he would be dishonored or would lose all
standing with the Admiralty for having deceived the Allies. Either
that or at the moment of his return to England he must resign.
Labarthe had no way of knowing then that the Admiral had already decided on just this action.

At Maryland on Friday, December 31, dinner was as usual—bad.
But we had a lot of guests, and there was enough whisky for us to
see out the old year gaily enough. Before the clock struck twelve,
each of us expressed a wish for the New Year. I well remember
Voigt's. "God keep us Hitler!" he said with fervor. That sent a
chill through us all.

Why on earth would he ask God to protect Hitler? "Oh, it's
quite simple," he said. "As long as Hitler is there, we will recognize
the danger of men like him, and the Germans will recognize it too.
But once he is dead, we will forget. Then, after having won the
war, we will lose the peace. The condition for peace that must be
imposed on the Germans, the one and only condition, is that they
keep Hitler at their head. That is the way to save them from their
lack of judgment and save us from our lack of memory. And, when
at last Hitler, heavy with years, will have died, every street sign
bearing his name in all of Germany must be religiously preserved.
Otherwise those poor Germans will founder again in their devotion
to some new guide, some new chief, some new Führer. There will
be the Hitler legend, like the Napoleon legend. Such men as these
can mislead nations in legend just as they misled them in life."

As for me, I would have preferred a far simpler solution for ending the war, to kill Hitler and kill him at once. I have never been
able to understand why the Allies failed to appropriate for this
high purpose some hundreds of millions of dollars or pounds sterling. Why had they not long since created a corps of specialists
who would have singlemindedly concentrated on the German
Führer as their target? Had they succeeded, millions of lives would

have been saved. But they did not even give it a try. And so it is that I hold a sorry opinion of all secret services, the Intelligence Service first of all. And I am all but confirmed in my belief that there exists a tacit sort of *camarilla*, a mutual protective society, among chiefs of state.

1942

January 1942

In mid-January, Churchill returned from the United States. Very soon afterward he called in General de Gaulle, to talk to him about Saint Pierre–Miquelon. This was hardly surprising in view of the irritations to which the Prime Minister had been exposed because of the General's behavior. And all this while he was engaged in the monster job of planning with the President and the Anglo-American staffs for every conceivable prospect of a global war.

Churchill was fully aware that his protégé the General was not to be included in plans for future operations. Eden had tried to get the Free French counted in the original roll call of the "United Nations," as the Allied forces were first called at the Washington conference. He had cabled his opinion that the United States had no right to exclude them. But they had been excluded—excluded because the President of the United States had no confidence that their chief would ever prove to be a loyal ally; excluded because the Prime Minister of Great Britain found himself no longer able to accept the word of their chief as a man or as an ally.

The General arrived in the company of M. Pleven. The Prime Minister was flanked by Anthony Eden and Major Morton. From what I was told, this is how the conversation went:

Churchill took the General to task, more or less in these words: "You gave me your promise not to undertake the Saint Pierre–Miquelon operation, and yet you went ahead and ordered your Admiral to do it!"

The General replied, more or less in these words, "Saint Pierre is a French territory. I am at home there [*J'y suis chez moi*]. I do not have to promise not to enter my own home!"

"But that is exactly what you did promise! Furthermore, you had Admiral Muselier perform an action that has upset relations between England and the United States. You let it be believed that this action was taken with my complicity. You have seriously hampered the policies of our new ally, whose contribution to the common cause is a thousand times more important than yours for the liberation of your own country."

An argument ensued as to whether Saint Pierre–Miquelon would or would not pass under the jurisdiction of General de Gaulle. Churchill said that the islands were French and would remain so. There had never been any question, the Prime Minister said, of their ceasing to be French, but he could not undertake to let them be governed by the General. All that would be the concern of the future government of France. Meanwhile the United States and Great Britain would keep representatives on Saint Pierre and Miquelon and would answer for the defense of the islands. An agreement between Great Britain and the United States would be reached on the whole matter.

General de Gaulle then demanded that certain of the provisions of this agreement remain secret. He found the affair humiliating and feared for his popularity. Churchill replied that the United States would most certainly refuse to allow any of the provisions to be kept secret. The General then asked to incorporate into the Free French Forces the volunteers recruited on Saint Pierre. Churchill's reply was that the agreement between the United States and Great Britain must be concluded first.

"But that is contrary to our agreement of 1940!" cried the General.

"The 1940 agreement was based on the supposition that you would have succeeded in recruiting a sizable body of volunteers. You have actually recruited only a paltry few. Things being as they are, I am thinking of revising our agreement."

This threat hardly fazed the General. He knew that, pushed to the wall, Churchill would give way, out of fear of Parliament and of English public opinion. This "mechanism," so to speak, would operate automatically. Actually, the exchange between the two men—of which I have given a simplified version—would have little interest if it had not been the subject for a report that General de Gaulle sent to Admiral Muselier, who was still on his island. This report, the Admiral was soon to state, did not check at all with the one prepared by the English. The discrepancy was brought to the Admiral's attention by his chief of staff, Captain Moullec, in a cable from London. The English account of the conversation had come into the Captain's possession, and he had every reason to consider it accurate. Moullec had also seen the version sent to the Admiral by General de Gaulle. Comparing the two, he realized that his chief was once more being led down the garden path. And so he sent his cable of warning.

How could such an explosive cable have been sent from Gaullist headquarters? To explain, I must go into some detail. Possibly the reader is not an expert in cryptography; very few people are. Cryptography is the art of communicating in code. Now, to code a message, one has a special dictionary, duplicates of which are in the hands of one's correspondents, and, supposedly, they are all carefully guarded. After every word in this dictionary there is a number or group of numbers. As an example, let me take *compte-rendu*, a French word meaning "minutes." The number after it is, say, 4745. (Anyone who receives this number in a coded dispatch consults his dictionary and alongside the number finds *compte-rendu*.) When one goes from code to cipher, one needs a key as well; with this key, 4745 becomes, for instance, 2632. This operation is called "ciphering," that is, giving a coded message an extra cover of secrecy. In a ciphered dispatch, the recipient finds an innocent grouping of numbers which to him, and presumably to him alone, indicates what key to use to decipher it back into code. (And the key can be varied infinitely.) When the key is applied to 2632, it becomes 4745, and, in the special dictionary, the number 4745 comes out *compte-rendu*. In this way one reconstructs the original message.

To warn the Admiral that de Gaulle was leading him into error, Commandant Moullec made use of a very secret key, the so-called "personal key," known only to him and to his chief. This is how the cable read before it was coded and ciphered: "To be deciphered by yourself alone. . . . Having had knowledge of the official minutes [*compte-rendu*] of the Churchill–de Gaulle meeting on January 22 . . . I must inform you that the atmosphere during the conversations was heavily charged. In this light, telegrams 2821 and 2849 from the General reveal grave misrepresentations. . . ."

General de Gaulle found out about this dispatch and about several others exchanged by the Admiral and Commandant Moullec, and he told the Admiral, on his return to London, that the decoding services of Carlton Gardens had succeeded in breaking the cipher.

"That," the Admiral replied, "is a technical impossibility." (And so it is, except in rare cases when a cipher is used too long unchanged or is varied according to some eventually recognizable pattern.)

Thereupon General de Gaulle rattled off several sentences from the dispatches which he seemed to have learned by heart. The Admiral himself goes on with the story in his book, *De Gaulle contre le Gaullisme:* "My reply was, 'General, you could only have come by your knowledge of the contents of these dispatches by bribing one of my signal officers!'

"That very day I began an investigation of the leaks and learned that one of the junior signal officers had been behaving strangely for some time. . . . As the investigation progressed, we learned that this man . . . had been having serious financial problems. Two officers of General de Gaulle's military cabinet had been cultivating his acquaintance. They had several times taken him out on the town and had advanced him sums of money. Under questioning, he confessed to having received money from the General's private funds and to having told about the messages he had seen being ciphered. He also stated that the General had personally interrogated him, not only about the messages but also about all the higher ranking officers on the General Staff of the Navy, and all others of any importance."

February–March 1942

On Saint Pierre the Admiral had handed over his command to Commander Héron de Villefosse and had left for London by plane, arriving on February 28. General de Gaulle himself went to meet him at the airfield, flanked by the National Commissioners. He was in an extremely cordial mood. In his own car he drove the Admiral to the Hyde Park Hotel and, before letting him off there, embraced him. The Admiral's staff officers, who were also part of the welcoming party, were very much struck by this.

Once alone with his own people, the Admiral asked for a full report on what had happened. He then went to see his colleagues in the British Admiralty. He arranged also to have a talk with General Odic, who until recently had commanded the Air Force in North Africa under General Weygand. General Odic's break with Vichy in answer to General de Gaulle's appeal had been widely proclaimed by the Gaullist radio. And also his expressions of horror at Vichy's servility to the Germans, at Vichy's meekness in the face of mass executions of French hostages by German firing squads. On his arrival in London, he had been taken to Carlton Gardens to meet the leader of the Free French Forces. Photographers were present to record the embrace between the two. But the interview between them ended badly.

General Odic reported that a great number of the pilots he had commanded in North Africa were ready to resume the fight, but on one condition: they did not wish to bind themselves to General de Gaulle personally by signing the oath. This brought a flash of anger from de Gaulle. Then General Odic made a reference to General Weygand, who then had not yet been recalled under pressure from the Nazis. "Weygand," he started to say, "is making ready the Army of Africa. . . ."

"Weygand is a traitor!" snapped the General. "And what's more, all those who have not yet rallied to me can stay where they are. As for you, you can go back to Africa, and I will go and fight you there!"

I have set down this story as General Odic told it to me at the time.

Later, General Odic did go back to Africa, following the Allied landings there. To Kenneth Pendar,[1] one of Ambassador Murphy's network of a dozen or so special consuls who prepared for the landings, he reported on some other choice bits from his conversations with General de Gaulle. When General Odic referred to "Republican institutions," General de Gaulle asked, "Do you still believe in those things?"

"I reminded General de Gaulle that the reason I had come to London was to try to prevent a Franco-German alliance which Vichy seemed about to accept. De Gaulle replied in these exact words: 'On the contrary, France must be in the war by the side of Germany to be able to prove the guilt of the men of Vichy.'

"I informed the British Government that honor forbade my becoming associated with the movement which I had unmasked, in the same manner in which it had prevented my remaining with the Government of Vichy. . . ."

To my way of thinking, General Odic perhaps did not follow de Gaulle's meaning. De Gaulle was simply trying to say that the guilt of the men of Vichy would become unmistakably clear, to those who still refused to see it, if Vichy were to declare war on the Allies.

On the morning of March 3, Admiral Muselier entered the Clock Room at Carlton Gardens. General de Gaulle had convened the National Committee, and the Saint Pierre–Miquelon affair was on the agenda.

[1] Kenneth Pendar: *Adventure in Diplomacy: Our French Dilemma* (New York: Dodd, Mead & Co.; 1945), pp. 203, 201, 204.

I was familiar with the setting, having had a look around it two or three times. The wall paneling of a light-colored wood extended almost to the ceiling. At one end, there was the sizable clock which gave the room, or hall, its name. The hands and numerals alone were visible; the works were concealed behind the paneling. As to what happened there that morning, I was informed in detail by a person who was present.

General Legentilhomme, Commissioner of War, his arm still stiff from the wound he had received in the Syrian action the previous spring, was already there. Then the Air Commissioner entered; and the Commissioner of the Interior, Labor, and Information; the Commissioner of Foreign Affairs; the Commissioner of Economic Affairs, Finances, and Colonies, who was also in charge of coordinating the work of the various civil commissariats. Finally, General de Gaulle made his entry. He shook hands all around and when he came to the Admiral he clasped his with a notable show of cordiality. He then proceeded to his chair under the big clock and asked the Admiral to report on the occupation of Saint Pierre–Miquelon.

Admiral Muselier limited himself strictly to the facts of the military, or rather of the naval, operation, touching not at all on any of the diplomatic or other aspects. When he had closed his portfolio, the General spoke: "This operation was handled perfectly. And now, messieurs, you see that I was right in ordering the occupation contrary to the opinion of our allies."

The Admiral answered, "I deliberately did not discuss the affair from the point of view of foreign policy. *But,* since you yourself have raised the subject, I wish to state emphatically that I do not share your opinion."

"We will be able to talk of that aspect of the question at some later date," the General said, indicating that he was about to bring the session to a close.

"No, General, with your permission we will discuss it now. And I wish here to declare that on two occasions during the operation Saint Pierre-Miquelon, I was not told the truth. I was even led to believe the opposite of the truth: for example, in the matter of the promise made the Americans, that the operations would not take place without their previous agreement, a promise made in your name, of course, General . . ."

"Messieurs!" called out the General, making a gesture to invoke calm. But the Admiral plunged ahead with the recital of his grievances: "On January 22, General, you had an interview with Churchill and Eden. You did not send me the official minutes of this meeting as prepared by the Foreign Office. On the contrary, I received an account [*un procès-verbal*] over your signature, General, and it did not agree at all with the Foreign Office report!"

Here the Commissioner of Foreign Affairs interrupted.

"There weren't any minutes prepared by the Foreign Office."

"I have them here," the Admiral said, drawing out of his brief-case a translation of the minutes in résumé which had been handed to his general staff by the English liaison officer. The Admiral then calmly read the two documents: the résumé from the Foreign Office and the report on the selfsame interview sent him by General de Gaulle. The discrepancies were startling.

The two texts can be found in Admiral Muselier's book, *De Gaulle contre le Gaullisme*. The report sent by the General gives the impression that the meeting was satisfactory. But one paragraph of the official text given out by the English reads: "The General replied that such procedure was contrary to the Churchill–de Gaulle agreement of 1940. The Prime Minister's response was that the agreement in question was based on the supposition that General de Gaulle would have rallied a sizable body of Frenchmen to the cause of resistance to the enemy. As this had not taken place, the Prime Minister was considering a revision of the agreement."

The General here broke in on the reading of the British text to deny its very substance. Two Commissioners—one of whom had been present at the meeting with Churchill—spoke up to say that the English account was incorrect. One of them cried out, "Anyway, I happen to know who drafted it. It was . . ."

Here it was the Admiral who interrupted: "Now, for the second time, I catch you in a flagrant lie. [He actually said: *en flagrant délit d'inexactitude*.] The first time it had to do with your pledge to the Americans that the operation would not be undertaken without their approval. The second time it is over these minutes from the English. You begin by saying that they do not exist. Then you state that you know who drafted them."

General de Gaulle was smoking cigarette after cigarette, his features expressionless. One would have thought that none of this concerned him. But at that point the Admiral turned to face him directly and declared that he, the General, was responsible for everything that had happened, since his commissioners did no more than carry out his orders. In conclusion the Admiral said, "I find it no longer possible to continue working with this committee. I herewith resign as National Commissioner."

The General calmly asked the Admiral to reconsider. The Admiral just as calmly replied that his decision had been reached only after long reflection; that he had in fact made up his mind in Halifax when he received the General's telegram reading: "Under these circumstances, I command you to rally Saint Pierre and Miquelon by your own means and without saying anything to foreigners." He had decided to obey, with the intention of resigning afterward. In the same message the General had said, "I assume the entire responsibility for this operation, which has become indispensable in order for France to keep her possessions." The Admiral said he was leaving him with this responsibility.

"In any case, if you persist in your decision," replied the General, "I am asking you to hand in your resignation in writing."

"That will be done this afternoon," the Admiral said. That same day he did in fact send the General a letter stating that he could no longer give him any assistance of a political character. The next day, March 4, the General not only accepted the Admiral's resignation as Commissioner of the Navy but also stripped Muselier of the command of the Free French Naval Forces, the fleet that he himself had brought into being before he had arrived in London. The General then appointed a new admiral, Captain Auboyneau, and by still another decree, he named the new admiral National Commissioner of the Navy.

Protests came in from the English admirals who worked with the Free French Navy. There was also a protest from Mr. Alexander, First Lord of the Admiralty and one of the Labor Party's representatives in the War Cabinet. Alexander's contention, voiced to his colleagues, was this: the land forces of the Free French were admirable, but they had not yet gone into action once against the Germans. The French Naval Forces, however, were participating day and night in the cruel battle of the Atlantic against the Nazis. Their men on sea duty numbered 3,500, and they had suffered losses of more than 600. They were performing the most indispensable services. As for Admiral Muselier, he was the founder and the soul of this magnificent little fleet. To relieve him of his command would bring recruiting to a halt and would seriously hamper operations at sea. As for General de Gaulle, said the First Lord, he had made war primarily on the Vichy French. He seemed to aspire to personal power. Was it up to the English to encourage him in this? His methods were disturbing. His concept of relations between allies was peculiar. No, Alexander contended, we must not, for him, sacrifice Admiral Muselier, admirable in combat, admirable in organization, and a faithful ally.

Churchill was exceedingly distressed. He shared the viewpoint of his associates in the War Cabinet and he agreed that General de Gaulle should be asked to leave the Admiral in his command. Eden and Alexander were charged with this *démarche.* But, as the Prime Minister feared, it failed. General de Gaulle stood firm, and Churchill could only acquiesce and undertake to calm the members of the Cabinet, to silence the English admirals, and to tell Admiral Muselier that it was up to him to give way and thus avoid a major crisis damaging to the Allied cause.

The Admiral did in fact efface himself. He did it with abnegation, that is, without submitting the letters of resignation from his staff officers, who were determined to stand by him, and also without revealing the scandal to officers in subaltern posts. And he did not let word reach the sailors of his little navy, who worshipped him. It was thanks to him that none of them left their ships.

At Westminster House, headquarters of the Free French Navy, the staff was in a state of effervescence, however. But the General saw no reason to worry; he knew that he had Churchill where he wanted him. On March 10, he prevailed upon the English to ask Admiral Muselier not to appear at Westminster House, where, pending the arrival of Auboyneau, his functions would be carried out by General Legentilhomme serving as an interim commissioner. This done, the General summoned the officers of the Navy to Westminster House at six in the evening. He made his appearance several minutes before the hour, in campaign uniform, kepi, and white gloves. The officers emerged from their various rooms and gathered in the main hall, and the General said, "Messieurs, since you don't have your greatcoats on, I will take mine off." He faced them and began to speak: "Messieurs, I am General de Gaulle. You are officers of the Free French Navy. Respect will be paid where it should be paid, and, most particularly to Admiral Muselier."

A *coup de théâtre:* at the very moment the General mentioned his name, Admiral Muselier himself entered the hall. "General," he said, "you have convoked all the officers of the Navy. I am an officer of the Navy, and here I am" (*"me voici"*).

There was a moment of silence. The General offered his hand to the Admiral and again spoke: "I wish to see each officer individually, beginning with the most junior."

He strode into the office normally used by the aides-de-camp. The Admiral followed after him. The General indicated by a gesture that the Admiral should leave. "My wish is to see each officer alone."

"General, in no military organization is it customary to interrogate officers other than in the presence of their chief."

"Admiral, you are committing a breach of military discipline."

"Not at all, General, but I know that certain officers are rather excited and I would not want any of them to put themselves in the wrong. Here in this headquarters I am solely responsible, and if anybody is to go to the Tower by virtue of the powers that reside in you, it will be me!"

The General was by now even more rigid than usual, and again he said that the Admiral was guilty of a breach of "military discipline." "Under the circumstances, the only thing I can do is leave this room." And putting on his gloves, he walked out. With the officers waiting at the door, he took an ominous tone: "Messieurs, rest assured that what must be done will be done. Our conversation can be resumed later." The General intended now to make use of the weapon he held, namely, his agreement with the English government granting him very special prerogatives—just how special, we will see.

At eleven o'clock next morning, he dispatched a note to the English government, beginning: "A penalty of thirty days' fortress arrest is imposed on Admiral Muselier." Then came the charge of which apparently the Admiral had been found guilty (by whom?). It was "insubordination."

If an incident of this kind had taken place in territory controlled by the General, Brazzaville for instance, there would have been no problem: the General had means to carry out the sentence. But he was on British soil. In a second note, then, he referred to "the agreements concluded in this respect"—meaning the agreements concerning jurisdiction, signed on January 15, 1941. He was within his rights.

How was Churchill to extricate himself from this situation? Was he to have Admiral Muselier jailed a second time? The first time, it is true, the charge was espionage—though the accusation turned out to be an invention of the security chief of Carlton Gardens. And now he was being asked to arrest the Admiral for insubordinate behavior to General de Gaulle.

What would people say? Difficulties would be raised in the Cabinet, where Alexander and others backed the Admiral against the General. And in the House of Commons several members were showing signs of distress. If the Prime Minister were asked a question from the floor, what was he to say? Was he to admit that by virtue of agreements concluded on the subject he had granted General de Gaulle the right to have Free Frenchmen on the soil of the United Kingdom sent off between two policemen to the Tower without a hearing, without a trial, without any recourse to British justice?

To realize the scandal that an admission of this sort could have provoked, one has to have lived in England to have known the respect felt there for habeas corpus,[2] for individual liberty, and for the complete independence of the courts. Murmurs were already being heard in the lobbies of the House. Two members in the know were heard raising an interesting question before a larger group: did the English people have *their* revolution a century before the French, only to be asked now to permit the use of the *lettre de cachet,* which supposedly had gone out of vogue in France too when Louis XVI lost his head? (And that, though it was after the English revolution, was a good century and a half ago.) And who had issued this *lettre de cachet?* A foreigner! And who was the victim? The only one of the French admirals who was faithful to his government's pledge not to conclude a separate armistice! He was in trouble because he had dared to protest an action by General de Gaulle, an action that was a serious breach of inter-Allied solidarity. And who was to provide the strong-arm to conduct the Admiral to the Tower? The British police, no less!

Churchill did not hesitate a moment. He gave instructions that General de Gaulle's request was to be refused—no matter how well founded it might be in the terms of the agreement he had himself signed with the General without dreaming of the uses it might be put to. But he had to take precautions lest the General set off another scandal, this time by loudly proclaiming that the English were faithless to their agreement. The Prime Minister set himself a double-barreled task: first, to prevail upon the Admiral to leave London voluntarily, and second, to get General de Gaulle to abandon his intentions to have the Admiral confined to a fortress.

---

[2] Actually, habeas corpus and other guarantees had been suspended for the duration (Attlee's speech in the Commons, May 22, 1940), but the Churchill government was constantly on the alert to prevent flagrant injustices.

Churchill worked it out this way: the Admiral would go to Ealing on sick leave, and Commander Moullec would convalesce at Kingston.

Churchill had hoped to get General de Gaulle away for a few days to his place in the country, but there the Prime Minister failed. General de Gaulle remained in London. He had a job to do. He went immediately and quietly to work at Westminster House, removing from their commands all of Admiral Muselier's principal aides. He did this by transfers, by confinement to quarters, by close arrest. Then, with his usual intelligence, he put into operation two potent weapons, as follows:

First, any officer in the Free French Navy who sided with Admiral Muselier would be excluded *ipso facto* from the Free French Naval Forces; and since the British had given him, as Chief of the Free French, the monopoly on enlistments by French citizens, any officer thought to be loyal to the Admiral would no longer be allowed to fight the common enemy. With service in the Free French Navy denied him, he could not enlist in any of the British services. Second, any officer of the Navy who refused to obey the orders of the Chief of the Free French would be considered to have violated his oath, dishonored himself, and be guilty of insubordination, and might find himself facing a court-martial.

I was all too familiar with the alternatives the officers of the Navy now faced. It was because of them that I had not been able to bring myself to sign the Gaullist oath. For the officers who had signed the oath—in other words, who had joined the Free French Navy after the Admiral had brought it into General de Gaulle's movement—there was a cruel dilemma and only one way out, really: to abandon the Admiral, go on with the war at sea, and thereby honor their pledged word.

There is no reason to name the few officers who were willing to take over the jobs at Westminster House vacated by shipmates punished in one way or another by the General. One of them said: "The General called me in and asked me, 'You are in fact a Free Frenchman?'

" 'Yes, General.'

" 'And I am in fact General de Gaulle, Chief of the Free French, to whom you have sworn obedience?'

" 'Yes, General.'

" 'Then give me your obedience!'

" 'Yes, General.' "

A perfect syllogism. And it would seem to prove one thing, apart from what the General here wanted it to prove, that a man should never sign an oath of allegiance to *one person*.

One of the officers who refused to knuckle under to General de Gaulle was Héron de Villefosse, who had been left in command on Saint Pierre. A model of rectitude, he fell prey to a case of conscience. For him what counted was his will to remain faithful to his admiral in adversity, regardless of all danger and sacrifice. From Saint Pierre the Commander sent off the following cable, unciphered: "Kindly transmit the following to Admiral Muselier: Learning that you are obliged to take a rest, I wish to send you, in my name personally and in that of all the officers on Saint Pierre, our most affectionate good wishes, in the hope that you will soon be able to resume your post at the head of the Free French Naval Forces. In our eyes, you are still the man who saved the honor of the French Navy in the darkest period of its history. Your name and your example are inseparable from the ensign bearing the Cross of Lorraine, which, by your orders, will continue to fly over warships of Free France. Respectfully, Villefosse."

This did not set at all well with General de Gaulle. The next day he sent this cable in reply: "For Captain de Villefosse, to be decoded by him: Hand over your command to the next senior officer on Saint Pierre and return to London immediately. Insubordination— General de Gaulle."

When Villefosse reached London, however, the General seemed to have forgotten that he was angry with him. De Gaulle knew very well that Villefosse was held in high esteem for his good faith, his idealism, his intellectual qualities, and his talents. He was often spoken of as an Alfred de Vigny become a sailor. The General welcomed him with a certain warmth. Captain de Villefosse might have taken the occasion to present his own case, but he chose rather to make himself heard on the subject of Admiral Muselier. To the General he spoke, as he did later in his book, of the courage of the Admiral, of his unselfish patriotism, of the physical ordeals he had experienced, which nevertheless never caused him to hesitate. He evoked for the General a picture of the Admiral on that terrible westward crossing of the North Atlantic, the corvettes rolling scuppers under in the tempest in which the *Renoncule* came close to foundering. He described the Admiral crossing in a ship's boat from the *Lobelia* to the *Mimosa* in mountainous seas, holding the tiller himself, swept by frozen spume from the crests of breaking waves, shouting encouragement to his men, who knew their danger all too well. He told the General of the Admiral's serious illness on snow-covered Saint Pierre: how, although he was spitting blood, he was in action night and day over frozen roads in a raging gale.

General de Gaulle listened, hands in his belt. Finally he looked intently at Villefosse: "Yes, of course . . . but all that . . . believe me, all that was taken into account when I made my decision."

What you will not find in the Captain's book, *Souvenirs d'un Marin de la France Libre,* is any mention of how he eluded temptation. If that day he had wished to make sure of his promotion to admiral, he would only have had to bend a little. But not so: he clicked his heels and took his leave without any of the small signs of submission which would certainly have sufficed, given the General's mood. The Captain had reached the door when the General called after him: "Villefosse, you behaved very well at Saint Pierre!"

The Captain was not to be moved. He had made up his mind not to go back into the service as long as Admiral Muselier was barred from it. And one must assume that the General, once he saw that the Captain's loyalty to his chief could not be shaken, no longer wanted him; otherwise, he could have exerted pressure on him, as he did on others.

Captain de Villefosse took off the blue and gold uniform of the French Navy, a uniform worn by his grandfather and sacred in his eyes. Denied the privilege of serving his country or its ally

Great Britain on the seas, where his competence lay, he stayed on in London, an *émigré*, and nearly penniless too. Later, he was to become a broadcaster on the French program of the BBC, earning enough to keep alive, though not engaged where he would be most valuable. He never complained. He had a first-rate mind, was pure in spirit, and was happy to remain so.

Although the winner, General de Gaulle was the loser too. In the upper reaches of government in London and in Washington where policy was made, a France incarnated by General de Gaulle would no longer be thought of as a reliable ally. And men in these high places began increasingly to consider that in the future organization of the peace, France, which in all likelihood would be Gaullist, could not be counted on to play a leading role.

It was at about this time that my relations with Carlton Gardens became very difficult. I still had some excellent comrades under that roof, but in my association with the top personalities it was possible, even probable, that I conducted myself in ways that might be considered disrespectful to their place of dignity in the General's embryo government.

One day in mid-February I had a lively quarrel with a certain commissioner. It was, as always, over the role they were playing in France, and my continuing refusal to incite the Resistance to acts of violence. That evening I received a letter from the Commissioner. He had this to say: "I do not understand the attitude of a person like yourself, who has set himself up in the offices of a foreign, though friendly power, so as to indulge in criticisms, not always well-intentioned, of your compatriots."

He was right when he said that I was on the payroll of the British; so were several of my associates on the BBC who were in the Free French. But he was quite wrong to suggest that I ever criticized the General before any of my English friends and co-workers; I was careful never to do that, but I did frequently criticize the English—and to their faces—for their unreserved support of the General's cause. I had to admit that there was a large element of truth in the Commissioner's letter. I immediately took a decision:

I would no longer accept a penny or even a scrap of bread for my work with the English. Either they allowed me to do my job without pay, or they would have to find someone to take my place. I told Anne that we would be leaving Woburn the next day. I put the letter of the Commissioner back in its envelope, and I slept soundly.

In the morning I went to see the head of the organization and told him what I had decided. But he was leaving us. David Bowes-Lyon was going to take his place, so it was with him chiefly that I talked about my problem. His first reaction was to break into laughter. His position in England was such that he could speak his mind with exceeding frankness. The reproach in the Commissioner's letter made him raise his eyebrows.

" 'A foreign, though friendly power'! I ask you, doesn't the man have any notion of what an alliance is supposed to be? How can anybody harbor such thoughts?"

"I don't think that he is wicked," I said. "It's just that he is a very poor sort, that's all." He pretended to have misunderstood my meaning. "Poor? That one? Come off it! The salaries and expense allowances of the General's commissioners come to I don't know how many times more than you earn here. So you receive English gold, do you? And they, the commissioners, what do you think they receive, rupees? They are paid in pounds, to be reimbursed by us, I confess, through the peanuts we are buying from them. Or to be reimbursed after the war by *notre dame la France.*"

By then he was very angry. He walked up and down in front of the fireplace that warmed his office, one of the Abbey's finest rooms. Then his anger subsided and he again broke into laughter. "I'll tell you what we are going to do. We will follow the example they themselves have set! We will no longer pay you a salary; we will simply loan you money until the end of the war. You will pay us back when you can. We will talk about it on the day of victory."

Seeing that I was not about to change my mind, he said, "All right then, it's agreed: I am asking you to work for nothing." I accepted his offer. "But you will go on living here?"

"No, I am going back to town."

"But if I invite you to spend weekends with us, you will accept?"

I said yes, I would come up from Saturday to Monday. I found that I could just as easily prepare my copy in London as at Woburn. I did go up as agreed—as invited, I should say—on weekends, with Anne or without her. The English had finally broken their habit of devoting Sunday to rest. It was on Sundays now that we did our best work.

I don't know whether the Gaullist commissioner thought that his letter might get me to leave Woburn Abbey. I am sure that he had in mind the salvation of my soul as well as the good of the cause he served with such abnegation. But if his hope had been to diminish my nefarious influence there, he failed badly. In fact, he achieved the exact opposite: from then on, everybody at the Abbey became out-and-out anti-Gaullist. And I found that no matter how hard I tried, I could no longer pass myself off as crazy in respect to the General and his movement. However, I must say that none of these little changes in viewpoint made the slightest difference; the General's cause had henceforth to be considered as already won in France.

There was no problem about our moving. We had only to see that the white mice were left safely in the care of the gardener's wife at Maryland. All our other belongings were piled into the car loaned us by Castellane, and we left the next morning, February 15, for London. Our apartment was rented. The Maison de l'Institut was full up. So we went first to a hotel and then to a furnished flat in Kensington. Anne was not well. In the bitter cold she came down with bronchial pneumonia. Then she recovered, and our life became more or less organized. I had no trouble finding translations to do, and other work.

Before leaving Woburn, we learned from a telephone message that Armand had arrived. After a roundabout odyssey of two months, he had finally landed in England. We could see him two days later, once he had been released from Patriotic School. Patriotic School was a black building, formerly a secondary school, near Wimbledon, and, to many, its reputation was as black as its exterior. Every new arrival from an occupied country had to pass some time there until the various English services were convinced that he was not a spy or some other kind of enemy agent. It was extremely disagreeable, but probably indispensable. Little Simone Weil, although she came from New York, had to spend two weeks there. Nothing about her was frightening but her intellect. Pierre Mendès-France, who arrived at about the same time as Armand, did better. When they asked if he had anyone who would vouch for him in England, he said, "Yes, of course."

"Who?"

"General de Gaulle."

"Do you know him?"

"Yes."

"Personally?"

"Yes."

The policemen could do nothing, once they had checked his story, but let him go. General de Gaulle, incidentally, saw Patriotic School in a sinister light. He believed, and wrote, that loyal Frenchmen were being seduced there to work for a foreign country, England: "a foreign, though friendly country."

You can imagine what joy Armand's arrival plunged us in. Anne spent an hour getting her hair done. Then there had to be a new hat. With a wide brim? A narrow brim? No brim? Perhaps a fur toque? That took longer than the hairdresser. Then off we went to the rendezvous, at Fitzmaurice Place. In London, Fitzmaurice Place is of course not a *Place* but a street leading into Berkeley Square. No trace of Armand. He had misunderstood or forgotten the address I had given him. We set out to look for him and very soon found him making a tour of Berkeley Square for perhaps the tenth time. There were tremendous embraces. We found and he found that none of us had changed by a hair in two long years. When Anne had enough of pecking her brother's cheeks, and we had talked about all our families, and about his long journey—he had come from the ends of the earth—I asked him if he had signed the enlistment oath.

"Me? Seven times! At each stop."

"Good, that will save us an argument. I suppose you know what you have let yourself in for. You are henceforth to obey any and all orders from *le Grand Charles*. Do you know that?"

"Why should I care? Besides: V*ive le Grand Charles!* I am going over to the Navy this afternoon to sign up for the eighth time."

That is what he did, as an ensign with one stripe. His oath, which I saw (each volunteer received a duplicate), was a little different from the one Professor René Cassin had refused to make the slightest concession in for me. The reference to "three months afterward" did not appear. Except for this detail, which I consider unimportant, it still constituted an act of allegiance to one man, designated by name, General de Gaulle. To refuse to obey any order of his, after signing this, spelled insubordination, rebellion, dishonor, not to speak of a court-martial and its consequences, at a time when one was not and could not be surrounded with the guarantees normal in France.

Nevertheless, we did have arguments with Armand. Because he is, of all the fighting Gaullists I know, the most intelligent and the most disinterested, I feel I should here, in a sort of spasm of objectivity, set forth his viewpoint, yielding him, in a manner of speaking, the floor. I do it the more willingly because I would have found it heart-warming in those years to have participated in the collective admiration for a man, as he and Anne found it. This is more or less what Armand said time and time again:

"General de Gaulle is the only French chief who, to my knowledge, said that the show was not over yet, that there was still hope—this in the face of the masochistic bleats from the Pétain–Vichy team about how the French people had to expiate their sins, about the purifying virtues of the barbed wire of a German concentration camp.

"His argument—I mean *le Grand Charles'*s—was capital for me. I had read *Mein Kampf* in German and in French. If Hitler won the war, I would never, never set foot in France again. I would live as an exile until my death. Our chances now, at the beginning of 1942, are not brilliant but they are better than nothing. Without the General, I would have enlisted with the English or the Canadians, but since we have a French chief, French ships, and French crews, so much the better. No hesitation is possible for me.

"I have heard about the three months of service after the end of hostilities. But there is no mention of them on the oath I signed. I would not find them excessive anyway. It is only sensible and wise to have a homogeneous French force in readiness when one has no idea what will remain of the police and other forces of order after the capitulation of the enemy and the dispersement of the Vichy authorities. Besides, there will certainly be more or less brutal convulsions in our country, not to mention possible foreign interference—possible and inadmissible. So, if your fears should prove justified—which I don't think they will—remember that the first rebellion is by far the most difficult. The moment Germany has been vanquished and France liberated, the matter will no longer be very important."

I won't burden you with what I answered: I have already expressed my point of view often enough. But I will mention the questions I asked him, so as to reveal more completely the ideas of a man I can call, without the slightest irony, a good Gaullist.

"Tell me, Armand, you will admit that the General, since the day he reached London, has had the ambition to see himself at the head of the French people if and when victory is won?"

"Do I admit it! That is what I hope for and, as far as it depends on me, what I intend to see!"

"You agree that he never has had, that he never will have, any intention of ceding his place to another?"

"I count on that, too! You are trying to say that he is doing all he can to block the road to any and all competitors? So much the better, a thousand times better! Not only is it he who picked up the flag. . . ."

"That was because there wasn't time for anyone else to pick it up ahead of him. He reached England in Churchill's plane while they were still fighting in France. . . ."

"Your because's don't interest me. The fact is that he was the first; that he made an agreement with the English whereby he is the recognized chief of the Free French; that he will be, I hope, chief of state. I am not saying that he has no faults. Who is without faults? But when one stops to think of the depths from which we have come and of the heights to which we may go, I say yet again: *Vive le Grand Charles!* Think back on the men of the Third Republic, on the members of our parliament who were such bad shepherds and showed it so tragically by leading us into catastrophe: that they should dare—as many of them will, beyond a doubt —to try to take the reins into their hands again! So, louder than ever I cry: *Vive le Grand Charles!*"

"Well, well! That was a fine tirade! But listen to me, Armand: what you say about the men of the Third Republic is quite right. But the regime under which they ravaged the nation was the very same regime which operated so well for France in the finest periods of our history. To my mind, this would seem to show what we are faced with is a national sickness, a malady afflicting the nation as a whole, that our problem has nothing at all to do with the regime but rather with the quality of certain generations, the quality of the individual man perhaps."

"Don't make it out that I do not agree. I think exactly as you do: the mediocrity of regimes is a problem far less serious than the absence of men of worth. And to say it straight out, Charles de Gaulle is the man who can save the nation!"

"Do you think he is honest?"

"In what sense of the word? Certainly he is *honest*. He has never pocketed any money that wasn't his!"

"But when a man has everything, why should he bother about money? Money is only a means to an end anyway. No, by *honest* I mean this: does he speak the truth to the nation? Or is he engaged in some vast deception?"

"How funny you are! A man cannot govern, or even, for that matter, live in the society of other men, without a minimum use of the lie! Look again into Molière—*The Misanthrope*, for instance— or into Labiche's *L'Auvergnat*."

"We were just now speaking of the lies told by our political leaders toward the end of the Third Republic: do you think that *they* helped matters?"

"Oh, come off it! Those fellows were just petty little liars of no account!"

Anne was well again and the spring was upon us. We were able once more to afford our apartment in Lowndes Square, and for a time Armand lived there with us. Thanks to him, our relations with the Gaullists became more agreeable. Those brought home were mostly combatants. As for the Carltonians, they no longer dared to yap. Yet one of them once asked Armand if he was seeing me.

"Yes, I live with him and my sister."

"Good! Then you can tell him for me that he is a proper *salaud!*"

"I can't agree," Armand replied, "but I will be happy to relay the message."

With Armand, I made a call on the author of this pretty compliment. He explained that I was accused by another Carltonian of having invented and spread around London an ignoble story about the General. My answer was that I never made up anything of the sort, much less told it around. The accuser was sent for and turned out to be a onetime comrade of mine. Like the good Christian that he was, he took it all back: he had been misinformed, etc. After this diverting scene, I found only smiles at Carlton Gardens, and even invitations to luncheon.

These I could not accept because I would naturally have had to return them, and, with the rationing, it was not easy. However, I did take up one invitation, from the comrade who had expressed his sorrow at having spoken ill of me. He wanted to make peace. He had hopes even of converting me to Gaullism. To return the favor, I invited him home one day. Introducing him to Anne, I said, "This is my former comrade . . ." And turning to him: "I warn you not to talk politics with Anne: not that she isn't a Gaullist, for she is. But she considers herself a royalist!"

At this, he opened his eyes wide and moved toward her, and for a moment I thought I was on the point of witnessing the scene from *Les Femmes savantes* where the learned Philaminte embraces

Vadius, "for the love of Greek," as she says. But no, my old friend opened his arms wide, and with deep emotion said, "You too, madame!"

I had to laugh. So it was for the love not of Greek but of the king of France.

Though we seldom entertained at meals, we often had people in after dinner. Pierre Maillaud usually appeared with a gift of some kind, a bottle or a *paté en conserve*, sometimes his ration of bacon or margarine. That was because he ate in restaurants, as his wife, Jeannette, was in the country with the children. When Pierre was with us, conversation was always lively. Before we turned to the topics of the day, there was a little routine parodying of the usual polite greetings, with nonsense citations of our own, usually borrowed from the masters. One of Pierre's which I always liked was borrowed from Anatole France: "I beat my servants and never pay them, and yet I am not sure that they are truly faithful to me." Maillaud came from a Protestant family with I don't know how many pastors in its ancestry. He himself went seldom to church, but he had an astonishing store of Biblical quotes which he liked to throw around, with or without relevance. "And they poured out for the men to eat. But while they were eating of the pottage, they cried out, O man of God, there is death in the pot. And they could not eat it." (I always looked forward to his offering this citation to his hostess at some dinner party.)

Apropos of General de Gaulle, when that gentleman was under discussion, as he frequently was, Pierre would intone, "Let what you say be simply 'Yes' or 'No,' anything more than this comes from evil."

Naturally, we talked war and politics. This might seem strange today in peacetime. It would in France, I know. But for us in 1942 the double subject was inevitable, and for the women as much as the men. It was like that once in France among the women at court; read Madame de Sévigné, or Madame de La Fayette's *La Princesse de Clèves* or the *Mémoires*. You won't find two pages without politics.

About General de Gaulle we never quarreled any more. Pierre

had become even more anti-Gaullist than I in that he considered the General personally responsible for the actions of all his services, his police included. He held to the belief that the evil a man commits through the instrumentality of another is evil of the third degree, the worst, which must be called Satanism. I was still not in agreement with Maillaud, however, about the attitude those of us who were then speaking over the radio should maintain. At that time Maillaud was on every night under the *nom de guerre* of Pierre Bourdan.[3]

Here I should perhaps explain how the BBC operation went. Each broadcast to France opened with a news bulletin. Then came five minutes made available by the British government to General de Gaulle or his spokesman. After that came a program called *Les Français parlent aux Français*. Needless to say, the General's five minutes, whether he came on in person or his spokesman did, consisted of a pure Gaullist propaganda line. The feature called *Les Français parlent aux Français* was scheduled immediately afterward; it was quite favorable to Gaullism in tone, and it *never*, by virtue of an agreement between the General and the English, broadcast anything even mildly critical of his cause.

My feeling was that the people of France, listening during the long, dark night of the Occupation, must inevitably conclude from the unanimity of opinion expressed by all that everyone on the BBC team was a simon-pure Gaullist. (Since the war, my inquiries have proved to my satisfaction that this was the case.) If our listeners happened to note, however, as many surely would, that certain commentators—Pierre Bourdan (Maillaud), for instance—were somewhat less than passionately Gaullist, they would conclude that among the followers of General de Gaulle all shades of opinion were represented. Within the frame of unanimity, they

[3] There was justification aplenty for the use of *noms de guerre*. In the Occupied Zone, the German police and their French associates did not hesitate to persecute families of well-known Gaullists. Van Moppès's aged father was deported by the Nazis and was never heard from again. In the so-called Free Zone, occupied after November 1942, Charles Maurras in *L'Action Française* shrieked for action against families of Gaullists, naming names.

would perceive an admirable diversity, and therein they would see evidence of a great liberalism around the General.

"You yourself are anti-Gaullist," I would say to Pierre Maillaud, and to Jacques Duchesne too.

"Up to a point," Maillaud replied, having to stop biting his thumbnail to do so.

"Héron de Villefosse is thoroughly anti-Gaullist."

"With just a nuance of admiration for the General."

"Very well. I'll wager you this. That when we go back to France, you and Jacques Duchesne will be hailed, the two of you, as Gaullists of the purest, most valiant breed, on a par with the Porteparole. Just wait and see."

This was the basic disagreement between us. I was certain that the anti-Gaullists who spoke over the BBC, under the rules in force there, were helping to reinforce the General's propaganda through their talent, their intelligence, and their very moderation. That is why, after a time, I gave up broadcasting. Before I decided to quit, I tried an experiment: I brought a different script each to Darcy Gillie and to Jacques Duchesne. Darcy Gillie, who was to become correspondent of the *Manchester Guardian* in Paris after the war, was at that time charged with censoring our scripts. I remember how that day his hands trembled as he tried without success to get me to make some changes in the text of the news commentary I had placed on his desk. I feel sure that he was unhappy at having to insist. My job as commentator then went to François Quillici, director of the weekly *La Marseillaise,* which was entirely controlled by Carlton Gardens. Duchesne likewise turned down the script I had given him. It was a letter to my father—though not quite as long as the one I am rewriting in this book. Duchesne felt that duty required him to make sure his team of broadcasters would not seem to be in discord about anything. I respected his preoccupation with high policy, without, however, sharing it.

Jacques Duchesne (actually his name was Michel Saint-Denis) and Pierre Maillaud were willing, though reluctantly, to be taken for Gaullists. They felt it their duty to bolster French hopes in a time of black despair. This was their only motive, as it was the only motive of Captain de Villefosse and not a few others. They considered it absolutely essential, when our country was so sorely tried, to present an appearance of unanimity among all the adversaries of the common enemy.

One of the frequent visitors at home was Jean Oberlé, a sworn Gaullist, sincere, and like Armand totally disinterested. But his admiration for the General did not prevent him from realizing that our listening public in France must be getting an image of the General which was at odds with the facts. When I said it was wrong to lie to our compatriots at home, even by implication, he answered: "There you go again, always with some fine big word in your mouth. Lie! Lie! Why not use a more agreeable word, like *illusion?* We must not destroy their *illusions!* They are so miserably unhappy in France! So they think *le Grand Charles* is perfect? Let them. They think that he does not want to govern after the war? Let them. They think that he is opposed to any exercise of personal power? So much the better! And they think that we are all of us with him? (As you yourself would be, if you weren't cracked!) Again, so much the better! Leave the mist on the windowpane, for their sakes! Let their vision go on being blurred."

I have yet to be convinced. I do not believe that the French people have to be treated like invalids, minors, imbeciles. I think the French were quite as able to hear the truth—and moreover deserved to hear it—as the English in 1940 when Winston Churchill told them he could promise nothing but "blood, sweat and tears." I think the French were as capable of heroism as the Dutch, say; even as capable as the Poles, who in far worse conditions, hopeless really, fought better than any of the other occupied peoples, and without having General de Gaulle to urge them on.

When Jacques Duchesne came to the house, our parties took on a literary flavor. He would frequently read, most admirably too, from the French classics. Mostly we played, we talked of this and that, and we sang. Many of our songs were improvisations and, naturally, based on political themes, since we talked politics so much.

André Labarthe came only rarely. When he did, he took the floor and kept it. He had tales to tell, like this one: "The other day I was invited to lunch with the General . . ."

"You? Really?"

"Of course. From time to time he makes an effort to salvage me. So, he invited me to lunch at the Connaught. I arrived and in the vestibule I saw, beside the General's kepi, an immense ivory cane."

"Immense? How big?" Oberlé asked.

"Much bigger than yours: a cane to match the General's height. We lunched in the General's private dining room. There were other guests, Colonel Passy and the good Père Cassin. Toward the end of the meal, I spoke up: 'General, in your vestibule you have an ivory cane the likes of which I have never seen before.'

" 'That,' replied the General, 'is a gift they gave me in Africa, a cane made of a single piece of ivory.'

" 'A single piece of ivory! I must say, for a cane like that, an elephant would have to have mighty long tusks!'

" 'Yes, indeed!' said the General, and he went on, his voice high, intoning the sentences as he does on the air: 'The elephants of Africa!—of Equatorial Africa!—the Elephants of French Equatorial Africa are the biggest elephants!—the biggest in the world!' "

"Of course!"cut in Oberlé. "France is a *grande dame* and naturally she'd have to have the biggest elephants!"

"But wait a minute, I haven't finished," Labarthe said. "After lunch, the General left the room for an instant. I slipped out to the vestibule and brought back the cane. I fooled around with it—and guess what! It unscrewed; it was made of *two* pieces of ivory! Passy and Père Cassin, who were watching me nervously, quickly turned their backs and went over to the window as if to look at the view. Just imagine if the General had come back before I'd finished screwing his cane back into one piece again—how embarrassing!"

Monica, the pastor's daughter, was indulgent as always. "That only goes to show," she said, "that the General can himself be taken in by a fake!"

At other times we quarreled. For example, apropos of Admiral Darlan, Van Moppès (who was known as "Momo") used to sing a little rhyme to the tune of the well-known radio commercial:

> *Un meuble signé Levitan*
> *Est garanti pour longtemps.*
> (Furniture signed *Levitan*
> Is guaranteed to last a long time.)

Van Moppès's version went like this:

> *Un amiral nommé Darlan*
> *Est garanti pro-allemand.*
> (An admiral named Darlan
> Is pro-German guaranteed.)

I spoke up; this was calumny. Darlan was anything anybody wanted to call him, certainly anti-English since Churchill had refused to take his word about the fleet, but he was *not* pro-German! Momo's answer interested me greatly, and at Christmas I had occasion to remember exactly what he had said.

"No, it's not calumny, it's an order—a military order! General de Gaulle gives the order: Attack Darlan! So we attack Darlan! General de Gaulle instructs us to guarantee that Darlan is pro-German; so we guarantee it! *C'est la guerre!* It was the same for Estienne d'Orves when he was shot in Paris. We get a command from on high: 'You are to state that Commandant Estienne d'Orves was shot as a spy in the moat at Vincennes by French *gardes mobiles* on orders from Admiral Darlan!' Very well, we state just that! The truth seems to be that old Darlan actually intervened with the Boches to try to save Estienne. But that doesn't make the slightest difference; at Carlton Gardens we do what we're told, don't we, Jean? They designate Darlan as the man to bring down? Good, we bring him down! We man the guns. We don't put up an argument about whether the shells from our guns are likely also to kill women and children! Am I right, Jean? It's for the chiefs that this kind of thing is painful! The little matter of getting Frenchmen to kill other Frenchmen takes a strong stomach!"

Van Moppès could be bitter after two or three drinks. Oberlé restored the peace. He stood up, his right hand on his cane, his left hand raised to command silence. Dropping his Parisian accent, he put on a Montauban accent, which is very soft and slightly nasal, and in a charming voice he sang for us, "A *Montauban y'a trois filles.*" Dr. Jacques Le Beau then gave us "*Nini peau de chien,*" so keenly reminiscent of the Paris we all missed so cruelly. Jacques Le Beau was the son of the governor-general of Algeria who had had everything ready in June 1940 to receive the French government. Jacques was not a Gaullist, but he looked after all Frenchmen, Gaullist or not, free of charge. He did his work at an English hospital, and he drew no pay; he was doing research in neurosurgery which later brought him renown. He was so poor that he never accepted an invitation to lunch or dinner; he saw no way of ever repaying it. But he would come in after dinner to sing to us of, among other things, the charms of Nini, her soft skin, her freckles.

We worked very hard at our distractions, as people are wont to when they feel miserable. Later, when Armand, then on corvette duty guarding North Atlantic convoys, would come down on leave from Greenock, in Scotland, we had even gayer, rowdier evenings. Armand would bring shipmates, such as Flohic, now commander, serving at the Élysée, who used to say that he was an *aspirant* with permanent rank, and Philippon, whom I remember as very small and very brave. At around two in the morning, our neighbors would knock on the wall; they claimed they had slept better during the bombings.

The girls who came were quieter. There was Madgia, secretary to General Sikorski, chief of the Polish government-in-exile. She would prepare marvelous dishes with even the poorest ingredients. There was also Sue, a cousin of Anne's, who was private secretary to one of General de Gaulle's national commissioners. Naturally we never talked about her boss, and, anyway, she was discretion personified. Anita and Elizabeth Kalerova represented still another country that had been overrun. They were from Prague.

Torcy had an idea based on the proposition that true confidences can be exchanged only between people who already trust each other. This seems indisputable. But it was frequently overlooked during the war. Let us imagine that an English agent, or a Gaullist agent, had gone to see my parents in Occupied France. Most probably they would have been extremely cautious and vague in their answers to any of his questions. And rightly so. Suppose I were in France and had occasion to tell persons who had hitherto not known me what I knew of the situation in England and of the policies of General de Gaulle's "government"; it is more than probable that I would be listened to with skepticism. And all the more so if I expressed myself unreservedly, incautiously.

Let us imagine, on the other hand, that I was able to speak directly with my parents, with my most intimate friends. I would naturally have believed everything they might have told me, and they would have listened with full confidence, without suspicion, to what I told them. In other words, messages exchanged between persons who know each other intimately have the greatest value; the other kind mean little.

Why then should we in London not get together various persons we knew who had close relationships with people of influence in France? That was what we did, and we met once a week in Torcy's apartment. Several of us had friends in France in positions to act effectively when the time came, who deserved to be kept accurately informed. My role in these gatherings was simply that of secretary. Soon we had quite a number of personal messages, and various addresses of the friends they were to go to. Naturally, we had to have some means to get them to France. And that depended entirely on the English. Our project was doing well until we had it brought to the attention of the Prime Minister. His response was immediate: we could do nothing along these lines without advising General de Gaulle; to let us proceed otherwise would be contrary to the British agreements with him. Colonel Maurice Buckmaster, chief of the British service for intelligence from France, informed me later that the English government had agreed not to recruit any of the Frenchmen in England to work with them in France. Churchill had acted like the lion in the fable, who let his claws be pared and his teeth pulled, so blind with love was he.

The whole project had to be abandoned. The General commanded all the avenues to France and the minds of the French, thanks to the powers the Prime Minister had granted him. But that was not enough to satisfy him. He disapproved of the English and the Americans maintaining even personal, friendly contacts in France with any military leaders or other persons under Vichy authority. If the English and the Americans kept up such contacts, he said, they would be showing respect for Vichy, diminishing his own authority, and discouraging the Resistance. He even went so far as to say that this might cause the French to become resigned to a German victory.

April 1942

On April 1, 1942, the General made a speech threatening the Allies. It was in this speech that he first substituted "Fighting France" for "Free France." This was intended to mean that he was henceforth chief of all *unfree* Frenchmen who were fighting in the Resistance as well as those who were *free* outside of France. What was more, he was the one and only leader of all Frenchmen worthy of the name. Then came the threat: if the English and the Americans, said he, did not go along with Fighting France, then Fighting France would no longer go along with them.[1] He went further

---

[1] *General de Gaulle's threats to the Allies*

". . . It all comes to this: Fighting France means to stand by her Allies, but on the express condition that her Allies stand by her. She maintains that, by fighting at their side, she will regain her independence, her sovereignty, and her greatness, provided her Allies respect these attributes in her. She is doing all she can to further their victory, but on condition that this victory be likewise her own. During the past fifteen hundred years she has acquired the habit of being a great Power, and demands that nobody, her friends least of all, should lose sight of this. In short, Fighting France has but one reason, one justification, for her presence in the camp of freedom: that of being France herself and treated as such by her co-belligerents . . .

". . . Who could seriously imagine that in such a matter Hitler's wishes

still: he wanted it clearly understood, as he had already told the British agents in Brazzaville, that if the Allies held back or were in any way reluctant in their support of General de Gaulle, the French people would resign themselves to victory by Hitler. If General de Gaulle in making this statement was really speaking in the name of the French people, if he did incarnate France, *was* France, I can only say that he was not speaking in my name, or in the name of my parents, or in the name of my friends. More than ever, I felt myself outside his ranks.

The General ended with the announcement that a new regime was to be set up in liberated France. His own, naturally. There would be, he said, *the greatest revolution in the history of France!* Nothing more or less than that! He said this, I assure you, and then lifting his arms to heaven, he cried out, "In the secrecy of her suffering, an entirely new France is rising . . ." That France, need I say, is the one you have before your eyes today. Yet I cannot begin to give you an idea of the transports of enthusiasm provoked

---

and dictates could be countered by anything other than the resistance of the French nation, galvanised by Fighting France? If the impossible were to happen, and France abandoned the struggle tomorrow, what ambassador could prevent Hitler, even for a moment, from disposing of the country as he pleased? We certainly do not believe that freedom's camp would ever want to risk losing France by giving way to such illusions.

". . . In the ghastly tragedy our people are living through, in view of all the favours Herr Hitler would be prepared to grant them were they willing to serve him, and remembering, too, the frightful regime of national demoralisation to which they are now subjected by the infamous champions of capitulation, how would it be possible to keep this nation as an ally if the Allies themselves failed to do whatever is necessary to uphold her in the fight? Who indeed, and in the name of what, could keep French territories, French forces, and French thought in the war, much less add to them, if the Allies themselves were to limit their support? . . .

". . . [It is] one thing which dominates the whole French question today— the face of revolution. For France, betrayed by her ruling and privileged classes, has embarked on the greatest revolution in all her history. . . . In the secrecy of her suffering, an entirely new France is rising, and she will be guided by new men. . . ."

Speech delivered by General de Gaulle at a luncheon given by the National Defence Public Interest Committee, London, April 1942. De Gaulle: *Memoirs, Documents* (1940–42), pp. 277–8.

by this speech. My good friend the Porte-pensée—as I thought of him—was afterward in a state. "A France entirely new!" he repeated. "You will come to her, you stubborn ones, you men of little faith, to this new France, more beautiful, stronger, greater, and with her Empire more prosperous (the Anglo-Saxons permitting) than at any time in her history! You heard him: the greatest revolution in her history! Let me tell you, messieurs, that it was worthwhile for France to have lost a battle, since General de Gaulle will raise her up to the only rank that becomes her, the very first rank among nations!"

That spring Armand embarked on a corvette. Life on these small craft was hard. But he preferred sea duty to the civilian posts—posts of great importance for someone his age—which had been offered him in the Free French organization.

The celebrated Pierre Mendès-France, former Under-Secretary of State in the Finance Ministry, deputy mayor of Louviers, arrived in England a little after Armand. He could have been a national commissioner, in other words, a minister. But he had not come for that. Besides, what he saw at Carlton Gardens confirmed his feeling that the best thing was to put on a uniform again. He made a statement to the press: "When the General continues the struggle against the common enemy, he answers the deepest wish of the French people." This carefully worded utterance was meant for people who can read between the lines. Could he have spoken more clearly? I don't know. He went back into service as a lieutenant-observer of aviation and saw to it that the planes always flew very low over France, dangerously exposed to ack-ack fire, so as to make quite sure that their bombs were dropped on German military installations and not on the French population.

When Armand left us for Greenock, where the corvettes were based, and then for the Atlantic, where he took part in the convoys from North America and later in convoys which carried supplies to the Soviet Union under savage German attacks, we had a new guest staying with us. He was Louis Roché. I mentioned earlier that he had been appointed after the armistice to the Vichy France legation in Dublin as Second Secretary. With Pierre Saffroy, the First Secretary, he later came back to England. I want here to mention the letter of resignation that Roché and Saffroy signed, in October 1941; it contains a fine statement of principle. "It would not be honorable in respect to the government of Vichy," they wrote, "to live off it financially when we feel ourselves incapable any longer of defending its policy." This point of view may seem normal enough, but one does not run across it so very often. In fact, their letter and their forthright statement bring to mind another quite opposite case involving an employee of the French Embassy in London.

Right after General de Gaulle's radio appeal, this man busied himself, in June and July 1940, making speeches on the BBC in support of the General. Meanwhile he was receiving his salary from the government of Marshal Pétain. Roger Cambon, then chargé d'affaires, called him in. Cambon said the speeches were all well and good—he in no way disapproved—but, he asked: "Who is paying you?"

Then he added, "Monsieur, you will call at the Chancellery, where they will give you a month's pay in lieu of notice." The man took the money. It is interesting to note how often the so-called "double game" has meant merely being paid by one side to carry out the policies of the other.

Louis Roché was in delicate health: he had frequent fainting spells, which scared us all. But not Mary, once again in our service as maid. She used to say, "It's nothing, nothing at all." She would then slap him hard a couple of times and say, "You must not pay any attention to these attacks: he'll forget all about it when he's over fifty." She was a dragon! Unhappily, at the year's end she was mobilized to return to nursing duty, in spite of her fifty years of age.

As soon as Roché found an apartment in London that was fairly decent—there were very few—he had his family join him. We then had a new arrival to take his bed. He was my cousin Roland, who reached London by way of Gibraltar. He had been in Morocco, where he had worked with the Americans. He did not at once sign the enlistment oath. What I told him about Carlton Gardens made him hesitate, but, impatient, hating inaction, he finally decided to join up with the General. He had hardly signed when he was attached to the celebrated BCRA,[2] the Gaullist equivalent of the French *deuxième bureau* and *sûreté générale*, and the opposite number, in their own opinion, of British Intelligence and Scotland Yard. He started as a lieutenant and shortly became captain.

He was as much disgusted by what he saw there as by what they expected of him. I reacted to his distress by saying, "You had only not to join them."

To that he would reply, "I will know how to break away in time."

He did break away, but it was through the portals of heroism. When he died, he did not cry out, *"Vive de Gaulle!"* but *"Vive la France!"*—two witnesses have attested to this. (The BCRA was full of heroic young men: that is not at all the question here.)

At the BCRA, which had its headquarters in Duke Street, later to become very famous indeed, they insisted that Roland give them the names and addresses of all Frenchmen who were working with the Americans in the North African Resistance. He refused, wisely. They then brought incredible pressure to bear on him. He told me that he never gave in to them. He was right. As for me, I was never willing to give a single name in France, or even to try to write to my parents through the intermediary of an agent, whether Gaullist or English. (But here let me say that I was never pressured to do so.) After the letter of mine that I had entrusted to the Foreign Office was turned over to British Intelligence, which then made improper use of it, I never did anything like that again. One should never have confidence in agents for whom the end justifies the means. The only good system would have been that suggested by Torcy and, as I have explained, rejected by the English for reasons they thought right.

Some day the full story of the BCRA will be told by persons

[2] Bureau Central de Renseignements et d'Action (Central Bureau of Intelligence and Action of the Free French).

other than I. I did not even want to listen to the things Roland tried to tell me. "If it is a secret," I would say, "why do you tell me?"

"It is because," said he, "I do not think such things *should* remain secret."

I have no desire to arouse indignation against General de Gaulle by relating incidents concerning the BCRA—far from it. But in respect to one of the most notorious stories to come out of Duke Street, I would like to show that the Chief of the Free French was entirely within his rights: this is the so-called "Dufour case," which attracted a great deal of attention. Read the version of it given by Captain Héron de Villefosse in his *Souvenirs d'un Marin de la France Libre*,[3] and then read the passages in General de Gaulle's memoirs in which he treats the same subject. It becomes immediately clear that General de Gaulle was right when he called Dufour a "deserter": the man did sign the enlistment oath of the Free French. And as a "deserter," what could he expect but conviction by a military tribunal set up by General de Gaulle in exercise of the

[3] *Commandant de Villefosse on the Dufour affair*

". . . Certain incidents like the Dufour affair revealed to informed persons, of which I was one, the increasingly more odious actions of the BCRA. Dufour, seriously wounded in the kidneys in June 1940, had played a part in the Resistance in 1940. He had established relations with the English Secret Services and had been obliged to escape to England. Called on May 18, 1942, by the BCRA, he was invited by Passy and his acolytes, Captains Wybot and Girard, to inform on the network and missions in which he had participated. Considering himself bound to secrecy, Dufour refused, and was tortured by Wybot and Girard. They struck him with a steel rod especially in the area of his wound, which caused him great suffering. They threatened to kill him, and also to rape in his presence a girl of his acquaintance whom they had arrested.

"Afterward Dufour was thrown into the French prison at Camberley Camp, where he was kept until the beginning of December 1942. At that time he made his escape and before the High Court of Justice in London filed a complaint officially against de Gaulle, Passy, Wybot, Girard, and four other officers. This affair was to come to trial, but, on the one hand, witnesses were threatened with reprisals against their families in France; and, on the other (and of this I am certain), Dufour agreed to withdraw his complaint, against payment of 3,000 pounds sterling, effected by the Gaullists."

Louis de Villefosse: *Souvenirs d'un Marin de la France Libre*, p. 248.

rights granted him by Churchill's government? De Gaulle was right, too, when he said that "all that is perfectly regular" (meaning legal). He was right when he said that if Dufour "was mistreated during the interrogations," he could avail himself of his "right to appeal to high French authorities." And General de Gaulle was right when he claimed that Churchill's government violated "the agreements signed by him with Free France by virtue of which French soldiers in Great Britain were answerable only before French military courts." [4] In other words, Dufour's arrest, of incontestable legality, derived from his having signed the enlistment oath, which compelled anyone signing it to obey General de Gaulle's orders and those of his representatives; it also derived from Churchill's decision to give the General power whereby to enforce his authority on the men who enlisted in his service and thereby accepted him as their master.

General de Gaulle was equally within his rights in refusing to allow the English to have anything whatsoever to say about the destination of the monies and the arms they supplied him with for distribution to the Resistance in France. Since Churchill's government granted sovereign rights to General de Gaulle, why should the General not have made sovereign use of these arms and these funds?

At long last, Roland stopped telling me about what he saw and heard at BCRA headquarters. From then on, we had no more arguments about such Gaullist activities. But, between Roland and Anne, things were not going well. They were wary of each other, these two, as if expecting at any moment to come to blows. Both

---

[4] The BCRA and similar organizations in London were of course under the general supervision of the British SOE (Secret Operations Executive), but the various British services could operate in France without having to inform the BCRA. This explains the BCRA's interest in Dufour, who had operated in France as a *British* agent.

Here I should say that incidents like the Dufour case, with torture, with threats—and more—to friends and family, were commonplace in Nazi-dominated Europe. In Paris, certain French Nazis such as the infamous Bony and Laffont almost equaled their masters in sadism. But to have it go on in London under the noses of, but out of reach of, the English police was extraordinary, to put it mildly.

were Gaullists; their fathers had both been career officers; but that did not help. One day at lunch Anne came forth with so many disagreeable remarks that Roland left the table and walked out of the house. When, days later, he let himself be talked into coming back to the house, Anne, almost childishly impulsive, ran to him and threw her arms around him. Nothing was said about their quarrel. That is her way in such situations, and it seems to be the right one. Sometimes, even today, Anne will say, "Evenings, when I draw the blinds in my room, I find myself thinking of Roland."

"Why, when you are drawing the blinds?"

"Because he did such a good job repairing the cords of the blinds we had in our apartment in London." That is how memory functions.

May 1942

Sparks flew again between the General and Churchill in the month of May. The English had reason to fear that the Japanese would make an attempt to establish a submarine base on Madagascar. Early in May, British forces landed at Diego-Suarez, at the northern tip of the great island. Churchill, in agreement with Roosevelt, had decided not to say a word to General de Gaulle.

"Our memories of experiences with him at Dakar, in Syria, and at Saint Pierre–Miquelon do not now encourage us to include him in this kind of operation"—this was the substance of what the English said. "Even granting that his presence might not bring a repulse, as it did at Dakar, or that we would not have to fight, as in Syria, for weeks against former allies and then after winning run into all sorts of headaches with the General, we think it better to go it alone and at a later time turn the island over to the Free French." There was another factor as well, security. Churchill remembered all too well how information about the Dakar expedition had leaked to Vichy. Blame for this was laid by many persons at the door of some of the men in the General's entourage, who were supposed to have had Cagoulard connections at one time. During the planning for the attack on Madagascar, Churchill several times stated flatly that his fears for the security of the project were a major factor in his decision to exclude General de Gaulle.

It should not be difficult to imagine the General's reaction when he was given the news, by telephone, on the night of May 4–5, that the British had landed on Diego-Suarez.

June 1942

Though the Free French forces had fought alongside British troops in minor engagements, for the first time since the armistice they were about to confront the Germans in a major battle, at Bir Hakeim, deep in the Libyan desert. To understand what took place at Bir Hakeim, it is perhaps well to go back in time a little. After the defeat of France, Mussolini had tried to extend his colonial empire in Africa. Marshal Graziani had some initial successes, but was later beaten by the troops of General Wavell. The Italians are good soldiers, on the very reasonable condition that the cause they are fighting for be one they can approve. The cause Mussolini proposed seemed to most Italians stupid and dishonorable.

The Germans came to the rescue of the defeated Italians, sending in the Afrika Korps under General Rommel, the "desert fox." The British were then defeated in their turn and had to retreat to Salûm in Egypt. From there, General Wavell launched a counteroffensive in the autumn of 1941.

General Rommel had suffered fearful losses, in tanks and in men. But he managed to withdraw behind the defenses at El Agheila by January 7. By then the British forces, their supply lines drawn tighter than a rubber band, were overextended. As long as they held Benghazi and the coast of Cyrenaica, they were able to bomb German-Italian supply ships coming into Tripoli and, in a measure, to protect Malta. But they did not hold Benghazi or any part of Cyrenaica very long, for Rommel made a surprising counterattack on January 21—totally unexpected, save by General de Gaulle, as he later wrote. It must be remembered that, for all the British could do, Rommel had a supply line from Italy, through Tripoli. British supplies had to go 20,000 miles around the Cape. In London, the sudden and at the time unexplained fall of Benghazi came as a terrible shock.

By late February, General Ritchie had dug in, under orders from his chief in Cairo, General Auchinleck, in a strong defensive position in the Gazala–Tobruk–Bir Hakeim position which General Wavell had earlier said was "the natural balance of the desert" between the source of Axis supplies in Tripoli and the source of British supplies in Egypt.

General Ritchie and General Auchinleck were under orders to use this position, known as the "Gazala line," as a springboard from which to strike back and recover Benghazi and the airfields commanding the waist of the Mediterranean. They took their time. Auchinleck was worried about a possible German attack through Anatolia or the Caucasus into Syria and eastward. He had kept two Empire divisions in Syria. He also felt the need to send reinforcements to the Far East. Called to order from London,[1] he agreed to stage an offensive utilizing the American tanks (Grants) and the new antitank guns sent him around the Cape. But, at the end of May, Rommel struck first. In London we heard of Churchill's quip about the man who was preparing cautiously

---

[1] Churchill, under severe pressure for a "Second Front," informed Auchinleck: "A very heavy counter-stroke upon the Russians must be expected soon, and it will be thought intolerable that 630,000 men (exclusive of Malta) on your ration strength should remain unengaged, preparing for another set-piece in July." *The Hinge of Fate*, p. 293.

with a paper funnel to blow a healing mixture of gunpowder down a sick bear's throat. "But the bear blew first." Indeed he did!

The Gazala line, the southern end of which was held by General Koenig's light division of Free French, was something new in desert warfare, as we learned later. Everywhere else in the desert, except at Alamein (where the Qattara Depression served as a barrier), the attacker could always sweep south around the end of any position and then take its defenders from behind. General Wavell had shown how it was done, and General Rommel had caught on fast. The British, therefore, had laid a very wide, solid minefield from Gazala to Bir Hakeim, forty miles south and east from the coast. This was studded with three forts, or "boxes," about a mile or so square, inspired by the British infantry squares at Waterloo, by Scapa Flow, and other precedents going back to the Macedonians. (The London men called them "castles.") These "boxes" were protected on all four sides by a ring of mines (set *in* the extended minefield) and by barbed wire, and, inside, by a tremendous concentration of artillery and antitank guns. The garrisons, supplied with food, water, and ammunition against a siege, would be sealed in. Behind, there were similar "boxes" at "Knightsbridge," garrisoned by the guards, and supposedly at Tobruk. Rommel was free to bypass these "boxes" and take all the desert real estate he wanted, but he would not dare go too far lest the garrisons, supported in principle by British tanks massed some distance behind them, should sally forth and attack his flanks.

The opposing forces at Alamein were almost evenly balanced, some ten divisions, roughly 130,000 men, and 500 tanks on each side.

The number of the French troops and the French losses sustained at Bir Hakeim have been a subject of controversy. But no longer, as today the official figures are available. According to the Historical Section of the Ministère des Armées, the troops under General Koenig's command at Bir Hakeim consisted of the First half Brigade of the Foreign Legion, the Second half Brigade

Colonial, the First Artillery Regiment, and the First Battalion of Marines. (The Battalion of Marines had been created by Admiral Muselier.)

On the moonlit morning of May 26–7 a British observer at Bir Hakeim, seeing a cloud of dust to the southeast, called out: "It's the whole bloody Afrika Korps." And so it was. Rommel was making an end-run with the intention of taking Tobruk on the second day and coming in behind the entire Gazala line as far as the coast (which his forces did in fact reach).

Rommel's armor had struck north to the sea, *behind* the Gazala line, and northeast towards Tobruk. But the attack failed and on May 30–1, unable to go back south around Bir Hakeim or to receive supplies by that route, he withdrew his forces *into* the line, hoping to force an opening with the help of the Italians on the western side. He was very badly off. According to his fellow generals, as they expressed themselves after the war, he should have struck south to knock out Bir Hakeim, but he did not. For at least one day the Afrika Korps was on the brink of defeat.

General Rommel personally intervened, arriving in front of the fortified place on June 3 and issuing a demand that the garrison surrender. General Koenig refused. On June 5, Rommel issued a second ultimatum. Koenig replied with gunfire. On the seventh, Rommel hemmed in the fort, and on the eighth he launched an attack. The Free French magnificently repulsed the attack, but the Germans renewed their assault in the ensuing days. The French held on.

You can imagine how anxiously we followed this combat from afar. And I believe the non-Gaullists such as I, in reaction against the political aims of the movement, had the most admiration for the combatants. Every afternoon I went to Carlton Gardens to learn the latest news, and then make them public in the *Courrier de l'Air.* On June 9, I transcribed General Koenig's declaration: "I will remain with our troops, who will defend their positions to the very end." That "to the very end" sent shivers through us all.

On June 10, I took a copy of General de Gaulle's message: "General Koenig, know and tell your troops that all France is watching you with pride." As I left Carlton Gardens, I ran into the General's spokesman. "Have you seen?" he asked. "It's happened! The General has ordered Schumann and Soustelle to go right on!"

"Go where? To Bir Hakeim?"

"Don't be childish! I mean he commanded them to fight to the finish. And you should see what effect that has had! The BBC, the morning papers, the evening papers, all of them, they can't say enough about the heroism of our men! All the more so because the British in Libya—excuse the expression—are taking it on the lam! We're teaching them a thing or two!"

Maurice Schumann was the General's mouthpiece on the radio; Jacques Soustelle was his mouthpiece in the British press. He inflicted upon the newspaper readers an intensive bombardment of French heroism: Valmy, Verdun, Du Guesclin, Bayard, Condé, Napoleon, Foch—whole columns of names filled the London papers. The *Daily Herald* said that the defense of Bir Hakeim was one of the most splendid exploits of the war. The spirit of Verdun still lived. They would not let go, said the *Daily Mail*. "*Allez-vous faire pendre!*" Such, said the *News Chronicle*, was the daily reply of the defenders of Bir Hakeim to Rommel (after Henri IV's famous words to Sully). It was delirium. The English are generous, sometimes too generous, in their admiration for foreigners—when they put their minds to it, that is. You see that in sports when foreigners are pitted against Englishmen. You see it also in war. Foch is far more celebrated in England than in France and had a monument in London long before one was raised to him in Paris.

June 10, 1942

In the street, on a newsstand, there was a poster with huge letters. I read it from a distance, but I could make out GREAT VICTORY, and also FREE FRENCH. Another poster screamed: ROMMEL BEATEN BY DE GAULLE'S TROOPS.

The *Daily Express* ran a cartoon showing Marianne, her hands raised, a ball and chain around her ankles. She was saying to Pierre Laval, who was reading a newspaper, "You see, I still know how to fight!" A black headline read: THE FREE FRENCH VICTORIOUSLY REPULSE ROMMEL.

June 11, 1942

The newspaper *France*, which printed communiqués from Carlton Gardens, said in its largest, blackest type:

KOENIG A BIR HAKEIM
"J'ai ordre de tenir: je tiens"
(I have the order to hold; I am holding)

It went on, in equally fat type, to tell of COUNTERATTACKS, ENEMY THROWN BACK, etc.

June 12, 1942

On June 12, we learned that on the night of June 10–11, after having inflicted heavy losses on the enemy and destroyed all their stores, the French had "won a fresh victory" by withdrawing from Bir Hakeim, on the orders of General Ritchie, and fighting their way through Rommel's encircling forces, to El Gobi, out of reach of the enemy.

June 13, 1942

Some days later, I was showing our English colonel the draft of an article I had written for the *Courrier de l'Air*. The colonel, although a Francophile, pursed his lips and handed it back to me, saying: "Very well. Write what you like. But I think that it would have been well for you to write as you usually do—I mean, limiting yourself to the facts. The facts here are not what you have set down. They are as follows. The garrison charged by General Ritchie with holding Bir Hakeim repulsed Italian[1] and German attacks from May 27 to June 10. On June 10, the camp being surrounded, General Ritchie authorized the withdrawal of the French troops, a withdrawal that General de Gaulle had requested. The English command furthermore did not want to have the Free

[1] Actually, the Italians found themselves in front of Bir Hakeim by mistake. Their orders were to avoid it and not to attack.

French, the first time they found themselves facing the Germans in battle, to get themselves killed to the last man, as happened with the British brigades at Ghât-el-Skarab; they had orders to hold out to the end, and that is what they did.

"On the night of June 10–11, the French garrison pulled out of the fortified camp, leaving its wounded behind, and fought its way through enemy lines to British trucks at Bug-Bug.

"The French suffered the loss of 1,150 men killed, wounded, and missing. At Bir Hakeim they left 53 cannon and 250 vehicles. They brought back with them 154 Italian prisoners and 123 Germans.

"On the twelfth, the Germans took Bir Hakeim. Their communiqué said they took it by assault. That is not so. Rommel lied. The place was evacuated, except for the wounded, before he entered, and the equipment was destroyed.

"If you see no point in saying all that in the *Courrier de l'Air*, print at least the official communiqué issued by General Ritchie, Commander-in-Chief of the Allied Forces in the sector: 'On orders from General Ritchie, the garrison of Bir Hakeim withdrew on the night of June 10–11. The troops of the Free French Forces, under the orders of General Koenig, during a period of sixteen days threw back powerful attacks by infantry, tanks, and planes. They inflicted heavy losses on the Axis powers. They played a vital role in thwarting the enemy's plans. Their magnificent fighting qualities have won for them the admiration of the United Nations.' "

I said that I would certainly print the communiqué but that if I presented the affair of Bir Hakeim as the loss of a fortified place after a courageous defense, Carlton Gardens would complain to the Foreign Office.

"Well, it's up to you to decide," Colonel S— went on. "But if you describe this action as a French victory and a German defeat, you will not be telling the truth. The English press was taken in by the propaganda from Carlton Gardens. The final impression was: the French held while the English ran away. Very well, remember what I am saying: it was the first time the Free French faced the Germans in battle. But it will be the last. There you have the results of all the clamor by the propaganda services of Carlton Gardens."

Much later, when I had an opportunity to check into what actually happened during those catastrophic days, I came to see that Colonel S— had gone a little overboard. Quite understandably, I grant, in view of the tremendous attention called to the French stand at Bir Hakeim. Of course, as I have indicated, it wasn't quite the first time the Free French had faced the Germans in battle. Several battalions had been in action a year earlier, under Wavell, and in January General Koenig's brigade had taken part in the capture of the German and Italian troops encircled at Salûm and Bardia.

I have also looked into the matter of the French losses at Bir Hakeim, about which there has been some unhappy controversy. Here are the official figures given me in 1963 by the Historical Section of the Ministère des Armées:

At Bir Hakeim:
officers: 44 killed or missing
soldiers: 1,104 killed or missing
During the sortie (June 10):
killed: 130
wounded: 198
missing: 829
(Most of the missing were prisoners.)

The manner in which the heroism of the French troops of Bir Hakeim was exploited—to use the words of Jean Oberlé, himself an excellent Gaullist—seriously vexed the English leaders. The great mass of the public, however, was suffused with new enthusiasm for General de Gaulle and for his army.[2] As for Churchill, he

---

[2] In his book about his life in London (*Jean Oberlé Vous Parle*), Jean Oberlé, a leading Gaullist, said this about Bir Hakeim:

". . . This remarkable action by the Free French Forces, by the French soldiers who had been fighting alongside the Allies in Africa for two years, was of course exploited by us. It was very natural, and our soldiers deserved being thus exalted.

was to write in his history that, in spite of the fine defense put up by the Free French against Rommel, the evacuation and loss of the site was a heavy blow and contributed in part to the loss of the Gazala line and the ensuing disasters, the loss of Tobruk among them, which saw the British retreat well into Egypt, to El Alamein, in fact.[3]

June 18, 1942

On June 18, 1942, the second anniversary of his first appeal, General de Gaulle spoke before more than ten thousand Frenchmen and Frenchwomen assembled in Albert Hall, then the largest hall in London. The national commissioners were all there. When the General stood up to speak, he raised his arms, making the V

". . . The English, very sporting, accorded the greatest acclaim to the men of Bir Hakeim. The English newspapers ran enormous headlines reading: 'The *Verduns* Are Still Holding Out.' Koenig and his men knew glory. Churchill in the Commons paid them homage, to acclamations from the House. As for Maurice Schumann, spokesman for Fighting France, he dished up Bir Hakeim with every kind of sauce. On each and every occasion he talked only of Bir Hakeim. I say it again, that was all we had to put our teeth into."

Since then, it has become an established historical fact that the men at Bir Hakeim had more than done their job. They had borne the full brunt of the Africa Korps for days—as long as they had been asked by General Ritchie, longer in fact.

[3] Sir Winston Churchill, in *The Hinge of Fate* (Volume IV of his *History of the Second World War*, p. 362), writes first of the destruction of the British brigade at Ghât-el-Skarab on June 1, and quotes Rommel as saying, ". . . The British defense was conducted with considerable skill. As usual the British fought to the last round of ammunition."

He then goes on: "Soon the enemy armour sallied from the bridgehead and renewed its attacks. The Free French were evacuated from Bir Hacheim after a very fine defense. This was a very heavy blow, and the next phase of the battle began, in far worse circumstances than the first; nor would the whole-hearted efforts of the Royal Air Force prevent the collapse that followed."

sign. He began by condemning the use of personal power, by Marshal Pétain. Then he raised a hymn to the empire and proclaimed that France was held by virtue of what he called a "sacred sovereignty" and "her benevolent influence." The nation, he said, was deeply conscious of its "imperial accomplishment" and of the ties that united it to its empire. Any blow struck at her sovereignty over it would be "profoundly odious to France."

To the delight of his audience, he took note of the fact that the Free French were accused of being difficult, and intransigent. But, he said, "in the extremity to which France finds herself reduced, no compromise, no transactions are conceivable." An eloquent mention of Bir Hakeim and a thundering peroration brought the hall to its feet. His final words were that once the liberation was accomplished, he would consider "our task finished. . . ." [1]

On the way out, I caught the arm of the good man from Carlton Gardens whom I had dubbed Porte-pensée. "Excuse me, sir," I said. "I beg your pardon, but tell me, does the last sentence in the General's speech—about his task being finished—does it really mean that he intends to retire, once French territory has been liberated?"

"You simply don't listen!" he replied with a show of irritation.

[1] Extracts from General de Gaulle's speech at Albert Hall, June 18, 1942

On the Empire:
". . . In the nation's fearful ordeal one element stands out as vital to her future and indispensable to her greatness. I refer to the Empire . . .
". . . the French people are alive to their imperial achievements and the profound solidarity which unites them to the Empire. . . . Any attack on her sovereign rights in the Empire would indeed be hateful to France."
On Bir Hakeim:
". . . When a ray of her reborn glory touched the bloodied brows of her soldiers at Bir Hakeim, the whole world recognised France."
When his task is finished:
". . . United for battle, we shall loyally fulfil our duty towards France, never resting until national liberation is accomplished. Then, our task completed, our part played, following all who served her since the dawn of her history, precursors of all who will serve her in her eternal future, we shall say to France, simply, in the word of Péguy: *Mother, behold thy sons, who have fought so hard.*"

De Gaulle: *Memoirs*, Documents (1940–42), pp. 424–9.

"You don't pay attention to the words and then you accuse the General of ambiguity! He did not say *liberation of our territory*; he spoke of *national liberation,* which is not the same thing at all! In his deepest thoughts the General considers that *national liberation* must be accomplished through revolution—and it will be the greatest revolution in the history of France! Hasn't he already said that? Good Lord, your trouble is that you don't know how to listen."

Several days later, Porte-pensée sent me a copy of the manifesto General de Gaulle was having printed in the clandestine newspapers of France. One sentence, underlined in red, repeated in different words what he had already said: "As the French people are uniting for victory, they are assembling for a revolution!" My friend from Carlton Gardens, a fine fellow, really, had written below the signature a few words for my personal benefit: "There is still time for you to become one of us!"

July 1942

From now on, General de Gaulle devoted a considerable part of his activities to organizing action in the French Resistance. In July, he prevailed upon the English to give official recognition to the change in the name of his organization: Free France became Fighting France. He had the leaders of the Resistance movements in France come to London. (He said that he "convoked" them.) He supplied them with funds. He brought even the Communists over to his side. But there, it seemed to me, the concessions made were mutual. Later, in Algiers, I saw Communist deputies who had just come out of an African concentration camp, where they had been since the outbreak of the war. They told me, "We will follow him to the end of the road [the liberation], but only that far. We know with whom we are dealing!" On the other hand, Léon Blum, an intelligent man and a good man, believed for a long time that General de Gaulle favored parliamentary democracy!

I was in Pierre Comert's office when a member of the Socialist Party, who was later to become a very important figure in France, presented his views on General de Gaulle. He had come to London to find out if the General was such a valiant champion of parliamentary democracy as the Socialist Party chief, Léon Blum, then still in prison at Bourassol, believed him to be. Here are the notes I took after listening to the visitor from France tell us, ingeniously and with a warm accent from the South of France, just how General de Gaulle managed to put the Socialist Party in his pocket:

". . . There we were, without any money. Our treasurer, with a display of scruples that were to his credit, did not want to let go of even a sou. Once the Party came back into existence officially, he said, it would find its treasury intact. Help reached us from several sources, including a really surprising one: Raymond Patenôtre[1] handed us enough money to bring out the issue of *Le Populaire* which carried the testimony of Léon Blum at the Riom trial. But very soon we were penniless again, in the soup. And I mean in the soup! Then it was that we had a visit from some representatives of General de Gaulle. We received these gentlemen with courtesy but no enthusiasm. Prudence, prudence above all! We remembered General de Gaulle's prewar friendships with the Right. With Marshal Pétain. We remembered his enthusiasm for a professional army [in the famous book published in 1934]. Not for us, thank you! We declared flatly to the gentlemen who were proposing to finance us: Messieurs, we will not eat of that bread! But, they said, renewing their offer, we ask nothing of you but that you be yourselves! The General would find it repugnant to exercise the slightest control over the use you make of what we are offering you! He has complete confidence in you. You are against Vichy? You are against Hitler? Well, that's enough for us. Besides, the General is not the kind of man you imagine him to be. The General favors the Left. Take note of how he speaks of our cherished and so efficacious unions!"

[1] A French press and industrial magnate.

Léon Blum's envoy closed his little talk by saying that in view of these assurances the Socialist Party accepted the financial backing offered them. But he had been sent to London to inform himself at first hand of the political tendencies of General de Gaulle and his entourage. . . . The General's entourage? Our friend from the South of France was soon in no position to criticize it. He became part of it.

This little tale could be matched by a hundred others, only one of which I will relate here. It really has little to do with General de Gaulle, but it shows, I think, the naïveté of certain persons and how he made use of people notable in their fields of operation. This story has to do with M. P—, a member of the Resistance who had recently arrived from France, and was subsequently to play an important role in the Gaullist organization. My friend Siriex telephoned me one day: "Jacques Soustelle arranged a press conference for this newly arrived hero of the Resistance, but the more important English journalists did not show up. It would seem that the London press is a little tired of the fireworks set off for each new arrival from France. In this particular case, they are wrong. The General is reserving for this man a post that it not exactly negligible. Perhaps you would be willing to arrange for him to meet your friends on *The Times*, the *Manchester Guardian*, and the *Daily Telegraph*."

So it was that I arranged a small luncheon for the Englishmen from the three papers mentioned, for the new man fresh from France, and for my friend from Carlton Gardens, who, by the way, was becoming less and less Carltonian and would shortly leave for a combat post. The English journalists knew their business. One of them, Iverach, was already tops in his trade. They put only a few questions to my guest. One of them asked: "What, in your opinion, is the comparison between the spirit of Resistance in Occupied France and in the Unoccupied Zone?"

"Indomitable in both zones!" he replied and then went on with an interesting exposé, a little as if he were on a lecture platform, not at a luncheon table. When finally, after some ten minutes, he stopped for breath, there was a second question: "Please be so good as to give us, monsieur, your estimate of the prestige of Marshal Pétain in Unoccupied France?"

"It is nil, absolutely nil!" he replied and thereupon launched into another, equally passionate address.

A third question: "In Occupied France, from which you have just come, do you have ways of informing yourselves on conditions in North Africa?"

"Alas, no! The Germans have effectively cut off metropolitan France from our three Algerian departments, etc. . . ."

A fourth question: "What do you think of the policy of the Americans in respect to France, Monsieur P—?"

"I consider it a major disaster! By the mere fact of keeping an ambassador in Vichy, President Roosevelt considerably strengthens the terrible influence of Pétain. Furthermore, Roosevelt maintains contacts, through his representatives, with anti-Gaullist officers. And this is discouraging to the Resistance. He should be told! To maintain relations with Vichy amounts to hamstringing our patriots and strengthening Pétain to a formidable extent! I repeat, Roosevelt should be told."

"You must know, monsieur, that the Canadians also maintain a diplomatic mission accredited to Marshal Pétain?"

"I don't compliment them on it! In North Africa notably, the Canadians are giving the impression that salvation may not necessarily come through Gaullism. That is a nefarious policy."

In reporting the questions asked by my English friends, I have not abbreviated them. They were laconic. But I have had to reduce to a mere résumé the answers, for these were so generously phrased as to seem now like an intervention in the Chamber of Deputies, now like a lecture in a university classroom. As a result, we were at the table a good two hours.

Once alone with me in the street, the three Englishmen exchanged smiles. They were amused by the thought of the newly arrived "Resister" successively assuring them that the Resistance was indomitable; that the Americans had knocked it flat; that the prestige of Marshal Pétain was nil; that the influence of Marshal Pétain was formidable; that the Occupied Zone was completely cut off from North Africa; that in North Africa people were coming to believe that salvation could be achieved without the intervention of General de Gaulle.

The General "convoked" several other patriots. Among them were men of incredible courage: Jean Moulin, Emmanuel d'Astier de la Vigerie, and Pierre Brossolette. After the war I came to know Emmanuel d'Astier when I worked as a correspondent for *Liberation* for almost a year. As for Pierre Brossolette, he came to our house in London. His courage frightened me, and I speak of him, of his memory, with the deepest respect. Perhaps I have said it already, but I will say it again, for it is a thought that has long haunted me: never would I have been able consciously, willingly, to risk suicide or torture, the concentration camp, physical and perhaps moral weakness and collapse. All the more then, do I, a distant and horrified spectator, admire the Resistance inside France. The comfort and freedom we enjoyed in London, despite the Nazi bombers in the skies, always made me ashamed.

Relations between the General and the British government, which had improved somewhat in June, deteriorated again in July. But with the Americans, things were going rather better. The reason for this was little known. General Marshall, the American Chief of Staff, wanted to open what was then being called, in anticipation, the "Second Front" in Europe, with the Allied forces invading France directly from England, as was actually to take place two years later in Normandy. But, as is well known, Churchill preferred to go around by North Africa and strike up through the Balkans, the "soft underbelly of Europe," a Churchillian phrase which was to become renowned, though never confirmed.

President Roosevelt had been favorable to this plan, but he saw that it met with little enthusiasm in Moscow. The Russians considered Danubian and Balkan Europe to be within their zone of influence. Furthermore, they were eager to have an Allied offensive get underway at the earliest, so that the might of the German armies engaging them deep within their homeland would be to some extent distracted. At that moment in history, the only other front on which the German Army and its Italian allies were engaged was Libya, Egypt actually.

Roosevelt had his reasons for not wanting the Russians to become discouraged. In the summer of 1942, he favored General Marshall's strategy of a direct strike at Western Europe. He had Churchill to convince, however. He was acutely aware of the Prime Minister's admiration for General de Gaulle. For all their many head-on clashes, Churchill had not ceased to consider the French general one of the ablest strategists of our time. If General de Gaulle believed that it would be possible to make a cross-Channel attack from bases in England, thus obviating the need for the roundabout action through North Africa *and* at the same time giving the Russians the relief they were clamoring for, his opinion would be helpful in winning over Churchill.

It was against this background that General Marshall, Admiral King, Chief of Operations of the United States Navy, and General Eisenhower, who had been chosen to command the Allied expeditionary force, went to see General de Gaulle in London, to ascertain his views on the matter.

"Naturally, I am in favor of a direct offensive in Europe," answered General de Gaulle.

"With England as a base of departure?"

"Naturally," said the General, and went on to add, "No other operation would bring matters to a head. Moreover, the best solution for France is the one that would shorten the trials of the invasion and hasten national unification."

On the following day, the Americans, delighted that General de Gaulle was of their opinion, went to tell the English: "General de Gaulle favors a direct offensive launched from Great Britain."

"How's that?" exclaimed the British, thunderstruck. "He told you that?"

"Yes, without the slightest hesitation."

"But to us he said just the contrary!"

"What? He gave you a contrary opinion?"

"Yes, exactly the contrary. You have only to look at what he told

Churchill in a note addressed to him on March 1, 1941: 'With reference to an offensive, French North Africa is the best possible base to start from in order to act later on the Continent.' "

The Americans could hardly believe their ears.

President Roosevelt's reasons for not wanting to discourage Stalin at that period should be better known than they are. He has been bitterly criticized, even in America (or should I say, particularly in America?), for having been, as his critics say, "taken in" by Stalin, for having believed in the good faith of that fearful tyrant, for having naïvely abandoned the peoples of Central Europe, the Danube, and the Balkans. There are people today who say: "If only he had followed Churchill's plans, if only the Allied armies had driven into the soft underbelly through Yugoslavia! All these peoples would have been saved! But no, not only did he reject Churchill's strategy, but, at Teheran, he was willing to recognize that Hungary, Rumania, etc., were within the Russian zone of influence. [Greece was recognized as being within the English zone, and Yugoslavia within a combined Allied-Russian zone.]"

This subject has been debated back and forth over the years, and all too often without much regard for the facts. I can remember being in Washington early in 1945 when Roosevelt's policy was being heatedly discussed. (I gather that it is still being argued and still with rather more heat than light.) At that time I had occasion to hear Alexis Léger discuss the broad lines of the President's policy. Léger was highly thought of in Washington. His gallant but foredoomed attempts, as Secretary-General at the Quai d'Orsay, to hold French foreign policy within reasonable lines were much appreciated in Washington. His dignified behavior at the time of his dismissal in the spring of 1940 by Paul Reynaud acting under the influence of the Baudouin–Hélène de Portes cabal was understood and admired by President Roosevelt, whom he often saw, and by his chief foreign-policy aides. Secretary of State Hull and Under-Secretary Sumner Welles were on friendly terms with him. In view of all this, I think it safe to say that Léger was very well informed indeed. I wrote down what he said in my presence on that occasion in 1945 not very long before Roosevelt's death.

"The President has ceaselessly concentrated on the one primary goal, winning the war; and ceaselessly he has been dominated by his preoccupation not to lose it. How to win? By a massive landing of Allied forces in Europe and by the development of a 'new weapon.'"

Here I should perhaps say that at the time in question nobody spoke of the "atom bomb." It was rumored that progress was being made toward the development of such a weapon, but this was one of the best-kept secrets of the war. Moreover, it was not until the Potsdam Conference in July–August 1945, after the defeat of the German Reich, that even the President, by then Harry S Truman, knew for certain that it would work. People who were aware that heroic efforts were being made to beat the Germans in developing something of the sort referred to it, if at all, as a "new weapon." (It is a fact of history that Truman did not hear of the "Manhattan Project," as it was called, until he assumed the presidency.)

Léger's remarks, as I set them down that night, continued: "How to lose the war? In either of two ways. Or in both. The first would be if the Russians were to call a halt, granting the Germans a truce, which would allow Hitler to move the larger part of his forces to the West to block an Allied landing in Europe. A German–Soviet truce is not unthinkable. Both the Russians and the Germans are tired.

"We like to think that the Russians would not dare abandon us. But Stalin is capable of anything. The President knows it, and, contrary to what is said by fools, places no trust at all in the man he chooses to call 'Uncle Joe.' he takes him for what he is, a bandit, quite capable of a second criminal understanding with the other great bandit, Hitler. And all the more so because the Russians are exasperated to see that England and the United States have suffered relatively few losses in manpower whereas the Soviet Union has already lost at least 10,000,000. Stalin has every reason to feel that the end of the war will find Russia exhausted, bled white, confronting an America and a Great Britain at the peak of their military might."

Léger then went on to speak of the second way in which the war might be lost. The fact that it well might have been lost seems to have escaped the attention of most of this generation. And, even then, when the situation was indeed, as Léger explained, very chancy, there were men who did not seem to think it could be lost. One had only to see the constant preoccupation of some Gaullists with matters of protocol, personal prestige, the enthusiasm of African crowds, etc., to wonder whether they were at any time worried at the prospect that the Allies would go down in defeat, and with them France.

"The second way in which the war could be lost: in spite of massive Allied bombings, German industry continues to manufacture arms in increasing quantity and of increasing quality. What will happen if the engineers and scientists of the Reich, who were the first to develop the hollow or armor-piercing charges capable of penetrating the armor of tanks, then the V-1 and now the V-2— what will happen, I say again, if they are the first to perfect a new, secret weapon? It is not impossible that they should be the first.[2] At the instigation of Albert Einstein, the President has had brought to the United States as many German and other European scientists, many of them of Jewish origin, as possible. It is rumored that he has decided to devote unlimited funds to the development of the 'new weapon.' But who will win the race?

"There you have the reason why the President is willing to pay a very high price *to keep Russia actively in the war*. And what is this price? It consists of two parts. The first is the opening of a second front in Western Europe. Roosevelt said, 'Yes, I will pay.' The English raised the question of manpower, saying, quite correctly, that an assault on the Atlantic wall would take many more men than an operation in the Balkans and Central Europe. The American answer, President Roosevelt's answer, was that the United States would supply the major effort in manpower and weaponry. In exchange, the Supreme Command would be American.

"Churchill wanted an offensive made in the Balkans. So did

[2] It was only near the end of 1944 that it became clear that the Germans would not have the atom bomb in this war. (Samuel A. Goudsmit: *Alsos* [New York: Henry Schuman; 1947].)

Roosevelt, but he was forced to give way in view of General Marshall's categorical objections, objections of a strictly military nature. According to the experts, six months of free maritime traffic would be required to feed an army capable of standing up to the Germans in Europe. If the second front were in the Balkans, this traffic would have to cross by way of Gibraltar; but the Germans would certainly cover the straits. And the Yugoslav ports would not be enough.

"The other demand of the Russians was that the Western Powers leave them Central and Balkan Europe as Soviet zones of influence. The President consented. He knows very well that the American people will not fight to prevent this.

"The President knows through bitter experience. He was unable to lead the United States into the war in 1940 when France was struck down and Great Britain was within inches of defeat. It took an attack by the Japanese on Pearl Harbor and the Philippines for a state of war with Japan to come into effect. And the United States did not declare war on Germany. Or on Italy. The Germans and the Italians had to take the initiative four days later. It is said that the American people are bellicose and imperialist. The truth is that the United States, of all the nations of the globe, is the most peaceful, the most difficult to lead into war.

"So—the Americans, who did not declare war to preserve the liberty of the French or the liberty of the English, will not declare it either to safeguard the liberty of the Poles, the Czechoslovakians, the Bulgarians, the Rumanians, or the Hungarians. The North Americans are the most generous people on earth. But they are also the most devoted to peace.

"That is why the President gave Stalin in advance what he could not keep him from taking. All he could hope for was that the tyrant's hand should not bear down too heavily on those unfortunate countries. The way to prevent this, since it had been decided not to use force, was to give the bandit as little reason as possible to be afraid."

That was how Alexis Léger sketched Roosevelt's policy to me. Nothing that I have seen or read since has given me any reason to think him wrong. In fact, later, during the Hungarian revolt, when a different administration was in power in Washington, I often thought back on this conversation and I understood why not one American went on his own to get himself killed in Budapest. And not one Frenchman either.

Summer, 1942

General de Gaulle wanted to go back to the Middle East, but Churchill was in no mood to grant him the necessary facilities. The Prime Minister was apprehensive lest the chief of the Fighting French, once in Beirut or Brazzaville and out from under British influence, might make some kind of sensational gesture or statement.

As a matter of fact, the General, by his own admission, was not in a very cooperative mood at that moment. He was aware of the negotiations going on between General Giraud, then in the Unoccupied Zone after his escape from Koenigstein, and Robert Murphy, President Roosevelt's personal emissary in North Africa. And he had every reason to believe that those negotiations would not favor him as a political leader.

Despite serious opposition in both the American and the English commands, Churchill finally made a plane available to the General, and, just before his departure, met with him at Downing Street. In his memoirs,[1] the General gives a lively account of this conversation of July 29, 1942.

> "Well," said Mr. Churchill, "you're off to Africa and the Levant."
> "I am pleased to be going to the Levant," replied the General.

[1] De Gaulle: *Memoirs*, Documents (1942–44), p. 29.

"Spears is making a nuisance of himself. He is causing us difficulties."

"Spears," continued Mr. Churchill, "has a lot of enemies. But he has one friend—the Prime Minister. When you get there, go and see him. I will telegraph to him and tell him to listen to what you say."

"They say," added Mr. Churchill, "that the independence of the Levant States is not a reality, and the people are not contented."

"They are," retorted the General, "at least as content in Syria and the Lebanon as the people in Iraq, Palestine or Egypt."

Before reading the passage in the General's memoirs, I had heard about this conversation from David Bowes-Lyon. He gave a slightly different turn to Churchill's response regarding General Spears. Imitating the Prime Minister's rather personal enunciation in French: "*Oui, je sais, je sais!* General Spears *avait beaucoup d'ennemis. Mais il a un ami: c'est moi!*" The meaning remains the same, but this version paints rather more clearly Churchill's complete loyalty to his friends, even to those who added fresh worries to the burden he bore, to those who were at odds among themselves.

August 1942

Early in August 1942, The General left London, austere and gray even in summer, for the blue skies of Beirut, for the enthusiasm of the crowds and the admiration and the deference of the Syrian and Lebanese notables. These people really knew how to demonstrate their devotion, however transient it might later prove to be.

From Beirut, he states, on August 27 "I was in a position to announce to our London delegation: The United States has now decided to land troops in French North Africa. The operation will be launched in conjunction with a forthcoming British offensive in

Egypt. . . . That is why, having need of us, they took the position indicated by their memorandum of July 9. Now their plans have changed. . . ."

Just what special precautions were taken by General de Gaulle in transmitting this interesting bit of intelligence to London are not revealed in his memoirs; the Germans would have been happy to know what he knew. The General also went out of his way to inform a bewildered American consul in Beirut that he was quite *au courant* of the project for the North African landings in conjunction with the British offensive from El Alamein (all but the actual dates, which had not then been set) and that he resented his exclusion from it. And a London representative of the Free French, claiming to have had his information about the top-secret plan from Vichy, New York, *and* two other unspecified places, voiced his protest. Understandably, all this provoked a flap among the Anglo-American planners. Robert Murphy, in a message to General Donovan of the American OSS, raised a question as to whether General de Gaulle, "who had adopted a hostile and arrogant attitude towards Great Britain recently over the Syria question," might not perpetrate some "treachery" in the event that the United States undertook some form of military intervention in French North Africa. Murphy advised Colonel Donovan to exclude the Fighting French "at the moment" from knowledge of his discussions in London with French underground leaders.[1]

From the Middle East, de Gaulle flew three thousand miles to

---

[1] At this time Commander Kittredge, aide to Admiral Stark in London, said in a report to Washington: "In general, the British are opposed to working with or through the Fighting French undercover resistance organization. . . . The British feel that there are leaks in the Fighting French organization, which have resulted in the Germans receiving advance notice of various plans and operations." (Langer: *Our Vichy Gamble*, p. 298.)

This bandying about of rumor, all too well informed, did not increase American or British enthusiasm about including the Gaullists in this enormously chancy operation concerning which the Commander-in-Chief, General Eisenhower, was later to say, "The situation was vague, the amount of resources unknown, the final object indeterminate, and the only firm factor . . . our instructions to attack." (Dwight D. Eisenhower: *Crusade in Europe* [New York: Doubleday; 1948], p. 77.)

Fort-Lamy. There, he gave General Leclerc "personal and secret instructions" to wait until the British Eighth Army had started its drive westward from El Alamein and *then* to strike northward and try to take Tripoli ahead of the English. When he reached Brazzaville, he was overwhelmed by the loving welcome given him, which exceeded even the warmth of the demonstration in Beirut. The demonstrations in Africa showed that there was unanimity behind General de Gaulle, *except* for the rebels, deserters, nonconformists, and the like, who were sweating out their punishments in prisons there.

While in Africa, as in the Middle East, the General not only had the satisfaction of popular acclaim; he had his worries too, and these came to him, naturally, from the Allies. When all the documents are published, they will show the enormous amount of time that General de Gaulle spent, during the war, fighting the Allies.

In contrast, the time devoted by Churchill to the Fighting French during this period is not considerable. The Prime Minister had other preoccupations, in the Far East, in the Atlantic, in Madagascar. And now, with the Americans, he was mounting the great offensive that was to acquire North Africa as the springboard for an attack on Italy. And there lay one of the causes of our tragedy in France: the British Prime Minister one day recognized de Gaulle as Chief of the Free French; he placed at his disposal the radio, arms, and pounds sterling, and then for almost a year hardly bothered with him. From time to time Churchill was importuned with complaints about the General, and his answer was to show the complainants the door. From time to time he went into rages against the General, but finally gave way to him, in recognition of the powers that he had himself granted him. And then he thought no more about him. (Heaven knows that in 1942 he had other things to worry about!)

Then he turned around and found himself face to face with a gigantic creature, like, he said, the monster created by Frankenstein. His little joke about this was all over London: he was Frankenstein and he had created a monster for his delight. But he maintained his friendship for the General, and quite sincerely.

September 1942

While in the Middle East General de Gaulle was trying to bring down General Spears, in London his commissioners were getting their lumps. Complaints were received from the Foreign Office to the effect that the General was constantly saying that Great Britain wanted to keep Syria and Lebanon for herself, when he knew this was absolutely false. Why then these gratuitous insults directed at the good faith of Great Britain? Did the General believe that an alliance could function under these conditions? Why didn't he return to London? There would be decisions to take which might interest France. In any case, if he did not want to return, let him not complain that he had not been consulted. He would do well to realize that a project was on the eve of fulfillment which should concern the Chief of the Free French.

The commissioners did as they were asked and informed the General, but he decided not to return as yet. On September 10, they were again summoned to the Foreign Office. Eden told them, in substance: "We are at Diego-Suarez; but in view of the Japanese threat in that part of the world, we may be obliged to extend our occupation to the entire island of Madagascar. If the General would be good enough to return to London as the Prime Minister has had the honor to ask him, we can talk over with him the possibility of entrusting him with the administration of the island. Otherwise. . . ."

This time the General decided to return, not, however, without taking a turn around the garden—to Brazzaville, in other words—so as to underline clearly the fact that he was taking his own sweet time. He returned to England on September 25. I well remember because it was on that day that the English for the first time had their planes drop over France leaflets calling on the people not to commit premature acts of resistance. Some of us had been asking for the past two years that this be done. I believe I never wrote a leaflet with so much pleasure.

The General had been in no hurry to return. And now Churchill was in no hurry to receive him. He had him cool his heels until September 29, the day he was to inform the House of Commons that British troops had taken over Madasgascar, and that they had done so without the prolonged fratricidal struggle that had bloodied the Syrian campaign. When the General was at long last ushered into the Prime Minister's office, it was to voice an angry protest. Madagascar was part of the France which he had assumed in his person. Churchill was violating rights that he had himself recognized as the General's.

In exasperation Churchill flung at him some words that would not long be secret, for in the next few days there were indiscretions, the voluntary kind. I heard several versions that varied in picturesqueness but were all essentially alike in substance. Here it would be simplest to choose the version General de Gaulle gives in his memoirs:

"Mr. Churchill then attacked me in a bitter and highly emotional tone. When I pointed out that the establishment of a British-controlled administration in Madagascar would constitute an interference with the rights of France, he exclaimed furiously: 'You claim to be France! You are not France! I do not recognize you as France!'

"Then, still as vehemently: 'France! Where is France now? Of course I don't deny that General de Gaulle and his followers are an important and honorable part of the French people, but certainly another authority besides his could be found which would also have its value.' I interrupted him. 'If, in your eyes, I am not the representative of France, why and with what right are you dealing with me concerning her world-wide interests?' Mr. Churchill did not reply."

What else could he do? General de Gaulle was absolutely right; his papers were in order. Churchill recognized him as Chief of the

Free French, then of the Fighting French, and, since the summer of 1940 as the sole authority entitled to negotiate in the name of France. The General had repeated on innumerable occasions that he was acting in the name of the French people, that he incarnated France, that he embodied in his person the whole apparatus of state and government. Never did Churchill publicly challenge the General's sweeping affirmation. Furthermore, the emotional out-bursts of the Prime Minister could hardly serve to move the man who, in all this, "thought of himself as merely doing his duty."

Churchill being thus reduced to silence, Eden took the floor. "He repeated the justification the British claimed to have for inter-fering with our affairs there. Then, losing his temper in his turn, he complained bitterly of my behavior."

Eden implied that the General was ungrateful. The Secretary of State for Foreigh Affairs, model Etonian and model Oxonian, the perfect gentleman, was nevertheless the son of his father, Sir Wil-liam, the terrible-tempered baronet who was known to hurl plates out of the window and who once, on a rainy day, threw out a faulty barometer, shouting. "Go yourself and see what the weather is like out there!"

The General, faced with two outraged Englishmen, maintained a sovereign calm. So he was ungrateful? He had certainly not for-gotten the help he had received from Churchill, from England. But the interests of France, which were his own, took precedence over all else. He could not forget this even to please Churchill, his friend.

François Mauriac has ably analyzed how it came about that General de Gaulle, in the perspective of the historical destiny he very early conceived for himself, "has tended" to identify his per-sonal fortune with the fortune of France. Further on, the General's faithful portraitist avers that this "is what gives his personality such an extraordinary flavor. The pride that is so often reproached de Gaulle springs from an auto-veneration directed not to himself but to that which he incarnates." Since François Mauriac has else-where stated that the General incarnates France in his person, **what he** says about him here could hardly be worded more aptly.

When Churchill, recovering his powers of speech, reproached the General with employing his Anglophobia to serve his own ends, he made the mistake of everyone who failed to see that the General considered France's interest and his own to be identical. "Mr. Churchill outdid him [Eden], shouting that my Anglophobia was dictated by a desire for prestige, and to see aggrandized my personal position in France." But if Mauriac is right when he states that the General *is* France, how could one speak of his personal position *in* France?

These great truths about General de Gaulle took a long time to seep into the brains of the men who were directing the English and American war efforts. It wasn't until the liberation that they accepted the evidence and comprehended that the General was indeed an incarnation of France. It is quite another question whether France herself had anything like an accurate idea of the man who was her incarnation!

Today France has an accurate idea of him. Those who stand to one side, who wish for some other regime, must admit that the majority of the nation came out, with their eyes open, for his form of government—a form of government in which, as François Mauriac so well puts it, "the foreign policy of France is the conception of a single brain and is executed according to the views and the tactics of one single man who consults with nobody." Those tactics are more military than diplomatic in origin.[1]

At the time of the violent scene between General de Gaulle and Churchill, with Eden in his corner, the General's National Com-

---

[1] *General de Gaulle's military tactics*

"But surprise must be organized. Not only by means of secrecy . . . but also under cover of a thick veil of make-believe. In our age . . . it is almost impossible to prevent information reaching the enemy. But, none the less, one may confuse him. If one is willing to hoodwink one's own camp deliberately, to mislead the very people one intends to employ, or by clever artifice . . . one can hide reality behind falsehood. . . . Cunning must be used to make him [the enemy] believe that one is where one is not, that one wants something quite different from what one does. . . ." Charles de Gaulle: *The Army of the Future* (New York: Lippincott; 1941). (Translated here by Jay Allen from the French edition published in London in 1940.)

missioner of Foreign Affairs, Maurice Dejean, did not quite grasp this concept of foreign affairs. Dejean evidently wished to represent a France other than the one incarnated by the General. He thought some few concessions might help restore good relations with the English and reestablish the old confidence. After all, Dejean had borne the full brunt of Great Britain's displeasure. The General knew this and in his memoirs describes how the Foreign Office, concentrating on him "the full force of all its departments and brandishing before his eyes the specter of a complete breakdown of relations—a diplomat's worst fear—affected him sufficiently for him to envisage what concession we could make to reestablish good relations.

"Concessions? I would not hear of them. Dejean therefore handed in his resignation."

With some little humor, Maurice Dejean recounted how it all came about. The General had him summoned and said to him, "You are a bad Frenchman [*un mauvais Français*]!"

"General, I am just as good a Frenchman as you are."

"That is quite possible, Dejean, but you are no longer Commissioner of Foreign Affairs."

My friend Paniguian was fond of Dejean and invited me to dine with him. I remember his telling me during this crisis with the General that his only ambition was to represent France in Prague, after the war. This struck me as not only a very pleasant ambition but also a modest one. His wife was courageous and gay. She used to say, "It is all right with me, our being on the beach. I will do housework or I will make hats." Luckily, Dejean was shortly afterward appointed as General de Gaulle's representative to the various refugee governments then in Great Britain.

Of those of all the sovereigns in exile, Queen Wilhelmina's political ideals struck me as the most nearly opposite to those of de Gaulle; she had decided that the government of Holland at the liberation should be entrusted to men who had stayed behind. The fact that she had been taken to London rather against her will weighed heavily on her heart. She seemed almost to feel herself unworthy, and her ambition was to abdicate and lead her life in wooden shoes. One day when she was presiding over a council of her ministers—and seemed to be half asleep, as was her custom— an argument arose on the subject of who should get which jobs after the liberation. She coughed and there was a sudden silence.

"Stop this kind of talk, gentlemen. It is not worthy of you. It is indecent! You seem to forget [and this was something she had never said before] that the moment we are back in Holland you will all hand me your resignations. And I will accept them. None of you will play any official role; the government will be in the hands of those who stayed behind in Holland."

This was told me by one of the Queen's ministers of that period. Another told me that he had stuck it out in Holland until almost the end of the war, and then he had received a secret message ordering him to present himself in London. There, he went to see the Queen.

"Why did you leave Holland?" she asked him grimly.

"But, Your Majesty, because you ordered me to."

"Oh, that's different. Very well, you are forgiven."

Respectful of her country's constitution and of its parliamentary system, she was, for all that she was queen, a firm adversary of personal power. She was convinced that the Dutch, like the English, the Swiss, and so many other peoples, were perfectly capable of handling their own affairs through their elected representatives.

Autumn, 1942

By the autumn of 1942 the Allied plan for a landing directly in France had been shelved. Preparations were underway, quite noticeably for those with eyes, for the operation in North Africa. A man had to be thick in the head and simple besides not to have an idea of what was about to happen. Hitler and certain French admirals proved to be just that. Among the remarkably obtuse French admirals I am thinking particularly of Admiral Prix Michelier, whose headquarters were in Casablanca. At Woburn, leaflets printed in both French and Arabic left us in doubt only about the date of the operation.

In October, Raymond Lacoste, an old friend of mine, returned to London from a lengthy and roundabout mission, and one evening came by with an officer of the French Navy who made an immediate impression on us. He was quite unlike most officers we knew: he was obviously very tough and very much a fighting man. He was Captain Maerten, who was in command at Diego-Suarez in May of that year (1942) when the British landed on Madagascar. There was a brief exchange of fire in which his friend Captain Fontaine was killed, for which he never forgave the British. A cease-fire agreement was then quickly agreed upon. Disagreeable though it is to have to say it, the British did not fulfill quite all the terms of the cease-fire. The French received the honors of war as promised, and at once. Keeping their side arms, they paraded before the English forces, who stood at attention. No complaint about that. But by the terms of the agreement all members of the French forces who wanted to go home to France were to be repatriated "at the earliest possible date." This promise was not carried out immediately. True, there were discrepancies between the French and English texts of the cease-fire, but the long delay in the matter of repatriation was deliberate. The War Office intervened in the matter, insisting that there would be no repatriation unless and until the Vichy government agreed to repatriate certain British sailors who had reached the coasts of French Africa from vessels torpedoed nearby. In other words, the War Office made use of the prisoners at Diego-Suarez as currency for an exchange. The cease-fire did not provide for anything like that.

Here it should be said that if the British had been prompt in honoring their agreement our sailors would have very shortly become German prisoners when the Nazi occupation was extended to include all of France in November, after the Allied landings in

North Africa. With North Africa back in the war, the sailors from Madagascar could instead reenter the service immediately. The English might excuse themselves in this way: they knew the landings were soon to take place, but they could not say so. However, I doubt that any such consideration entered into the matter.

At Cape Town, Captain Maerten had been separated from his men and then sent on to England to present his case for their early repatriation as agreed. He had a second objective: to forestall a renewal of hostilities on Madagascar. The British, with South African units predominating, were only in Diego-Suarez. The rest of the huge island was still under Vichy control.

Once in London, the Captain sought out his old shipmate, Admiral Auboyneau, now Chief of the Free French Navy, and went to stay with him. Although they shared the same ideals, they spent their days happily exchanging insults on the subject of General de Gaulle and his politics. Captain Maerten was eager to see the Free French and the Vichy navies united again in the common cause. He strongly believed that General de Gaulle was needlessly antagonizing the officers and men of the Vichy ships, far and away the largest part of the Navy. Quite obviously, Admiral Auboyneau would have disagreed.

Captain Maerten was given to overplaying the role of a rough, uncultured man of the sea. He was really not that, but his pose seemed the result of a loathing for a type of officer he liked to call a "notary," or worse, a "flower pot." Actually he was and is a very intelligent fellow. In London he kept his eyes open. He saw any number of Englishmen and Frenchmen and concluded that he should at least make an attempt to work through General de Gaulle, or anyway try to obtain his blessing.

Admiral Auboyneau undertook to arrange the meeting, and he thought he should go along with his old friend. When the audience was over, the Captain told me all about it in his usual harsh tones and jocular manner.

"Auboyneau had me steer a course ahead of him. There was the General, seated behind his desk. He got to his feet. Look, it's all very well to be told in advance, but when you actually see him, he

looks really tall, taller than you ever imagined! He made some
sort of gesture which seemed to mean we should be seated. So we
sat. Silence. I waited for the General to open the conversation. But
he said not a word. So I plunged right in: 'General, I have heard a
lot about you.' Silence. Evidently that was not what I was supposed
to say. Again I took my courage in my hands and I said, 'General,
now about General Weygand. . . .'

"Then he opened his mouth and spoke. He said, 'General
Weygand is a worm-eaten plank!'

"Again silence. But I kept to my course and said, 'General, now
take Admiral Auphan, there is an honorable man . . .'

"He cut straight across my bows. 'Don't mention Auphan to
me,' he snapped. 'He's a . . . !'

"He did not say exactly what he considered Auphan to be, but I
could imagine. Silence again. So I gave Auboyneau a poke in the
ribs. 'Say something!'

"Auboyneau did say something. He said, 'General, my comrade
Maerten thanks you . . .'

"The General got to his feet. Ring off the main engines!"

Maerten, however, did get on well with Admiral Muselier, who
was quick to understand what he had in mind. Together with Lady
Warwick, Anthony Eden's sister, the Admiral arranged for Maerten to make contact with British Intelligence. By now he was aware
that an important Allied operation was in the works and he did not
have to be psychic to guess that its objective was North Africa.
What he asked of the Intelligence Service was authorization and
the means to go on his own to warn his friend Admiral Auphan
that there was little time to lose if he wanted to get the French
fleet back into action. Auphan and Darlan were so close that telling
one would amount to telling the other.

The English were reluctant to underwrite anything that would
upset General de Gaulle, however, and Captain Maerten's idea of
a personal mission was nipped in the bud. He could do nothing
through the Americans either, as they were in direct contact with a
number of persons in North Africa, although, as it turned out,
none of these people had the slightest influence with the French

fleet. The Captain did get permission to send Admiral Auphan a letter through the British, but it was never delivered. He showed me a copy. It was a very good letter as far as it went but obviously was not very explicit.

One can only speculate on what might have happened if Captain Maerten had been allowed to go personally to warn Auphan. Might he not have saved the French fleet and enabled it to go into action again? Might he not have been able to prevail upon Admiral Darlan to make arrangements in time for the French fleet to escape from Toulon? Might he not even have been able to prevent the monstrous naval engagement off Oran and Casablanca by informing French commanders like Admiral Michelier of the enormous strength of the American and English expeditionary forces?

President Roosevelt was determined that General de Gaulle would not be told about the plan (known as "Torch") for the North Africa landings. Still less did he want his cooperation. Churchill did not want it either. He had already bypassed him in the Madagascar affair. To arrive off North Africa with General de Gaulle would mean a repulse as at Dakar or a bloody fight to the finish as in Syria. If there were to be battles with disciplined Vichyites—as there were indeed to be—they would have to be brought to an end very quickly lest the Germans be given an opportunity to arrive in strength. As they did in fact arrive in Tunisia.

Since his return from the Middle East, General de Gaulle had taken still more firmly in hand the direction of the Resistance in France. He began his moves to unite under his authority, and his alone, all the various Resistance groups. Although their political objectives *after* the liberation would inevitably differ greatly, they were still more or less united toward the common goal. In the complex operation to bring them firmly under his control, the General showed remarkable adroitness. It was this quality that later, in 1958, brought an accolade from François Mauriac. The great novelist then wrote, with evident relish: "And with all that, cunning too, God bless him!"

General de Gaulle's subtle maneuvers in the fall of 1942 had one aim: to bring patriots of the most diverse tendencies to see in him the person who would establish, or reestablish, whatever regime it was they dreamed about. In this the General was completely successful.

Take, for example, Georges Mandel. He saw General de Gaulle clearly, he thought, as the man who was to restore the Third Republic. Georges Mandel, Minister of the Interior in the Reynaud Cabinet in the tragic weeks of 1940, was a figure of heroic proportions. He had been the intimate collaborator of Georges Clemenceau, the Tiger of World War I. At Clemenceau's side he had seen the Third Republic triumph in the great, though costly victory of 1918. He knew all too well that the defeat of 1940 was not to be laid to the parliamentary regime under which the Third Republic had reached such heights, but to the use to which it was put by a generation exemplifying the Darwinian theory in reverse. For in its last years the Third Republic did seem to be in the hands of people who personified the survival of the weakest.

From his prison cell at Le Pourtalet, whence he was taken to be shot, or rather murdered, Georges Mandel succeeded in sending out an admirable letter to General de Gaulle.[1] Mandel told de Gaulle that when the liberation came, the whole Vichy chapter, its legislation, everything, must be erased with a stroke of the pen. And at all costs, legality must be observed.

Many another distinguished figure of the Third Republic believed that General de Gaulle had but a single political ambition, and that was to restore a parliamentary regime. Édouard Herriot, president of the Chamber of Deputies, thought that. So did Léon Jouhaux, head of the Confédération Générale du Travail (the

---

[1] *Extract from Georges Mandel's letter to General de Gaulle*

In prison, at Le Pourtalet
August 20, 1942

". . . Since June 17th, 1940, our unfortunate country has been handed over to leaders who are, in varying degrees, in the service of the enemy. If France comes back into the war, it will be necessary to begin by *effacing with a stroke of the pen all the political measures they have taken and to restore the Republic.*" De Gaulle: *Memoirs,* Documents (1942–44), p. 40.

French Trade Union Federation). Also Léon Blum, leader of the Socialist Party.

From the prison of Bourassol, where he was then incarcerated, Léon Blum managed to send out a note to the French National Committee in London in which he affirmed his certainty as to the restoration of the parliamentary regime in France.[2] There was absolutely no reason, he said, to fear any attempt at establishing "personal power," despite the current rumors, as he called them, concerning General de Gaulle's "former political ties" and also those of "a part of his present entourage."

The volunteers of the Secret Army were convinced that they were risking their lives not only to liberate France from the invader but to reestablish democratic government. Their statutes made this clear. These volunteers of course were to consider themselves bound by the oath of enlistment. Their primary mission, according to Instruction No. 5, issued by General Delestraint, was "to fight to liberate French soil from the German yoke." Their second was "to aid General de Gaulle to maintain order at the moment of liberation and to establish in France a democratic regime."

What is equivocal here is the use of the word "democratic." In the West, a democratic regime is generally considered to function through intermediaries: deputies, congressmen, members of the House of Commons, senators—all representatives of the nation and entrusted by the nation with the management of power. And paid to do it. But if one consults the book *De Gaulle,* by François

[2] *Extract from a note sent by Léon Blum to the French National Committee in London*

Bourassol, October 1942

". . . This interim Government can only be set up by one man and in one name: that of General de Gaulle. . . . I am not unaware that there are fears, even distrust, of General de Gaulle: rumours based on his former political liaisons, on part of his present entourage, a fundamental aversion to the appearance of personal and military power. But I do not share these opinions. . . . I should add that neither this [interim] Government nor even France herself will be able to exist for long in the true sense of the word without the co-operation and help of the Anglo-Saxon democracies. All these guarantees should suffice." De Gaulle: *Memoirs,* Documents (1942–44), p. 62.

Mauriac, who is the authority on the deeper thoughts of the General, one discovers that he has given the word another meaning entirely. "De Gaulle, the only revolutionary," he writes, "is in the final analysis the only democrat in the absolute sense because he insists that the people must make their decisions without intermediaries."

To convince the French people of the strictly democratic intentions of General de Gaulle was one thing. To convince leading men in England and, above all, the leading Americans in authority during the war, was quite another thing.

Adroit though he was, the General did pass up one unequaled opportunity to present himself as the champion of the Republic. In August, Marshal Pétain abolished the permanent bureaus of the Senate and the Chamber. Presidents Jeanneney of the Senate and Herriot of the Chamber protested energetically. "You have nullified the councils general. You plan to abolish national representation. . . . It is no longer enough for you to have forbidden any activity whatsoever to the legislative assemblies. . . . You are putting an end to their very existence. . . ." Herriot was arrested immediately.

On hearing of the Marshal's action—actually, it was Laval's— the official Gaullist organ in London, *La Marseillaise,* applauded. Its editor, François Quillici, wrote: "So Herriot and Jeanneney are out of a job. . . . Their hard luck leaves me cold. . . . What have they done? Like Candide, they have cultivated their garden." He thought Laval's action was motivated by fear that on the day the Allies landed in France the Chambers would be summoned. The idea of these people "with their presumptuous tripe" coming to meet the Free French volunteers, he found laughable. Subsequently de Gaulle himself rectified this position slightly; after all, he was about to invoke Herriot's support in his appeal to President Roosevelt.

De Gaulle's real opportunity had come a little earlier, when a plan had been presented to him for rescuing from France Mandel, Herriot, Gamelin, Daladier, Blum, and Reynaud, his former chief. With money enough, such a rescue, fantastic though it sounds, might not have been too difficult. After all, General Giraud's escape from the fortress of Koenigstein had been managed for less than 10,000 francs. The plan originated in America, where it was feared for the lives of these men, notably Blum and Mandel. (Mandel was indeed shot.) To Henri de Kérillis, deputy and spokesman for the group that was prepared to finance the project, one of the General's entourage wrote: "Your proposal made a very bad impression on several people who have influence with the chief. The prospect of having three ex-Premiers, a former Minister, and the former Generalissimo on Allied soil struck them as catastrophic for the General's future. . . ."

Pierre Comert was on intimate terms with the American Ambassador, John G. Winant. Torcy saw much of him too and was a close friend of his Counselor, H. Freeman Matthews. As for me, I used to meet several times a week with Americans who, although occupying less exalted positions, were well informed, men like Wallace Carroll and William Tyler, who became good friends of mine. My work with them was on a voluntary basis. They themselves worked with the English in a climate of confidence that the Free French at Carlton Gardens had no idea of; I know, because the Carltonians used to express before me their pity for the English, who, they assured me, were under the thumb of the Americans.

October 1942

There was no doubt that the greatest reservoir of power was in the United States, and it was due to increase miraculously as the war went on. General de Gaulle was fully aware of this. He also knew that the United States and Great Britain would continue to stand stubbornly together. From all the evidence, France at the end of the war would have a role to play in the reconstruction of the world only to the extent that she had the confidence of both England and the United States. This would be true in Europe. It would also be true in Africa, in the Middle East, and in the Far East. No Anglo-American confidence, no weight in international conferences—not even invitations to these conferences, perhaps. Isolation, impotence, nullity.

Neither was there any reason, as the General discovered belatedly, to count on Stalin to support him against Roosevelt and Churchill, whether in international conferences or in some bilateral relationship. Stalin would send the French not one loaf of bread, not one rifle. Only Stalinist propaganda.

It was therefore in the interest of France to have at the head of her government someone who had the confidence of both Churchill and Roosevelt. But President Roosevelt had been quoted as saying, of General de Gaulle, "I cannot imagine a man in whom I have less confidence." The consequences for France would be catastrophic if the President's opinion of de Gaulle was not modified in time. In October 1942, practically on the eve of the Anglo-American landings in North Africa, the General took extreme measures to improve Roosevelt's opinion of him. He sent to Washington, to see the President, André Philip, a Socialist, a Protestant, and an undoubted believer in the democratic process. To him he entrusted a letter for Roosevelt, dated October 26, 1942, which constitutes a document of fundamental importance to any study of General de Gaulle.

Roosevelt had been led to believe that the Allies could count on most of the French military leaders in North Africa to reenter the war against the Germans when the Anglo-American landings became a reality. General de Gaulle tried to counter this idea. "Perhaps you think," he wrote, "that one day those leaders [of Vichy France] will take up arms at our side. Alas, I do not believe it."

On this level, the last-minute efforts of General de Gaulle had not the slightest effect on the President. Less than two weeks later, General Eisenhower would be collaborating—or, it might be more proper to say, would be working hand in hand—with French military chiefs, even with Admiral Darlan in North Africa.

But that was only a secondary point. The principal effort made by de Gaulle in his letter was to try to prove that the two essential suspicions of the United States were unfounded. And what were these suspicions? The first was that General de Gaulle was attempting to pose as the government of France. The second, that General de Gaulle aspired to the exercise of personal power in liberated France. The General rejected both accusations and stated categorically that *he did not in any way or manner pose as the government of France; and that neither he nor his associates would dream of imposing a personal rule on France.* To top off these affirmations, the General cited the fact that such men as Blum, Herriot, and Jouhaux, all staunch believers in parliamentary democracy, had put themselves at his disposal. He cited too, as a fact, the supposedly intrinsic opposition of the French to any exercise of personal power. If he himself, he wrote, and his associates "nourished such base designs to exploit the future freedom of the French people, we should be showing a curious ignorance of our fellow countrymen. . . . Who would be fool enough to imagine that he could set up and maintain a regime of personal power in France? Whatever services he might have rendered in the past, the dreamer who attempted such a thing would be up against unanimous opposition."

Roosevelt asked André Philip to thank General de Gaulle for this remarkable letter. But he sent no reply. As a matter of fact, the letter was annotated for the President by a high State Department official, who was not impressed by it.

October–November 1942

In this momentous October we were following with anxiety the advance of the Nazi armies to the oil fields at Maikop, with Baku not so far ahead, and to the Volga at Stalingrad. We found some comfort in Hitler's dismissal of General Halder, the Chief of his General Staff. And some of our more optimistic Russian experts made us happy when they pointed to the long, exposed flank of the Germans along the Don. Somebody, I forget who, had read a Russian book on how Stalin during the Russian Civil War had brought about General Denikin's defeat by an attack between the bend in the Don and Stalingrad, whence came its name. We had to wait until mid-November for the Russians to spring the trap on the Sixth Army at Stalingrad. We understood that a massive Russian offensive was impending and we knew what—besides winter—they were waiting for. Churchill had been to see Stalin, who claimed to be greatly worried about Hess in England, to explain with some diffidence why the promised "second front" could not be opened in Europe in 1942 and to try to soothe him with an alternative, two in fact, in North Africa, at opposite ends of the continent. The first of those operations was known—we learned later—as Lightfoot and the second as Torch.

After the Prime Minister's return to London, we heard that Stalin, while bitterly disappointed by the Allies' inability to launch a "Second Front" on the French coast, had been so far mollified by Churchill's optimistic prospectus of the double-ended North Africa offensive as to come forth with a most uncharacteristic remark: "May God prosper this enterprise!" At this time, or shortly afterwards, we began to hear too about "the soft underbelly of Europe," another of Churchill's memorable phrases. As nearly as I can discover, it was first used by Churchill in one of his enthusiastic exposés to Stalin on the vulnerability of Italy to attack from North Africa. To back up his argument, Churchill drew a rough sketch of an alligator, showing that only on its soft underbelly was it without protection. The Russians quickly grasped the idea.

It was on October 23 that we learned with more excitement than surprise that the Eighth Army, with two new generals, Sir Harold Alexander as over-all commander, and Sir Bernard Law Montgomery, had struck back in deadly earnest at El Alamein with an opening salvo from a thousand cannon. This was to be a hard-fought battle. Field Marshal Rommel was in the mountains out-side Vienna, on sick leave because of an ailing liver, and was sum-moned by a frantic call from Hitler. When he reached his com-mand post, the battle was all but lost. Yet it was to continue for many days more.

It was a beefed-up Eighth Army that struck, with fresh supplies of tanks, bombers, and fighters, many of them American—giving them complete mastery in the air—and a new morale. After the disasters of Gazala, Tobruk, and all, they had miraculously stood firm along a forty-mile front at Alam Halfa during the first days of September. A German expert on the Panzer battles called this stand "the turning point of the desert war."

It was not, however, until two months after Alam Halfa that Montgomery, blithely ignoring the Prime Minister's impatience, considered himself ready to begin his great drive. When he began it that night with his thousand-gun salute, there was no stopping him. This time there was no desert flank to be turned by either side, for the Qattara Depression was the finest tank trap imagina-ble. In England, we French and our friends were pleased to know that among the three armored and seven infantry divisions of Montgomery's command there was a French division under Gen-eral Koenig, along with a Greek division and two Polish divisions. They had been placed on a rise called Quaret el Himemat, oppo-site their old enemies, the Ariete Armored Division. After the breakthrough, they would be reinforced by the Second Light Divi-sion.

The Führer's orders to Rommel not to give an inch arrived a little late, but by then the decision was not Rommel's to make. On November 2–3 came the breakthrough, and by the third, Rommel, Hitler's orders in his pocket ("Show the troops the way of victory or death"), began to draw back. On the fourth, British armor was out in the open heading west. The goal was Tunis—so Churchill's orders read—and Tunis was 2,000 miles away.

General Alexander's exuberant cable to London on November 6 was understandable. "Ring out the bells! Prisoners estimated now 20,000 [the figure was to go higher], guns 400. . . . Eighth Army is advancing. . . ." Four German divisions and eight Italian divisions had been obliterated. The *Luftwaffe* was hardly to be seen. Rommel's deputy, General von Thoma, was a prisoner, along with nine Italian generals. Churchill, however, decided to wait a while before ringing out the bells. Later he wrote, "Before Alamein we never had a victory. After Alamein we never had a defeat." [1]

On November 8 would come the Torch operation, and on November 19 the Russians would strike north and south of Stalingrad, trap the German Sixth Army, and begin the overwhelming attacks that thenceforth never ceased for long.

November 8, 1942

Then came another historic Sunday.

Long before dawn the BBC began repeatedly broadcasting a message in French: *Allo Robert. Franklin arrive! Allo Robert. Franklin arrive!*

This was clear enough to anyone listening in attentively at that hour, whatever his nationality. And many anxious Frenchmen in North Africa who were in on the secret had their sets tuned to the BBC all night long. Robert Murphy, in Algiers, was President Roosevelt's representative in North Africa. The eight hundred ships which were already just off the Atlantic coast of Morocco and off Algeria in the Mediterranean were about to send ashore large American and British forces. At about five that morning of November 8, 1942, the USS *Texas*, in the Atlantic only a few miles off Rabat, the Moroccan capital, and Port Lyautey, broadcast messages in French, over the French official wave length, that were far more specific and also of most immediate import. The time had been carefully chosen. Only in the very early hours of Sunday morning

[1] Churchill: *Hinge of Fate* (Boston: Houghton Mifflin; 1950), p. 603.

was this wave length not monopolized by Radio-Morocco's programs of music enjoyed by the native population. Sets in French command posts were normally left on low the entire night, just in case orders of any urgency had to be transmitted by the authorities there, acting in Marshal Pétain's name. So it was that many a French officer was shocked into wakefulness by the voice of Franklin D. Roosevelt, in French, coming from the set at his bedside with a message of startling import to him and all his kind in Morocco, Algeria, and Tunisia: American forces were at that very moment going ashore, if they were not already ashore. (The news that English troops were along was withheld for the time being, and for good reasons.)

General Giraud was in Gibraltar, whence he was to fly to Algiers to take command of the French Army of Africa, a considerable force. On his escape from the German fortress of Koenigstein, he had gone to Vichy, and now, having come from France by submarine, he was about to lead French troops back into combat. Or so it was announced and so it was at first believed.

In Algiers and Oran, as in Casablanca and Rabat, a certain number of Frenchmen were in on the secret: the moment they heard the BBC broadcasting over and over again "*Allo Robert. Franklin arrive!*" they were to fall to and, in their various roles, help get the Allies safely ashore.

In London, General de Gaulle was sleeping. It was only just before five o'clock that morning that the English had him awakened. A member of the entourage was given the task of breaking the news to him. It has been said that his first reaction was to exclaim, "*Eh, bien!* I hope the Vichy people will toss them back into the sea!" I find it hard to believe that he entertained even for a moment a hope that the Anglo-American forces would be thrown back into the sea for having dared to disembark without his permission. Actually, on that very day he went on the air and declared his full support of the landing. He called upon all Frenchmen in North Africa to aid the Allies and to so conduct themselves "that our Algeria, our Morocco, our Tunisia may serve as the base for the operation that will liberate France." However, I can personally attest to the consternation of any number of Carltonians during the morning when they learned that General Giraud was to take command of the French Army in Africa. As things turned out, this news was premature—but what news! General Giraud, who had been wounded and taken prisoner during the First World War, who then made his first escape, returning to combat in 1917 and covering himself with glory, who had been wounded seven times and wore five stars on his sleeve—now placed at the head of an army ten times larger than that of the Free French! A parallel enterprise, indeed. And as rivals go, what a rival! One that, at first sight, would not seem easy to topple.

The Carltonians who felt this way showed a woeful lack of faith in their General; he had displayed not inconsiderable talents at coping with opposition from whatever quarter. They also gave credit to General Giraud for far too much intelligence and ingenuity. To tell the truth, he had little of either. As a matter of fact, when Giraud had learned, in Gibraltar, that the Supreme Command of the Allied forces in Africa was to be in American hands, not his, he had begun to sulk. Nobody could attribute much cunning to him! It took him all of twenty-four hours to make his decision.

The story of the Anglo-American landings in North Africa has been told many times, but not always accurately. Any number of legends developed afterward. One that has been slow to die has it that due to the careful and highly picturesque groundwork by American agents the operation proved to be all but bloodless. Technically, this was not the case. A certain number of Frenchmen, military as well as civilian, were indeed let in on the secret in advance of the landings but were led to believe that the landings were months away; they were told the truth only on the eve of the actual operation. And all too obviously they were not men in high positions. They carried no weight with the naval officers who valued their oath to the Marshal above all other considerations, and so fought back. This was the case with most of the Navy. It was the Navy which in Algeria and Morocco put up the fiercest kind of resistance. In Tunisia they did worse: they allowed the Germans to take Bizerte, Tunis, and nearly all of Tunisia.

The most typical and most tragic resistance was offered to the American forces at Casablanca, then the principal French naval port on the Atlantic. The considerable portion of the fleet there was under the command of Vice-Admiral Prix Michelier. Michelier had been advised by his services late in the night of November 7–8 that huge Anglo-American convoys were well into the Mediterranean. Michelier, being a clever fellow, had come to the conclusion that the Allies were going to try to land in Tripoli; or in Tunisia, behind Marshal Rommel's Afrika Korps, then staggering after El Alamein; or in Algeria—but certainly not in Morocco. He had no idea of course that another enormous convoy, this one directly from the United States, was moving into position just off the Moroccan coast. Thus, when he was alerted by General Béthouart, a veteran of the ill-fated Norwegian expedition of the spring of 1940 (who was in on the secret), that there was indeed a powerful American fleet speeding toward the western coast and that it would land in Morocco, the Admiral did not believe a word of it. The Resident General in Rabat, still General Noguès, the veteran soldier-politician to whose cheeks, he said, the armistice of 1940 had brought a blush—for three whole days, until he decided to bend to the will of Marshal Pétain—was likewise alerted. In fact, a serious effort was made by Frenchmen and Americans in on the conspiracy—some OSS men among the latter—to immobilize him. It failed. Over a secret telephone wire that his informants (and would-be saviors) had neglected to cut, he called his admiral. He wanted to know just how large the supposed fleet might be, for if the Americans arrived in sufficient force to resist a German attack through Spain, and possibly a combined German and Spanish attack (Spain had heavy troop detachments in the Spanish Moroccan Zone), he would consider greeting them with open arms.[1] If, however, this

[1] So he later told any number of Americans, complaining that Ambassador Murphy had not taken him into his confidence. But, according to Mr. Murphy, General Noguès had earlier expressed himself as quite unwilling to gamble even if promised a sure thing. The Ambassador had asked him in October, somewhat obliquely, what he would do if the United States were "to reach a position where it could send half a million men to North Africa, fully equipped with planes, tanks, guns, warships, and all the rest." The General's

was merely a raid, or an expedition on the scale of the attack on Dakar, it must be repulsed. Otherwise, thought the General, we'll have the Germans installed for good and all in North Africa.

What did his admiral reply? That he saw nothing. That in his opinion there was not an American ship within five hundred kilometers of the Atlantic coast of Morocco, except perhaps a small reconnaissance force. General Noguès thereupon gave orders to round up those who were conspiring to seize him.

Actually it was a formidable amphibious force moving up for a three-pronged attack against Port Lyautey in the north, Fedala and Casablanca in the center, and Safi to the south. Had there not been a thick haze, the battleships, cruisers, destroyers, and transports would have been visible from the shore well before dawn. The powerful new USS *Massachusetts* was below the horizon and remained there to cope with the *Jean-Bart's* forward batteries and those defending Casablanca harbor. Now, Admiral Michelier, who had come from the Franco-German Armistice Commission of Wiesbaden, had only been in command since October 20. He did not believe in a landing, as one was announced every other day. And in order to save gasoline he refused to go out and reconnoiter by plane as proposed by the general commanding the Air Force. He was therefore, he said, taken totally by surprise. Once the "reports" of an American fleet were so amply confirmed, he gave orders for his subordinates to resist—which they did "with a courage worthy of a better cause," as British Admiral Troubridge said, speaking of French resistance at Arzeu, east of Oran. When all the French ships had been sunk or knocked out of combat by the sixteen-inch guns of the *Massachusetts* and the eight-inch guns of the cruisers, and the *Jean-Bart* had been struck first by a bomb from a Flying Fortress from Gibraltar, which sank her by the stern in shallow water, then by a direct hit from the *Massachusetts*, which silenced her; when, on the French side alone, more than 450 sailors had

---

reply was "explosive." "Do not try that. If you do I will meet you with all the firepower I possess. It is too late for France to participate in this war now. We will do better to stay out. If Morocco becomes a battleground it will be lost to France!"

been killed—Admiral Michelier still would not obey Admiral Darlan's belated order to cease fire. And he did not have the good luck to get himself killed.

At the eastern end of French Africa, in Tunisia, there was another admiral, the Resident General in Tunis, a man by the name of Esteva known in the Navy as the "virgin admiral." He was an austere sort, given to walking barefoot in religious processions and considered very nearly insane with pride. Wishing at all costs to remain faithful to his oath to Marshal Pétain, he welcomed the Germans, whose troop-carrying transports began putting down at El Alouina airport in Tunis on November 9. He also gave orders to Admiral Derrien, who commanded the French naval base at Bizerte, to offer no resistance. When the Germans arrived at the Admiralty in Bizerte, called La Pêcherie, poor Derrien, once such a good sailor but now in a state of near blindness, had forgotten to scuttle the small naval craft in the channel leading to the base (thirteen vessels, some say; fifteen, according to others), and they fell into the hands of the enemy. This dishonorable incident might seem to confirm the opinion of those who thought the Germans would be able to get their hands on the greater part of our fleet. But, as I see it, the Bizerte affair was an accident, useful only as an argument. As an argument it is of course irrefutable. The old admiral, as I said, was half blind, and blinded even more by his oath to the Marshal and his concept of discipline. He is dead now. He was tried and convicted, and lived on for several miserable years. But how was it that this admiral, who had never had any fear of death, did not, once the foolish blunder had been committed, go off and get himself killed too? He had only to attack some German with his saber, if he had no other arm at hand. I fail to understand.

The French Army in Tunisia had the right, the normal reaction: the Germans were landing, so they fired on them. They disobeyed the Marshal, disobeyed Admiral Esteva, did not wait for Admiral Darlan in Algiers to terminate his maneuver of turning about. But the Army did not control the ports. It could only withdraw westward, toward Algeria, leaving the sea frontier, which the Navy controlled and was now handing over to the enemy.

On that Sunday in London, Admiral Muselier, learning of the landings, came right over to the Admiralty. He had been eating his heart out because of the inactivity to which he had been reduced by General de Gaulle. He was vehement and convincing. "I can take Bizerte for you. And save Tunisia. Parachute me, along with fifty men, into Sidi Ahmed. I know every inch of the fortified camp of Bizerte. I was major-general at Sidi Abdallah. I was commander of the Navy in Tunisia. I was the man who drew up the defense plan for Bizerte and installed the batteries against an attack from the landward side." (The Italians in Tripolitania had been making threatening noises long before the war.)

I was to see for myself, the following spring, just how murderous the fire from these batteries was against American tanks.

Admiral Muselier's proposition pleased the Admiralty. The risk was not great. A detachment of fifty men—why not? The returns could be enormous. The proposal was passed along to the War Office, and they were tempted too. But—to use Admiral Muselier, who was at outs with General de Gaulle? To use him without the General's consent? The English hesitated.

"But," the Admiral said, exasperated, yet conciliatory, "you need never admit that you have made use of my services. Don't give out my name. I'll dress as a parachutist—the nationality doesn't make any difference. What matters is that we act quickly, very quickly—this evening! The Germans are pouring in. They won't be easy to dislodge once they have dug in!"

The operation proposed by Admiral Muselier did not take place. If it had and had succeeded—and there was no reason why it should not have succeeded that Sunday night, or Monday or Tuesday, before the Germans were there in any great force—it would perhaps not have been necessary to spend six long months, as the Admiral remarked later, to throw the Germans out of Tunisia. Six months and how many lives, French, English, and American?

The Allied landing in North Africa had a personal epilogue for Anne and me. There was again a French Army and a French Navy in the war against Germany, and I could now join up as a volunteer without having to sign any enlistment oath to anybody. I had waited exactly twenty-eight months for this.

My request was transmitted to the French Admiralty in Algeria by the American Naval Attaché in London.

I believe I explained that on arriving at Woburn I had signed the Official Secrets Act, which consisted of a promise not to reveal any secret information I might have learned. I never had to get involved with what the British call Intelligence, which means information about this and that; much less with the Intelligence Service. Anyway, I have a kind of horror of secret organizations; I am simply not cut out for that kind of work. But it must be evident that at Woburn I was somewhat in the know about Anglo-American military operations. Anyone who possessed such information needed special authorization to leave England. I had asked for a pledge, when I entered Woburn, that I could give up my work and leave the United Kingdom when I wished. This promise was scrupulously and immediately kept. Furthermore, it was on an English ship that I reached Algiers to resume my service in the French Navy. But in Algiers the formalities took weeks.

Meanwhile an unexpected event took place. Admiral Darlan, Chief of the French Fleet, was in Algiers at the time of the landings. He had come to see his son, Alain, who was seriously ill with polio. There is no doubt that the Admiral had had advance notice of the Allied intentions. He had known what was afoot, but he had not been told the date (neither had anyone else, even those who were to be active in the conspiracy). As we know, he had previously established contact with Allied emissaries. For some time now, he had been ready to turn his coat. But he did not want to gamble; he wanted to be quite sure that the Allied forces were strong enough to resist German retaliation through Spain. Admiral Darlan, like General Noguès, had lived too long under the threat of a lightning, inexorable strike by the German Panzers and the *Luftwaffe* at a time when the British would inevitably have arrived with too little too late. He was not altogether convinced that the Allies had it in them to pull off this operation.

General Mast had insisted to Ambassador Murphy and General Clark that Giraud was their man, *not* Darlan. Then Giraud balked, and when finally he was talked into going along with the Allies, it became immediately clear that he was *not* their man. "A good division general, nothing more!" said Darlan scornfully. When on November 11 the German Army moved into the hitherto Unoccupied Zone and began airlifting troops to Tunisia, Admiral Darlan's mind was finally made up for him. And the minds of all the other Vichy proconsuls (except for Admiral Esteva in Tunis).

It was all very confusing. And the French officers who had conspired with Ambassador Murphy to help the Allies land were either in prison awaiting court-martial for treason, like General Béthouart in Morocco, or in hiding, like General Mast in Algeria.

As for General de Gaulle, he had publicly announced that he was washing his hands of the whole business. Nervous Carltonians did not know which way to turn. One day they had a "parallel entrepreneur" in General Giraud; the next day, two "parallel entrepreneurs," Giraud and also Admiral Darlan, claiming the Marshal's blessing. And then they were down to one, Darlan, a very serious contender. Or so thought the Carltonians of little faith. But not General de Gaulle, for he knew that his mission, now and henceforth approved and backed by the fervent patriots of France, could not fail just because of Admiral Darlan. Who could deny that the Admiral's all too recent past as a minister in Marshal Pétain's government had made him odious? He had acquired the reputation, fully confirmed from London, of wishing for the victory of the German Reich. That was not a true picture of Darlan at all—but you recall that on the Gaullist broadcasts from London a refrain was sung affirming that Darlan was pro-German. And that same French program on the BBC affirmed that Darlan had endorsed the execution of Commander d'Estienne d'Orves by French *gardes mobiles* in the moat of the Château de Vincennes. And who was Commander d'Estienne? One of the heroes of the Free French Naval Forces. Attached to their *deuxième bureau*—otherwise, Free French Naval Intelligence—he had been sent from London on a secret mission to France, where, in Brest, the great French, now

German base, he was to keep an eye on the two powerful German cruisers, the *Scharnhorst* and the *Gneisenau*. He was about as gifted for espionage as I am for being Pope; he was almost immediately caught by the Germans. But Carlton Gardens declared that he had fallen before a French firing squad, and with Darlan's approval.

The fact that Admiral Darlan not only *did not* agree to the execution of Commander d'Estienne but intervened vigorously, if vainly, with the German High Command in Paris to prevent it was never broadcast on the BBC. And so in November and December 1942 Admiral Darlan still bore the ugly mark of being considered, among other things, the man who had approved the execution of one of the noblest heroes of Free France.

When Admiral Darlan made his startling appearance in North Africa, there was a storm of protest in England and the United States. (Interestingly, the Russians were not at all shocked.) General Catroux, speaking for the Gaullist organization, called the Admiral the "worm in the fruit," and everybody knows what happens to a worm when it is found in a fruit: it must be eliminated.

In that November, when he also made his spectacular appearance on the North African stage, General Giraud was widely known as a soldier of great valor. General de Gaulle, unhappy about Giraud's emergence as a "parallel entrepreneur," gave much publicity to a letter that General Giraud had written to Marshal Pétain after his escape from Koenigstein. In this letter, General Giraud promised obedience to the Marshal. Much was made of this, of Giraud's having now broken a promise that, as an officer of the Army of the Third Republic, he presumably had no reason to make. (Actually the letter was written at the moment when Pierre Laval, hard-pressed by the Germans, was trying to force Giraud to return voluntarily to the cell from which he had escaped with the help of pro-Allied elements in Vichy.)

A Gaullist in Moscow informed the Kremlin that General Giraud's escape from Germany had taken place in circumstances that were considered in London to be "highly suspect." General Giraud was pictured to the Kremlin as a lackey of the capitalists, French,

American, *and* German. Another Gaullist, in Pretoria, had some
extremely severe strictures to make concerning General Giraud,
but, it seems, in quite a different sense from those of his colleague in
Moscow. And shortly General de Gaulle himself was to make
known his thoughts regarding the French military chiefs of North
Africa.

November 11, 1942

On November 11, 1942, to mark the anniversary of the armistice
ending World War I, General de Gaulle bid all the French in
London to attend Albert Hall. He made his appearance on a ros-
trum behind which rose an immense Cross of Lorraine. During the
entire ceremony, a white-gloved lieutenant held above the General's head a flag fringed with gold.

General de Gaulle spoke. He affirmed that this celebration was a
celebration of Fighting France, and that it was from Fighting
France *alone* that France expected the struggle for her liberation to
be directed. "In truth every day France gives a plebiscite in favor of
Fighting France. It is towards Fighting France that the Nation
turns. It is in Fighting France that she recognizes herself. It is from
Fighting France . . ." Here there was a long pause, and then his
voice thundered: ". . . And from Fighting France *alone* that she
expects the direction of her struggle."

From the packed hall came a roar of approval.

The General's reasoning was not hard to follow. Yes, he was the
incarnation of Fighting France. So it was by him, and him alone,
that France wished to be led. The General became still more explicit: he would smash all "parallel entrepreneurs." "Therefore we
suffer no one to come and divide our country's war effort by any of
these so-called parallel enterprises—that is, divided enterprises—to

which the secret but all powerful expression of the national will, moreover, will soon do justice. Therefore it is in the name of France that the French National Committee speaks when it calls for the help of all to wrest our country from the enemy and from Vichy, to re-establish French liberties, and to cause the laws of the Republic to be observed." [1]

There followed a thunder of approbation.

Then from the back of the balcony a voice was raised, the timid, thin voice of an elderly man, General Eon, a former officer of the Zouaves, now retired. Holding a paper in his hand, he read from it, audibly enough in the sudden stillness caused by the untoward interruption. What he read was an appeal to General de Gaulle, a supplication to him to join forces with General Giraud. Eon explained that General Giraud now had ten times as many troops under his command as General de Gaulle; that he was de Gaulle's senior in rank and in years; that he had led his armies in combat and had been victorious; it was to General Giraud, therefore, that the command should go. In the light of all this, Eon begged General de Gaulle to put himself at the disposition of General Giraud.

Eon had scarcely finished, and was folding up his petition to put it back in his pocket, when he was set upon by indignant Gaullists. [2]

The retribution that was visited upon Admiral Darlan was not in his being wiped out by an assassin's bullet, crushed like the worm in the fruit. It was in the shattering realization that he was not to be obeyed, he the high chief for so many years—not by the French

---

[1] De Gaulle: *Memoirs,* II, p. 51.

[2] "When, from the top of one of the balconies, a retired general who had taken refuge in England raised his voice to adjure me to subordinate myself to Giraud, the poor man was immediately dragged from his seat by outraged groups and expelled from the hall, pursued by the shouts of the crowd." De Gaulle: *Memoirs,* II, p. 50.

"The nation cannot allow a handful of men who symbolize capitulation, collaboration, usurpation, and who against the liberators have used and abused the discipline of others, to go on using and abusing this discipline today to travesty honor and duty. . . . The nation will not allow them to defile our liberation. . . ." General de Gaulle on the radio, December 6, 1942.

fleet or by the admirals who until only weeks before had been under his orders: the admirals at Toulon, not to mention those at
Alexandria, Dakar, and Martinique (who came over later on).
From Algiers he sent orders both in code and unciphered to his
admirals—"his," as he thought—in Toulon, where the French high-
seas fleet lay. He commanded them, begged them, pleaded with
them to set up steam and flee from Toulon to rejoin the war in
North Africa. And they mocked him.

The witless admirals remained until the end faithful to the oath
they had sworn to Pétain. Unawares, they had in advance abdi-
cated the free exercise of their conscience into the hands of another;
this is a very common form of suicide.

The Germans occupied the so-called "Free" Zone on November
11, in an operation long prepared and appropriately called "Attila."
They did, needless to say, promise—word of honor and all that—
not to occupy the perimeter around the Toulon naval base. This
was to be left in the hands of French troops; and Admiral Auphan,
Marshal Pétain's Ministry of Marine, did begin a bit belatedly to
fortify it. On November 25, Hitler decided to carry out a plan likewise prepared in advance, which was to win for the Reich at last the
French warships it had hungered for for so long. The French army
units were ordered to evacuate the perimeter; their places were
then taken by marines. Even then, the French admirals in Toulon
were not particularly alarmed. In the early morning hours of November 27, the Nazis reached out for the fleet. The French officers
and crews, suddenly awakened, were ordered by Admiral Jean de
Laborde to scuttle. In his opinion it was then too late to get underway and try to escape south in the open waters of the Mediterranean. Such, briefly, was the tragedy of Toulon.

Was it really so impossible to try to get away or, when all the
chips were down, to fight it out and die? For all my three years or
so of sea duty in the French Navy, I am not competent to state
with any degree of assurance that it would have been possible.
However, today, as I look back on that black day, I see that Anne's
reaction to the news from Toulon, her immediate reaction, was the
right one and that mine, which was that escape was impossible, was

wrong. First, let me explain that in London we were at first most inaccurately informed. The news of the tragedy of Toulon did, after all, come from behind what were then without argument German lines, and it was not until days later that we had the picture whole and clear. The early reports indicated, not that the squadron had scuttled, but that they had blown themselves up— that their last act had been heroic, that there had been many more victims than there would have been in an attempt to escape, no matter how desperate.

The newspaper *France* appeared in London on Saturday morning, November 28, carrying huge black headlines:

HITLER HAVING DECREED THE OCCUPATION OF TOULON,

FRENCH FLEET SCUTTLES ITSELF,

ARSENAL, MUNITIONS DEPOTS

OIL TANKS, COASTAL BATTERIES BLOWN UP

Most of the commanding officers remained aboard their ships and went down with them. Arms in hand, the crews fought to keep the enemy from reaching the ships. They suffered heavy losses.

AT TEN HOURS NOT A SINGLE SHIP

REMAINED AFLOAT

This was the version of the tragedy first published in London. On that day I was working with our English associates on the next edition of the *Courrier de l'Air*. The two Englishmen were as deeply moved as I. "What can be done," they asked, "to show our sense of solidarity with the French? How to tell them of our admiration for the action of those French sailors in blowing themselves up with their ships? How unfair of us ever to have doubted them! Mers-el-Kebir now seems more than ever an unjustified attack!" And so on.

A suggestion was made for a symbolical gesture of solidarity: all ships of the Royal Navy would fly their flags at half-mast for an hour. Officers at the Admiralty agreed. But the proposal was cut short by Churchill. He had his reasons. He said that he intended himself to speak on the "Toulon affair." And speak he did; here are his words: "In the smoke and the flames of Toulon, the French

Navy redeemed its honor." By this, one was given to understand that the honor of the French Navy had been lost. The Prime Minister's remarks seemed somewhat less of a compliment than any of us had expected—and a belated justification of British behavior at Mers-el-Kebir.

When I went home on the evening of November 27, I knew only the version of the events at Toulon which appeared next morning in *France*. In other words, I then believed that thousands of French sailors had been killed in circumstances that could only be considered heroic. When I told Anne the story as I then knew it, her reaction astounded me. "*Les salauds!*" she exclaimed angrily. "I will never speak to any of them again. I adored them. Now I hate them! Imagine, to end like that when they could have sunk their fangs into the Germans!"

I tried to explain to her how impossible it had been for them to escape from Toulon: the ships were not in combat readiness, they undoubtedly were low on fuel—and, whatever the reasons, nothing could match the courage of officers going voluntarily to their deaths in such circumstances, going down with their ships in the best tradition of the Navy. It was Anne, however, who proved to be right. Nothing whatever was done at Toulon to fight back. To deny them our ships, yes. But not to leave them something to remember us by.

If I felt any need to respect the chronology of events, I would have to leave for later the story of Toulon as it was told me on board the cruiser *Jeanne d'Arc* by a shipmate who had been through it all. When he came aboard, we gave him the usual party, with drinks into the small hours, to which every fresh arrival from France was entitled. When the party came to its ritual end, I got him out on the afterdeck and asked him to tell me in detail all that he had seen and done on that blackest day in French naval history, blackest in our time, anyway. Here is the story he told me, with no interruptions on my part.

"I was on the Mars,[3] at the Noël dock. That night, November 26 to 27, I was the duty officer. Toward four o'clock in the morn-

---
[3] A destroyer.

ing, I was awakened by the helmsman on watch, who said, 'Lieutenant, I hear sounds from over by Le Mourillon.' I went up to the bridge, and there were indeed sounds from the direction of Le Mourillon. And also from Fort Lamargue. I heard planes too. I woke up the Commandant. He came up to the bridge. The entire roadstead by then was brightly lit by flares dropped by German planes. There were also mooring mines. From the direction of the arsenal we heard explosions. The Commandant went to his cabin and came back with a sealed envelope. It contained the orders to scuttle.

"The gongs sounded battle stations. The radio of the *Strasbourg* was already sending out its orders. The signal light at her masthead was blinking the same message to all ships: *Scuttle! Scuttle! Scuttle!* Our commanding officer gave orders to abandon ship. First the personal effects of the officers were carried ashore. When everybody was on the pier, a duty detachment set off the explosive charges. The ship went down fast, without capsizing. It was not exactly gay; but it was a good show.

"The Germans did not arrive until 7.30 hours. Our complement, officers at the head, surrendered. The Germans did not look all that happy. They separated us from the crew and led us off to Saint-Anne. It was not until twenty-four hours later that were we allowed to return to pick up our personal belongings. And everything had been rifled. My wife's picture had been torn to shreds and the pieces scattered on the ground. *Salauds d'Allemands!* They had us just where they wanted us!"

On two points only had my new shipmate displayed any anger: over the separation of crew and officers, and over the rifling of his personal effects. I asked him, "How much fuel did you have? Enough for you to have reached Algiers?"

"On the ship? Oh, yes, but the fires had been banked the night before to economize on oil. We would have needed perhaps two hours to get up steam, and then there was another problem: one out of eight of our crew were on shore leave."

"You could have turned up your fires and tried to make a run for it?"

"Perhaps, but there were mines."

That's true, there were mines. And the prospect of dive bombers. There is no use going further into this; it is all too maddening. It should go down in the history of France as an illustration of the defects engendered, under the Third Republic, in the officer corps of the French Navy: a fatuous pride, mixed with naïveté (a man had to pretty naïve to believe that the Germans would not break into the Toulon perimeter); a monstrous concept of honor (as in the insane adherence to the oath to Pétain); a gradual disappearance of the fighting spirit, along with an increasing preoccupation with the nation's politics and with family life.

There is no branch of the service, I believe, where the commanding officers have anything like the power they have in the Navy. This is of course all the more so when ships are at sea. The signal given a squadron in maneuvers: "Follow the Admiral" (*à l'imitation de l'Amiral*), is symbolic of this immense authority. It is this which in a defeat makes the admiral all the more responsible. In the French Navy, the petty-officer corps (*la maistrance*) excels. The sailors are very good. But the Navy as a whole is as worthy as its leaders, no more and no less. The Vichy admirals were bad. But the little Free French Navy was superb and aroused the admiraton of the English, who in naval matters know whereof they speak. The number of French career officers serving their ships was infinitesimal. In their fighting spirit, the Free French naval units took their inspiration from Admiral Muselier, who organized them.

With my reputation as an anti-Gaullist so solidly established, the men of the Free French Naval Forces should have found my company poison, particularly after Admiral Muselier left. But not at all. This might be taken to mean that they themselves were not so very Gaullist. When I left London, the friend who came to live with Anne was the wife of the captain of one of the most famous of the corvettes flying the Cross of Lorraine, a ship which itself had been decorated with the Croix de Guerre. And it was due to the Free French Navy that I was able to obtain enough clothing coupons to outfit myself.

December 1942

On Christmas Eve, we had a few friends in and sang a few songs. With us was Monica, the daughter of a dean of the Anglican Church, and some friends of mine whose repertoire of songs was somewhat less than edifying. Our complete lack of solemnity at parties (Imagine, in wartime, and with our country invaded) would have distressed any really serious-minded person. But no one like that had been invited.

When we got tired of hearing our own voices, somebody had a brilliant idea: we should play "Murder." For this game to be any fun, it must be played with the stern respect for rules that the British manage to inject even into their lighter moments. It was well before midnight when Lacoste, for some reason that has escaped my memory, left the party and went home. After some four or five murderers had been ferreted out by our detectives, there was another murder, and Anne, who had drawn an ace and was supposed to find the guilty party, failed; and that called for a forfeit. We decided that she had to telephone Lacoste, who ought to pay a forfeit too for deserting us. She was not to say who she was but simply to sing the *Internationale* for his delight. It was well known that Lacoste ate Communists for breakfast, just as in most towns and villages in France there was always some stoutly anticlerical person who was called an "eater of priests." And of course Anne professed royalist sentiments.

With great good humor, she did her part, and to perfection. We then went back to our game. The lights were off and then, just when a new murder was about to be committed, the telephone rang. So as not to break up the game, I went to the extension phone in our bedroom. It was Lacoste. He asked had I heard the news.

"What news?"

"They have murdered him!"

"Who?"

"Darlan!"

"Come off it, Lacoste," I said. "You are trying to pay us back!"

"Pay you back for what?"

"For the *Internationale* over the phone just now. It was Anne."

"Ah, so it *was* Anne! I wondered. Now tell her for me that she is *mignonne,* and an idiot too. But about Darlan, it's true."

"You are pulling my leg."

"No, no, no! I swear it. Telephone *The Times* if you don't believe me."

I went back to the others, turned on the light, and I told them. I did not telephone *The Times*; the Agence Française Indépendante confirmed Lacoste's story. Darlan had indeed been killed earlier that day in Algiers.

We then and there lost our taste for "Murder." There ensued a wild argument as to who was behind it. We had lots of theories. But need I say that we reached no verdict? We found ourselves recalling the angry denunciations, the incitements, for they were often just that. "Darlan to the scaffold!" The jingle over the radio. "Darlan is the worm in the fruit." "Darlan gave the orders to execute Commandant d'Estienne d'Orves."

The next day we learned that young Bonnier de la Chapelle, who fired the shot, had been put up against a wall. He had expected to be saved, that some powerful person would intervene, that the rifles of the firing squad would not be loaded, that he would be whisked off to safety. As we know, no powerful person did anything, unless it was to speed up the execution. The rifles *were* loaded. And Bonnier de la Chapelle took his secret to his grave. The investigation came to nothing. There are not a few persons still around who know a lot about what happened. Their stories are, some of them anyway, convincing. But they can give no proof. The old *cui prod est* test is of little help because the important personages who could be said to have derived benefit from the elimination of the Admiral of the Fleet were many. And most of them— or, let us just say many of them—were above reproach.

Some candidly expressed their pleasure. For instance, General Mark Clark. But not General de Gaulle. Oh, no! He declared to Charles Peake, an English diplomat in charge of liaison between the Foreign Office and Carlton Gardens, that the murder of Admiral Darlan was a "detestable crime."

1942-43

Winter, 1942–43

Not very long before I left London for North Africa, a stranger rang our doorbell. It was about five o'clock in the afternoon, and Anne was alone. She opened the door. A man stood there whom she had never seen before. She described him as well dressed, good-looking but coarse, and, as to manners, quite evidently not a disciple of Lord Chesterfield. He asked for me. Anne said I was out, but, thinking he might be some friend of mine, she asked him in.

He presented himself. He was Inspector X of Scotland Yard, Special Branch. To prove it, he showed his credentials. He then said, "Kindly telephone Whitehall 1212 to make sure that I am who I say I am."

Anne demurred, saying that she could see the picture on his credentials went with his face.

"No, no, *please* telephone."

So he was, as he said, Inspector X of the Special Branch, which handles counterespionage and is supposed to keep an eye on foreigners.

"Sir, what is it you want? My husband is not here, so perhaps you could come back later, when he gets home."

"Do you know what your husband does?"

"What do you mean, what he does?"

"I mean what his job is."

"But he works, and for you the English, with the English officials. And, incidentally, without pay."

"Do you know about any of his other activities?"

"Why do you ask that?"

"You can't guess why?"

"No, I can't. My husband does do translations . . ."

"Do you know whether he belongs to a secret society?"

"A secret society? Of course not!"

"Husbands don't always tell their wives everything they do."

"If that is true, how would I be expected to know what he does?"

"But what about you yourself? Do you, by any chance, know Monsieur Pleven?"

"I have met M. Pleven socially."

"Do you know what he does?"

"Of course! He is a commissioner with General de Gaulle. But he does not keep me informed of his work."

"You don't see yet why I am asking you all these questions?"

"No, I really don't."

"And Colonel Dewavrin—or, as he calls himself, Colonel Passy —do you know him?"

"No, not at all."

"What about Captain R—? Do you know him?"

"Yes, he is my husband's cousin."

"Do you know what he does?"

"He is an aviator."

"You don't know anything else about him?"

"I have a vague idea that he is involved in the Resistance in France, and that, naturally, is secret."

The inspector opened his cigarette case and found it surprisingly empty. "Would you have a cigarette, please? I am out of them."

Anne got up, found cigarettes, and when the inspector fumbled around looking for his lighter or matches, she lighted his cigarette for him. This policeman, I might say, if you have not already guessed it, was young and not overly bright. He said, "I just wanted to see if your hand was steady."

Anne then understood that she was dealing with a fool, but she was bemused by him. He continued to think up questions. He asked about nearly all the French in London, Gaullists or not. Her answers became more and more laconic. Suddenly he asked, "You could not by any chance give me a cup of tea, or could you?"

A request of this kind sounds absurd. But not as absurd in England as elsewhere. In London a man asks for a cup of tea as in Paris he would ask for a glass of water. And one does not refuse, even in a time of rationing. So Anne went to the kitchen and was soon back with a cup of hot tea. She surprised our young ace from Scotland Yard rummaging through the papers on my desk. He had in his hand a letter of no particular importance from Ambassador Charles Corbin. She snatched it out of his hands. He was grinning, obviously thinking himself a veritable Sherlock Holmes for having devised a stratagem by which to get her to leave him alone near my desk.

Finally he started to leave, but turned to say, "As soon as I am out of the door, I'll wager that you are going straight off to telephone your husband."

"Certainly!"

"Wives all do that. Allow me to give you a word of advice: don't talk to him on the telephone about my call."

"And why not, pray?"

"I am telling you this in your own interst, and in his. Your line might be tapped . . ."

"Well, if it is, it is tapped by you, the police."

"There are different branches. . . . It does not look at all nice to have had a visit from an inspector of the Special Branch, which deals with counterespionage and with the criminal activities of foreigners."

The second he was out the door, Anne did call me, to ask me to come home as quickly as possible. There was a note of urgency in her voice. I was at Bush House, where a part of Political Warfare had its offices. A quarter of an hour later I reached home. Anne recounted the visit she had just had. I was taken in by the apparent calm with which she told the story. She asked me, what does this mean? What was I going to do about it? etc. I answered as calmly as I knew how, trying to reassure her that the detective's visit could mean nothing unpleasant for us, and I said that I would make a visit or two myself, one on the inspector in question. And, incidentally, she should not have let him in.

Now, making an about-face, and white with anger, she spoke her piece: So this is how I took it! She had just been subjected to harassment during one whole hour by an infamous police agent, and I dared tell her that there was nothing unpleasant in it! So I would make one or two visits, would I? And she should not have let the man in! So this was how I protected her! Well, in that case, she would protect herself!

No sooner said than done. She began by telephoning the inspector: "You warned me, sir, not to talk about your visit? Let me tell you that I will talk about it to everybody in London. I will talk about it to General de Gaulle. He will hear how a Frenchwoman is treated in England! I will tell —— [giving Torcy's real name], and tell him what kind of problems a woman faces who is the wife of a non-Gaullist in England. I will talk about it to the Foreign Office and let them know how the English police treat French people who stayed with them in England to volunteer their services! Working for you, the English! I will talk about it to the press. I will talk about it to the whole wide world!"

And she proceeded instantly to carry out this fine program. It was useless for me to try to explain the reasons for the stupid, offensive visit she had had to put up with. She was in no mood to listen. In fact, she was already on her way. I went out too. She went directly to see Torcy. Unhappily, he was out, for he could have explained it all away for her. At Carlton Gardens, it was my friend Paul-Henri Siriex who received her. He said that he was completely in the dark, that the English were disagreeable with Gaullists too. Of that she could be sure, he said as if he meant it. But, but . . . She had vanished, on her way to Bush House. There she was instantly received by Colonel S——, who declared that it was outrageous for the police to do such a thing, that she would receive an apology, etc. But he did not tell her the reason for the inspector's investigation. And actually I don't think she cared much about that.

My first call was on the inspector at New Scotland Yard. He received me affably and with a big smile. The smile soon went.

"You went on purpose to see my wife," I said, "when you knew she would be alone. Such a thing is intolerable! I am going at once to the Foreign Office to lodge a complaint. They will be asked to present their apologies for your actions and for your behavior to my wife. You are afraid? I understand. For it is fear that is behind your investigation, as I happen to know. The English police must bear the blame. You have allowed foreigners on British soil to commit iniquitous offenses against other foreigners. But don't ask me to give you the smallest scrap of information about any of my compatriots. Just allow me to tell you that your so-called surveillance of foreigners here is very badly carried out!"

At the Foreign Office, I saw Christopher ——. He was distressed. He said that Anne would receive a letter of apology.

She did in fact receive such a letter. And, on the eve of my departure for North Africa, a luncheon was given for us, for the two of us, by the General Staff of Political Warfare. Present were David Bowes-Lyon and his wife, and Pan, and Colonel S—.

Now, to get down to cases. There was a reason for the interrogation at home. This is the story.

The Prime Minister was worried lest some Member of Parliament should rise in the Commons to question him about what was going on in Duke Street, the headquarters of the BCRA. The House of Commons would not have liked to learn that, within less than a mile from where they were sitting, foreigners were using on other foreigners police methods forbidden by English law. Churchill had ordered an investigation, and our inspector was one of those engaged in it. That he should have been stupid and bad-mannered in ways policemen often are is hardly surprising. Inspector Younger, the man who arrested Admiral Muselier, was not exactly smart either. Anyway, the conception of New Scotland Yard as an institution populated by gentlemen only, because the inspectors wear bowler hats and striped pants and carry umbrellas, is fantasy right out of the mystery stories.

Once the investigation was completed, what was Churchill going to do? To finish my account, I must get a little ahead of the story. The Prime Minister was to make one last effort later on, with the dossier of the investigation in hand, to relieve himself of his responsibility to the French and to his own people for having accorded certain special powers to General de Gaulle. To accomplish this end, he had enlisted the assistance of President Roosevelt, to whom he had said, in substance: You were not mistaken in your judgment of General de Gaulle. I now admit that it would be wrong to allow the French people to think of de Gaulle as an ally after our own hearts and as a democrat by our definition of the term; we would be guilty of deceiving them most gravely.[1] There is still time, before we land in Europe, to make the truth blaze out, to enlighten public opinion not only in France but in England and in the rest of the free world.

Roosevelt at first showed little enthusiasm for an operation that he considered tardy. He was afraid that its effect in France might be the exact opposite of what was intended, that it might strengthen the General in the eyes of the French, who would then see him as a defender of the nation's interests against a perfidious Britain and an imperialist America, each of which de Gaulle had said was hoping to profit by our country's weakness to lay hands on our colonial empire. Roosevelt was of the opinion that at the eleventh hour they should pay as little attention as possible to General de Gaulle; leave him strictly alone.

Nevertheless, he consented to take the initiative, but no more than that. Here is how he was to do it, and this was what was so interesting about the report compiled by Scotland Yard, a report that will certainly not see the light of day for fifty years, if then. It was agreed, then, between Roosevelt and Churchill that Churchill would have the report made ready. In Washington, Roosevelt would contrive to make some allusion to its existence, and in London a confidential memorandum based on it would be circulated. This would provoke questions in the House. Churchill would be

[1] I agree with you that no confidence can be placed in de Gaulle's friendship for the Allies . . ." (Prime Minister Churchill to President Roosevelt, *Foreign Relations of the United States*, 1943, Vol. II, p. 159.)

asked to deny the existence of such a memorandum. He would reply that unhappily the memorandum was indeed official and that it was based on true facts, but that he could tell the House no more, except in a secret session. Behind closed doors, he would open the dossier. The Members of the House would then be of the unanimous opinion that Great Britain should revise its attitude toward General de Gaulle.[2]

This scenario was played to the letter. But not to its end. On July 22, 1943, Robert Boothby, a Conservative Member, questioned the Prime Minister as to the authenticity of the memorandum and asked to know what steps were to be taken to put an end to the propagation of such shocking lies. Churchill stood up and, to the amazement of most of the Members, declared that the memorandum did exist and that he took full responsibility for it. But, he went on to say, it was a confidential document and he was not disposed to discuss it in other than a secret session, if the Chamber wished for one.

No such secret session ever took place. Why? Because the whips of the Conservative Party told the Prime Minister, in effect: "Don't even think of it! If you give an explanation of the memorandum, if you open the dossier, the Opposition will accuse you of

---

[2] On July 12, 1943, in the Washington *Post* and the Des Moines *Register and Tribune*, Ernest Lindley, a Washington correspondent with high Administration contacts, published a story to the effect that "copies of a statement of British policy toward General de Gaulle" had been placed in the hands of British and American officials in Washington. According to Lindley, the statement indicated that while the British had stuck with de Gaulle through thick and thin, they had begun to modify their policy and now felt: (1) that he could no longer be considered a reliable friend of Britain, that he had left a "trail of Anglophobia" wherever he went; (2) that he had tried to play Great Britain against the United States and the United States against Britain; (3) that he had tried to create friction between the British and French in Syria; (4) that he had "Fascist and dictatorial tendencies," etc. And that de Gaulle was "chiefly concerned with his own political power. He is behaving as an opponent of Great Britain and the United States, rather than as any ally."

On July 16, the London *Times* printed an editorial comment by the Washington *Post*: "We are asked to believe . . . that Mr. Churchill is capable of making one statement of his views to the Commons . . . and another contrary statement for the benefit of British and American officials. . . ."

frivolity, carelessness in allowing General de Gaulle to act in this manner over such a long period of time on the very soil of Great Britain; for recommending him to the English people over so long a time as such an excellent ally; for recommending him to the French people as the very model of a democrat; for making arrangements with him in England's name which grant him exorbitant powers and from which today you cannot extricate yourself; for helping him to build up his standing in France; for backing him even when he assumes instransigent positions in respect to yourself. And as for your own standing here in Great Britain, it is not as strong as you think it is. You could even lose, the next time the country goes to the polls. Why give the Opposition another stick to beat you with?"

So it is that the dossier still rests in the archives. Churchill did not ever open it before a session of the Commons, secret or otherwise. Yet the concession he made to his party in this matter was not sufficient to ward off defeat in the first elections after the war. There were of course other factors. But the Conservative whips were right: Churchill was no longer quite as popular as he thought.

Before leaving England for Algiers as a naval officer, I went back to Woburn Abbey to say goodbye, alone because Anne was down with a bad throat. My diary tells me that it was on Wednesday, January 6. That evening, at Maryland, there was a party in honor of Sir Reginald Leeper, who had been appointed Ambassador to the Greek government in Cairo. This was to be my last visit. Our goodbyes were said with the belief that we would see each other after the war, if not before. In fact, most of us did meet again, with the exception of the two or three who died.

Everyone told me that Anne would be looked after. She was to keep on with the *Courrier de l'Air* until a replacement had been found for me.

What I was never to see again was the London blackout, if you can properly claim to see it when you have to feel your way like a blind man. A thick fog, a "pea-souper," complicated matters even further. I remember a night when I had to take the tube home, as there were no taxis, and no buses running. When I emerged at Knightsbridge Station, it was so dark, what with fog and the blackout, that I truly could not see my hand in front of me. Our house was only a few steps from the station and I knew the way blind: you turned at the corner of the Harvey, Nichols store, then felt your way along the bars of the iron fence fronting our building (one of the few such fences that had not been taken down and melted for purposes of war); then you counted, one door, two doors, the third door was yours! Once in the vestibule, with the door closed behind me, I was blinded by the lights. Mary cried out in horror, "But your hands, sir! *Please*, please don't touch anything!" My hands were as black as if I had worked all day in a coal mine.

On nights when along with the blackout there was heavy fog, and I was only just able to make out the blank fronts of bombed stores boarded over, buses passing by like ghosts, street lamps that were now nothing but hazards to pedestrians groping their way on the sidewalk, I used to promise myself that if ever I was able to return to England after the war, I would enjoy to the fullest the lighted buses, the bright show windows, the street lamps spilling their comforting pools of light on sidewalk and street. And, in fact, in 1945 I did go back to London for several years and not an evening passed that I did not remember the lengthy tunnel of darkness—three years and more—and revel in the lights of a great capital no longer besieged, fully alive again.

On the evening before I was to leave, a number of friends came by. Persons of the most diverse and contradictory convictions met without insulting one another. Among them were, for instance, Pierre Brossolette, who was to die in the Resistance, and Captain Maerten. The Captain, on the morning after Admiral Darlan's assassination (Christmas morning), went out in search of a post office that was open for business. Finding one at last, he sent off a telegram in French to the Admiral's widow: "I weep with you over the death of my well-beloved chief." There you have Captain Maerten! He and I had hardly a single thought in common. But courage and fidelity are not virtues that you run into every day.

At four in the morning, a few of the faithful were still standing by, standing, that is, in a manner of speaking. Pierre Maillaud, Jean Oberlé, Michel Saint-Denis, Robert Battefort, Monica, and several others were up, but two of the girls had gone to sleep on our bed, waiting for their escorts to be ready to take them home. Among the indefatigable males still there, I remember a young English naval officer named W—. He had been in on the landings in Algiers on November 8 and was one of the first men ashore. He was aboard the destroyer HMS *Broke* when at dawn on November 8 she rammed through the boom blocking the southern entrance of the harbor. At twenty-five knots, with every gun firing, she touched at the mole. There was just time for W— to jump to it, but heavy fire from the batteries around the Admiralty, manned by our furious French sailors, forced her to draw away. W— made a run for it and barely managed to clear the ornamental iron barrier at the entrance to the mole. The *Broke* got away, but not before she had been so badly holed that she sank under tow. Our young officer in the uniform of His Majesty's Navy walked unconcernedly up the hill into town. For all anybody seemed to care, he could have been a mail carrier. Yet at that moment the American and British troops were still miles outside Algiers. Fighting was going on inside the town between the young men recruited by Ambassador Murphy and his French friends to try to immobilize the authorities for some hours, and the authorities, who were fighting back. Soon recognized as English, W— was riotously welcomed, dragged off the streets, which were dangerous, and plied with drinks. And all the while, French officers under oath to Marshal Pétain were spreading death and destruction in the harbor among the allies of France.

W— had great admiration for Captain Wharton, R.N., British naval liaison officer on General Eisenhower's staff. He wanted, before I left England, to write me a letter of introduction to him. The complications on the eve of my departure were in large part due to having engaged the services of a former chief steward on a passenger ship who claimed to know how to mix twenty-seven different kinds of cocktails. He undertook to demonstrate, and

W— was fascinated. Whence his problem later in the evening when he sat down to write the letter. He tried a pen, but it had three nibs. He asked for a typewriter, but it was under some kind of spell: he struck at a key and a quite different letter appeared on the paper. Wisely, he gave up. He said to me, "You aren't leaving until tomorrow night and you have to go by Bush House in the morning? The note will be ready for you." And he left, accompanied by Michel Saint-Denis, who was a partisan of red wine as opposed to cocktails.

Toward noon the next day, I went by Bush House. On the fifth floor I found W—, who had not forgotten the letter for Captain Wharton. I thanked him for the letter and asked, "Did you get home all right last night in the blackout despite the absence of taxis?"

"Yes," he said. "But I did not go to my place. I don't know whether you noticed the state Michel was in. By Jove, if he did not drink three bottles of claret all by himself! You understand, of course, that I did not want to leave him. He would never have found his own door! So I went all the way home with him and spent the night there." I said goodbye to W— and went down to the fourth floor, where the French section of the BBC had its offices. Reigning there was Michel Saint-Denis. He was also to give me a letter, for his son, who lived in Algiers. I said, "Well, I know that you got home safely. W— accompanied you."

"You saw how he was. How can a man let himself get into such a state! He must have sampled each of those twenty-seven cocktails three times—it's incredible! With the cold outside last night, it would have been unchristian to let him go home alone. He would never have recognized his own door. And he would have waked up on the sidewalk with a fine case of pneumonia."

While making my farewell rounds that day, I thought of going to see Simone Weil, but eventually did not. This is a matter for regret, I can even say for remorse. How wrong I was! I was so afraid that we would get into an argument, as we did in the past, way back to the days when we were classmates. But at that time our bone of contention was different: she then used to tax me with militarism. She herself was the apostle of a pacifism which was all the more astonishing for the miraculous powers she attributed to a refusal to use force under any circumstances. In those days she was out to refute Pascal's dictum, "Justice without force is impotent; force without justice is tyrannical." We were then at an age when in an argument the weapons we used were quotations from great writers.

I knew that she had, so to speak, changed sides from the Left. She was cruelly hard on herself and now she accused herself, as she has written, of having been before the war in a state of "criminal error." Before leaving New York, she had carried on a correspondence with Maurice Schumann, who had been her classmate and mine. She had arrived in London gift-wrapped and tied up with ribbons for General de Gaulle. After landing, she had spent two weeks in Patriotic School to prove that she was not an enemy agent, and then she had been assigned to the section under André Philip. Great use was made there of her prodigious intelligence and her formidable command of dialectics in establishing the various theses on the legitimacy of General de Gaulle, on the suppression of political parties, and on the nobility of the Free French movement.[3]

---

[3] *Words of Simone Weil in London*

"There is in his [General de Gaulle's] words an accent of sincerity and honor which is persuasive. . . . The needs of Freedom itself, so essential to the intellect, call for a corresponding protection against suggestion, propaganda, influence by means of obsession. These are methods of constraint, a special kind of constraint, not accompanied by fear or physical distress, but which is none the less a form of violence. Modern technique places extremely potent instruments at its service . . . and human souls are its victims. Naturally, the State is guilty of crime if it makes use of such methods itself. . . . It should . . . prevent their use. . . . A few straightforward measures of public salubrity would protect the population from offenses against the truth . . . the human soul's most sacred need . . . protection against suggestion and falsehood. . . . Any man who has the power to persecute or to deceive other men should be forced to take an oath not to do it." *Ecrits de Londres,* pp. 69, 82, 87. Pub-

When we were young, I was never able to succeed in getting *la petite Weil* to change her opinion in the slightest about anything at all. In that winter of 1942-43, she believed with all her heart and mind in the absolute sincerity of General de Gaulle. Anybody who dared to express doubt would have been ground to bits by that amazing intellect of hers; it was certainly, as a thinking machine, the most peremptory, the best oiled, the most rapid I have ever encountered. It was capable of producing fifty arguments an hour. And this thinking machine could only slow down and come to a halt through the action of its own built-in brake. The truth is, she had always to discover for herself or not at all. Nothing better illustrates the marvelous talent of General de Gaulle than Simone Weil's absolute faith that any exercise of personal power was abhorrent to him.

Dear little Simone Weil! Of one thing I am sure: they are going to try to appropriate her memory for themselves. And why not? Those pretenders who made use of the letters of Léon Blum, of Georges Mandel, of Édouard Herriot, and of the homage paid to the head of the Free French by so many patriots who died to prove that General de Gaulle was a true-blue champion of parliamentary democracy—why should they not be capable of laying hand on the beloved memory of *la petite Weil* and appropriating it as one more stone for the monument they are raising? After all, it makes no difference to me, and I am not trying to say that little Simone Weil was not a Gaullist, for she was.[4] What is sad is that she should be dead. And dead because of what? I have been told that it was grief because she was not able to be in France to play her part in the

---

lished in English under the title *The Need for Roots* (New York: G. P. Putnam's Sons; 1952).

Words of François Mauriac

"All right then, yes! One must deceive men, or at least mislead them, in order to save them." Mauriac: *De Gaulle*, p. 93.

[4] I now know that shortly before her death Simone sent in her resignation to Carlton Gardens. M. André Philip, Commissioner of the Interior, did not accept it.

Resistance. I believe this. She had a vocation for martyrdom—how could she console herself for being at Carlton Gardens, in the very headquarters of the privileged? She even refused, in London, to eat more than was allowed to ordinary Frenchmen under the Occupation, and her death in a sanitarium in Ashford, Kent, was the result.

Even the fighting Gaullists, as she must have seen, were privileged in comparison to the Resistance fighters in France. And the very rare Frenchmen in London who were not Gaullists like Maillaud or anti-Gaullists like Torcy were still privileged, compared to the French inside France. I have already said this? Good. I could not repeat it too often.

For this young non-Catholic saint, General de Gaulle was above all else a symbol, as he was for the majority of the French people, a symbol of a truth which was *in her,* of a truth which was *in them.*

But what is the truth of France?

It is not that I wish to give my own definition—heaven forbid! For me it is enough to love France; and even more so when she is sick. As she was. As she is.

To love a sick France is to detest her sickness. Marshal Pétain is deserving of glory, eternal glory, for having held the flag at Verdun; but not of laurels for having been the symptom, if not the cause, of the malady in the throes of which the nation denied its allegiance, and its ideals of liberty, equality, and fraternity. In its sickness it denied too its great virtue of clear thinking. General de Gaulle is deserving of glory, eternal glory, for having picked up the flag in 1940. But there are no laurels on his brow, for he is the symbol, if not the cause, of the disease which continues. It is a disease that drives the weak and bitter survivors of generations decimated by the world wars to renounce their liberties, entrusting power to one man; to renounce lucidity and candor for obscurity and deceit; to show themselves not as brothers to other nations, but full of distrust; not thankful, but ungrateful, toward the very nations that saved us all.

I have tried here to reestablish the good name of some Frenchmen of the older generations, such as Comert, Muselier, Torcy, who resisted the evil. The cure will come. The nation is very old—it has existed for almost a millennium—but, with the new generations, it will soon be one of the nations with the largest proportion of young people. One day, through them, France will show the world again her traditional virtues of clear thinking, of cheerfulness, of courtesy, of generosity. Both for herself and for the other nations, she will again have as her ideals *Liberté, Egalité, Fraternité.*

I dreamed of those things on board the English warship as it skipped gaily on the Bay of Biscay, off the coasts of Gascony, off the coasts of Occupied France, as I headed toward other ships, French ships, on which I could, without swearing an oath to the person of Marshal Pétain or General de Gaulle—more than two years late, but at long last—make war.

Dramatis Personae

Bowes-Lyon, the Honorable David. Born 1902, died 1961. The sixth son of the Count of Strathmore; brother of Queen Elizabeth, the wife of George VI. Toward the end of 1942 and the beginning of 1943, provisional head of the Political Warfare organization at Woburn Abbey, before becoming a member of the British Embassy in Washington.

Cambon, Roger. French diplomat, born in 1881. Minister-counselor of the French Embassy in London at the moment of the Franco-German armistice, he sent his resignation to the government of Marshal Pétain, remaining faithful to the English alliance. Stayed on in London through the war. Son of Ambassador Jules Cambon and nephew of Ambassador Paul Cambon, the two greatest figures in French diplomacy under the Third Republic. Loyal to the entente cordiale, to the principles of solidarity among Western democracies and of a parliamentary regime with full separation of powers. Outspoken adversary of the Vichy government, but he approved neither of the political role General de Gaulle took upon himself nor of his long-range ambitions.

Cameron, Norman. Scottish poet, born in 1905, died 1953. *Collected Poems*, with an introduction by Robert Graves (London: The Hogarth Press). Translated Villon, Verlaine, and Rimbaud into English.

Cassin, René. Professor of Civil Law, born in 1887. One of the first and most important associates of General de Gaulle. National Commissioner of Justice and Education in London from 1941 to 1943. Now honorary president of the Conseil d'État. Compagnon of the Order of Liberation.

Castellane, Boniface, Marquis de. French diplomat, born in 1897. Became French chargé d'affaires in London upon Roger Cambon's resignation.

385

Comert, Pierre. Born 1880, died 1964. French journalist and diplomat. Graduate of the École Normale, agrégé in German. Scholarship *Tour du Monde*. Correspondent of *Le Temps* in Vienna and Berlin, 1908–14. Press attaché in London, 1917–19. Director of Information Services at the League of Nations. Director of Press Service of the French Ministry of Foreign Affairs as Minister Plenipotentiary. Reached London in June 1940 and founded the French daily *France*. Supported General de Gaulle's military actions to continue the war against Hitler and Mussolini, but approved neither of the battles waged against other Frenchmen while there were so many foreign invaders to fight against, nor of the General's political views.

Corbin, Charles. French diplomat, born 1881. Ambassador of France in London, June 1940. Sent his resignation to Marshal Pétain's government at the time of the armistice, without, however, approving of the political enterprises of General de Gaulle.

Courcel, Geoffroy, Chodron de. French diplomat, born 1912. Ordinance officer, then chief of secretariat to General de Gaulle in London. Now French Ambassador in London.

Gamelin, Maurice. French general. Born 1872, died 1958. Commander-in-Chief, Allied Land Forces, 1939–40. Replaced by General Weygand, May 19, 1940. Arrested 1940, he was transferred to Germany in 1943, and remained prisoner until 1945.

Léger, Alexis. French diplomat, born 1887. Better known as the poet Saint-John Perse. Secretary-general of the Ministry for Foreign Affairs. Dismissed from office by Paul Reynaud in May 1940 and deprived of French citizenship by Marshal Pétain, he lived in exile in Washington, where he worked for France in a private capacity but refused to join the political organization of General de Gaulle. Awarded the Nobel Prize for Literature in 1960.

Maillaud, Pierre. French journalist and politician. Born 1909, died 1948. Director, Agence Française Indépendante, created in London in 1940 by M. P. L. Bret and Maillaud. Under pseudonym *Pierre Bourdan*, principal French commentator for the BBC, 1940–44. Member of French Parliament and Minister after the liberation.

Monnet, Jean. French statesman and economist, born 1888. Took part in organization of Franco-British Common Defense Program, 1940. After the French armistice, engaged in supplying Britain with arms as a member of the British Supply Council, Washington, 1940–43. After the Allied landings in North Africa, became Commissioner for Armament, Supplies, and Reconstruction, French National Liberation Committee, Algiers, 1943–44. Created Plan Monnet, 1947.

General Commissioner, Plan for Modernization and Equipment, France, 1947. President, Preparatory Conference of Schuman Plan, 1950. President, European Coal and Steel Community, 1952–55. Chairman, Action Committee for a United States of Europe, 1956. Together with Pope John XXIII, received American Presidential Medal of Freedom, 1963.

Moppès, Maurice Van. On the staff of the French section of the BBC, 1940–44.

Muselier, Émile Henri. French admiral. Born 1882, died 1965. Established the Free French Naval Forces in Gibraltar, June 1940. On reaching London, he agreed to put himself under the command of General de Gaulle, as Commander-in-Chief of the Free French Naval and Air Forces. First to use the Cross of Lorraine. Ousted by General de Gaulle following violent disagreements in 1942. During World War I, Muselier served as ensign and in 1915 as Captain of Marines on the Yser. Wounded several times. Grand Officer of the *Légion d'honneur, Croix de Guerre*, Knight Commander of the Bath, Compagnon of the Order of Liberation.

Oberlé, Jean. French painter and writer. One of the leading members of the French team on the BBC, 1940–44.

Palewski, Gaston. French politician, born 1901. Paul Reynaud's Chief of Secretariat, 1940; then collaborator of General de Gaulle. Director, Political Affairs, London, 1940. Commanding officer of Free French Forces, East Africa, 1941. Chief of Secretariat for the General, 1942–46. Now president of the Conseil Constitutionnel. Compagnon of the Order of Liberation.

Pleven, René. French politician, born 1901. Began with business career, as London representative of the Automatic Telephone Company. In 1940, became principal collaborator of General de Gaulle. Under the Fourth Republic, he was Prime Minister, 1950–51, and again 1951–52. Presently a member of Parliament and of the Union Démocratique et Socialiste de la Resistance (UDSR). Compagnon of the Order of Liberation.

Reynaud, Paul. French politician, born 1878. As Prime Minister, March–June 1940, he brought into his government Marshal Pétain as Vice-President of the Council of Ministers and General de Gaulle as Under-Secretary of State for War. Resigned June 17, 1940, after defeat in Parliament, giving way to Marshal Pétain. At first on good terms with the Marshals' government, he was then interned by Vichy, then by the Germans until the end of the war. Now a member of Parliament in France.

Roché, Louis. French diplomat, born 1903. Secretary, French Embassy in London, 1940; then at French Legation, Dublin. Resigned in 1941. French section, BBC. Now French Ambassador in Vienna.

Saffroy, Pierre. French diplomat, born 1921. Secretary of Legation, Dublin. Resigned, October 1941. French section, BBC. Refused to sign Acte d'Engagement to General de Gaulle, and to take a diplomatic appointment until the end of the war. After the war, he became French Minister in Munich.

Saint-Denis, Michel. Born 1897. Director, French section of the BBC, 1940–44, under pseudonym Jacques Duchesne. Administrator and secretary of the Théâtre du Vieux-Colombier; founder and director of the Compagnie des Quinze, and intimate of his uncle, Jacques Copeau.

Schumann, Maurice. French journalist and politician, born 1911. Radio spokesman for General de Gaulle. Fellow student of mine and of Simone Weil in Alain's class at the Lycée Henri IV in Paris. Now a member of Parliament in France, and president of the Commission of Foreign Affairs of the National Assembly.

Spears, Sir Edward L. Bart, KBE, CB, MC. Prime Minister's personal representative with French Prime Minister, and Minister for Defence, May–June 1940; Head of British mission to General de Gaulle, July 1940; Head of Spears Mission, Syria and Lebanon, July 1941; First Minister to republics of Syria and Lebanon, 1942–44.

Torcy—pseudonym designating a French diplomat in London. (I took his name from Jean-Baptiste Colbert, Marquis de Torcy, nephew of the celebrated Colbert who was Minister of Louis XIV at the end of his reign. In his modest way, he played a considerable role, displaying qualities of rectitude and abnegation which made him, like Louis XIV's minister, a model for all diplomats.)

Weil, Simone. French philosopher and mystic, born 1909. Agrégée and professor of philosophy, she was a classmate of mine and of Maurice Schumann at the Lycée Henry IV. Died of tuberculosis and grief in London, 1944.

Weygand, Maxime. Born 1867. French general and close collaborator of Marshal Foch in World War I. Paul Reynaud, as Prime Minister, called him to replace General Gamelin as Commander-in-Chief on May 19, 1940, when the Franco-English Army was already three quarters destroyed. He gave battle and lost. Refused to capitulate as Reynaud asked him to do, but insisted on an armistice. The Prime Minister did not replace him with another general determined to continue the war. After the armistice, he reconstituted a French army in North Africa. Opposed collaboration with the Germans, but remained loyal to Marshal Pétain and did not rally to de Gaulle, which earned him the General's ill-will. The Germans demanded his recall from North Africa in November 1940. Arrested by the Gestapo, November 1942, and kept prisoner in Germany until 1945. He was placed at the disposition of the High Court of Justice by the French government, and obtained a dismissal of all charges brought against him. Died in Paris in 1965. General de Gaulle refused to allow funeral services in the Chapel of Les Invalides, customary for French military leaders. Holder of the Grand Croix of the *Légion d'honneur* and also the Médaille Militaire, the highest possible decoration for a French general.

Index

391